The Grief Taboo in American Literature

Loss and
Prolonged
Adolescence
in Twain,
Melville, and
Hemingway

Pamela A. Boker

The Grief Taboo in American Literature

Literature and Psychoanalysis

GENERAL EDITOR: JEFFREY BERMAN

The Grief Taboo
in American Literature

Loss and Prolonged Adolescence in
Twain, Melville, and Hemingway

Pamela A. Boker

New York University Press
NEW YORK & LONDON

NEW YORK UNIVERSITY PRESS
New York and London

© 1996 by New York University

Reprinted with permission of Northwestern University Press: From Herman Melville, *Moby-Dick; or, The Whale,* ed. Harrison Hayford (Evanston and Chicago: Northwestern University Press/Newberry Library, 1988), and *Pierre; or The Ambiguities,* ed. Harrison Hayford (Evanston and Chicago: Northwestern University Press/Newberry Library, 1971).

Reprinted with permission of Scribner, an imprint of Simon & Schuster: From *In Our Time* by Ernest Hemingway. Copyright 1925, 1930 Charles Scribner's Sons. Copyright renewed 1953, © 1958 by Ernest Hemingway. From *The Snows of Kilimanjaro and Other Stories* by Ernest Hemingway. Copyright 1927, 1933, 1936 by Ernest Hemingway. Copyrights renewed: 1955, © 1961 by Ernest Hemingway; © 1961, 1964 by Mary Hemingway. From *Islands in the Stream* by Ernest Hemingway. Copyright © 1970 by Mary Hemingway. From *Death in the Afternoon* by Ernest Hemingway. Copyright 1932 Charles Scribner's Sons. Copyright renewed © 1960 by Ernest Hemingway. From *For Whom the Bell Tolls* by Ernest Hemingway. Copyright 1940 by Ernest Hemingway. Copyright renewed © 1968 by Mary Hemingway. From *The Garden of Eden* by Ernest Hemingway. Copyright © 1986 by Mary Hemingway, John Hemingway, Patrick Hemingway, and Gregory Hemingway. From *A Farewell to Arms* by Ernest Hemingway. Copyright 1929 Charles Scribner's Sons. Copyright renewed 1957 by Ernest Hemingway. From *A Moveable Feast* by Ernest Hemingway. Copyright © 1964 by Mary Hemingway. Copyright renewed © 1992 by John H. Hemingway, Patrick Hemingway, and Gregory Hemingway. From *Men Without Women* by Ernest Hemingway. Copyright 1927 Charles Scribner's Sons. Copyright renewed 1955 by Ernest Hemingway. From *Across the River and Into the Trees* by Ernest Hemingway. Copyright 1950 by Ernest Hemingway. Copyright renewed © 1978 by Mary Hemingway.

Library of Congress Cataloging-in-Publication Data
Boker, Pamela A., 1955–
    The grief taboo in American literature : loss and prolonged
adolescence in Twain, Melville, and Hemingway / Pamela A. Boker.
        p.   cm. — (Literature and psychoanalysis ; 8)
    Includes bibliographical references and index.
    ISBN 0-8147-1228-2 (alk. paper)
        1. American fiction—Men authors—History and criticism.   2. Grief
in literature.   3. Melville, Herman, 1819–1891—Knowledge—
Psychology.   4. Twain, Mark, 1835–1910—Knowledge—Psychology.
5. Hemingway, Ernest, 1899–1961—Knowledge—Psychology.
6. Psychoanalysis and literature—United States—History.
7. Masculinity (Psychology) in literature.   8. Repression
(Psychology) in literature.   9. Loss (Psychology) in literature.
10. Adolescence in literature.   I. Title.   II. Series.
PS374.G75B65 1996   95-4390
810.9′353—dc20   CIP

For BESSIE
In Loving Memory

Give sorrow words; the grief that does not speak
Whispers the oe'r fraught heart, and bids it break.

—Shakespeare, *Macbeth*

It is the image in the mind that binds us to our lost treasures, but it is the loss that shapes the image.

—Colette, *My Mother's House*

He oft finds med'cine who his grief imparts.

—Spencer, *The Faerie Queene*

Sorrow concealed, like an oven stopp'd,
Doth burn the heart to cinders where it is.

—Shakespeare, *Titus Andronicus*

Contents

Foreword

As New York University Press inaugurates a new series of books on literature and psychoanalysis, it seems appropriate to pause and reflect briefly upon the history of psychoanalytic literary criticism. For a century now it has struggled to define its relationship to its two contentious progenitors and come of age. After glancing at its origins, we may be in a better position to speculate on its future.

Psychoanalytic literary criticism was conceived at the precise moment in which Freud, reflecting upon his self-analysis, made a connection to two plays and thus gave us a radically new approach to reading literature. Writing to his friend Wilhelm Fliess in 1897, Freud breathlessly advanced the idea that "love of the mother and jealousy of the father" are universal phenomena of early childhood (*Origins*, 223–24). He referred immediately to the gripping power of *Oedipus Rex* and *Hamlet* for confirmation of, and perhaps inspiration for, his compelling perception of family drama, naming his theory the "Oedipus complex" after Sophocles' legendary fictional hero.

Freud acknowledged repeatedly his indebtedness to literature, mythology, and philosophy. There is no doubt that he was a great humanist, steeped in world literature, able to read several languages and range across disciplinary boundaries. He regarded creative writers as allies, investigating the same psychic terrain and intuiting similar human truths. "[P]sycho-analytic observation must concede priority of imaginative writers," he declared in 1901 in *The Psychopathology of Everyday Life* (*SE* 6213), a concession he was generally happy to make. The only exceptions were writers like Schopenhauer, Nietzsche, and Schnitzler, whom he avoided reading because of the anxiety of influence. He quoted effortlessly from Sophocles, Shakespeare, Goethe, and Dostoevsky, and was himself a master prose stylist, the recipient of the coveted Goethe Prize in 1930. When he was considered for the Nobel Prize, it was not for medicine but for literature. Upon being greeted as the discoverer of the unconscious, he disclaimed the title and instead paid generous tribute to the poets and philosophers who preceded him.

And yet Freud's forays into literary criticism have not been welcomed uniformly by creative writers, largely because of his allegiance to science rather than art. Despite his admiration for art, he viewed the artist as an introvert, not far removed from neurosis. The artist, he wrote in a well-known passage in the *Introductory Lectures on Psycho-Analysis* (1916–17), "is oppressed by excessively powerful instinctual needs. He desires to win honour, power, wealth, fame and the love of women; but he lacks the means for achieving these satisfactions" (*SE* 16376). Consequently, Freud argued, artists retreat from reality into the world of fantasy, where they attempt to make their dreams come true. While conceding that true artists manage to shape their daydreams in such a way as to find a path back to reality, thus fulfilling their wishes, Freud nevertheless theorized art as a substitute gratification. Little wonder, then, that few artists have been pleased with Freud's pronouncements.

Nor have many artists been sympathetic to Freud's preoccupation with sexuality and aggression; his deterministic vision of human life; his combative, polemical temperament; his self-fulfilling belief that psychoanalysis brings out the worst in people; and his imperialistic claim that psychoanalysis, which he regarded as his personal creation, would explore and conquer vast new territories. He chose as the epigraph for *The Interpretation of Dreams* (1900) a quotation from *The Aeneid* "Flectere si nequeo superos, Acheronta movebo" ("If I cannot bend the Higher Powers, I will move the Infernal Regions"). Although he denied that there was anything Promethean about his work, he regarded himself as one of the disturbers of the world's sleep. The man who asserted that "psycho-analysis is in a position to speak the decisive word in all questions that touch upon the imaginative life of man" (*SE* 19208) could hardly expect to win many converts among creative writers, who were no less familiar with the imaginative life of humankind and who resented his intrusion into their domain.

Freud viewed psychoanalysts as scientists, committed to the reality principle and to heroic self-renunciation. He perceived artists, by contrast—and women—as neurotic and highly narcissistic, devoted to the pleasure principle, intuiting mysterious truths which they could not rationally understand. "Kindly nature has given the artist the ability to express his most secret mental impulses, which are hidden even from himself," he stated in *Leonardo da Vinci and a Memory of His Childhood* in 1910 (*SE* 11 107). The artist, in Freud's judgment, creates beauty, but the psychoanalyst analyzes its meaning and "penetrates" it, with all the phallic implications thereof. As much as he admired artists, Freud did not want to give them credit for knowing what they are doing. Moreover, although he always referred to artists as male, he assumed that art itself was essentially female; and he was drawn to the "seductive" nature of art even as he resisted its embrace, lest he lose his masculine analytical power. He wanted to be called a scientist, not an artist.

From the beginning of his career, then, the marriage Freud envisioned between the artist and the analyst was distinctly unequal and patriarchal. For their part, most creative writers have remained wary of psychoanalysis. Franz Kafka, James Joyce, and D. H. Lawrence were fascinated by psychoanalytic theory and appropriated it, in varying degrees, in their stories, but they all remained skeptical of Freud's therapeutic claims and declined to be analyzed.

Most artists do not want to be "cured," fearing that their creativity will be imperiled, and they certainly do not want psychoanalysts to probe their work; they agree with Wordsworth that to dissect is to murder. Vladimir Nabokov's sardonic reference to Freud as the "Viennese witch doctor" and his contemptuous dismissal of psychoanalysis as black magic are extreme examples of creative writers' mistrust of psychoanalytic interpretations of literature. "[A]ll my books should be stamped Freudians Keep Out," Nabokov writes in *Bend Sinister* (xii). Humbert Humbert speaks for his creator when he observes in *Lolita* that the difference between the rapist and therapist is but a matter of spacing (147).

Freud never lost faith that psychoanalysis could cast light upon a wide variety of academic subjects. In the short essay "On the Teaching of Psycho-Analysis in Universities" (1919), he maintained that his new science has a role not only in medical schools but also in the "solutions of problems" in art, philosophy, religion, literature, mythology, and history. "The fertilizing effects of psycho-analytic thought on these other disciplines," Freud wrote enthusiastically, "would certainly contribute greatly towards forging a closer link, in the sense of a *universitas literarum*, between medical science and the branches of learning which lie within the sphere of philosophy and the arts" (*SE* 17 173). Regrettably, he did not envision in the same essay a cross-fertilization, a desire, that is, for other disciplines to pollinate psychoanalysis.

Elsewhere, though, Freud was willing to acknowledge a more reciprocal relationship between the analyst and the creative writer. He opened his first published essay on literary criticism, "Delusions and Dreams in Jensen's *Gradiva*" (1907), with the egalitarian statement that "creative writers are valued allies and their evidence is to be highly prized, for they are apt to know a whole host of things between heaven and earth of which our philosophy has not yet let us dream" (*SE* 98), an allusion to his beloved Hamlet's affirmation of the mystery of all things. Conceding that literary artists have been, from time immemorial, precursors to scientists, Freud concluded that the "creative writer cannot evade the psychiatrist nor the psychiatrist the creative writer, and the poetic treatment of a psychiatric theme can turn out to be correct without any sacrifice of its beauty" (*SE* 944).

It is in the spirit of this equal partnership between literature and psychoanalysis that New York University Press launches the present series. We intend to publish books that are genuinely interdisciplinary, theoretically sophisticated, and clinically informed. The literary critic's insights into psychoanalysis are no less valuable than the psychoanalyst's insights into literature. Gone are the days when psychoanalytic critics assumed that Freud had a master key to unlock the secrets of literature. Instead of reading literature to confirm psychoanalytic theory, many critics are now reading Freud to discover how his understanding of literature shaped the evolution of his theory. In short, the master-slave relationship traditionally implicit in the marriage between the literary critic and the psychoanalyst has given way to a healthier dialogic relationship, in which each learns from and contributes to the other's discipline.

Indeed, the prevailing ideas of the late twentieth century are strikingly different from those of the late nineteenth century, when literature and psychoanalysis were first allied. In contrast to Freud, who assumed he was discovering absolute truth, we now believe that knowledge, particularly in the humanities and social sciences, is relative and dependent upon cultural contexts. Freud's classical drive theory, with its mechanistic implications of cathectic energy, has given way to newer relational models such as object relations, self psychology, and interpersonal psychoanalysis, affirming the importance of human interaction. Many early psychoanalytic ideas, such as the death instinct and the phylogenetic transmission of memories, have fallen by the wayside, and Freud's theorizing on female psychology has been recognized as a reflection of his cultural bias.

Significant developments have also taken place in psychoanalytic literary theory. An extraordinary variety and synthesis of competing approaches have emerged, including post-Freudian, Jungian, Lacanian, Horneyan, feminist, deconstructive, psycholinguistic, and reader response. Interest in psychoanalytic literary criticism is at an all-time high, not just in the handful of journals devoted to psychological criticism, but in dozens of mainstream journals that have traditionally avoided psychological approaches to literature. Scholars are working on identity theory, narcissism, gender theory, mourning and loss, and creativity. Additionally, they are investigating new areas, such as composition theory and pedagogy, and exploring the roles of resistance, transference, and countertransference in the classroom.

"In the end we depend / On the creatures we made," Freud observed at the close of his life (*Letters*, 425), quoting from Goethe's *Faust;* and in the end psychoanalytic literary criticism depends on the scholars who continue to shape it. All serious scholarship is an act of love and devotion, and for many of the authors in this series, including myself, psychoanalytic literary criticism has become a consuming passion, in some cases a lifelong one. Like other passions, there is an element of idealization here. For despite our criticisms of Freud, we stand in awe of his achievements; and even as we recognize the limitations of any single approach to literature, we find that psychoanalysis has profoundly illuminated the human condition and inspired countless artists. In the words of the fictional "Freud" in D. M. Thomas's extraordinary novel *The White Hotel* (1981), "Long may poetry and psychoanalysis continue to highlight, from their different perspectives, the human face in all its nobility and sorrow" (143n.).

JEFFREY BERMAN
Professor of English
State University of New York at Albany

Introduction

Toward a Theory of Repressed Grief in American Literature

The concept for this book was formulated several years ago, when, as a graduate student in American studies (with a secondary emphasis in psychoanalysis), I was asked to draw some conclusions about the traditional American literary canon. I recognized two common themes that consistently appeared in American literature written by male authors, from the Puritans, through the early Republic and Transcendentalism, and well into the mid-twentieth century. These were loss, and male adolescence; or, more specifically, the disavowal of grief over a willfully discarded past, and the fact that much of America's greatest literature appears to be designed for adolescent boys.

I had, of course, discovered nothing new here as both themes appeared as general topics of scholarly interest in American literary criticism as early as 1923, the year D. H. Lawrence wrote *Studies in Classic American Literature.* Perry Miller was one of the first American scholars to point out that the American experiment was based upon America's estrangement from its paternal and historical past, emphasizing, as many others have since, that America sought to formulate an independent self-definition based on a radical "isolation" from its English heritage.[1] Additionally, the New Critics of the 1950s maintained an opinion that the typical hero of American fiction was a wide-eyed, innocent new Adam, an idealistic wanderer out to explore the Edenic vastness of the American wilderness, the winding rivers, and the uncharted seas.[2]

As I studied these themes more closely, however, what struck me as perplexing was not the ideas themselves, so much as the connection that American literary critics have made between them. Throughout the history of American cultural and literary criticism the frequent emphasis on loss and male adolescence converged in the commonly held view that the American Adam was a self-willed orphan who had adopted the spirit of the American experiment by rebelliously cutting himself off from his past, and who therefore, as R. W. B. Lewis proposes, was "happily bereft of ancestry" (5).

Partly because I was approaching American studies with an eye for psychoanalytic patterns of thought, but primarily, I believe, because I was engaging my material with a feminine sensibility that was attuned to emotional vulnerability and the dynamics of interpersonal relationships, my suspicions were aroused with regard to the motives behind these fictional themes, and even more so, behind the prevalent attitude of exuberant optimism with which they were viewed by so many American male critics. Despite the fundamentally tragic nature of the experiences of rebellion, separation, and loss out of which the "American Adam," like the American colonies themselves, was engendered, the themes of uncompromising self-reliance and a willfully chosen orphan identity have been viewed by a certain masculine critical perspective as celebrated events that, for the most part, were devoid of emotional consequences. In time, I began to develop the notion that an attitude has persisted in American studies, as in American democratic ideology, in which the continuous reinvention of the self, the effacement of past generations, and the absence of a father figure in the aristocratic tradition, somehow served to inhibit the expression of mourning that is so critical to the process of separation and mature identity formation. This celebratory attitude has obstructed critics from recognizing the underlying psychological mechanisms and the paralyzing effects of adolescent idealism and the repression of grief in American thought and fiction.

This book, then, seeks to remove a masculine blind spot that has obscured emotional and psychological understanding of some of America's greatest fiction writers and their works. The opening premise behind this critical undertaking can be reduced to two psychoanalytic tenants: namely, that "unmanifested grief will be found expressed to the full in some way or other," and that a "person without emotional ties to people or places is removed, not free."[3] What I am suggesting, in other words, is that the inability to mourn over one's emotional deprivations, particularly in relation to one's parental figures and to a lost personal and historical past, is not an heroic capacity as male American critics have chosen to believe; it represents, rather, a psychological incapacity to assimilate and work through problematic and fractured object relationships.

Emotional honesty, vulnerability, and expression, along with the valuing of personal ties, are customarily associated with a feminine sensibility in patriarchal culture. Therefore, it is not only the repression of grief and the inability to mourn that will be explored in this study, but also the repression of "feminine" impulses and the female herself (primarily, the figure of the mother) as central ingredients in the creative processes and the fictional products of the male American author. In a sense, the principal thesis of this book is about wrestling with the feminine element in its most generative form.

In its methods and motives, therefore, *The Grief Taboo in American Literature* may be recognized as partially a feminist enterprise. As such, its ultimate goal is to dismantle the myth of an American male canon by exposing the feminine/maternal principle, which serves as a central impulse in the formation of works of fiction hitherto purported to be constructed exclusively by a masculine imagination. Using the lives and fiction of Herman Melville, Mark Twain, and Ernest Hemingway as examples, I will demonstrate that, despite the apparently successful efforts of American male culture to control and displace female power, our male authors continue to struggle internally with the maternal/feminine in the form of their conflicting desires for separation from, and fusion with, the intrapsychic and symbolically depicted image of the mother. To encode the maternal and female voice in texts composed by male authors is, in effect, to articulate a non-phallic masculinity at the heart of the traditional male canon, which would, as Kaja Silverman proposes, "at the very least, permit female subjectivity," and certainly male subjectivity as well, "to be lived differently than . . . at present."[4] Such a venture would also, Silverman maintains, force a "collapse of that system of fortification whereby sexual difference is secured," and thereby encourage a fundamental reconciliation of American masculinity with a previously denied, or unrecognized, internal femininity.[5]

By exploring the psychological incapacities in the creative processes and fictional works of three of America's most prominent, most criticized, and most talked about fiction writers, we can reach a new and deeper understanding, not only of their works, but also of each of them as individual creative artists, and together as representative American authorial figures. Perpetual adolescence, the repression of loss and grief, and the repudiation of feminine identification (or of the mother/woman herself), are the related psychological incapacities that play a vital role in the creative processes and fictional imaginations of Melville, Twain, and Hemingway. While these emotional conflicts may be viewed in biographical terms as psychological inadequacies, more importantly, they may also be seen as significant assets in the development of the artistic product. Understanding this paradox, whereby the attainment of maturity and direct emotional expression are not necessarily beneficial to the American writer, is another of the primary aims of this study, since to accept this paradox is also to acknowledge the psychoanalytic assumption that all great art is in some way a sublimation of repressed, or unconscious, psychic conflicts and impulses. The unworked-through unconscious psychic conflicts experienced in the course of masculine separation-individuation that impede maturity, the conscious acknowledgement of grief, and the psychological debt owed to the mother and the mother-child relationship, are, in this case, the linked psychic impulses that will be brought to the surface and illuminated in the fictional texts of the three authors under consideration.

In order to understand how arrested adolescent development did not inhibit these writers' creativity, or, to take the question a step farther, how it actually may have fostered the production of brilliant art, we will have to wait until the later discussions of the individual authors and their works. At this point it should be enough to mention that the stage of adolescent narcissism and idealization is a particularly rich creative period of psychic development, full of symbolic and metaphorical nuances, primitive myth-making potential, and the power to imaginatively bend the world to one's creative will. Ernest Hemingway may have been on the mark, therefore, when he responded to an accusation that he was "frozen in adolescence," by proposing: "Perhaps adolescence isn't such a bad place to be frozen."[6]

Additionally, gender identity theorists generally agree that masculine maturity in America, as in most Western cultures, historically has hinged upon the male's successful ability to distance himself emotionally from the mother, and that this mandated separation produces true American "tough guys" who strive for autonomy and independent achievement apart from feminine influence.[7] The failure to achieve this fulfillment of the masculine separation-individuation process results in a prolonged emotional dependency on the mother, on mother-child relational conflicts, and on one's lingering infantile feminine identification, all of which are symbolically displaced and defended against by American men, as they are by the three authors investigated in this book.[8] At the same time, however, such a seemingly negative fixation on these adolescent and infantile developmental issues allows these male authors to gain intuitive and psychological access to their own universal primitive conflicts, most especially to the creatively rich, mysterious, and bountiful images of the preoedipal mother, as well as to the compelling psychic dramas of regressive and imaginative primary-process thinking.[9]

One of the reasons I have chosen the trio of Melville, Twain, and Hemingway for this study is that they are three of America's best male authors, whose established reputations mark them as representative figures within the literary canon. Indeed, it is likely that the works of Melville, Twain, and Hemingway attained their status as representative American literature in the latter half of the twentieth century in part because they reflect the repressions and common defenses of an entire adolescent patriarchal culture.[10] As articulations of the prolonged mother-loss and father-hunger inherent in the male adolescent's struggle both to attain and to retreat from masculine maturity—a contest that I believe is left perpetually unresolved in the literature of America—the fiction of Melville, Twain, and Hemingway strikes a deeply meaningful and psychologically powerful chord in a narcissistic and fundamentally adolescent male culture. Through an awakening, only recently possible in critical thought, to the psychological and developmental problems that continue to plague American culture, we can see that the male author—himself a perpetual adolescent—created better fiction than even he knew.

Inspired by the consistent convergence of the themes of arrested adolescent development, idealism, repressed, or tabooed, grief, and disavowed feminine/maternal identification in American literary, historical, and cultural thought, I initially endeavored to discover whether a similar relation existed in the individual psychological domain of the lives and literary works of three of America's most distinctive writers of fiction. In this respect, I found a degree of confirmation far greater than I had hoped for or expected. In each case, the key to unlocking the connection between the aforementioned themes was provided by the object relations hypothesis, rooted in the mother-child relationship, that an early experience of emotional loss or deprivation often results in a defensive response to all subsequent experiences of separation and loss, through which grief and mourning are denied conscious and direct expression. Indeed, it was increasingly apparent, with every new avenue of psychoanalytic inquiry I pursued, that many of the texts of American literature that have in the past few decades been explored from a wealth of different critical perspectives come alive in a new and thoroughgoing way (particularly for feminist readers such as myself) when the preoedipal conflicts and the imaginatively transformed figure of the mother—or the author's own feminine sensibilities of which this figure is the mirror image—are identified as dynamic underlying forces in the textual narrative.

Among the goals that I have set out to achieve in *The Grief Taboo in American Literature*, therefore, is a demonstration of where and how grief, or feelings and feminine identification in general, are denied by these authors as an unconscious revolt against lingering maternal dependency. I also intend to show how adolescent idealization and an ideological identification with patriarchal culture serve as totems to protect against the acknowledgment of the grief and feelings that are always and everywhere present but never directly expressed.[11] In short, I seek to expose the vulnerability of a willfully and defiantly constructed American masculinity in the very places where that vulnerability is denied and defended against.

Herman Melville's inability to vent openly his grief over loss grew out of intense feelings of guilt over that loss, and it transformed his grief into various forms of aggression. Through the act of writing, Melville found a way to sublimate his repressed grief, and to act out his early emotional conflicts, which, by virtue of the fact that they were suppressed into the realm of the unconscious, appeared in his fiction in fixated form. Melville's fictional protagonists, like the author himself, appear to be trapped within early infantile and adolescent conflicts, which they are unable to get beyond in the course of their fictional dramas—leaving them to traverse perpetually the psychic landscape of aggression, guilt, and repressed grief. In the opening chapter on Melville's *Moby-Dick*, I intentionally refrain from drawing upon biological data, or the kind of psycho-biographical analysis just proposed with regard to Melville himself. I do so in order to establish the important fact that the text taken by itself can stand up to a psychoanalytic inquiry of repressed grief, fixated masculine development, and feminist undercurrents; and even more importantly, that the novel is a timeless and brilliant work of art for the precise reason that it functions so successfully as a self-contained, universal psychological drama.

On the other hand, in the extended discussions of the life and fiction of Mark Twain and Ernest Hemingway, I demonstrate in detail how artistic expression functioned for both of them, personally, as a way of dealing with the issue of emotional deprivation and loss. The manner or style of creative expression that each adopted supplied them with artful strategies for repressing, or indirectly expressing, the grief from loss:

Twain, through the use of humor and nostalgic fantasies of a lost ideal past (both of which disguise emotional pain behind a facade of pleasure and optimism); and Hemingway, through a masterful narrative technique in which painful emotions, or emotional vulnerability itself, are communicated only by way of silent reference and implication. For both of these authors the motive, and the consequence, of their taboo against grief can be traced to a fixation on preoedipal and adolescent conflicts, to their corresponding commitment to adolescent idealism, and finally, to their efforts to keep at arms length the inevitable encroachment of their grief and loss—grief and loss associated with eventual disillusionment with the idealistic fantasies that they initially used to protect themselves against the disappointments and emotional pain of growing up.

Methodological problems inevitably arise in any critical investigation. One of the difficulties in tracing, through the lens of psychoanalysis, the themes of tabooed grief and fictive mourning in the works of three authors whose personal histories and creative styles are as diverse as the distinct historical moment of which they were a product and a part, is that there will be gaps in the aetiology of their personal and artistic development that cannot be bridged, except through grossly artificial means. For this reason, I will not attempt to draw psychoanalytic parallels between Melville, Twain, and Hemingway, except to point out, wherever applicable, how their unique experiences of early deprivation and loss led to similar reactions: an arrest in the development of the masculine individuation process, a partial (yet significant in relation to their development as artists) inability to grieve openly over loss, and their use of many of the same strategies to deal indirectly with their repressed—and therefore, chronic or protracted—grief.

As befits any posthumous psychoanalytic exploration of literary figures and their works, I try to discharge the task with an awareness of the limitations one confronts when attempting to offer a dynamic formulation for a "patient" one has never met. As a methodological premise, I grant the fact that genius can never fully be explained or dissected. Nevertheless, I also assume that it is possible to identify and to illuminate the underlying forces that shaped the content and structure of an artist's work. I also intend to offer a combination of object-relations theory, developmental psychology, and feminist psychoanalysis as interpretive models, or frames of reference, through which diverse and seemingly disparate biographical and literary elements may be ordered to generate new theories for present and future inquiry.

Throughout this psychoanalytic investigation of American literature, I adapt my methodology to the literary and biographical material at hand, often switching gears, combining theoretical applications, and even occasionally pursuing two psychoanalytic narratives at once, rather than seeking to make the literary narrative conform to a pre-determined analytical schema. The narrative of repressed grief in the text of Melville's *Moby-Dick*, for example, is best understood by calling upon developmental and object-relations psychoanalytic theories that elucidate the dynamics of the child's early attempts to achieve autonomy against the pull of regressive separation anxiety, as well as by calling upon clinical and theoretical studies on adult male fantasies of the all-providing, and yet smothering, preoedipal mother. Whereas, in my investigation of the evolution of Mark Twain's identity as a humorist in America, I employ D. W. Winnicott's findings on the effects of emotional deprivation and maternal disappointment on the child's formulation of a secure sense of self. The theories of John Bowlby on sibling loss and pathological mourning also prove extremely useful in understanding the creative role that guilt and repressed grief play in Twain's novels and short fiction. Ernest Hemingway's life and fiction present a different analytical challenge, in that genetically stimulated depression and self-image problems (stemming partly from the pressures exerted upon him by twentieth-century American culture) contributed to his motives for denying and displacing overt grief and mourning in his life and fictional narrative, and to his singular incapacity to confront (or to work through) his experiences of loss and grief in later life. In this case, current and classical psychoanalytic theories on the formation of the ego ideal in adolescence, and on the effect that a negative self-concept has on the development of a depressive disorder, effectively serve to open up Hemingway's fictional texts as narratives of repressed grief and denied emotional vulnerability.

To view each of these three authors and their works independently, or as separate case studies, each with a psychoanalytic integrity unique unto itself, is not to disregard the richly revealing literary, cultural, and biographical commonalities that they share: Indeed, when embarking upon this study, one of my central aims was to highlight such commonalities amongst the three. To cite one example of the numerous parallels existing, not only among the three writers, but also with American culture at large, it may be observed that Melville, Twain, and Hemingway all share a family configuration in which the father is emotionally inaccessible to the son and in which the mother plays the role of the children's primary caretaker. Furthermore, Melville and Twain were twelve years old when their fathers died, while Hemingway's father, who suffered from a depressive and/or nervous disorder, increasingly distanced himself from his son when Ernest was also about twelve years old.[12] In addition, all three writers had exceptionally strong, and somewhat narcissistic, mother figures, fostering intense and prolonged dependency ties and the intrapsychic formation of a clinging and yet rejecting maternal figure.

Despite their differences, the early nuclear families to which Melville, Twain, and Hemingway belonged mirror the typical American family configuration in which the father is out of the home for most of the day while the mother assumes almost exclusive care of the children.[13] As is characteristic of this family scenario, Melville, Twain, and Hemingway were deprived of an intimate personal relationship with their fathers as young boys, and so denied the opportunity to be initiated personally into the world of men, which would also have enabled them to achieve a clear separation from the mother. Instead, they sought to achieve a masculine identity structure by identifying with an abstract heroic paternal ideal, thus circumventing the critical reality-testing (or negative oedipus complex) phase of development.[14] Although it remains to be seen how this developmental dynamic played a part in the creative process and fictional imagination of each of these three authors, suffice it to say for the present that they shared an emotional dependency on the mother, an experience of paternal disappointment, and many of the developmental problems, as well as the creative benefits, that accompany the prolongation of the stage of adolescent idealism.

It is worth pointing out that this modern father-son dynamic is markedly different from the classical oedipal father-son conflict. To persist in the identification of one's self with a flawless, exalted ego ideal—as did Melville, Twain, and Hemingway, and American patriarchal culture at large—is to engage in a narcissistic fantasy of self-perfection that frequently precludes the successful development from adolescence to adulthood. According to psychoanalysis, the heroic paternal ideal not only embodies the threatening oedipal father, but is also an extension of a primal or infantile experience of God-like narcissistic omnipotence more closely identified with the child's fantasized image of the all-powerful parents, particularly the early preoedipal mother. The tendency toward paternal idealization and utopian thinking, therefore, is more of a regressive than an oedipal choice on the part of the son.[15] The important recognition to be made here is that the American character, and by extension American literature, cannot be understood (as it often has in the past) solely in terms of a Freudian oedipal paradigm; indeed, gender theory enables us to recognize a more complicated dynamic at work in the American male's masculine identity development. Hence, it is part of the intention of this book to reposition much of what has been labeled as "oedipal" conflicts in American fiction as a crisis in the American male writer's, and his hero's, preoedipal and object-relations development, in which he stubbornly retains a regressive, infantile narcissism through his insistence on taking a utopian, grandiose ideal as his chosen ego-ideal self object.

The fact that the heroic paternal ideals with which Melville, Twain, Hemingway, and their fictional male protagonists sought to identify are considered to be masculine or paternal ideological constructs, and that the feminine, preoedipal, or maternal origin of which they are echoes is disavowed, can be understood in terms of the defensively constructed masculinity of a patriarchal culture that denies its mortal and maternal origins, as well as the personhood of women and mothers. In American culture, as in American literature, when the real or subjective figure of the woman and mother is omitted from one's view of the world, from all that is important (that is to say, masculine), the figure chosen as a female or maternal substitute is going to be male, or a masculine ideal. In a world without women, as in a Renaissance stage-drama, the men are forced to play a plurality of roles, assigning to each other the parts of mother and wife. Contemporary psychoanalytic and feminist theory, however, enables us to uncover the disguised gender roles in the male fantasies of American fiction: to see the feared and repressed feminine in the black slave or the young boy, and the idealized mother in the rivers, the sea, and the ecstatic moments of sexual union and death.

When reconstructing the past according to present modes of analysis—whether historical, sociological, or psychoanalytical—one inevitably runs the risk of distorting historical experience. The compensation, of course, is that the past often can be made to come alive in a new way that is meaningful within present historical and psychoanalytic contexts. Equally valid is the related conviction that much of the significance of a literary text or historical event lies dormant until a new and expanded method of inquiry or perceptive apparatus allows us to recognize its abundant interpretive potentialities. Such, I believe, is the case with the present investigation of repressed grief, arrested adolescence, and repudiated emotional vulnerability in American fiction. We have arrived at a cultural moment where we can see, and in fact are especially receptive to acknowledging, the feminine sensibilities that are embedded in the patriarchal literary texts of a male-dominant culture. In the last twenty years or so we have gained a greater understanding of gender roles, particularly of masculinity, as constructed entities. This understanding has allowed us to recognize, and break down, the masculine defenses against feminine identification that previously were unconsciously erected by the American male writer.

To attempt to bridge the gap between the cultural narrative and the individual psychoanalytic narratives in the fiction of Melville, Twain, and Hemingway, as I have begun to suggest, is also to risk falling into the trap of reductive analysis. I would, however, like to leave open the possibility of such a line of interpretive thought for the reader to accept or reject at will by proposing that the unique psychological circumstances that fostered the creative impulse in these writers, and the psychological themes with which they were personally involved, both fed upon and fed into the psychological and ideological issues that were brewing within the collective American psyche. The rejection of the past and the passing of one generation to the next, especially from father to son, has not, since America's early beginnings, been invigorated by an appropriate sense of grief and mourning, and this indicates that the theme of repressed grief was already at work in American thought and ideology much earlier than the mid-nineteenth century when Melville appeared on the literary scene.

"Stranded Vessels:" Utopian Thinking and Compulsive Self-Reliance in Early American Literature

The typical jeremiad that proliferated throughout colonial America in the mid-seventeenth century assumed as its premise a positive, abstract vision of a "new" and purified England in order to supplant, and to compensate for, the griefs suffered and the pains endured in the real, but willfully shed, social and religious past. Using the workings of divine providence as a justification for their rebellious undertaking, the Puritans severed themselves physically, spiritually, and ideologically from their "real" or historical father. Instead, they erected an heroic utopian ideal in the form of an impossible-to-attain spiritual perfectibility, and developed a notion of themselves as "heroic sufferers" who endured religious "purgative pain" for the sake of their divine American mission as God's chosen people.[16]

Calling upon a secular (that is, a political and economic) kind of divine prophesy at work in the destiny of America, Thomas Paine in his 1776 pamphlet, "Common Sense," encouraged a second major national break with the past, this time through America's declaration of independence from England. The unification of the colonies into a separate independent state, Paine writes, "like an act of oblivion, shall bury in forgetfulness every former dissention."[17] All past attachments and griefs, Paine implies, can be wiped from America's collective memory merely by proclaiming the willful intention to do so: "All plans, proposals, &c. prior to the nineteenth of April, i.e. to the commencement of hostilities, are like the almanacks of last year; which, though proper then, are superceded [sic] and useless now" (37). "We have it in our power to begin the world over again," Paine adds in the appendix to his political circular: "The birthday of a new world is at hand" (66). Within the macrocosm of American government and culture, then, remorse and grief over a lost past are all but snuffed out in the name of progress, idealism, and freedom.

Within the microcosmic universe of the individual, the American doctrine of self-reliance, self-creation, and rebirth was personified by Benjamin Franklin in his now famous autobiography. Here, he proclaims his intention to pursue "the bold and arduous Project of arriving at moral Perfection," and in doing so advocates as distinctly American the capacity to disavow one's restricting and limiting real past, and to reshape a potent and exemplary self out of sheer wilfulness and ambition.[18] Franklin's wholehearted investment of psychic energy into fulfilling such an idealized scheme necessitated the rigid subordination of emotional vulnerability to will, and of the grief over a rejected personal and historical past to an indefatigable optimism. Franklin's remarkable ability to succeed and profit from his scheme of self-discipline, however, exemplifies just how far one can go in a patriarchal culture through a steadfast adherence to this American utopian ideal.[19]

When Alexis de Tocqueville visited America in 1831, he noted not only the virtues but also the adverse consequences of "extreme equality" and the peculiarly American "doctrine of self-interest."[20] In a passage that anticipates the romantic tone of Hawthorne or Poe, de Tocqueville proceeds to describe these negative attributes, not as pernicious, but as profoundly sorrowful: "Thus, not only does democracy make every man forget his ancestors, but it hides his descendants and separates his contemporaries from him; it throws him back forever upon himself alone, and threatens in the end to confine him entirely within the solitude of his own heart" (194). Again, the isolation inherent in the truly democratic system of equality and self-reliance portends a grief and sadness concerning one's separation from the past, from one's fellow human beings, and from one's own emotional, or "feminine," sensibilities, that must be subjugated to the higher cause of personal success, intellectual mastery of the world, and self-rule.

The New England Transcendentalists, appropriating for their own use elements of English and German "romanticism," French and English poetry, and Oriental literature, created a "living religion" removed from inherited biblical theology and doctrine. The Transcendentalists saw "the image of God . . . stamped on nature," celebrated the divine powers of the individual mind and senses, and in turn invested godliness in the image of a universal Divine Mind.[21] As the Puritans had before them, the Transcendentalists were obliged to deny the disappointments and limitations of the Fall, or of loss and compromise in general, and instead to engage optimistically and fully in the ideological search for a perfectible, autonomous self. Once again, the repression of grief over a lost and discarded past was justified and sublimated by the compelling desire to recapture in some way the "Paradise" of individual wholeness or oneness. For the Transcendentalists, however, it was not the biblical garden of Edenic maternal plentitude, but Mother Nature, with whom they aspired to achieve divine, spiritual symbiosis. They sought, as William Henry Furness explains, a "grand Interpretation of Nature—the Revelation of her mysteries."[22]

The Transcendentalist belief in the primacy of the individual, initially advanced and supported by the democratic doctrine of absolute equality and self-rule, was adopted most prominently by Ralph Waldo Emerson, who, through his writing and preaching, transformed it into a credo that expanded to cult proportions in America. True to the adopted spirit of American democratic self-reliance, Emerson believed that the human mind was complete in and of itself, and hence had no use for either the historical or the personal past. "There is no history; There is only Biography," he writes. "You can only live for yourself. . . . The new individual must work out the whole problem of science, letters, theology for himself"; he "can owe his fathers nothing."[23] Gay Wilson Allen, in his biographical work on Emerson, proposes that the doctrine of self-reliance satisfied Emerson's pressing urge to occupy a position of "emotional invulnerability."[24] Indeed, while there is evidence to suggest that Emerson suffered deep pain and sorrow after the deaths of his first wife Ellen in 1831, his brother Charles in 1836, and particularly his son Waldo in 1842, his brief outpourings of grief are countered by an overwhelming effort to deny the consolation that grieving provides—by intellectualizing about the uselessness of succumbing to one's feelings, and by extolling the superior virtues of maintaining a willful optimism.

Possessed by a strange discomfort in the face of his own lack of emotions, Emerson, in a letter to a friend shortly after the death of young Waldo, admits that: "I chiefly grieve that I cannot grieve; that this fact takes no more deep hold than other facts. . . ."[25] Emerson's confessed inability to grieve, however, did not diminish or eradicate his grief. His inviolate optimism and proudly flaunted emotional insularity were, in fact, memorials to the losses for which he refused to grieve adequately at the time they occurred. In his 1844 essay, "The Tragic," Emerson writes: "Some men are above grief, and some below it" (*Essays*, 1292). Emerson, of course, includes himself among those "higher" natures who are "above grief"; and to those like himself he counsels: "We must walk as guests in nature,—not impassioned, but cool and disengaged" (1293). "The intellect," he concludes, "is a consoler, which delights in detaching, or putting an interval between a man and his fortune, and so converts the sufferer into a spectator, and his pain into poetry" (1295). Because Emerson's poetry and philosophy of discipline, self-reliance, and impervious autonomy evolved to a significant degree as a displaced grief response for his repressed and unacknowledged emotions, they are, especially in their heightened optimism and flagrant grandiosity, themselves a totemic testimony to the grief and real human emotions that they perpetually seek to transcend.

In many ways, Henry David Thoreau played the part of Emerson's adoring yet rejected, and dejected, "son," whose compulsive adherence to an elevated image of the father resulted in the same repression of emotional vulnerability and fixation at the adolescent stage of development that afflicted his spiritual father, Emerson.[26] Thoreau inherited from Emerson the legacy of grandiosity and extreme self-absorption at the expense of an articulated emotional life and strong interpersonal relationships. Thoreau's emulation of this father figure, combined with his inability to achieve real intimacy with him, or, in fact, with anyone, is characteristic of the kind of democratic father-son relationship about which de Tocqueville had years earlier complained. The "old have no very important advice to give the young," Thoreau proposes in *Walden*. "One generation abandons the enterprises of another like stranded vessels."[27] Surely if any man was ever, as de Tocqueville warned, confined "entirely within the solitude of his own heart," it was Henry David Thoreau.[28] Like Emerson, Thoreau incorporated his awkward and inept social skills and his incapacity to establish intimate personal relationships into a formal philosophy by glorifying the virtues of independent solitude and attributing to the natural world an emotional depth sufficient to sustain the emotional needs of the individual. In 1851, he writes in his Journal: "I *really* can communicate with my friends and congratulate myself and them on our relation and rejoice in their presence and society oftenest when they are personally absent."[29]

The grief and loss that Thoreau undoubtedly felt from being so removed from his fellow human beings are denied overt expression, but they are clearly recognizable in his compulsive denial of loss, his avoidance of emotional pain, and his tendency to universalize or generalize about his sorrow. The psychosomatic lockjaw, poor health, and inability to write that afflicted Thoreau after the death from lockjaw of his brother John in 1842, was probably a displaced manifestation of the grief that fails to appear in Thoreau's writings or Journal during this time. When writing about the death of Emerson's son Waldo, Thoreau, as Emerson himself did, sublimated his sadness over Emerson's son's death into a forced and chilling positivism: "Neither will Nature manifest any sorrow at his death, but soon the note of the lark will be heard down in the meadow, and fresh dandelions will spring from the old stocks [sic] where he plucked them last summer."[30]

America's idealism, optimism, and exaggerated emphasis on the self, which were transformed by Thoreau from an ideology into a style of daily living, all achieve a culmination in the poetry and philosophy of Walt Whitman. In "Starting from Paumanok," Whitman embraces the American democratic spirit of rebirth, and along with it a celebratory rejection of the past, by describing America as: "A world primal again, vistas of glory incessant and branching, / A new race dominating previous ones and grander far, with new contests, / New politics, new literatures and religions, new inventions and arts" (*Leaves*, 26–27). Through the spiritual tenor of his poetry, Whitman enacted an apotheosis of the myth of America as a promised land of perpetual regeneration.

Furthermore, if the Transcendentalists, Emerson and Thoreau included, failed to identify Nature as a nostalgic fantasy of a return to, or merging with, the preoedipal mother—the timeless, serene womb and the quiescence of egoless, non-being and death—Walt Whitman's explicit poetic imagery made the regressive nature of the American male's unconscious desires abundantly clear. Whitman's "poetry of democracy" openly proclaims its elaborate fantasies of symbiotic fusion. In Whitman's imagination, the democratic credo, "E Pluribus Unum," becomes a dynamic means of ecstatically realizing "One's Self" through the total dispersion of the self into the "All": "A vast similitude interlocks all," Whitman writes in the poem "On the Beach at Night Alone;" and by this he includes: "All spheres, grown, ungrown, small, large, suns, moons, planets, / All distances of place however wide, / All distances of time, all inanimate forms," and so on.[31] Although Whitman, unlike Emerson and Thoreau, claimed to experience intimacy with others, it was an intimacy with the "All"—with everything and everyone—that renders the feasibility of real intimacy with any constituent part of that universal (or with any one individual), at best abstract and impersonal, at worst impossible or delusionary.[32] The young Whitman, the poet who proclaimed that "at thirty-seven and in perfect health I now begin," can rather easily be cast in the role of the "aborted adolescent" who is entangled in a nostalgic state of chronic mourning for his own undifferentiated infancy. As Lawrence observes: "Everything was female" to Whitman, and he was "[a]lways wanting to merge himself into the womb of something or other. . . Anything, so long as he could merge himself" (*Studies*, 176). Whitman thus differs from so many of his predecessors in the openness with which he voices his nostalgic longing for feminine/maternal identification, a position that inevitably has been interpreted by an American male culture as a homoerotic, and therefore a deviant, vision of masculine maturity and individuation.

Of all of America's most popular nineteenth-century writers, however, Nathaniel Hawthorne perhaps perceived most truly and deeply the danger of repressing one's dark and negative emotions. Hawthorne recognized that to separate oneself from one's dubious desires—indeed from all those feelings and natural instincts that make one human—is to repress forcibly from consciousness that which cannot be concealed indefinitely. Such emotions, therefore, will inevitably surface and take their toll in other tragic ways on the human mind and heart. "Young Goodman Brown" and "The Minister's Black Veil" are two of Hawthorne's most psychologically penetrating dramatizations of the dire consequences that come to those who attempt to disavow an irrepressible part of their instinctual and emotional reality.

"My Kinsman, Major Molineux," and "Roger Malvin's Burial," in fact, could function as ur-texts for the present psychoanalytic investigation of American literature in that they demonstrate the pernicious consequences of repressed grief, specifically in relation to the lost son and the absent father. In "My Kinsman, Major Molineux," one may recognize the theme of the boy's loss of innocence as a result of his inevitable discovery of the imagined heroic father as a less than ideal figure. The tragic tone of the tale's ending, however, is conveyed not only through the boy's disillusionment with the paternal ideal, but also through his defensive denial of emotional loss, and his inability, or unwillingness, to grieve over this loss. "Roger Malvin's Burial" relates the story of a son, Reuben Bourne, who, out of self-interest, abandons his dying "father," a secret which he keeps to himself for years afterward. Because of his guilt, the adolescent Reuben is unable to allow himself to grieve properly over his "father's" death, and so lives a dark and overcast life of chronic grief and shame until he becomes a father himself and his repressed guilt returns as an ominous and unconscious inner destructive force. When Reuben's son, Cyrus, reaches the same age as Reuben when he made that fateful journey with his "father" years ago, he is "mistakenly" murdered by Reuben while hunting in the woods, thus expiating the father's guilt and finally allowing Reuben to grieve openly, not only for the son who lies dead on the forest floor, but also for the father who, both literally and psychologically, was never adequately "buried" by his son at the time of his death.

There are, of course, more ways to read Hawthorne's stories than as psychoanalytic narratives of repressed grief and failed masculine individuation.[33] To state what I assume is obvious to the experienced critical reader, the psychoanalytic readings of the fiction and literary imaginations of Melville, Twain, and Hemingway that I offer in this book—while they may, in certain instances, seem to refute or overturn previously proposed interpretations—are not intended to undermine or usurp prior literary, cultural, or analytical approaches, but rather, to complement and enhance them. The vigor of my approach is justified, I believe, by my conviction that a new and penetrating understanding of some of America's most notable and cherished literary figures and their texts can be gained by pursuing a direct and focused psychoanalytic reading.

Also for the sake of introduction, it should be pointed out that there is a wealth of first-rate American fiction that lies outside the thematic range of aborted adolescence, repressed grief, and denied feminine sensibilities investigated in this study. The fiction of William Dean Howells, Edith Wharton, G. W. Cable, and Henry James, for example—whose works are often referred to as the late nineteenth- and early twentieth-century "novels of manners"—frequently address the themes of emotional vulnerability, the pains and pleasures of the individual's development toward maturity, and the sociological significance of loss, disillusionment, and death, in an effort to portray the subtleties and diversities of life in American culture. Similarly, the naturalistic novels of Frank Norris, Jack London, Theodore Dreiser, and James T. Farrell evaded the issue of repressed emotional vulnerability particularly because they confronted head-on the griefs and losses inherent in the individual's struggle within the family and the community: by emphasizing, rather than attempting to deny in any way, the inevitably bleak and pessimistic fate of mankind.

Nineteenth- and twentieth-century American women writers have been, one might broadly say, grounded in many of the literary, social, political, and psychological concerns of the novels of manners, naturalism, and realism that I have just mentioned. In the most general terms, women writers have dealt with loss, mourning, and separation in a fundamentally different way than their masculine counterparts. Whereas male writers often respond to loss and death with a suppressed anxiety toward, and an unconscious fear of, deprivation, abandonment, and emotional vulnerability, women authors tend to express a more immediate and conscious emotional reaction to the threat of interpersonal loss and separation. Nineteenth-century women writers mainly chose to portray women's roles in the family and in society (a literary subject that was, to say the least, de-emphasized by most American male writers), and therefore, the themes of loss and separation were dealt with primarily in social and inter-relational terms. In their novels and stories, social and religious funeral rituals surrounding death and loss were consistently viewed by women characters with a sincerity that seemed to allow them to acknowledge their sorrow, and to work through the process of mourning in an orderly and timely fashion. In the writings and fiction of women, from Anne Bradstreet and Mary Rowlandson in early Puritan America, to Harriet Beecher Stowe and Emily Dickinson in the nineteenth century, and to Willa Cather, Susan Glaspell, and Carson McCullers in the twentieth century—grief and mourning over death and loss are overtly and conspicuously manifested (if not exaggerated) through social and psychological vehicles of emotional expression.

At the same time it may be granted that the separation-individuation process of adolescent girls in American society, as it is frequently depicted in the fiction of women writers, is fraught with its own difficulties, often having to do with the girl's prolonged attachment to, and identification with, the mother. An avenue for further investigation of tabooed grief in American fiction might be an exploration of women's mechanisms of defense against experiencing both the grief of self-loss resulting from an actual, or intrapsychic, separation from the mother imago, and the grief of loss from death. These feminine mechanisms of defense might include self-sacrificing empathy, moral or religious rationalizations, the belief in a "better" life after death, and denial based on the biologically supported fact that a woman can "live on after death" through her reproductive capacity, and therefore can find refuge in a kind of "immortality" that is inaccessible to men.

Let it suffice that not all of American fiction falls into the thematic categories highlighted in this investigation. Nevertheless, the thematic patterns of repressed grief, perpetual adolescence, and denied feminine identification can be found in many of the writings that traditionally have been identified as distinctly American in tone, spirit, and content; in those works, in other words, that celebrate freedom, self-reliance, idealism, and masculine prowess. The lamentable consequence of what R. W. B. Lewis describes as America's chronic innocence and habit of forgetfulness is that we have repeatedly returned "decade after decade and with the same pain and amazement, to all the old conflicts, programs, and discoveries."[34] Since the age of Emerson, Lewis declares, we have been a "one-generation culture." To recognize in our greatest myths the preoedipal mother, the fundamental dejection, the unresolved infantile and adolescent conflicts, and the instability of our cultural myths and language, may mean that we can break the cycle of the repression, repetition, and return of repressed grief, not only in our inherited cultural ideology, but in our present and future critical outlook as well.

*Conspiracies in Adolescent Idealism: Interpreting the American
Literary Imagination*

For the most part, American literary criticism has participated in the
democratic spirit of optimism by valorizing the repression of grief, and
the disavowal of the paralyzing emotional consequences of separation
and loss, and by viewing these repressions and denials as necessary to the
fulfillment of the "imperial" American self and the utopian ideal of
perfectibility. Early literary and historical critics, for example Stuart
Sherman in his essay "What is a Puritan?" identify the essentially heroic
attributes of the Puritan as "dissatisfaction with the past, courage to
break sharply from it, a vision of a better life."[35] In addition, what have
been labeled as the "self-reflexive" theories of American literary language
were designed by the New Critics—F. O. Matthiessen, Charles Feidelson, Jr., and Richard Poirier are good examples—in an effort to make
sense of the American writer's symbolic, allegorical, and mythic use of
language to escape or transcend historical, social, political, and emotional
determinism, and to create instead an autonomous, self-referential language—a "world elsewhere."[36] These early commentators on American
literature, even those who attack the idealism of American culture, have
set the critical tone for the traditional literary canon by accepting the
mythical terms of America as a New World Garden. As males themselves, they seem to have identified with the authors they have described,
and, joining them, appear to have suppressed the emotional content of
experience. Consequently, they, like their literary subjects, have distanced themselves from important aspects of social and interpersonal relationships.

On the other hand, many of these literary and cultural theorists have
recognized the immaturity of America's idealism, and the emotionally
and spiritually debilitating consequences of its transcendent utopian fantasies. Perhaps it was because D. H. Lawrence came to American literature with an eye for a most un-American form of spirituality and un-
veiled sexuality that he was able to perceive a repressiveness,
childishness, hollow idealism, and will to power in the mind of the
male American fiction writer.[37] Similarly, Leslie Fiedler has repeatedly
observed that it is "maturity above all things that the American writer
fears."[38] According to Fiedler, American fiction is "in flight from the
physical data of the actual world, in search of a (sexless and dim)
Ideal" (29).

Following the same line of thought, Richard Chase points to the inclination of American writers to "veer toward mythic, allegorical, and symbolic forms."[39] The characters in American literature, Chase adds, are not "complexly related to each other or to society or to the past," but transcend class, race, and their human and historical origins (xi). As Yvor Winters has observed, "the choice between abstractions inadequate or irrelevant to experience on the one hand, and experience on the other as far as practicable unilluminated by understanding, is tragically characteristic of the history of this country and of its literature."[40]

Richard Poirier and F. O. Matthiessen, among others, have critically addressed the influence of democracy and freedom on the styles and themes of nineteenth-century American writers and poets. However, it seems they, too, have been captivated by a national optimism that drew their attention away from the psychological and cultural significance of grief in American literature. Although R. W. B. Lewis recognized the "tragic spirit" in the imaginative vision of early American writers, he focused primarily on the influence of hopeful innocence on their works and perhaps was diverted from the investigation of grief by his belief that the literature of America is "uninvigorated by a sense of loss."[41]

While much of the existing scholarship, particularly in its emphasis on the innocence and idealism of the American literary hero, has touched upon the issues of immaturity and arrested adolescence in America's male writers and their texts, none has systematically pursued or fully explored the insights that psychoanalysis has to offer in reaching a meaningful understanding of the male separation-individuation struggle, and the dynamic and integral role that the taboo against grief plays in this faltering developmental process. Biographers such as Van Wyck Brooks, Leon Howard, Leon Edel, Peter Griffin, and Bernice Kert have recognized the adolescent nature of our writers' most "mature" works. Melville, Twain, and Hemingway in particular have received considerable attention in this regard by these and other critics, such as Philip Young, Richard Chase, Kenneth Lynn, and Earl Rovit, all of whom address these authors' concern with father absence, the presence of father surrogates, the nostalgic yearning for youth and childhood, and the conspicuous scarcity of direct emotional expression in their works.

In the last two decades, dozens of books and literally hundreds of articles have dealt with the theme of the absent father and the lost son in an America that has remained since its rebellious beginnings a "culture of separation." The subject of "constructing masculinity" and the question of what it means to be a male in America are, today, the primary focus of psychoanalytic and psychiatric institutes across the country. These concerns, however, are emanating almost exclusively from the fields of sociology, psychology, and feminist theory. Comparatively speaking, literary criticism has not yet begun to apply these questions retrospectively to American literature, where I believe they are most deeply buried and most cleverly disguised, and therefore most profoundly in need of consideration.

The American Orphan-Hero

The fictional works of Melville, Twain, and Hemingway are representative of so much of American literature written by males in that they present us with the archetypal suicidal orphan, the perpetual adolescent who is simultaneously seeking and escaping from masculine maturity. One of the ongoing controversies surrounding American literature is whether its central mode is one of escape or quest. The answer, of course, is that it is both. The fictional adolescent orphan seeks both to escape from maternal dependency and to quest for the ideal father. In a parallel movement he also attempts to escape from, or disavow, the real, disappointing father and to quest for the fantasized omnipotent and narcissistically gratifying mother. Typically, in this saga, the American orphan is also trapped within his own transcendent idealized universe in which the real father is replaced by an heroic paternal ideal, and the real mother is abstracted—split into good and bad entities—and projected onto the American landscape as freedom and the fullness of nature, or, alternately, onto a land-bound, smothering, and restricting social domesticity.

Within the images and characters of the male author's texts, therefore, the reader should be able to identify the author's own discarded and outwardly projected parent images. Like one of the first mythical orphans, Oedipus, the American orphan/author is a wanderer, seeking to encounter the lost or absent parents in his fictional wanderings. But the archetype of the American Oedipus is what might be called a "compulsive wanderer," who forever defers mourning for his lost parental objects.[42] In embarking on his search the American orphan/author usually gives up his emotional ties and responsibilities, which, in effect, compels him to pursue the active fulfillment of his own death-wishes. He is, therefore, a suicidal orphan who is on a voyage to join the lost, the dying, and the dead. His voyage to adventure is, in itself, an act of mourning, and as psychoanalysis tells us, it is not only the loss of actual objects for which he mourns, but also for his own lost "capacity to love."[43]

Because he searches, and as long as he searches, the American orphan precludes himself from feeling the grief and love that motivate his search. His wandering, itself, is thus its own defense against pining, disappointment, and sorrow.[44] The seeking and finding of a lost object is an essential component of grief, but, as the predominance of the themes of death, murder, and killing in the American hero's adventures illustrates, the seeker, with no direct emotional reaction possible, will experience his emotions in indirect ways: He displaces his hostility onto children, Indians, blacks, or, largely, the other, and projects his repressed desires onto his American wilderness landscape.

The fictional orphan's journey through his metaphorical American terrain, as with the author's imaginative travels through his self-created world of fiction and fantasy, provides the illusion that his adolescent trap is not internal but external, and his romanticizing guards him against the conscious awareness of the psychological reality of his search. By leaving home the traveler is under the illusion that he has cut himself off from his emotional past—from love, loneliness, and grief. Hence, what was once something real in the lives of these authors has been transformed by them into something remote in fictional space. But, as one psychoanalyst wrote of Oedipus, like so many orphans and adopted children, he is "inexorably drawn to his past during his adolescence . . . haunted by his severed origins" and continually obsessed with his eternal search for them.[45]

Mourning ends when searching stops, psychoanalysis tells us. However, the American author's family-romance search for his lost and ideal parents is doomed to perpetuity because—romanticized, fictionalized, and rendered predominately through the unconscious—it is irrevocably removed from the real objects that he seeks. The utopian Ideal perpetually sought after by the American orphan, as Leon Edel says of Thoreau's Walden, is "a mood, a fancy, a fleeting dream. Someone who looks for the unattainable must keep on looking as Thoreau did—the hound, the bay horse, the turtledove always eluded him," and, as Edel conclusively reminds us: "There are no utopias in the real world" ("Mystery," 64). Consequently, the fate of the dreamy and rebellious American orphan is always to wander, to "light out for the territory," as Sam

Clemens once wrote to his mother, always to "be so situated . . . that I can 'pull up stakes' and clear out whenever I feel like it."[46]

Repressed Grief, Adolescent Idealism, and the Disavowed Feminine: A Revisionary Reading of Melville, Twain, and Hemingway

We can glimpse the patterns of repressed grief, fixated adolescent idealism, and disavowed feminine sensibilities, through a revisionary reading of three short works of fiction, one by each of the authors to whom the remainder of this study will be devoted: Melville's "The Paradise of Bachelors and the Tartarus of Maids," Hemingway's "Cross-Country Snow," and Twain's "The $30,000 Bequest."

"The Paradise of Bachelors and the Tartarus of Maids" can indisputably be said to relate to the indignities of nineteenth-century industrialization. Equally supportable is the argument that the two parts of this story pit against each other Melville's personal conflict between the freedom and ease of bachelor life, and the seemingly insurmountable and intolerable responsibilities of sexual involvement, with its resultant economic and emotional burdens of home, family, and career. But additionally, "The Paradise of Bachelors and the Tartarus of Maids," also may be said to depict, respectively, the youthful joy and repose of the conscious mind that has repressed and silenced the sorrows, pains, and grief of adult accountability, and the dark, terrifying, and grief-filled contents of the repressed unconscious.

The narrator of the story, invited as a guest to dine with a group of prominent London lawyers—all "Brethren of the Order of Celibacy"—shares with these bachelors an opulent repast: roast beef, game-foul, and ox-tail soup, topped off with claret, sherry, and a pinch or two of choice snuff, garishly offered in a silver horn adorned with "two life-like goats' heads, with four more horns of solid silver."[47] The bachelors who reside at "No. ———, Elm Court, Temple," behave like adolescent boys, or more accurately, pre-pubescent, even infantile-like, men, who seek only primitive sensual gratification—comfort, warmth, and nurturing. Psychoanalytically, there is no irony or paradox in the fact that Melville's image of masculine idealism and heroism (the bachelors' every action has a military parallel—all are "manoeuvrings" of their manly "forces") is interchangeable with infantile or maternal womb imagery; with, as Melville says, "Eden's primal garden" (318). What *are* utopian fantasies and visionary ideals if not social and political re-enactments of a lost and longed-for primitive, infantile omnipotence? Melville describes his adolescent male paradise as a "cool, deep glen, shady among harboring hills"; an "oasis" and a "refuge" that is "charming," "delectable," and "dreamy" (316 and 318). The masculine utopia of perfect freedom, brotherhood, and primal gratification is, in effect, a regressive male fantasy that owes an unacknowledged debt to the mother, and to female biology in general. However, this debt cannot, indeed must not, be consciously paid without also acknowledging the pain and sacrifice of women that literally and figuratively engender the paradise that these males enjoy. With "wives or children" comes "pain" and "trouble," Melville says, and all of these must be forgotten and denied in order for these men to "give the whole care-worn world the slip" (316). But the price of enforcing this taboo against grief is dire. One must have a "stony heart": turn a cold eye not only to wife and children but to all the struggling and grief-filled real world. In order for a paradise of bachelors to be made possible, therefore, somewhere there must exist a Tartarus of maids.

Whitewashed from the outside, no one would suspect the oppression and dejection of the inhabitants within the paper factory of Melville's Tartarus of maids. The world's griefs are frozen within "an unfeeling earth," the forests all around "strangely groaned," and the cold wind "shrieked through the shivered pass, as if laden with lost spirits bound to the unhappy world" (325). The maids themselves are pale and pallid, "blue with cold," as if living a death-in-life. They are machines—"the vaunted slave[s] of humanity"—slaves of "the Sultan," their bachelor boss, Old Bach. There are no men to be found anywhere in the paper factory, where these maids diligently go about their menial tasks day after day without end; Old Bach presides from afar, and the narrator does not seem to recognize as masculine the "dark-complexioned man" who governs the paper factory, nor the boy-guide, "Cupid," who, despite his youth, possesses a cold "cruel-heartedness" (331).

The thematic task Melville appears to have assigned to the narrator of the tale, a "seedsman," is to draw a parallel between the paradise of bachelors at the Temple court, and this oppressive, lifeless paper mill: to reconnect with both a destructive and a constructive synthetic force the bright, complacent conscious, and the chilly, yet blood-boiling, repressed unconscious. The seedsman senses the parasitic, master-slave dynamic between these two symbolic locales, intuiting their "inverse similitude" by surmising that perhaps the rags that are ground into pulp for making paper might be "some old shirts, gathered from the dormitories of the Paradise of Bachelors" (330). Based on this possibility, and the knowledge that the bachelors—all of whom are lawyers—consume an enormous quantity of paper, the narrator conjectures that somehow a demonic and insidious association between them does in fact exist. But, as Melville implies, the bachelors' lives of comfort and ease thrive by sucking the life-blood out of their own souls, by denying life's pain, troubles, and woes, which, as Melville intuitively suspects, means that they must disavow, along with death and grief, their own mortal, biological, and maternal origins.

One last detail of Melville's story, which is almost forgotten by the time the reader reaches the end of "The Tartarus of Maids," is the knowledge that the true and original Brotherhood of the "bold Knights-Templars" is "no more" (317): "a moral blight tainted at last this sacred Brotherhood," the "worm of luxury crawled beneath their guard, gnawing the core of knightly troth" (317). Hedonism, greed, and selfishness ate away at "these degenerate Templars," transforming them all into "hypocrites and rakes." In short, their taboo against grief, pain, and reality froze their hearts, destroyed their souls, and set one against the other until none of the original Brotherhood remained. As in Hawthorne's story, "Roger Malvin's Burial," the repressed grief has inevitably returned, and without the warmth and fecundity of emotional intimacy and sexual contact this brotherhood of bachelors became a self-destructive, and eventually an extinct, species.

Well over a half-century after Melville, in 1855, wrote "The Paradise of Bachelors and the Tartarus of Maids" for magazine publication, Ernest Hemingway published his first collection of short stories, *In Our Time*, in which may be found a story that portrays a strikingly similar adolescent male conflict. In "Cross-Country Snow," Nick Adams, whom we think, but do not know for certain, is married (we know only that his girl, Helen, is having a baby in about seven months), laments with his friend, George, the approaching end of their adolescent life of carefree pleasure. The two young men are taking their last ski-run in before assuming, with great reluctance and some degree of anxiety, the responsibilities of adult life: Nick, with regard to his pregnant girlfriend (or wife) and anticipated fatherhood, and George, with his return to school. Enjoying the last few moments of their own Melvillean fraternal brotherhood, as males united by their common devotion to the sport of skiing, Hemingway explains that "George and Nick were happy. They were fond of each other."[48] Their passion for skiing is so intense that they can hardly find words to describe it. "There's nothing really can touch skiing, is there?" Nick asks his companion. George, in an obvious gesture of repression, not only of his grief but of the pleasures he must now surrender, replies to Nick: "It's too swell to talk about."

Longing to retain forever their adolescent freedom from obligation to family and career, George fantasizes, "don't you wish we could just bum together? Take our skis and . . . our rucksacks and not give a damn about school or anything" (110). Nick enthusiastically agrees; and although he is just getting accustomed to the upcoming birth of his first child, he confesses that "No," he does not "want" to "go back to the States" (111). Evoking the Dantean "Black Notch" of Melville's Tartarus of maids, George says, "It's hell, isn't it?":

> "No. Not exactly," Nick said.
> "Why not?"
> "I don't know," Nick said. (111)

Nick knows he is not emotionally ready for his adult responsibilities, but he will take the plunge regardless. He accepts the inevitable loss of the perfect skiing experience that he knows he will never be able to get anywhere in the States. He admits, in other words, that he will never be as self-indulgent and carefree once he gives up the joys of his youthful independence: "that's the way it is everywhere I've ever been," Nick says about the deficient skiing in the States. "Yes," George agrees, and knowing full well that Nick is referring to the inevitable loss of far more than just good skiing, he replies to Nick, "that's the way it is" (112).

Hemingway strategically withholds Nick's open acknowledgment of grief over the loss of his secure and inviolate shared adolescent male pleasures, as well as the inner terror he feels about growing up. Instead, he conveys Nick's emotional vulnerability through the young men's compensating fantasy that a regression to their former carefree bliss remains a distinct future possibility:

> "Maybe we'll never go skiing again, Nick," George said.
> "We've got to," said Nick. "It isn't worth while if you can't."
> "We'll go, all right," George said.
> "We've got to," Nick agreed. (112)

As in Melville's story, the real source of adolescent anxiety that Nick is experiencing has to do with the dark, mysterious, and to use Melville's

words, "unbudging fatality" (*Stories*, 284) of the forward march of female biology and sexuality, which Hemingway relates indirectly through
Nick and George's encounter with the pregnant waitress in the ski
lodge. Although he never noticed it before, Nick now observes that the
waitress's "apron covered swellingly her pregnancy" (*In Our Time*, 109).
Like the maids in Melville's paper factory, the waitress in Hemingway's
story is both unmarried and a servant to these perpetual adolescent
"bachelors." At first all Nick and George want from her is "cake," a
sweet to satisfy their oral desires. But her swelling belly makes Nick
feel uncomfortable, as does her coldness toward them. George explains
somewhat callously that the girl is "from up where they speak German
probably and she's touchy about being here and then she's got that baby
coming without being married and she's touchy." "How do you know
she isn't married?" Nick asks him. "No ring." George says. "Hell, no
girls get married around here till they're knocked up" (110).

    The reader is led to envision the girl's private life, in which the father-
to-be will now, like Nick himself, be forced to make a commitment to
the future mother of his child. Female biology has destroyed the young
girl's spirit, as well as (and perhaps as a result of) her boyfriend's
manly independence. Both female sexuality and female sensibilities (e.g.,
emotional vulnerability and commitment) are incompatible with the ecstatic joys and freedom of bachelorhood, for the adolescent male who
longs to retain forever his ideal, female-exclusive, and hedonistic life of
pleasure. Just as these themes reach back to Melville's story, so Hemingway describes skiing in the same preoedipal terms as Melville describes the drinking, conversing, and snuff-taking of the bachelors at the
Temple court. Descending down the hill at top speed, Nick experiences
the "rush and the sudden swoop" of flying through the soft snow, which
"left him only the wonderful flying, drooping sensation in his body"
(107). "Crouching so," in a fetal-like position, Nick feels himself "float
up and drop down," and turns to look at George who was "coming
around in a beautiful right curve, crouching, the legs shot forward and
back . . . the sticks accenting the curve like points of light, all in a wild
cloud of snow" (107–8). The oceanic sensations and aesthetic perfection
of the experience of skiing parallel the infantile elation and sensual gratification of the libertine feast of Melville's bachelors.

    Hemingway's vision of adolescent masculine idealism, like Melville's,
contains unmistakable echoes of quintessential infantile omnipotence;
but, as with Melville's bachelors, Hemingway's young males have disa-

vowed the maternal and feminine origins of their idealistic fantasies, appropriating the feminine components of experience for their own use and pleasure. There is little doubt that Nick, on some level, desires to return to his girl in the States, and that George wants to return to school, yet so powerful is their overriding taboo against growing up, and all that it entails, that they cannot see clearly their opposing desires and their gratitude toward women. What they also do not realize, but Hemingway suggests, is that their paradise of male freedom and ease is pleasurable mainly because it offers a contrast to their "other" life of adult obligations. Should Nick and George take off skiing forever, not only would they grow weary of one another's company, but the magic of escape and refuge would be drained from skiing, sport, and vacationing, just as the bachelor's life in the cloistered Temple court seems so tempting and appealing to Melville because it represents a "refuge" from the griefs and burdens outside. Hemingway, like Melville, intuits this connection, and conveys it indirectly through the anxious inner psychic conflict of his male hero. Hence, as in Melville's story, the repression of grief and loss, the longing for continued adolescent autonomy and idealism, and the fear of female sexuality, all become linked psychological elements that threaten to overwhelm the adolescent male, encroaching fears that he defends against by engaging in the regressive fantasy of a return to a former insular state of gratification and omnipotence.

With the slight difference of Mark Twain's unique approach to the issue of conflicted sexuality, his 1902 story, "The $30,000 Bequest," contains as its moral the same incompatibility between idealism and moral and emotional honesty. Again we find the deleterious consequences of investing one's psychic energy too heavily in an idealistic, romantic fantasy. The plot of Twain's story is relatively simple. A young married couple, the Fosters, with dreams of accruing enormous wealth in order to make their lives perfect, discover that a distant uncle plans to leave them a fortune upon his death. Becoming wholly immersed in dreams of their impending fortune, the husband and wife completely lose touch with reality, spending all of their free time "day-dreaming" and "castle-building," intoxicated "with their beguiling fantasies," so that their "dream life" and their "material life" soon become "so intermingled and so fused together that we can't quite tell which is which, any more." [49] In the end they find out that their allegedly rich uncle Tilbury had indeed died, but without a cent, and that he had, as he originally had warned them, made them the promise of wealth "not for love, but because money had given him most of his troubles and exasperations, and he wished to place it where there was good hope that it would continue its malignant work" (597–98).[50]

In Twain's novels of boyhood adventure, his romantic idealism more closely resembles the nostalgic idealism of Melville's and Hemingway's stories in that it takes the form of a regressive wish to remain perpetually within the Edenic paradise of carefree boyhood. "The $30,000 Bequest," however, like Twain's earlier stories about the effects of money on the human spirit and interpersonal relationships—"The £1,000,000 Bank-Note" (1893), and "The Man That Corrupted Hadleyburg" (1899)—raises the themes of idealism, optimism, and repressed grief to the macrocosmic level of American culture as a whole. The romantic idealism of Twain's married couple is none other than a young and utopian America's romantic "American Dream" of immense financial success, and the unlimited omnipotence and power that such acquisition can offer.

The pursuit of wealth is an integral component of the American myth of freedom, self-reliance, and personal fulfillment. Twain's story makes it clear that money is not life-enhancing but the vehicle of a destructive romantic myth that replaces humanistic values with materialistic and hedonistic ones, undermines religious sentiments, and inclines even the warmest of human hearts toward icy selfishness. The Eden of eternally deferred financial independence that the Fosters create for themselves, like Melville's Paradise of Bachelors and Hemingway's male fantasy of adolescent irresponsiblity, fails, ultimately, to bring them the satisfaction that they seek. Instead, it satisfies only insofar as it insulates the Fosters from an undesirable, and seemingly oppressive, reality. Indeed, the hoped-for utopian social and economic liberation of Twain's Foster family might well have been recorded by a Benjamin Franklin, an Emerson, or a Thomas Paine; for, as Paine writes in "Common Sense" about America's liberation from England and future prospects in 1776: "America doth not yet know what opulence is; and although the progress which she hath made stands unparalleled in the history of other nations, it is but childhood, compared with what she would be capable of arriving at, had she, as she ought to have, the legislative powers in her own hand" (66). As their name implies, the "Fosters" belong to the company of fictional American orphan heroes. Like an independent America after 1776, they have willfully broken all ties with their personal and historical past in the hope of becoming the self-appointed "kings" of their own powerful and imperial financial domain.

Whereas Melville and Hemingway deal with the issue of sexuality in the perpetual adolescent's psychic drama by emphasizing the incompatibility between masculine and feminine gender roles, Twain intuitively depicts this problem by confounding the gender identities of his fictional man and woman. The greedy couple, Saladin and Electra Foster, possess the "curious and unsexing" nicknames, Sally and Aleck. Husband and wife have been unsexed (or rather, their genders have been reversed), Twain seems to imply, for the very reason that their utopian idealism has neutralized their sexually based intimacy as a couple. The drive for power and riches, like Melville's and Hemingway's fantasy of freedom from domestic cares, perverts the natural order of family and society, and widens the gap between categories of gender and social class.[51]

Furthermore, the news of the imminent fulfillment of their romantic, idealistic dreams of wealth and fame had not arrived for more than a few hours before it began to destroy the natural, emotional ties within the Foster family. That very night, the "good-night kisses" from their children "might as well have been impressed upon vacancy, for all the response they got" (598). All of the Fosters' genuine and spontaneous grief for the impending death of their apparently magnanimous uncle is repressed by their greater selfishness and greed. "He's probably out of his troubles before this; it's a hundred to nothing he's selecting his brimstone-shovel this very minute," Sally exclaims with excited anticipation. His wife is horrified by her husband's sudden and uncharacteristic insensitivity. "But why should you *want* to talk in that dreadful way?" she accuses him. "How would you like to have people talk so about *you,* and you not cold yet?" (600). Each week they eagerly scan the obituaries, hoping to discover that their uncle at last has died:

"Let us be humbly thankful that he has been spared; and—"
"Damn his treacherous hide, I wish—"
"Sally! For shame!"
"I don't care!" retorted the man. "It's the way *you* feel, and if you weren't so immorally pious you'd be honest and say so." (602)

The Fosters' romantic and aesthetic idealism has inspired in them a disavowal of the emotional consequences of loss and death, and has resulted in a new divisiveness within their marital and social relationships. Long-held friendships disintegrate, and previously practiced charitable impulses and religious feelings fall by the wayside, as the Fosters begin to spend all of their time planning and managing their future investments. When the parson's wife, Mrs. Bennett, calls on the Fosters to elicit their support for a charitable cause, she is rudely turned away, and Aleck now probes intently the various local and city newspapers, "with an eye single to finance . . . as diligently all the week as she studied her Bible Sundays" (606).

Satirizing the insidious and ludicrous consequences of romantic idealism, Twain notes that Sally and Aleck are already "beginning to roll in eventual wealth," and humorously points out that the couple was "actually worth a hundred thousand dollars in clean, imaginary cash" (607). The Fosters no longer care whether their two daughters married for love; now their "changed financial condition had raised up a social bar between their daughters and the young mechanics" (607). With their "fictitious finances" (611) the Fosters inhabit a fictitious house and build fictitious churches and universities. "How wonderful it all seems, and how beautiful!" (618). Their daughters would marry royalty; they would all live happily ever after. They would make a new start, become reborn as duke and duchess, or better, king and queen. The past is forgotten, the utopia of the future is suddenly everything. Emotional ties mean nothing now; personal feelings have no place in the Fosters' life: grief, loss, suffering, need, remorse—they were above them all.

When the Fosters finally receive news of their uncle's death (but not yet of his poverty), in a typically American fashion their sorrow over the imminent loss of their past life is indistinguishable from their wild elation over their future possibilities: "The Fosters were trembling with grief, though it felt like joy" (620). Then the boom was lowered; their uncle had died without a penny. Having invested all of their psychic energy in an impossible, grandiose ideal, and consequently, having fully lost touch with reality, and with their hearts and souls, it was not a part, but all of the Fosters' reality that came crumbling down around them. For two years after they receive this news, the Fosters lived "in mental night, always brooding, steeped in vague regrets and melancholy dreams, never speaking; then release came to both on the same day" (621). There was nothing fortunate about the fall of Sally and Aleck Foster. Moralizing, but without true repentance, Sally concludes that for a mere illusion—a "transient" dream of future "feverish pleasures"—"we threw away our sweet and simple and happy life—let others take warning by us" (621).

Though distinctly different in both style and substance, the dramatic conflict depicted in these three stories partakes of the centuries-old masculine American ideals of freedom, self-reliance, and the pursuit of happiness. The irony of this American masculine utopian vision of paradise is that it both calls upon, and in itself embodies, an infantile fantasy of narcissistic fulfillment and omnipotence, as well as the retained intra-psychic image of the bountiful, all-providing preoedipal mother, yet it thrives on the imperative masculine denial of female biology, of the personhood of women, and of the acknowledgment of inner "feminine" sensibilities, such as emotional vulnerability and the overt expression of grief and feelings. This irony inherent in the male adolescent's problematic separation-individuation struggle, typical of each author's unique fictional style, is symbolically and metaphorically conveyed by Melville, disguised by Twain within a disarming humorous storytelling voice, and indirectly presented by Hemingway through the defensive and evasive thought processes of his fictional characters. Each author, therefore, has mastered a stylistic technique that functions defensively to repress the male adolescent's grief from loss, emotional deprivation, and disillusionment in the heroic paternal ideal. But through the very act of repressing grief, that grief has become the life-blood that pulses to every extremity throughout the body of their fictional imaginations. Thus, pain and grief are nowhere, and yet, everywhere, in the literature of America. This is the strange paradox of our national heritage; rather, it is the estrangement of the American orphan-hero from his own heart that has unmistakably been recognized, but, I believe, never adequately understood.

There is no question that by embracing, for generation after generation, the adolescent spirit of idealism, America has burgeoned and prospered with the ardor and rapidity of any true Renaissance culture. This book neither desires, nor attempts, to deny this fact. Instead, it seeks to look beyond and beneath the celebratory tenor of the American democratic spirit with the hope of identifying the developmental, emotional, and gender-specific sacrifices that have been made in the name of the American Dream. For it is the losses, internal psychic conflicts, disillusionments, and unacknowledged griefs also suffered by America in the course of its history that our greatest fiction writers have felt compelled to dramatize for us again and again. Melville's Ishmael, Twain's Huck Finn, and Hemingway's Nick Adams embody within their literary frames the inspiring, enduring, yet also paralyzing and ultimately doomed, masculine idealism of a fundamentally adolescent culture.

On the level of the individual, America's masculine ideals reflect the visionary and utopian thinking most characteristic of the adolescent state of mental and emotional development, which should inevitably be tempered by the compromises, limitations, and contingencies of reality in the course of the individual's progressive development toward maturity and adulthood. As so frequently occurs in Hemingway's stories, for the adolescent boy who circumvents identification with the real, biological, and fallible father—and by-passes with it much of the reality-testing process—when the moment of inevitable disillusionment in the heroic, masculine ideal arrives, all of life becomes one titanic gloomy sorrow. As young Joe concludes in Hemingway's story, "My Old Man": "I don't know. Seems like when they get started they don't leave a guy nothing."[52] The same may be said for Melville's young hero, Pierre Glendinning, who never entertained a negative thought in relation to his adolescent, idealistic image of a perfect father, an unblemished, queenly mother, and a wholly uncorrupted home of Saddle Meadows, so that the news of Mr. Glendinning's infidelity, and of Mrs. Glendinning's disapproval of her son, strikes Pierre like a death-blow. There is no such thing as a partial emulation of the heroic paternal ideal for the romantically inclined American male adolescent. When Pierre discovers that his father was a seducer, "his whole previous moral being was overturned"; all of Saddle Meadows is blighted, and "the whole man droops into nameless melancholy."[53] For Melville, if one cannot have the paradise of bachelors, then one must have the Tartarus of maids—total satisfaction or total deprivation—there is no middle ground.

Certainly, the same may be said of Hemingway's youthful and idealistic *code hero*.[54] As Hemingway repeatedly reminds us, if his masculine hero does not know that he can execute a task perfectly, that is, with complete practical and stylistic mastery, he should never think of attempting it. Such inflated, grandiose idealism, as Twain instructs us in his story, is an invitation to disaster, just as surely as Melville's Brotherhood of the bold Knights-Templars, by repressing life's griefs and sorrows—and with these their own humanity—is doomed to extinction. During the last conversation A. E. Hotchner had with Hemingway before Hemingway committed suicide in July 1961, he gently inquired of his ailing friend why he so ardently wanted to kill himself. Hemingway, Hotchner writes, "hesitated only a moment; then he spoke in his old, deliberate way":

"What do you think happens to a man going on sixty-two when he realizes that he can never write the books and stories he promised himself? Or do any of the things he promised himself in the good days?"

"But how can you say that? You have written a beautiful book about Paris, as beautiful as anyone can hope to write. How can you overlook that?"

"The best of that I wrote before. And now I can't finish it."

"But perhaps it is finished and it is just reluctance . . ."

"Hotch, if I can't exist on my own terms, then existence is impossible. Do you understand? That is how I've lived, and that is how I *must* live—or not live. . . . That's the way a champ should go out."[55]

Although many of Ernest Hemingway's difficulties in his last few years of life were due to clinical depression, chemical and electro-shock treatments, and the irreversible effects of alcoholism, much of his despair in the end, as this conversation with Hotchner clearly suggests, resulted from the inflexibility of his grandiose idealism, and his inability to yield to, grieve over, and move beyond, his profound sense of life's inevitable disappointments, and his own personal disillusionment.

Mark Twain's cynicism and melancholy in later life is well known. According to Twain's secretary, Isabel Lyon—who perhaps spent more time with him than anyone else toward the end of his life—Twain often would rant and rave about the "damned human race," which, as he writes in the sketch "The Czar's Soliloquy" (1905), was nothing but an absurd "joke," and a bad one at that.[56] In a letter to his friend, William Dean Howells, in 1878, Twain complained bitterly that "in truth I don't ever seem to be in a good enough humor with ANYthing to *satirize* it; no, I want to stand up before it & curse it, & foam at the mouth,—or take a (club & beat it) club & pound it to rags & pulp."[57] As Twain confessed in a letter shortly after Susy's death, he would proceed in this manner to "rage until I get a sort of relief."[58] Through his humorous satires, Mark Twain upheld the high moral standards and the utopian vision of America's youthful innocence that his country appeared to him to have betrayed through avarice and greed in the late nineteenth and early twentieth century. But like Hemingway, his intractable and unbending moral vision of American idealism caused him endless personal anguish and grief. Twain surrounded himself in later life with an adoring company of young girls, whom he called his "Angel Fish," partly, perhaps, as an unresolved grief response for his favorite, beloved daughter Susy, who died in 1896 from meningitis at age twenty-four,[59] but also, more generally, because they, like the imaginative world of his fictional, nostalgic boyhood fantasies, allowed him to return in spirit to a time that predated his personal and ideological griefs and losses: to a time of real—not pretended or fictional—innocence, emotional honesty, and idealistic adolescent dreams.

Who among us would not have paid whatever price was necessary to have been able to sit with a despondent and willfully isolated Melville during his last years, in the dimly lit livingroom of his New York City apartment, and assure him that the dreams of greatness that he had cherished and hoped would be his when the world received his soul-bearing masterpiece, *Moby-Dick*, would indeed, in the years to come, be fulfilled far beyond the limits of his most inexpressible desires. But as for Hemingway and Twain and the heroes of his own fiction, Melville saw partial success as tantamount to total loss, making grief inevitable, but mourning for that grief, and overcoming it, impossible. Like Hemingway, Melville wanted to be a "champ," and if he could not live like a champ, he would die as one, and leave the recognition of his greatness to posterity. Dr. Henry A. Murray, perhaps Melville's most fervent admirer, and, certainly, one of his most ardent sympathizers (if such a one can be singled out from the rest of us), summarized the progressive course of Melville's ambivalent love affair over the years with victory, and its only alternative, death, as follows:

The essence of Melville's outlook in *Mardi* (1849) can be credibly represented, I would say, in these words: "If I fail to reach my golden haven, may my annihilation be complete; all or nothing!" Two years later in *Moby-Dick:* "I forsee my annihilation, but against this verdict of Fate I shall hurl my everlasting protest." In *Pierre* (1852): "I am on the verge of annihilation but I can't make up my mind to it." In 1856, to Hawthorne in Liverpool: "I have pretty much made up my mind to be annihilated;" and in *Billy Budd* (1891): "I accept my annihilation."[60]

In a sense one might justly criticize these American authors for defending a utopian vision that essentially ignores the subjective and biological reality of women and mothers, and that is certain, should we choose to follow it, to lead us to the same position of disappointment, disillusionment, and despair that they ultimately came to inhabit. At the same time, we owe them a substantial debt for boldly bearing the burden of grief and loss, thus permitting those of us who followed to reap the pleasures and benefits of a still-unblemished American Dream. Through a dedicated and thorough attempt to understand the strategies of defense these American writers employed to defy and repress their anger, inner conflicts, and grief, we are better able to estimate the enormity of the contribution they have made to American history and culture. But in doing so, in perpetuating for our inheritance the American spirit of ecstatic freedom, self-reliance, and individual moral and ideological nobility, they invited personal defeat upon themselves, and embraced their heroic annihilation. This book seeks by exploring a particular viewpoint to understand how their personal despair could result, paradoxically, in such a powerful, and enduring, literary and cultural victory.

1. "Circle-Sailing": The Eternal Return of Tabooed Grief in Melville's *Moby-Dick*

Then there is the matter of my mother's abandonment of me. Again, this is the common experience. They walk ahead of us, and walk too fast, and forget us, they are so lost in thoughts of their own, and soon or late they disappear. The only mystery is that we expect it to be otherwise.

—Marilynne Robinson, *Housekeeping*

Getting over it so soon? But the words are ambiguous. To say the patient is getting over it after an operation for appendicitis is one thing; after he's had his leg off it is quite another. After that operation either the wounded stump heals or the man dies. If it heals, the fierce, continuous pain will stop. Presently he'll get back his strength and be able to stump about on his wooden leg. He has "got over it." But he will probably have recurrent pains in the stump all his life, and perhaps pretty bad ones; and he will always be a one-legged man. There will be hardly any moment when he forgets it. Bathing, dressing, sitting down and getting up again, even lying in bed will all be different. His whole way of life will be changed. All sorts of pleasures and activities that he once took for granted will have to be simply written off. Duties too. At present I am learning to get about on crutches. Perhaps I shall presently be given a wooden leg. But I shall never be a biped again.

—C. S. Lewis, *A Grief Observed*

Our voyaging is only great-circle sailing, and the doctors prescribe for diseases of the skin merely. One hastens to Southern Africa to chase the giraffe; but surely that is not the game he would be after. How long, pray, would a man hunt giraffes if he could? Snipes and woodcocks also may afford rare sport; but I trust it would be nobler game to shoot one's self.

—Henry David Thoreau, *Walden*

Herman Melville's *Moby-Dick* provides an ideal starting point for my investigation of the theme of tabooed, or unresolved grief in American literature. It also helps to establish the usefulness of object relations and feminist psychoanalytic theory in illuminating the novel in this fundamentally new way. The novel functions so well toward these ends, partly because it explores with sophistication and complexity the literary and psychoanalytic issues that will be taken up again in even greater depth in the fiction of Mark Twain and Ernest Hemingway, and partly because many of the claims that this study will make about the repression of grief in American literature and the vicissitudes of the American orphan-hero's separation-individuation process have already been glimpsed by Melville's critics in this most canonical of American novels; consequently, their attention allows me to focus upon the exemplary, or representative, qualities of these thematic claims.

The self-willed American orphan, who both embraces his independent orphan status, and at the same time mourns over his isolation and essential state of deprivation and loss, makes a striking appearance in this epic American novel. Ishmael's heroic stature in the novel is defined by his emotional posture as an orphan insofar as it is predicated upon a valiant, yet ultimately unresolved, struggle with a fundamental ambivalence—an ambivalence created by the author's repression of grief and inability to mourn openly. Throughout *Moby-Dick* the American orphan repeatedly acts out his conflicted desire, alternately to cling to and to distance himself from his personal past: to regress to a state of comforting dependency and yet, at the same time, to break away toward radical autonomy. This central crisis, in what may be called the young male's separation-individuation process, becomes a major concern for the fictional heroes of Mark Twain and Ernest Hemingway as well. Although for different reasons, these three authors were unable to conceive of an adequate resolution to their heroes' ambivalence, which disposed the American orphan hero toward a permanent state of arrested development, and condemned him to an endless struggle with his adolescent conflict, in which he perpetually straddles the borderline between maturity and immaturity.

Moby-Dick also lends itself to a demonstration of how the absent, or implied, figure of the mother, and the son's early relationship with her, play a central and pervasive role in the imaginative construction of what has previously been considered to be a masculine text. Despite her exclusion as a principal character in American fiction, the mother/woman occupies a prominent thematic place in the aetiology of the orphan hero's psychic drama. She is the repressed object of desire that continually returns, and only by evoking her symbolic presence can the American male author work through his conflicted grief in relation to her. Whether the influence she exerts is positive or negative, at any one point in the young male protagonist's psychological drama, to omit her is to risk underestimating the rich literary and psychoanalytic resources of the author's creative faculties. By reinstating her presence and influence within the thematic and psychological context of Melville's narrative, I hope to reinvigorate the novel as a feminist text, and, in doing so, recover the book for many of these essentially "lost" readers.

Melville's fixation, in *Moby-Dick*, on the theme of clinging versus distancing, or attachment versus loss, which the fiction of Twain and Hemingway also play out in various ways, can be traced, within the novel, to a fundamental experience of early deprivation and loss that directly affects not only the content but the narrative style of the American writer's fiction of tabooed grief. Melville, like Twain and Hemingway, used logocentric, patriarchal reasoning, or as Melville wrote in his novel *Pierre; or, the Ambiguities,* "all-stretchable philosophy,"[1] to seek conciliatory patterns that transcend personal sorrow, and to make sense of their experiences of loss, deprivation, and disappointment. Yet, their rationalizations served merely to give a narrative and dramatic form to their grief, rarely to resolve it. Consequently, their fictions as a whole became monuments to their chronic mourning and unresolved grief.

In developmental psychology the conflict of clinging versus distancing is the dominant crisis belonging to what is called the "rapprochement phase" of psychic growth, which occurs somewhere between the ages of one and three years.[2] It is the time when the child longs to explore his or her emerging autonomy and freedom, yet only within the safe assurance that the child's mother, or some other familiar and comforting object, is able to provide. When this feeling of connection is lost or suddenly disappears, the frightened child feels as though its whole inner world is dissolving, as though it is being abandoned, with emotional and physical rescue nowhere in sight. According to Daniel N. Stern, "[s]eparation loss (even momentary) is probably the most anguishing experience" a child can have. The primary caregiver, Stern explains, "is a psychological oxygen, without which, within seconds, the child experiences panic. And part of the panic of separation is most likely a feeling of becoming fragmented, of losing boundaries, of disappearing into a lonely, empty infinity."[3] From the point of view of the child, Stern contends, such isolation and abandonment feel as if the self is "dissolving like grains of salt in the ocean of space" (98). The anxiety of separation, Stern also maintains, does not change significantly when one becomes an adult: "The separation reaction is basic to us all and may not change much from the age of twelve months till death" (99).

In both its main plot and its many multiple sub-plots, *Moby-Dick* dramatizes the desolating consequences of abandonment and isolation. Young Pip's abandonment upon the broad and vast "open sea," which Melville describes as an experience of "intolerable" and "awful lonesomeness," is but a central moment in an entire novel of isolation and deprivation that resonates outward to envelop the tragic story of the fated *Pequod* and its crew.[4] The repetitious sections on the anatomy of the whale that dissolve into unresolvable philosophical speculation, and the compulsive repetitions of variations on the *Pequod's* story through the gams, all point to a problem of rapprochement-phase ambivalence that Melville was compelled to deal with repeatedly in the novel, yet could not seem to resolve. Longing for protection *and* escaping from confinement simultaneously lead Ahab and Ishmael to traverse backwards and forwards across this psychic terrain, but this strategy also holds the authorial figure, Melville himself, in a constant position of dual possibilities.

Specifically, Melville's affixed gaze on the "good" nurturing mother and the "bad" smothering and disappointing mother, like the whale that cannot fuse the two distinct views of reality captured separately by each eye,[5] became something of a primal scene that he could not get beyond in the book; thus, the novel as a whole takes shape as an anatomy of a fixation in narrative form. Through the dramatization of this fundamental conflict in the novel's plot, exposition, and characterizations, Melville draws the reader into his own efforts on behalf of Ishmael and Ahab either to repair, work through, or repudiate the anger and grief that he feels toward the ambivalently loved good/bad mother—which is acted out on several different levels in the novel. Hence, he allows us to participate regressively in his ongoing struggle with a primary ambivalence, in effect encouraging us, by perpetually reaching out to us and hectoring us, to engage in a kind of ego-merging with the author's own creative impulse in the book. In this way the rapprochement theme that thrives on Melville's own psycho-philosophical indeterminacy informs the psychological power that he masterfully manages to sustain throughout the book.

In the essay "Hawthorne and His Mosses," written during the composition of *Moby-Dick*, Melville confesses that the drive toward radical separation and autonomy—toward orphanhood—was an important motivating force in his conception of the novel. "Would that all excellent books were foundlings, without father or mother," he writes, "that so it might be, we could glorify them, without including their ostensible authors."[6] Melville admits that what he aspired to as a writer was complete "originality," a radical break with one's personal, historical, and literary past.[7] It is "better to fail in originality," Melville proposes, "than to succeed in imitation." Like a child seeking a new form of empowerment through an assertion of his or her emerging sense of autonomy, Melville senses that true greatness can be achieved only through separation and isolation.[8] According to Leo Bersani, Melville, in *Moby-Dick,* participates in a nineteenth-century American "experience of an impossible dream: that of a literature without debts, which would owe nothing to the past." Bersani then draws an allegorical parallel between America and the *Pequod,* claiming that: "by insisting on the *Pequod's* nearly total break with the land and the past, Melville simultaneously evokes the origins of America as a house for exiles from everywhere and makes those origins absolute. That is, he evokes the possibility of exile as a wholly new beginning and brutally deprives it of the comforting notion of loss."[9]

Melville's orphan-hero Ishmael is, like Melville himself, a self-willed orphan. When Ishmael begins his narrative with the injunction, "Call me Ishmael," he too is expressing a willful desire to assume an orphan identity as the disinherited son (3). Having no father or mother, Ishmael is a "loose-fish" that has been "abandoned . . . upon the seas of life" (396–97). He will forge an original self out of his complete isolation, as he forges the narrative of *Moby-Dick* out of his experience of abandonment on the sea when the *Pequod* and its crew sinks and disappears into the "closing vortex" of the black ocean (573). For both Melville and his narrator, then, *Moby-Dick* can be understood as an act of mourning, a product of greatness resulting from the grief of loss, separation, and isolation. Indeed, as Melville tells us by way of Ahab's final epiphany: "my topmost greatness lies in my topmost grief" (571). Ahab's greatness, however, like Melville's aspirations for the greatness of his novel, lies not in the expression of grief from loss but in the willful denial of grief; in, as Bersani observes, the "brutal" deprivation of the "comforting notion of loss."[10]

What Melville is advocating for both himself and for Ahab is to prolong the mourning process indefinitely by displacing one's grief from abandonment and isolation into a motivating force that drives one on to greatness. Ahab, Melville informs us, was abandoned by a "crazy, widowed mother, who died when he was only a twelvemonth *[sic]* old" (79).

It is perhaps possible, and indeed Melville seems to imply, that Ahab's mother was "crazy" from grief at having been made a widow. As John Bowlby or D. W. Winnicott might suggest, a mother preoccupied with her own grief would have functioned as a poor mirroring mother to her newborn infant.[11] The feeling of deprivation and abandonment that the infant Ahab would have felt from his grief-distracted mother is confirmed when she dies and abandons him forever. Throughout Ahab's life at sea, which he began as a "boy-harpooner of eighteen" (543), he carried within him the emotional pain of his "privation":

forty years on the pitiless sea! for forty years has Ahab forsaken the peaceful land, for forty years to make war on the horrors of the deep! . . . When I think of this life I have led; the desolation of solitude it has been; the masoned, walled-town of a Captain's exclusiveness, which admits but small entrance to any sympathy from the green country without—oh, weariness! heaviness! Guinea-coast slavery of solitary command! (543)

One may well assume from this that Ahab channeled his repressed grief from maternal abandonment into a desperate, aggressive rage against the outwardly projected image of his abandoning, persecuting "bad mother"—Mother Nature, the sea, and their concomitant, the white-whale breast of Moby Dick.[12] Given the tragic nature of Ahab's mother-infant relationship, Ishmael speaks truly when he intuits that "all the anguish" of Ahab's "present suffering was but the direct issue of a former woe" (463–64).

If, however unconsciously, Melville was acting out an unresolved rapprochement-phase conflict in the novel, then it becomes significant that the mother, at this stage of development, is a figure of great ambivalence to the child, who both longs for her comforting protection and seeks to escape from her smothering confinement.[13] To the child she is the prototype of all the good and evil in the world. It sometimes happens, however, as in the case of Ahab, that the trauma of maternal abandonment transforms the mother into a predominantly bad object. In order to preserve the image of the "good mother," the child internalizes the aggressive or persecuting image of the "bad mother," which results in a masochistic personality structure.[14] The psychological motive for Ahab's early integration and outward projection of the "bad mother" was to preserve the untainted image of the "good," nurturing mother. Indeed, so split off from Ahab's projective conception of an evil reality has the good or "sweet mother" become, that he "knowest not how" he came to be, and hence concludes that he is "unbegotten" (508).

The aggression toward the "bad mother," that is internalized in order to retain the uncorrupted image of the desired "good mother," may then take one of two courses. It may remain internalized and take the form of persecutory, destructive attacks against the self, leading ultimately to suicidal fantasies. Or, it may be projected outward onto the external world—onto God and nature. In the latter case, God and nature become narcissistic mirror images of the sinful blackness within the self—external objects that may then be attacked or hated. The guilt from Ahab's early hatred and rage toward his mother results in a fear of retaliatory persecution from the threatening external object, which is now identified as the locus of absolute evil, and is itself a remnant of the "bad" pregenital mother. As some critics already have suggested, to feel cursed and persecuted by Moby Dick, as Ahab does, is to suffer the malevolent attacks of his own hatred and aggression that are first projected onto the bad object and later turned upon himself.[15] Within this sado-masochistic dynamic, the white whale is, for Ahab, both the agent and the instrument of evil.

Through Ishmael's analytical musings on Ahab's "malady," Melville makes it clear that, for the *Pequod's* captain, the loss of Ahab's leg symbolizes all the "intellectual and spiritual exasperations" and "woes" he has suffered in his life (184). When Moby Dick bites off Ahab's leg, Ahab takes it as an opportunity to project his repressed grief and outward aggression onto a single, tangible object: "ever since he lost his leg last voyage by that accursed whale, he's been a kind of moody—desperate moody, and savage sometimes" (79). This dynamic of projection, and the metaphorical displacement of intangible and ineffable psychological issues onto tangible, symbolic objects, parallel Melville's sweeping projective displacement in the novel of an inner ineffable ambivalence onto philosophical indeterminacy. By pondering intellectually and attempting to understand rationally his pressing and unresolved psychological issues, Melville, like Ahab, was, to some extent, able to transcend his own personal suffering.

In the past, Melville's Freudian critics have viewed the white whale as a symbol of the father, interpreting Ahab's ivory leg as an emblem of oedipal castration. If Ahab's leg is indeed a phallus, however, it is one that belongs equally to the devouring, "bad" phallic mother. Ahab's artificial limb is a memorial to the grief from loss that was denied expression and replaced by his monomaniacal hatred and rage against a persecuting, malignant object of evil. Yet, below the stump where

Ahab's leg ends, as he confesses to the carpenter, he is still sensible, though only vaguely, of his lost wholeness. Accordingly, this phantom leg that Ahab still feels is the absent, yet still present, mother who was, and is, the source of all his unconscious loving desires and all-too-conscious present rage and woe.[16]

The theme of Ahab's rapprochement ambivalence resulting from maternal loss is further developed by Melville's duplication of the experience of maternal deprivation in Ishmael's life as well. Ishmael, like Ahab, suffers from an early traumatic experience involving the mother. In addition to being an orphan, having been abandoned by both his parents, Ishmael is raised by a stern stepmother, whose "conscientiousness" is a thinly disguised emotional coldness and perhaps even cruelty (26). So deprived of love is Ishmael, as he relates his story in "The Counterpane" chapter, that he would rather be beaten by his stepmother than abandoned by her and exiled to his room, where he must remain alone for hours. The psychological moral of Stubb's dream in the "Queen Mab" episode, in which Stubb is disturbed at having been kicked by Ahab, but finally decides that such abuse from "a beautiful ivory leg" should be deemed "an honor," is that aggression can indeed be interpreted as a form of expressed love (132). Ishmael's stepmother refuses even to grant him such a perverted acknowledgment of her love; and the indifference she shows him, by "condemning" him "to lie abed such an unendurable length of time," confirms his feelings of maternal abandonment (26). Despite Ishmael's absence of apparent grief and anger toward his stepmother, and his equivocal rationalization of her cruel behavior, Melville emphasizes the traumatic impact that this incident had upon Ishmael when he, as narrator, confesses that the experience made him feel "a great deal worse than I have ever done since, even from the greatest subsequent misfortunes" (26).

Ishmael, in concluding his narrative in "The Castaway" chapter of how poor Pip became a "lonely castaway" on the "shoreless ocean," portends that it will soon be "seen what like abandonment befell myself" (414). And yet, Ishmael's description of his childhood experience of abandonment more closely mirrors Pip's devastating ordeal than his own final installment in the tale of *Moby-Dick*. The "awful lonesomeness" of Pip's deprivation on the sea, Ishmael explains, "is intolerable": "The intense concentration of self in the middle of such a heartless immensity, my God! who can tell it?" (414). Ishmael, of course, can and does tell, in painful detail, what such an experience of abandonment is like. It is to see and feel "among the joyous, heartless, ever-juvenile eternities . . . God's foot upon the treadle of the loom"; and for Ishmael, to identify with the omnipotent power of an almighty deity is to feel as "heartless" and "indifferent as his God." Ishmael can describe Pip's ordeal because when he, himself, lies for "several hours broad awake" (26) in his bed, Ishmael experiences the same "intolerable" "intense concentration of self" that poor Pip feels lying face down in the black ocean, that "jeeringly kept his finite body up, but drowned the infinite of his soul" (414). Melville, with intuitive psychological insight, metaphorically describes Pip's traumatic experience of near-drowning as an example of the rapprochement-phase panic of a child who, according to Stern, is too suddenly or prematurely separated from his "home base," which makes him feel "stunned and disoriented: his breathing changes," as if he were deprived of "psychological oxygen," and he is overwhelmed by a feeling "of disappearing into a lonely, empty infinity" (*Diary*, 95–98).

Whereas Ahab projects the internalized aggression toward the "bad mother" onto the external world—onto God and nature—Ishmael's corresponding response to the hated mother is to retain his internalized aggression, where it takes the form of suicidal fantasies. By the end of Melville's first paragraph in *Moby-Dick*, he has already established the psychological connection in Ishmael's mind between tabooed or repressed grief, aggression, and suicide. Ishmael takes to sea, Melville writes, because, as Ishmael confesses:

It is a way I have of driving off the spleen, and regulating the circulation. Whenever I find myself growing grim about the mouth; whenever it is a damp, drizzly November in my soul; whenever I find myself involuntarily pausing before coffin warehouses, and bringing up the rear of every funeral I meet; and especially whenever my hypos get such an upper hand of me, that it requires a strong moral principle to prevent me from deliberately stepping into the street, and methodically knocking people's hats off—then, I account it high time to get to sea as soon as I can. This is my substitute for pistol and ball. With a philosophical flourish Cato throws himself upon his sword; I quietly take to the ship. (3)

Ishmael's aggressive inclination to knock "people's hats off" is manifested internally in his identification with Cato, who threw "himself upon his sword." In view of the tragic ending of the novel, Ishmael's decision to embark on this whaling voyage is a kind of suicidal act. Yet it is not aggression by itself that drives Ishmael but a more originary and deeply repressed motive: the *"striving for realization"* of mourning.[17]

While Ishmael is aware of his periodic tendency to let his "hypos" get "an upper hand" on him, his impulse to linger in front of "coffin warehouses" and participate in the mourning ritual of other people's funerals is an unconscious act, "involuntarily" motivated by his own unacknowledged grief.

Like Perth, the blacksmith, Ishmael may have viewed whaling as a suicidal mission, and so took to sea with "death-longing eyes" (486). Perth knows that by his excessive drinking he provoked the deaths of his beloved young wife and children; therefore, he feels a strong inclination to deal out the same punishment of death upon himself. But, being among those "who still have left in them some interior compunctions against suicide," he ships off to sea and buries himself in "a life which . . . is more oblivious than death" (486). To go "a-whaling," then, for both Perth and Ishmael, fulfills a death-wish that contains within it a powerful desire to undo the devastating losses they have suffered. But, because of the unworked-through guilt that accompanies their grief— Perth's in relation to the "Bottle Conjuror!" (485), and Ishmael's to the repressed retaliatory aggression toward his parents and stepmother— their mourning process was impaired. Unable to grieve unimpeded by guilt, their grief became chronic, destined never to bring them the consolation they seek.

Ishmael's masochistic aggression, like Ahab's enraged, persecutory aggression, is perpetually fueled by an internally erected taboo against the conscious acknowledgment of his grief. As psychoanalysis tells us, "one can never overestimate the immense grief" that lies at the source of masochistic aggression. Behind the child's hatred of the "bad mother" is an aching desire to be loved, and a deep sense of unconscious or tabooed grief at having been abandoned, as it were, by the "good mother." [18] Therefore, as critics have often intuited about Melville's novel, Ishmael and Ahab are psychological mirrors of one another. [19]

For Ishmael, the Whalemen's Chapel that he visits shortly before setting sail on the *Pequod* functions as a metaphor, not for mourning or achieving catharsis through grief, but for the impossibility or inability of ever grieving fully and completely for lost loved ones. Perhaps many of the widows and mothers who lost their husbands and sons at sea unburden their hearts through grieving and prayer, but Ishmael cannot help but perceive in their appearance that they are suffering from an "unceasing grief." "I feel sure," he says to himself (perhaps because he describes his own inner state), that all those who are there possess "unhealing hearts" that "bleed afresh" with each reminder of their loss (36). Because we see only what Ishmael sees, every word and image in the chapel drives home the inevitability that personal loss results in chronic, unresolved mourning.

To have "perished without a grave" (36), or, in other words, to be lost at sea and denied the comfort of a funeral ritual that might provide a sense of closure for one's grief and mourning, is an ideal metaphor for the unresolved and unacknowledged grief from the abandonment and loss that afflicts so many of the characters in Melville's novel. Significantly, the first tablet Ishmael sets his eyes upon in the chapel reports that an unfortunate sailor "lost overboard" drowned "Near the Isle of Desolation" (35). For the whalemen, as for Ishmael, Perth, Ahab, and Pip, comforting death can merely be presumed to be the consequence of being lost at sea, while abandonment and desolation are the more certain, and the more devastating, fate of the orphaned sailor.

For the masochistic Ishmael who, like Perth, is unable to achieve catharsis through grieving, the punishment of death would indeed relieve him of his guilt. It is understandable, then, that when Ishmael, while sitting among the tombs of the dead sailors in the Whalemen's Chapel, considers the possibility that the "same fate" of death may be his, he finds himself suddenly growing "merry again" (37), just as later on in his voyage composing his will gives the feeling that he is "a quiet ghost with a clean conscience" (228). Experts on suicide suggest that the suicidal fantasy is motivated not only by a desire to punish *oneself* for hating the love-object by whom one feels abandoned, and to punish the beloved object herself, but also in order to give the fantasy omnipotent mother a second chance to rescue her abandoned child.[20] Hence, the ending of *Moby-Dick*, in which the outcast and abandoned "orphan," Ishmael, is rescued by the good mother-ship, *Rachel*, "in her retracing-search after her missing children," can already be prefigured from page one of the novel (473).

Throughout *Moby-Dick*, Ishmael appears preoccupied with the kind of rapprochement-phase ambivalence that characterizes the child's, and later, the adult's, polarized and ambiguous relationship with the split good/bad mother. The theme of ambivalence as transferentially projected onto linguistic and philosophical indeterminacy is, in fact, the subject of many of the most notable and provocative chapters in the novel, including "The Whiteness of the Whale," "Moby Dick," "The Doubloon," "The Try-Works," "A Squeeze of the Hand," "The Monkey-Rope," and "The Mast-head." A child who experiences deprivation in relation to the maternal object will often, as an adult, engage in clinging and distancing behavior with others, and will maintain throughout adulthood a bifurcated worldview in which everything is either good or bad, black or white, comforting or smothering.[21] Fascinated by the whale, whose eyes allow him to view two "distinct picture[s]" at once, Ishmael is obsessed—in his own philosophical, monomaniacal fashion—with the fact that, as a man, he can never "examine any two things . . . at one and the same instant of time" (330).

Through his cytological discourse (the anatomy of the whale sections in *Moby-Dick*), and his musings on the analogies between the self and nature, Melville compulsively reiterates his philosophy of indefiniteness and ambivalence, by which the "[w]onderfullest things are ever the unmentionable" (106). In his hopelessly bifurcated reality, Ishmael can only attempt the "classification of the constituents of a chaos, nothing less is here essayed" (134). To explain the "ineffable" (188), "unfathomable" (263), "impenetrable" mystery of God and nature, Ishmael confesses, "would be to dive deeper than Ishmael can go" (187). The mysterious Mother-Whale-Self, like Ahab's cryptic doubloon, "must remain unpainted to the last" (264). As is characteristic of a rapprochement-phase crisis, Ishmael is both fearful of returning to an engulfing maternal utopia and, at the same time, unwilling to accept the impossible divisiveness of a heterogeneous reality. Trapped in an adolescent universe of indefiniteness and ambiguity, Ishmael must perpetually choose between the "open independence" of the sea, and the "treacherous, slavish shore" (107).

In the figure of the good sailor, Bulkington, Ishmael sees the incarnation of the fundamental ambiguity of all things. Through Bulkington, Ishmael recognizes the differences between the "safety, comfort" and "succor" of the port, and the "direst jeopardy" to one's freedom that the port also represents; and between the "highest truth" of "landlessness," and the threat of being left to "perish in that howling infinite" of a perpetually "shoreless" existence (107). No wonder Bulkington, as Ishmael comments, "interested me at once," when he first encountered him at the Spouter-Inn (16). For, in Bulkington, as in Ahab and himself, Ishmael perceives that "in the deep shadows of his eyes floated some reminiscences that did not seem to give him much joy" (16). Ishmael senses in Bulkington the repressed grief that is the mark of true greatness in a man; as Ishmael is later to realize, "all men tragically great are made so through a certain morbidness" (74). It is not grief but the taboo against grief that leads to greatness, and Bulkington shows no sign of grief. Instead, his grief has become a monomania through which he pursues "the intrepid effort of the soul to keep the open independence of the sea; while the wildest winds of heaven and earth conspire to cast her on the treacherous, slavish shore" (107).

Although Melville does not mention the cause of Bulkington's grief, the nature of his symptoms, and Ishmael's affinity towards him, lead one to conclude that the traumatic loss of some beloved object motivates his compulsive wandering. According to experts on grief and mourning, wandering is a form of searching that, "by its very nature, implies the loss or absence of an object." [22] Therefore, wandering is "an essential component" of chronic or unacknowledged grief. As one noted authority on "pathological wandering" proposes: "Is it not possible that the desire for adventure abroad, for voyages of exploration, etc., is in some individuals a sublimation of an abnormal compulsion to wander?" [23] The *Pequod* is a ship-of-death, but not because of the tragic fate that awaits it; its end represents merely the fitting burial for those among its crew who were seeking death before the vessel ever shipped out, and who finally joined, in death, those beloved whom they had lost long ago.

For a healthy resolution of the rapprochement crisis, both the "good" and "bad," comforting and disappointing, aspects of the mother must be fused and internalized, thus preparing the individual for the limitations and compromises of reality. [24] Instead, Ishmael's trauma in relation to his mother, like Ahab's, results in a pathological resolution of the rapprochement crisis, through which he internalizes the "bad mother" in an effort to preserve the untainted image of the omnipotent, "good mother." As both an internal and external psychic entity, the idealized "good mother" becomes the source of all love and plentitude, the prototype of utopian perfection. In the course of the novel Ishmael periodically attempts to recapture a regressive experience of maternal utopia—a blissful merging or "melting" into the lost "good mother." For Ishmael, as with the Transcendentalists, she becomes Mother-Cosmos-Nature, into which his ego longs to dissolve and, hence, undo the trauma of abandonment by repairing his lost feeling of narcissistic omnipotence. At the same time, he fears the annihilation of the self and the loss of control that such a state of egolessness represents.

Throughout his voyage on the *Pequod*, Ishmael habitually engages in a regressive fantasy so as to reunite with the lost "good mother" of his orphan past. Janine Chasseguet-Smirgel describes this regressive fantasy as a "desire to discover a universe without obstacles, without roughness or differences, entirely smooth, identified with a mother's belly stripped of its contents, an interior to which one has free access" (*Sexuality*, 77).[25] This fantasy calls to mind the biblical story of Jonah, who entered the belly of the whale and emerged again unharmed. At one point in his cytological narrative, Ishmael recalls the opportunity he once had to enter, without confronting obstacles, the "great white, worshipped skeleton" of the whale:

To and fro I paced before this skeleton—brushed the vines aside—broke through the ribs—and with a ball of Arsacidean twine, wandered, eddied long amid its many winding, shaded colonnades and arbors. But soon my line was out; and following it back, I emerged from the opening where I entered. I saw no living thing within; naught was there but bones. (450)

This literal or physical fulfillment of a maternal utopian fantasy has a parallel, on the level of mental functioning, in Ishmael's primary drive to rediscover a state of egolessness, which he manages to achieve temporarily in the chapters "A Squeeze of the Hand," "The Mast-head," "The Try-Works," and "The Monkey-Rope." In these episodes, this time on the level of mental functioning, Ishmael escapes heterogeneous reality by returning to a state of homogeneity—an essentially anal universe ruled by the pleasure principle, with no limits or boundaries between objects. Chasseguet-Smirgel refers to this utopia as an entirely "malleable" universe formed by the "melting of thought into an undifferentiated mass" (84). The task appointed to Ishmael and his companions in "A Squeeze of the Hand" is "to squeeze those lumps" of sperm "back into fluid" (415). When immersed up to his elbows in the vat of sperm, Ishmael feels "divinely free from all ill-will, or petulance, or malice, of any sort whatsoever" (416). "I squeezed that sperm," he says, "till I myself almost melted into it."

The belief that all goods are held in common also characterizes most utopian fantasies. According to Chasseguet-Smirgel: "There must be a single identity among the citizens" in a utopia; in effect, the "maternal breast must belong to everybody" (95–99). The similarity between Chasseguet-Smirgel's description of the utopian maternal fantasy and Melville's depiction of Ishmael's emotional response to his pleasurable regressive experience is striking. "Come; let us squeeze hands all round," he proposes, "nay, let us all squeeze ourselves into each other; let

us squeeze ourselves universally into the very milk and sperm of kindness" (416).

Ishmael experiences a similar kind of ego-merging with Queequeg, in
"The Monkey-Rope" chapter, when, connected to the savage by the
rope-line, he perceives "that my own individuality was now merged in a
joint stock company of two" (320). "The Try-Works" chapter represents
Melville's most perfectly constructed fantasy of his regressive passion to
return to an undifferentiated state of maternal chaos, "preceding the
introduction of separation, of division, of distinctions, of naming, of
paternal law" (Chasseguet-Smirgel, 88). The try-works is the anal vessel
that transforms heterogeneous reality back into a homogeneous, unified
universe. Lured by the burning mass into an "unaccountable drowsi-
ness," Ishmael falls into a trance-like state of egolessness, so "that whatever swift, rushing thing I stood on was not so much bound to any
haven ahead as rushing from all havens astern" (424). Again succumbing
to an "unseasonable meditativeness" during his post on the mast-head,
Ishmael is "lulled into such an opium-like listlessness of vacant, unconscious reverie," that "at last he loses his identity; takes the mystic ocean
at his feet for the visible image of that deep, blue, bottomless soul,
pervading mankind and nature" (158–59). Melville's imagery suggests
that Ishmael finally attains a regressive, intra-uterine state, in which, as
Ishmael observes about himself, there "is no life in thee, now, except
that rocking life imparted by a gently rolling ship; by her, borrowed
from the sea" (159). The sea, itself, often becomes an alluring, "tranced,"
and "mystical" haven of maternal bliss for Melville (4–5). Ishmael
speaks, in the very first chapter of *Moby-Dick*, of "thousands upon
thousands of mortal men fixed in ocean reveries," longing to free themselves from their social responsibilities and the restraints of the land (4).

Melville also perceived that the maternal womb—the "insular Tahiti"
(274)—of his utopian fantasies could also be, as Chasseguet-Smirgel
says, "a murderous anal trap" (107). In depicting the alluring danger of
maternal regression—of whaling and voyaging at sea—Melville again
dramatized the child's ambivalence or rapprochement crisis with the
good/bad mother. The "live sea," he cautions, "swallows up ships and
crews" (274). Indeed, Melville goes so far as to identity the sea as a
devouring mother, "a fiend to its own offspring" (274). In his early
south-sea novels, *Typee, Mardi,* and *Omoo,* the friendly, comforting and
solicitous nature of the hero's relationship with the natives, particularly
with a gentle and seductive female figure, is always overcast with a sense

of fear and anxiety regarding the possibility that the hospitable natives will suddenly become inhospitable, turning against their visitor and perhaps even cannibalizing him.[26]

To be a "joint stock company of two," Ishmael says, in "The Monkey-Rope," is to risk "that another's mistake or misfortune might plunge innocent me into unmerited disaster and death" (320). Rather than strive to attain an impossible cerebral utopia, one should, as Ishmael cautions, in "A Squeeze of the Hand," "lower" one's hope of happiness to a more "attainable felicity" with wife and family (416). To lose oneself in the "elusive thoughts" of an "enchanted mood" is to risk toppling from the mast-head into the sea, "no more to rise for ever" (159). Finally, the terrible danger of losing one's self totally in the horrible maternal, chaotic "blackness of darkness" of the try-works induces Ishmael to conclude: "Look not too long in the face of the fire, O man!" (424). To retreat, or regress, too far from the light and order of heterogeneous reality into the maternal embrace, to rush too wildly "from all havens astern," is, as Tashtego nearly discovers, to be "smothered in the very whitest and daintiest of fragrant spermaceti; coffined, hearsed, and tombed in the secret inner chamber and sanctum sanctorum" of the whale/mother (344). It may be a "precious perishing," but it is a perishing nonetheless.

While the regressive lure toward unconscious, egoless merging with the lost "good mother" serves to undo the grief and loss of maternal abandonment, it also results in a terrifying feeling of engulfment and annihilation of the self. The psychologist, Henry A. Murray, was captivated by the fiction of Herman Melville because he saw in it, years before Freud's "discovery" of the unconscious, "the dazzling and bewildering shapes" of the "inner world" of the human mind. Melville, Murray enthusiastically believed, was the first "literary discoverer of . . . the Darkest Africa of the mind, the mythological unconscious."[27] The mysterious depths of the unconscious in both classical and contemporary feminist psychoanalysis has often been compared to "the primitive abyss of Dionysos . . . the mother's womb" (Chasseguet-Smirgel, 128, 138).[28] The same question that Chasseguet-Smirgel poses about Freud might also be posed about Herman Melville. How could Freud, she asks, seek to "explore the Unconscious—the Mother's body—and to send a flood of light into its dark depths, without lurching himself into the abyss" (139)? By way of an answer, she proposes that Freud's identification with Judaism provided him with an armor against engulfment in the form of his tools of investigation—reason, analysis, intellect, separation, and division—all of which belong to the paternal dimension of reality (135–39). But, whereas Freud had Judaism to wear as a diver's suit, complete with mask to observe coldly, and oxygen tank to breath without gasping, Melville had science, or rather, cytology; and also language, or more specifically, metaphor. By balancing the dangerous, chaotic, darkness of the unconscious in *Moby-Dick* with intellectual, cytological narrative, Melville could, so to speak, keep one foot on the shore, while allowing the other to be immersed in the mysterious sea of the unconscious.

Moby-Dick, Melville's perilous voyage into the depths of the unconscious, is buoyed throughout by a preponderance of historical, paternal symbols, metaphors, and similes, derived from ancient Greek texts, the Bible, Shakespeare, mythology, biology, nineteenth-century culture, and more.[29] Safely suited within the protective paternal confines of his cytological and analogical armor, Melville, in *Moby-Dick*, dove as deep into the maternal "invisible spheres" (195) of the unconscious as a mortal can go. On the level of narratology, then, Melville dramatized a rapprochement-phase conflict in which science (cytology) and language offered a refuge from engulfment in the joyous, yet self-annihilating, cosmos of the mother. In this way, Melville created a tension in the narrative text that paralleled the contextual, or philosophical, rapprochement conflict depicted throughout the novel.

For Melville, Moby Dick, the white whale, is the cosmos of the mother. He is both the "colorless" object of Ishmael's passive desire for divine unconscious egolessness, and the "all-color" object of Ahab's aggressive desire for divine super-conscious egomania.[30] While Ishmael longs to submit regressively and passively to the "inscrutable" in nature, Ahab will jealously "strike through the mask" of "visible objects" in nature in order to discover that power "beyond" that presides "over all creations" (164). Ishmael's passive-aggressive, and Ahab's willful-aggressive, search for the utopian body of the mother are both displacements of the same desire to repair an original experience of maternal abandonment depression. Comrades in abandonment and grief, Ishmael and Ahab share beneath their "hypos" and "haughty agony" a common desire to repair their emotional wounds and find refuge in a regressive mother-infant paradise. Thinking back to when he was "a boy," gazing at the sea from "the sand-hills of Nantucket," Ahab dreams of his own immortality, which brings to mind Ishmael's mystical utopian vision of "immortal infancy." In his quiet gazing, Ahab says to himself: "There's a soft shower to leeward. Such lovely leewardings! They must lead somewhere—to something else than common land, more palmy than the palms" (565).

In "The Gilder" chapter, Ishmael and Ahab partake of the same utopian maternal fantasy of returning to a state of blissful "immortal infancy." The "mystic mood" that Ishmael speaks of, in which "fact and fancy" melt into "one seamless whole," unmistakably evokes the longed-for image of the maternal womb:

> Oh, grassy glades! oh, ever vernal endless landscapes in the soul; in ye,— though long parched by the dead drought of the earthy life,—in ye, men yet may roll, like young horses in new morning clover; and for some few fleeting moments, feel the cool dew of the life immortal on them. . . . Where lies the final harbor, whence we unmoor no more? In what rapt ether sails the world, of which the weariest will never weary? Where is the foundling's father hidden? Our souls are like those orphans whose unwedded mothers die in bearing them: the secret of our paternity lies in their grave, and we must there to learn it. (492)[31]

Like Ahab, however, Ishmael mistakenly thinks that the ideal he is searching for is the "foundling's father," whereas to be "begotten" by "unwedded mothers" is to embrace a utopian fantasy of symbiosis with the mother in which, as Plato emphasizes in The Republic, "fathers will not know their sons, nor the sons their fathers" (Chasseguet-Smirgel, Sexuality, 95).[32] Ahab's desire to be "welded" with God the Father is a demonic, patriarchal version of Ishmael's fantasy of dissolution into the Mother-Cosmos.

This same merging and confusion of gender identification has previously occupied a significant place in Melville's biographical criticism. According to a number of his critics, in his own sea voyages, as well as in his early fictional accounts of those journeys—Omoo, Mardi, Typee, and White-Jacket—Melville was presumably seeking a father figure who might allow him to transcend his disappointment with his biological father, Allen Melville, who died a bankrupt when Melville was twelve years old. However, there is evidence in all of these novels that points to the additional possibility that Melville's search for the father, like Ahab's, contained within it a more primal wish: to re-find the exotic and satisfying refuge of the comforting and nurturing mother. Charles Haberstroh, for one, believes that Melville's young sea-faring protagonists represent Melville himself, who, as a child, felt "abandoned" and "impotent" in relation to his father and his highly prized older brother, and who hoped to find repose in the "safe bosom of some father's seeming strength."[33] Yet, despite Haberstroh's thesis that Melville was searching for an heroic *paternal* ideal, the oceanic images of comfort Haberstroh employs describe not paternal masculine support but the peace and serenity of the maternal womb:

The orphan's discovery of a lost parent would constitute an entry into a tireless and timeless world of golden peace: the final escape, the final freedom from doubt, the final and safe pillow for the head of the troubled child . . . a soft suspension of the need to think, or hope, or fear. Past and future, memory and desire will dissolve into an eternally placid present: a bay from which one hears the beating of the sea waves, but where the currents of the sea have no authority. (13)

Frederick Rosenheim suggests that Melville went to sea to repair his poor sense of self-esteem; in other words, to seek a narcissistic identification with his important and prosperous male Melville and Gansevoort relatives and ancestors (some of whom, including Captain John De Wolf, and Melville's cousins, Guert and Leonard Gansevoort—as well as his own father—had achieved considerable recognition as seamen).[34] Like Haberstroh, Rosenheim evokes, through the powerful father's image, the loving care of the good nurturing mother. In the father/monarch/god, he maintains, Melville yearned for a person "who will adore him, protect him and tend to him like a helpless babe" (7).

Believing that he was seeking a powerful and protective father, Melville, according to Rosenheim, found instead devoted women figures, such as Yillah, in *Mardi*, who would love and adore him, and soothe the rage he felt at "his mother for not adoring him enough, for abandoning him as he distortedly saw it" (7). Appropriately, then, the threat of cannibalism is also omnipresent in Melville's regressive fantasies of mother-son reunion. Cannibalism offered Melville the perfect objective correlative for the threat of castration, which he enacted to punish his oedipal longings, and the threat of engulfing annihilation, to punish his preoedipal or regressive desire to return to the embraces of the fantasy archaic mother.

At bottom, therefore, it is not only the father, but also the mother, whom Melville's protagonists set out to seek. For Melville, as for Ishmael, paternal inheritance was not something which he sought, but rather, something from which he wished to disconnect himself. Again, as Melville explains in his essay "Hawthorne and His Mosses," he felt he had to dissociate himself from his historical past—to embrace his "foundling" or orphan status—in order to attain the independence, originality, and spiritual grandeur he sought. One might say, then, that Melville's interest in the mother's body was sublimated in a more logical and psychologically acceptable search for self-esteem, through a longing to identify with a powerful *paternal* figure.

The psychoanalytic origins of the feeling of awe that Ahab seems to have in relation to his "fiery father," and to Moby Dick as well, further support the hypothesis that Melville's search for a powerful, phallic father figure disguised a more primal wish to be unconditionally embraced by the mother, at the hands of whom he believed he had suffered a devastating experience of emotional, and perhaps also physical, deprivation.[35] Freud explained the feeling of awe, in his essay, "A Disturbance of Memory on the Acropolis," as phallic awe, or the child's oedipal need for and fear of the father, which Freud believed that he himself felt in relation to the Parthenon temple.[36] Recent revisions of Freud's theory of awe, however, trace the preoccupation with feelings of oceanic and religious awe to a skewed experience with the preoedipal mother that occurred "well before self-object differentiation," and re-routed "the awe experience in the direction of anxiety or fear."[37] Current definitions of maternal awe as "reverential dread," mingled with "wonder," "mystery," and "the ineffable," come remarkably close to describing both Ishmael's emotional relationship with Nature and the Self, and Ahab's relationship to the great white whale, Moby Dick. Hence, if Freud, while in Athens, mistook the "temple" of the mother's body for a paternal, phallic temple, then it is reasonable to assume that patriarchal psychoanalysis, like Ahab himself, misconstrued the "Temple of the Whale" (458) and all that is "ineffable" in nature, including the creative principle of the universe, for a phallic father figure.

Maternal awe, it is now believed, results from the child's narcissistic identification with the split-off "bad mother," which in turn leads to a masochistic (passive-aggressive) or sadistic personality structure. In such individuals a crisis often results, resembling that of the rapprochement-phase crisis, in which "grandiosity and terror may coexist or alternate" in the adult, who finds it "difficult to untangle the web of dread and rage, humiliation and triumph, megalomania and devastation" within himself or herself (Harrison, "Awe," 191). Both Ahab's and Ishmael's ambiguous and awe-filled relationship with God and Nature, therefore, may perhaps be explained in terms of an early narcissistic identification with the persecuting, abandoning mother. But whereas Ahab focuses on the malignant projection of the early "bad mother," eclipsing, and hence losing sight entirely of, the "good mother," Ishmael apotheosizes the ideal "good mother" and, through an attempted regressive fantasy of fusion with her, seeks to attain a limitless narcissism and the oceanic bliss of mystical egolessness.

While the son's identification with the powerful father might repair a fundamental lack of self-esteem, only with the original ambivalently loved mother—or some symbolic substitute—can he work through his fixation at the rapprochement phase of development. Furthermore, if it is remembered, for a true resolution of the rapprochement crisis, or the phase of radical ambivalence, the images of the "good" and "bad" mother must be fused, a fusion which cannot occur until the persecutory guilt associated with an abandonment trauma is changed to depressive guilt, and the grief of loss at its core realized, activating a long-postponed mourning for the lost maternal object (Chasseguet-Smirgel, *Sexuality,* 125). Whatever critical interpretations have been generated to account for what Queequeg means to Ishmael, he certainly, in some respects, partakes of Melville's image of the good, nurturing mother. Queequeg's tomahawk, the "hatchet-faced baby" (27), produced from the communion of love between Ishmael and the savage, can be construed both as an oedipal product of father-Ishmael and mother-Queequeg (in which case the tomahawk signifies Ishmael's castration fear and feminine identity), and as the offspring of mother-Ishmael and father-Queequeg. In both scenarios, however, Ishmael is enacting a feminine/maternal identification.

Snug and warm under the bedcovers with Queequeg, Ishmael reflects upon the savage's hand that lies across the counterpane, an image which brings to mind the "phantom" memories of his austere stepmother. But extract the "bad" from Ishmael's memory of his mother, or in Ishmael's own words, "take away the awful fear" (26), and one is left with the "good mother," Queequeg. Queequeg's arm and the comforting maternal quilt "blended their hues together," making them, in effect, one. Unlike Ishmael's own mother, Queequeg can be counted upon to rescue a person from near death, particularly death from abandonment and drowning.[38] Before setting sail, Queequeg rescues the drowning greenhorn from the jaws of the black sea; later, he pulls Tashtego back from a "delicious death" (344) from drowning in the vat of warm sperm; and of course it is Queequeg's coffin that, in the end, saves Ishmael from the "suicidal" fate he envisions for himself when he resolves to go on a whaling voyage.

Even more importantly in terms of Ishmael's rapprochement crisis, Queequeg represents the healthy outcome of the child's ambivalence toward the splintered, good/bad mother. He is a heathen and a Satan worshipper—"the devil himself" (22), and yet he is also an omniscient and omnipotent nurturing mother-companion to Ishmael. Queequeg is complete unto himself, an incarnated fusion of all the goodness and evil in the world. Tattooed from head to toe, he wears the "mysteries" of "the heavens and the earth," as well as his entire personal history, on the *outside* of his body (480). For Queequeg, the "bad" does not need to be hidden or repressed in order to preserve the purity of the "good." To internalize Queequeg's inner wholeness—to allow himself to be "mysteriously drawn to him"—is, for Ishmael, to partake of Queequeg's "silent, solitary twain" (51). The "strange feelings" of "melting" that Ishmael experiences when he is snuggled up so close to Queequeg so as to become a part of him are the melting of the barrier between his severed worldview; in other words, of his own barricade between the good/bad mother. Therefore, as if magically: "No more my splintered heart and maddened hand were turned against the wolfish world" (51). Although, as D. H. Lawrence complained, in the rest of the novel "Queequeg is forgotten like yesterday's newspaper" (*Studies*, 156), it is Queequeg's love for Ishmael that plays the critical role of saving Ishmael's life at the end of his tale. Queequeg's coffin, on which is engraved the secret to all the good and evil in the world, which was once writ on Queequeg himself, is the emblem of overt mourning for the ambiguously loved, and now lost, maternal rescuer.

The fact that Queequeg plays an emblematic role in the latter half of the novel does not in any way detract from the important place he occupies as, quite literally, a life-and-death ingredient in Ishmael's story. His absent presence, like the absent presence of Ahab's lost leg and the lost maternal object, reveals the critical relevance of symbolic thinking in Melville's psychological drama and creative process. Perhaps partly for this reason *Moby-Dick* did not receive enthusiastic critical attention until after the discovery of psychoanalysis in the later nineteenth and early twentieth centuries, a discovery which allowed for a perceptible recognition of the emblematic psychoanalytic factors in the novel. In a similar way, the reader of *Moby-Dick* perhaps had to wait until the advent of feminist literary and psychoanalytic theory in the latter half of the twentieth century to identify, and hence, to fully appreciate, the vital critical import of the mother/woman's absent presence in Melville's novel.

Near the end of *Moby-Dick*, Melville gives Ahab several opportunities to transform his persecutory guilt into depressive guilt, as if toying with the possibility of psychological salvation. In "The Symphony" chapter, Melville lures Ahab infuriatingly close to an integration of his divided soul with the lost and repressed "good mother," and therefore to a catharsis of his aggression through grief. As before, the mildness of "a clear steel-blue day" inspires reveries in Ahab and Ishmael of the "innocency" of a "Sweet childhood"—a symbiotic oneness fantasy with the pregenital mother that is described by Ishmael as a state of "immortal infancy" (543). In evoking this archaic universe, Melville envisioned a wedding between the "feminine air" and the "masculine sea," which in *pregenital* experience corresponds to the "gentle," "snow-white" nurturing, "good mother," and the "strong," "murderous," phallic, "bad mother" (542). Through his narrative, Melville again merges Ishmael's experience of trauma with Ahab's, as he imagines Ahab's reconciliation with the cast-away good mother:

That glad, happy air, that winsome sky, did at last stroke and caress him; the step-mother world, so long cruel—forbidding—now threw affectionate arms round his stubborn neck, and did seem to joyously sob over him, as if over one, that however wilful and erring, she could yet find it in her heart to save and to bless. From beneath his slouched hat Ahab dropped a tear into the sea; nor did all the Pacific contain such wealth as that one wee drop. (543)

With his defenses down momentarily, Ahab opens his heart to comfort not only from the rejected and rejecting "step-mother," but to his companion, Starbuck, as well: "Close! stand close to me, Starbuck; let me look into a human eye" (544). Neither Ahab nor Melville seems able, or willing, to explain why, suddenly, "Ahab's glance was averted" from the course of emotional salvation, except to ask what "cruel, remorseless emperor commands me; that against all natural lovings and longings, I so keep pushing, and crowding, and jamming myself on all the time; recklessly making me ready to do what in my own proper, natural heart, I durst not so much as dare?" (545). Surely Ahab's unrelenting passion for greatness and immortality is responsible for his sudden and recalcitrant refusal to carry his mourning response any farther, as it is fueled and motivated by his denial of grief, and the displacement of that grief into wandering and searching, willful aggression, and angry protest.[39]

When his ivory leg is "snapped off" during the final chase after Moby Dick, Ahab again weakens somewhat in his resolve to defy his "natural loving and longing," and confesses to Starbuck: "Aye, aye, Starbuck, 'tis sweet to lean sometimes, be the leaner who he will; and would old Ahab had leaned oftener than he has" (560). On the last day of the chase, Ahab, for a third and final time, reaches out a human hand to his first mate: " 'Starbuck. I am old;—shake hands with me, man.' Their hands met; their eyes fastened; Starbuck's tears the glue" (566). Attempting to dissuade Ahab from his belief that courage and greatness are solely dependent on the denial of expressed grief, Starbuck pleads with Ahab: "Oh, my captain, my captain!—noble heart—go not—go not!—see; it's a brave man that weeps" (566).

It is the young Pip, however, who presents the greatest threat to Ahab's repressed grief and resulting monomaniacal resolve. Like Ahab and Ishmael, Pip has been abandoned by the "heartless"-seeming devouring "bad mother" sea. Even before his abandonment trauma at sea, however, Pip, as a slave, occupied an orphan identity, having been separated forcibly from both mother and father. Here Pip is "carried down alive to wondrous depths" in the mother-belly of the sea, "where strange shapes of the unwarped primal world glided to and fro before his passive eyes . . . among the joyous, heartless, ever-juvenile eternities" (414). Partaking of the infinite, mysterious creative powers of the Cosmos, Pip "saw God's foot upon the treadle of the loom" (414); but now, having attained what for mortal man is impossible, Pip has forever lost his "mortal reason" (414). Having been all but destroyed by maternal abandonment, Pip now shares the same trauma that Ahab and Ishmael once suffered. "There is that in thee, poor lad," Ahab says to the distracted boy, "which I feel too curing to my malady" (534). When Pip vows that he will "never desert" his master, Ahab comes too close to the emotional "cure" of worked-through mourning and forgiveness that he fears will sever him from his immortal anger and woe, and replies sharply to Pip: "Weep so, and I will murder thee!" (534). But before Ahab utters this murderous refusal, Pip speaks more profoundly and directly than anywhere else in Melville's novel of the original trauma of emotional deprivation, and the only true cure, of Ahab's divided heart and rage-filled monomania. Taking the comforting and protective hand of Ahab, the boy exclaims to his captain: "Ah, now, had poor Pip but felt so kind a thing as this, perhaps he had ne'er been lost!" (522).

In these temptation episodes, Melville permits Ahab to perceive lucidly that salvation, or the resolution of his internal conflicts, might well be achieved were he to acknowledge the grief and sorrow beneath his persecuting and persecutory rage and aggression. Without these moments of consciousness, however, Ahab could not attain the Aristotelian status of a true tragic hero. Otherwise, he would be merely the figure of a possessed madman. And so, with a clear understanding of his fate, Ahab will confront— "Forehead to forehead"—the evil, leviathan white-whale breast at last; the fate of the *Pequod* is "immutably decreed" (565, 561).

There is something truly uncanny and disturbing about Ahab's tragic end, however, in which he is tightly strapped forever to the *outside* of the terrible white whale that he has spent the better part of his life attempting to hunt down. Had Ahab been devoured by the whale and, like Jonah, been allowed to experience the blissful satisfaction of returning symbolically to the comforting mother's womb, his end would represent the fulfillment of a universal archaic myth. Instead, he dies a "lonely death" disconnected from his ship and crew, and, like his "lonely life," he must spend eternity "still chasing," searching, and grieving for the lost object of desire, never attaining the consolation of the comforting notion of loss (571).

As for Ishmael, he, along with the *Pequod* and its remaining crew, is sucked down toward the "closing vortex" of the devouring mother-sea. In his description of the disaster, Melville evokes the images of Ishmael's Jonah-like passage into the longed-for belly of the mother and then out again:

When I reached it, it had subsided to a creamy pool. Round and round, then, and ever contracting towards the button-like black bubble at the axis of that slowly wheeling circle, like another Ixion I did revolve. Till, gaining that vital centre, the black bubble upward burst; and now, liberated by reason of its cunning spring, and owing to its great buoyancy, rising with great force, the coffin life-buoy shot lengthwise from the sea, fell over, and floated by my side. (573)

Ishmael becomes the sole survivor of Ahab's, and the *Pequod's,* "death-longing" voyage. Embraced at last by the comforting and annihilating maternal sea, the *Pequod* and crew are digested into a chaotic, undifferentiated mass in the belly of Mother Nature. Ishmael's survival, by means of Queequeg's floating coffin, is psychoanalytically appropriate to Melville's novel as a whole, in which both mother and father have been seen to play a critical role. The image of paternal, symbolic language—Queequeg's coffin and Ishmael's, and Melville's, "immortality preserver"—rises from beneath the dark, impenetrable core of the engulfing maternal sea to save the narrator—the teller of the tale—from annihilation. Symbolic and metaphorical language, which belong to the paternal domain, combine with the mysterious, chaotic depths of the maternal unconscious, to create a balanced equation, or primal scene, in which both parents participate in the creation, or in Ishmael's experience, the preservation, of life.

In the novel's final scene Melville thus encapsulates the dynamic life-giving primal scene—the balanced interplay between the maternal and paternal elements in nature—that he had repeatedly acted out in *Moby-Dick*, but which he could not seem to get beyond. The reader, having struggled along with Melville through his multifarious variations of the primal scene, participates with Ishmael as well in this final act, which is, after all, merely the prologue of Ishmael's narrative that, with the circling of the eternal return of repressed grief, brings us back to the novel's first chapter. Similarly, Ahab's outwardly projected conflict with the good/ bad mother, like Ishmael's inwardly projected (toward suicidal fantasies) conflict with her, merge and separate throughout the novel to form a pulsating rhythm of perpetual mourning for an ungrieved-for experience of early deprivation and loss.

Since it has been my intention, in this chapter, to introduce the theme of tabooed grief as it appears *within* the text of a key work of American literature, I have proceeded with my investigation, for the most part, without engaging in the kind of weaving of fiction and biography that I shall rely upon more heavily in the extended subsequent discussions of Twain and Hemingway. For the sake of completing and enriching my exploration of *Moby-Dick* in this chapter, however, it is nevertheless appropriate to conclude by providing a few biographical details about Melville that can serve as a basic foundation for my critical analysis. The numerous, and in many cases, excellent biographical and psychoanalytic studies of Herman Melville suggest that he, like Twain and Hemingway, experienced a problematic childhood relationship with both his mother and father, which related specifically to an early object-relations trauma of combined maternal abandonment and disappointment in the father.

As a youth, Melville apparently suffered a double loss in relation to his father, Allen Melville: first, through his father's death from pneumonia when Herman was twelve years old; and second, through the disappointment that Melville's biographers believe he felt as a boy upon discovering that his father died a bankrupt—a disillusionment in the paternal ideal that was replayed in Melville's life through the death and bankruptcy several years later of his older brother Gansevoort.[40] The anger, disappointment, and general ambivalence that the twelve-year-old Melville must have felt toward his father, and the guilt from his aggressive thoughts, would likely have been repressed when Allen Melville died, a repression which would have made a direct emotional response to his father's death exceptionally difficult.[41] Like both Ishmael and the blacksmith, Perth, in *Moby-Dick*, Melville's grief over his father's and brother's death may have been obstructed by the guilt that he felt at having survived, or been "left . . . standing," while his "virtuous elder brother" and father were "plucked down" by death (485). Also, like both Ishmael and the blacksmith, Melville may then have viewed whaling as a suicide mission, taking to sea with "death-longing eyes" (486).

While Neal Tolchin, in *Mourning, Gender, and Creativity in the Art of Herman Melville*, may have been somewhat too narrow in attributing Melville's incapacity to grieve to a Victorian propriety against the overt expression of grief, Tolchin was right, I believe, in his unwavering conviction that one of the motives in Melville's composition of *Moby-Dick* was to act out an unresolved, and therefore chronic, mourning response for a lost parent. The grief from father-hunger and the son's devastating disillusionment in the heroic paternal ideal that become openly dramatized in *Pierre* are, for the most part, eclipsed in *Moby-Dick* by the more originary unresolved conflict with the rejecting and rejected mother. Perhaps it is this unworked-through father-son conflict that led Henry Murray to conclude that while "Ishmael survived the wreck" of despair and loss in *Moby-Dick*, "there was still," in Melville, "some energy, some grief, some hate—'deep volcanoes long burn ere they burn out.' *Pierre* is the burning out of Melville's volcano" ("Introduction," xiv). Melville's later novel is, indeed, the psychological sequel to *Moby-Dick*, in that it draws into the rapprochement equation the son's unresolved relationship with the ambivalently loved, real and ideal—disappointing and heroic—father.

That Herman Melville also suffered from "separation anxiety," or what John Bowlby calls an "insecure attachment," in relation to his mother,[42] Maria Gansevoort Melville, is an established notion, primarily owing to the biographical studies executed by some of Melville's most competent psychoanalytic and literary critics. However, while some critics, such as Newton Arvin, Lewis Mumford, Ludwig Lewishon, and

Leonard Pops, contend that Herman's unsatisfied desire for unconditional love from his mother took the form of oedipal rivalry with the
favorite son Gansevoort, others, most notably Edmund Bergler, Henry
A. Murray, and Frederick Rosenheim, believe that Melville's separation
anxiety in relation to the maternal figure originated in infancy from a
traumatic and premature weaning experience.[43] Before the age of one,
Herman and his two older siblings were afflicted by a severe case of
whooping cough, and it was this, Rosenheim suggests, that perhaps was
responsible for Maria's early weaning of the infant Herman from the
breast.[44] In his later life, Melville persisted in experiencing himself as "an
outcast, an Ishmael." According to Rosenheim, "Melville never forgave
his mother for ending his blessed babyhood" (12). The lonely-wanderer
protagonists of all of Melville's major novels, Rosenheim affirms, were
images of Melville himself, who "felt lost, deserted, thrust away from his
mother's breast." "It is the memory of this loss," Rosenheim concludes,
that "keeps [Melville] bitter" (22). Melville's admission to his niece later
in life that his mother "hated him" has suggested to several biographers
not only his mother's feelings toward him but his own repressed aggression toward her.[45]

My elucidation of the rapprochement-phase crisis, acted out on many
textual and contextual levels in *Moby-Dick*, both takes as its premise,
and further supports, the convincing argument set forth by Bergler,
Murray, and Rosenheim, that the psychological conflicts that infused
and inspired Melville's fiction were rooted in his unresolved trauma of
abandonment in relation to the pregenital mother. Melville's anger toward his mother and his lingering feelings of abandonment and grief,
combined with his longing to recapture his too-suddenly lost exclusive
infantile relationship with her, may well, therefore (as in the case of
Ishmael and Ahab), have led him to internalize the aggressive or persecuting image of the "bad mother" as the only way to preserve his
intrapsychic image of the loving "good mother." In this way, Melville
might readily have inhabited in fantasy the masochistic and sadistic
personality structures of both Ishmael and Ahab.

Certainly, embarking on a whaling journey was for Melville (and as
he reveals in *Moby-Dick*, it was also, for Ishmael), a kind of suicidal act
that was motivated not merely by aggression and masochism alone, but
by a deep underlying striving to mourn for his own imagined orphaned,
abandoned, and isolated self. *Moby-Dick* as a whole represents the or-
phan-Melville's cathartic preoedipal struggle. It is perhaps for this reason

that, after writing the novel, Melville felt "spotless as the lamb," while at the same time the demonstrative and violent primitive aggression released through the uncensored rage of Ahab led Melville to feel that he had also "written a wicked book."[46]

Melville's general philosophical views about life, which can be seen not only in *Moby-Dick* but in *Pierre, The Confidence Man,* and in most of his short fiction, are that wisdom is woe, that the world is divided into the irreconcilable ambiguity of good and evil, and that the loss of Paradise results in the predominance of evil in the world. These beliefs conform to the thinking of a child, who sees reality as a consequence of tragic loss, and whose psychic development is caught up in a recurring and unresolved rapprochement crisis of hopeless indefiniteness and ambiguity, where one is compelled to choose between clinging and distancing—between the "open independence" of the sea or the "treacherous, slavish shore" (*Moby-Dick,* 107). The loss and deprivation that Melville experienced as a child in relation to both his father and his mother thrust him into a state of ambivalence and abandonment depression that remained with him for the rest of his life. These early conflicts, as dramatized in Melville's fiction, are, metaphorically, the "long coils of the umbilical cord of Madame Leviathan, by which the young cub seemed still tethered to its dam" (388). The depressive protest, "I prefer not to," of Melville's Bartleby is perhaps the final submissive, "human sort of wail" of a young cub that has forever lost its dam (524).

Of all of Melville's superb and uncanny insights into the hidden nature of mankind and the world, one of his most significant realizations is his assumption that if greatness is to be had (meaning, of course, that if greatness is to be had by *him*), it would depend not on the cathartic indulgence of grief through mourning and tears, but on the strict enforcement of the taboo, or repression, of grief. According to Edwin S. Shneidman, Melville "had an enormous appetite for recognition and fame."[47] A person's accomplishments, Melville wrote, in *Redburn,* "are but tombstones that commemorate his death, but celebrate not his life." Melville "was partially dead during much of his own life," Shneidman concludes, because he cared more about his "post-self"—his reputation as a great writer—than about his living self.[48] Whatever the exact causes of Melville's overriding conviction that life is loss, and living is grieving, his life itself was a striving for the realization to mourn, and all his fictions were epitaphs.

When viewed through the dual lens of object relations and feminist psychoanalysis, and scrutinized according to current theories of attachment, separation, and pathological mourning, the fictions of Mark Twain and Ernest Hemingway also begin to take shape as elegiac narratives that act out the author's repressed and displaced mourning. Twain, through his humorous fiction, and Hemingway, through his narrative of omission, succeeded, as Melville also did, in making a virtue of loss and grief by sublimating these painful emotions into their art, eventually coming to flourish and prosper both personally and artistically on the creative displacement, or indirect expression, of their grief. Because of the prolonged absence of conscious grieving, they, like Melville, remained fixated in a position of adolescent ambivalence in relation to their disappointing, and therefore emotionally lost, parent figures, wavering one moment to the next from regression to childhood and feminine identification, to the assertion of autonomy and masculine identity. Finally, because the repression, disavowal, and displacement of grief had become an integral part of their artistic processes and personal identities, they began, ultimately, to hoard their grief, transforming the one thing they wished to rid themselves of into the very thing upon which their creative unconscious, and their psychic equilibrium, thrived.

2. "My First Lie, and How I Got Out of It": Deprivation-Grief and the Making of an American Humorist

When young lips have drunk deep of the bitter waters of Hate, Suspicion and Despair, all the Love in the world will not take away that knowledge.
—Rudyard Kipling, *Baa Baa Black Sheep*

Mr. Clemens laid all the faults of all mankind to the mothers for they alone— *alone*—have the teaching of their children. . . . I sat on that stiff little chair defending the mothers and I couldn't say what I ought to have said because I was blind with the suddenness of his attack.
—From Mark Twain's secretary Isabel Van Kleck Lyon's *Diary*, June 6, 1906

Sam Clemens began his career as a humorist and storyteller as a young boy, when he reportedly came home in the evenings heavily laden with an assortment of tales about his day's adventures. He would always recast his stories comically, relating them in a humorous and entertaining manner,[1] and although there was always a pretense of truthfulness, his listeners could never be certain as to how much of the story was true, and how much was pure fabrication. In his mother's experience: "Sammy is a wellspring of truth, but you can't bring up the whole well with one bucket.—I know his average. . . . I discount him 90 per cent for embroidery, and what is left is perfect and priceless truth, without a flaw in it anywhere" (Sanborn, 33).[2]

There is, in fact, hardly a speech, story, or novel produced by Mark Twain which is not, at least in part, a product of autobiography. All of Twain's works of fiction, he once claimed, were based on "incidents out of real life." Each one of his books, he said, "writes itself," and, "I never deliberately . . . 'created' a character in my life." Instead, Twain confessed, he would recollect a character, and then allow it to go "hither and thither as fancy dictates."[3] Perhaps the most revealing statement that Twain ever made about his own process of fiction-making is contained in an enigmatic claim, which appears in a journal entry from 1894: "If you tell the truth you don't have to remember anything."[4] For Twain, the process of remembering was clearly a form of lying, and thus, memory functioned as a means for transforming his life history into fiction.

It is therefore frustrating, if not fruitless, to attempt to decipher what is fiction and what is fact in the fabric of Twain's life and writings. How, then, is the psychoanalytic critic to approach Mark Twain's works, where autobiography is virtually inseparable from fiction, where the fiction itself is motivated and informed throughout by autobiography, and where what is told is inextricably bound up with his urge to exaggerate or "lie"? An answer is suggested by the psychoanalytic assumption that, in analysis, the process of retelling is equally as significant as the retold story, incident, or dream. The psychotherapist also knows what Twain's mother recognized, and what the psychoanalytic critic is forced to accept; namely, that words can be lies. It is, therefore, not merely the words themselves that are most revealing to the analyst, but the overdetermined, emotional themes, embedded in the stories that are told.

The overdetermined themes in Mark Twain's autobiographical and fictional writings are those of death, loss, loneliness, hostility, and deception. While critics, such as Bernard De Voto, have acknowledged the presence of many of these themes in Twain's work, they have, for the most part, attributed them to the tragedies which Samuel Clemens experienced in his later years. Included amongst these tragedies are the death of his younger brother, Henry, when Sam was twenty-two years old, the death of his daughter, Susy, from meningitis, in 1896, and the death of his wife, Livy, in 1904.[5] These events are believed to be of most significance because of the fact that it was only in Twain's later years that these darker themes came to the surface in his writing and began wholly to occupy his creative imagination. However, De Voto's biographical theory of Twain's later writings of "despair" does not take into account the fact that these grief-filled themes may also be found embedded in many of his works that were written well before these tragedies.

The aim of the following two chapters, therefore, is to substantiate the hypothesis that these overdetermined, darker themes were a prominent part of Sam Clemens's creative imagination from his early childhood and adolescence, and that his fixation on the emotional issues of his childhood and adolescence played a critical role in the evolution of his career as a humorist. I will attempt to locate, in Mark Twain's life and fiction, the origins of his identity as a humorist, for it is only through an understanding of how Twain used his humor to repress and to disguise his feelings of grief, abandonment, and disappointment that the causes of these underlying emotions can be discerned. I will also suggest that Samuel Clemens's persona as the humorist, Mark Twain, evolved as a compromise formation out of his disappointing relationship with his mother, Jane Lampton Clemens. This, in turn, fostered an anxiety, or rivalry, in Clemens, in relation to his comparatively well-behaved siblings. This sibling rivalry, as I will demonstrate in the chapter that follows, led to a pathological, lifetime obsession with grief, death, and mourning after three of his siblings died during his childhood.

This current chapter will demonstrate in the case of Mark Twain, as the previous chapter suggested in relation to Herman Melville, how an early experience of grief—specifically, the grief that results when one is deprived of the mother's unqualified love and attention—directly affected the creative writer's artistic process. While a study of grief and loss as they appear throughout a major work of Twain's fiction is reserved for a later chapter, here many of his lesser known stories and sketches, and his most openly autobiographical narratives, are examined in order to provide clues to the early development of his identity as a writer of humorous fiction. In the course of this chapter I will also suggest one explanation as to how Twain's creative impulse became redirected from private aims to cultural ones; or, more specifically, from his mother and family as audience, to the community of Hannibal, and finally to America and the world at large. An answer will be proposed for the question of why Mark Twain believed that in America the only way to communicate the truth was through "humorous and mendacious stories."[6] This will also entail a consideration of why, in fact, America was so overwhelmingly receptive to Mark Twain's games of rebellion and repression. In other words, how and why did his American audience conspire in the repression of the negative emotions, such as grief and hostility, which were embedded within the motives and content of Twain's humor and fiction?

In the case of Samuel Clemens, humor became a strategy of defense to combat and compensate for childhood deprivation and loss. Young Sam's adoption of the persona of a humorist evolved directly out of his defensive impulse as a child to deny or repress feelings of guilt, hostility, and grief. Humor became a means of deflecting his anger and grief, just as voyaging at sea and the writing of fiction did for Melville, and allowed Twain to sublimate these negative emotions into a more acceptable outlet of expression. Although his identity as a humorist may have originated as a defensive personality structure, and as a displaced manifestation of grief and guilt, because of the positive reinforcement that it came to provide for him, Twain's humorous persona, like Hemingway's grandiose, heroic self-image, took on a life of its own, encouraging a developmental fixation at this fundamentally adolescent stage of psychic growth.

Prior to Sam Clemens's Hannibal stage debut when he was fifteen, he had often used his humor and creative impulse to mediate between his mother and his childish ego. Thereafter, his humorous art occupied an intermediary position between himself and the world. Twain's remarkable ability to make people laugh became, in his teens, a usable transitional object between himself and the external world, and eventually he learned that his humor could publicly insulate him from his own aggression and that of his collective audience.[7] Humor became a safe haven in which Twain could act out both his desire for love and fame, and his animosity toward those whom he resented but whom, like his mother, he could not risk "hurting" through unmitigated aggression. Perhaps it is significant, in this regard, that "mark twain" is also a riverboat-piloting term, meaning "safe water."[8]

Van Wyck Brooks was correct when he sensed that Twain possessed "a mind that has not found itself, a mind that does not know itself"; but he was wrong, as I hope to show, in his belief that Twain's humor represented a "miscarriage" of his creative life.[9] Instead, I want to suggest, Mark Twain's humor was the strategy by which he adapted his repressed, "real" self to what he perceived as a persecuting world. To use D. W. Winnicott's terms, Twain's humor was the "false self" vehicle that enabled him to express his "true" self and opinions. Humor was not a compromise in Twain's creative life, as Brooks believed; rather, it served as an indispensable vehicle for Twain's moral, creative impulse. It enabled him to enact a transference of his inner hostility and sense of emptiness and abandonment, which developed out of his childhood experiences, onto America at large, and to receive from his wider cultural audience the love and approval that, as a child, only his humor could win from his mother.

Susan Gillman has recently demonstrated how Twain's texts turn against themselves to expose reality as "fictions of law and custom."[10]

However, her explanation of Twain's personal disillusionment with reality is psychoanalytically implausible. She suggests that Twain first determined that imposture was a social problem, and thereafter turned "that eye inward on himself and his own art." Such an interpretation, however, contradicts the paradoxical self-image that afflicted Twain from his early childhood until his death. This self-image can be characterized by Twain's two statements—I "never speak the truth," which he admitted in an interview at the age of sixty-five, and the claim he made, in *The Autobiography of Mark Twain*—"I was always honest; I know I can never be otherwise."[11] Furthermore, while Sam Clemens was essentially interchangeable with Mark Twain, he had also to deal with the fact that, as his mother once commented, "I've got no son named Mark."[12] I intend to demonstrate that these paradoxes of identity were not introjections of Twain's observations of the external world, as Gillman thinks, but that they were psychic realities which emanated from what Jacques Lacan might call a "psyche as text," that was forced to turn against itself at the earliest stages of self-development and identity formation. In the external world the young Sam Clemens merely found confirmation of his negative self-image, and the distorted sense of justice he learned from his mother, in the hypocrisy of society, traditional religion, and the self-deceptions of the human psyche.

Six years before his death, in April 1910, Twain came to the realization that he had "been forced by fate to adopt fiction as a medium of truth. Most liars lie for the love of the lie; I lie for the love of truth. I disseminate my true views by means of a series of apparently humorous and mendacious stories" (*Life As I Find It,* 334), and he admitted, with the utmost sincerity, in *The Autobiography of Mark Twain,* that only after one is dead is it possible to speak one's opinions directly.[13] In the following discussion, I will attempt to identify this force of "fate" to which Twain consistently felt he was obliged to submit. Twain's deeply felt skepticism and distrust of a reality based on "a fiction of law and custom," or on what structural psychoanalysts would call the "Father's word," resulted from a severe disturbance in "basic trust" in relation to the mother-object. The consequences of this, according to Erik Erikson, are a "negative-identity" structure, an incessant childish need to earn love and approval from others, and a feeling that one must always hide or disguise one's true self beneath a more socially acceptable identity.[14] In this sense Twain, as Edwin Shneidman says of Melville, "was partially dead during much of his own life"; his humorous persona was a living monument to a repressed, or "dead," self whose grief, hostility, and opinions, he believed, had to be kept hidden and disguised.

Mark Twain was intrigued by babies. Perhaps this interest was inspired by his belief that the "circumstances and environment" into which a baby is born, and which surround his or her earliest life experiences, have a decisive influence on the infant's future character and life's work.[15] As Satan explains in "The Mysterious Stranger": "A child's first act knocks over the initial brick, and the rest will follow inexorably" (213). My concern, however, is not with the particulars of Mark Twain's deterministic psychology, but rather, with the "experiences and circumstances" of his own infancy, and with his retrospective interpretations of what he believed his own "first childish act[s]" to be (214). Here, what will be discovered is that behind Twain's philosophical convictions about determinism lay a deeper suspicion that his own life had, at some time before he could remember, got out of his control, and that his own character and life's work had somehow been influenced by forces which he felt he could never quite identify.

The experience of early infancy may well have been fraught with an inordinate amount of stress, both for Sam Clemens and his mother, as he was born nearly two months premature, and began his life, in 1835, during one of the coldest and most uncongenial winters in Missouri history. About his early childhood, as he relates in *The Autobiography of Mark Twain*, he knew only what his mother and others had told him; namely, that he was "a sickly and precarious and tiresome and uncertain child" (11). Several of Twain's biographers, as well as Twain himself in *The Autobiography of Mark Twain*, report that when he asked his mother many years later whether she feared he would not live, she surprised him with the retort, "No—afraid you would" (*The Autobiography*, 11). Although this remark has often been humorously noted by Twain's critics, it carries a grave message, as it suggests either that the infant Sam was so critically ill or impossibly unmanageable that he could not function as a normal baby, or that Jane Clemens had a warped or, even worse, vicious sense of humor when it came to her son. Mark Twain, of course, could not actually remember what he was like as a baby. His narratives and statements about himself as a young child are imaginative interpretations of his mother's words, and of his estimation of himself as an adult. When his own first child, Langdon Clemens, was born, in 1870, Twain wrote a letter from the newborn child's point of

view to the Reverend Joseph Twichell and his wife, informing them of
"his" birth. The sadness and vexation that the child apparently feels
revealed more about Mark Twain's self-pitying identification with the
infant than about the true state of mind of his son:

> I came into the world on the 7th inst., and consequently am about five days old
> now. I have had wretched health ever since I made my appearance. First one
> thing and then another has kept me under the weather, and as a general thing I
> have been chilly and uncomfortable. . . . At birth I only weighed 4½ pounds
> with my clothes on. . . . Life seems a serious thing, what I have seen of it—and
> my observation teaches me that it is made up mainly of hiccups, unnecessary
> washings, and colic. But no doubt you, who are old, have long since grown
> accustomed and reconciled to what seems to me such a disagreeable novelty.[16]

It is probable that the sickly, temperamental, and hyperactive Sam
Clemens made his mother's caretaking task inordinately difficult. But
there is also reason to suspect that Jane Clemens was not up to the
challenge of adapting to her son's exceptional needs. She was frail in
health, and willful and erratic in her behavior. As a neighbor once
reported, Jane Clemens "was always one to say what came to her tongue
first." The same person added that on "general principle, anything she
liked was good for her and anything she didn't like was bad for her."[17]
The family physician, Dr. Meredith, also complained about Mrs. Clemens: "Try and pin her down to a routine. It can't be done. Several times
I've left medicine for the children and found she's switched to some old
Negro remedy" (Varble, 123). Adding to her list of anxieties, Jane
Clemens feared that her third son, Sam, would die in infancy as had her
second son, Pleasants Hannibal, only a few years before. Many years
later, when her sister, Patsy, died in childbirth, Jane Clemens asked her
brother-in-law, John Quarles, if she could raise the child as her own.
John Quarles declined the offer, implying that she had let three of her
children die already, and so could not be trusted with an infant's care.
"You don't notice a child is sick till it's got a hectic flush," he accused
her. "Patsy once said so, herself" (Varble, 197). While Mrs. Clemens
was at times anxious and oversolicitous of her children, at other times
she exhibited a heightened self-absorption and indifference toward them.
An acquaintance of Jane's made the observation that she "loved cats and
was apt to have one on her lap. When someone said to her, 'I believe
you like cats better than children,' she denied it indignantly, but explained that the advantage of a cat was that you could always put it down
when you were tired of holding it" (Webster, 531).

Perhaps Jane Clemens's excessive apprehensiveness about her new-born son's poor health and fractious disposition prevented her from responding appropriately to his unique needs.[18] Nonetheless, Sam Clemens survived his infancy, but as his mother admitted, it was a consequence of neither her own, nor Dr. Meredith's, efforts. "The baby did it for himself," she said. "He had to, to live," implying that it was the baby, not the mother, who mastered the art of conforming to the world's demands (Varble, 123). If Jane Clemens was, indeed, incapable of expressing her love by adapting to her baby's spontaneous demands, Sam Clemens was apparently sufficiently gifted to earn that needed love by adjusting to and coping with his mother's eccentric habits of nurturing.

There is no indication that, by the time he was a youngster, Sam Clemens's naturally impulsive and hyperactive nature had abated; if anything, he had grown even more excitable and ungovernable. According to Albert Bigelow Paine, "Little Sam . . . was a wild-headed impetuous child of sudden ecstasies that sent him capering and swinging his arms, venting his emotions in a series of leaps and shrieks and somersaults, and spasms of laughter as he lay rolling in the grass" (*Mark Twain: A Biography*, 32). Jane Clemens confirmed the unwieldy character of her obstreperous child when she admitted to him, years later, that he "gave me more uneasiness than any child I had" (Paine, 29). While Sam's mother at first referred to her infant son as a "difficult" and "demanding" child, his consistently bad behavior as he grew into boyhood eventually led her to label him as "disobedient." Unlike his well-behaved brothers and sisters, particularly his younger brother, Henry — who, like Sam's friend, Simmons Hicks, "was born honest" — Twain came to believe that he was born "without that incumbrance — so some people said" (*The Autobiography*, 52). Undoubtedly, Twain's mother was one of those "people" who repeatedly reminded young Sam of his inherently dishonest character.

In a revealing little sketch, entitled "My First Lie, and How I Got Out of It" (1900), Twain depicted himself as having already become an established, inveterate liar at the age of nine days old. Through the voice of this week-old infant, the Twain/narrator mentions having made the observation "that if a pin was sticking in me and I advertised it in the usual fashion, I was lovingly petted and coddled and pitied in a most agreeable way and got a ration between meals besides. It was human nature to want to get these riches, and I fell. I lied about the pin — advertising one when there wasn't any."[19] Whether the unsuspecting victim of this infant's con game for the prize of love was his own mother or some other fictional caretaker, it is clear that, in Twain's adult mind, a definitive and predictable connection existed between willful disobedience, deceit, and maternal attention. Whereas in circumstances of healthy and adequate nurturing the infant's basic needs are responded to by the caretaker with seemingly magical spontaneity, Twain's week-old baby experiences no such positive mirroring. For him, reality is something to be mastered; and while his desire for love is strong and hopeful, he feels as early as nine days old that he must resort to lies and deception in order to obtain this prize of love.[20] If, to begin with, the baby in Twain's story had any sense of deserving maternal attention, after his "fall" from innocence, through his lies and deception, any remnants of this sense must certainly have been dispelled.

The numerous examples of Sam Clemens's boyhood mischief, scattered throughout the first fifty pages of *The Autobiography of Mark Twain*, provide further evidence for the supposition that his relationship with his mother was marked by strong ambivalence and an active domestic air of mutual deception. In most cases, however, Sam's mischievousness as a boy was matched by Mrs. Clemens's own cunning methods of entrapment. For instance, one winter evening, when Sam returned from playing hooky from Church, unaware that he was wearing his Scotch plaid cloak inside-out (with the bright plaid lining on the outside), his mother, instead of asking him directly why this was the case, attempted to trick him into telling a lie.[21] She remarked, "It must have been impossible to keep warm there on such a night" (36). Sam unfortunately "didn't see the art of that remark" and foolishly claimed to have worn his cloak throughout the entire church service. The ruse was quickly uncovered by his mother. "You wore it with that red Scotch plaid outside and glaring? Didn't that attract any attention?" This time Sam "took the consequences"; but with his exceptional talent for adapting to and picking up on his mother's cunning ways, it is unlikely that the next time he would fail to anticipate and successfully evade his mother's "art," through his own superior use of deceptive tactics.

From these stories one may begin to identify the psychological dynamic that characterized Sam Clemens's childhood relationship with his mother, and which, if we accept his sketch about the "first lie" he ever told as a reflection of his own feelings toward his mother, governed his attempts to master the world from earliest infancy. Forrest G. Robinson, who perceptively analyzes the "dynamics of deception" in Mark Twain's fiction, confirms the hostile, deceptive interactions between Sam Clemens and his mother in his investigation of the relationship between Tom Sawyer and Aunt Polly. In *The Adventures of Tom Sawyer*, Robinson claims, "the woman and child unconsciously collaborate in the creation of a pleasurable contest of wills."[22] Although this statement, I believe, is for the most part valid, it leads one to question what part of the exchange between mother and son is "unconscious," and what exactly Robinson means by the paradox of their "pleasurable contest"? As the following passage, from *The Adventures of Tom Sawyer*, openly reveals, there is a profound element of aggression and hostility driving Aunt Polly's interrogation of Tom.

> While Tom was eating his supper, and stealing sugar as opportunity offered, aunt Polly asked him questions that were full of guile, and very deep—for she wanted to trap him into damaging revealments. Like many other simple-hearted souls, it was her pet vanity to believe she was endowed with a talent for dark and mysterious diplomacy and she loved to contemplate her most transparent devices as marvels of low cunning. Said she:
> "Tom, it was middling warm in school, warn't it?"
> "Yes'm."
> "Powerful warm, warn't it?"
> "Yes'm."
> "Didn't you want to go in a-swimming, Tom?"
> A bit of a scare shot through Tom—a touch of uncomfortable suspicion. He searched aunt Polly's face, but it told him nothing. So he said:
> "No'm—well, not very much."
> The old lady reached out her hand and felt Tom's shirt, and said:
> "But you ain't too warm now, though." And it flattered her to reflect that she had discovered that the shirt was dry without anybody knowing that that was what she had in her mind. But in spite of her, Tom knew where the wind lay, now.[23]

Robinson claims that "when the contest is finally joined the issue of compliance with rules appears in its true colors, as the merest pretext for an exhilarating round of artful deception and cat-like pursuit" (32). What Robinson attests to here, but does not directly state, is that the conscious elements of the game—the rules themselves, and the content of the dialogue between woman and child—are of secondary importance to both parties involved, while of primary significance is the game itself— its carefully designed structure, and the unacknowledged motives of the participants. The "game" of cat and mouse played by Tom and Aunt Polly allows them to act out both their love, and their hostility, toward one another. This is the unconscious, ambivalent motive of love combined with aggression that lies behind Tom and Aunt Polly's game, and that explains the seemingly paradoxical coupling of "pleasure" and "contest" that Robinson observes in Twain's mother-son relationships.

If the above analysis is correct, then the many episodes of underhanded gamesmanship between mother and son which appear throughout Twain's fiction and autobiographical works indeed merely represent the humorous surface dramatics of the son's repressed anger and frustration at having to lie, deceive, and play false to his moral, loving, filial self. Therefore, what we should find at the root of Twain's fictional representations of artful boyhood deception is a powerful and profound feeling of maternal disappointment and abandonment. "Hunting the Deceitful Turkey" was written by Twain in 1906, and although it appears in numerous editions of his collected stories, it has been neglected by Twain's critics. In this remarkable little story it is possible to see, most cleverly demonstrated, the depths of a young boy's feelings of yearning, betrayal, and defeat in relation to the mother figure.

The narrator of the story is a young boy who has gone out on one of his uncle's early morning turkey-hunts. Ironically, the mother turkey is lured out of hiding by blowing through a leg-bone of a previously captured turkey, which, the narrator observes, is yet another example of (Mother) "Nature's treacheries."[24] Mother Nature herself, Twain is suggesting, is "badly mixed" in a love/hate relationship with her offspring: "half the time she doesn't know which she likes best—to betray her child or protect it" (*Mark Twain's Short Stories*, 626). As the narrator explains, the hunt begins when the threatened "mamma-turkey" engages in a peculiarly "immoral device" of evasion (627). She pretends to the hunter that she is lame, and tells her young brood to lie low until she has "beguiled this shabby swindler out of the country." From then on, the pursuing young hunter and the elusive mother-turkey engage in a strategic contest of wit and deception, obeying rules of conduct, which, like those between Tom and Aunt Polly, and between young Sam Clemens and his mother, are somehow mutually understood. "I letting on to be thinking about something else," the narrator explains, "but neither of us sincere, and both of us waiting for the other to call game but in no real hurry about it, for indeed those little evanescent snatches of rest were very grateful to the feelings of us both" (627). Maintaining the same air of condescension which we saw revealed in Tom's secret thoughts about his aunt, the narrator assumes in advance that victory will be his: "I judged that I was safe to win, in the end, the competition being purely a matter of staying power and the advantage lying with me from the start because she was lame" (627). But, much to the boy's surprise and disappointment, he is unable to catch his prey. Instead, it is he who becomes the victim, when the mother turkey suddenly "flew off" to a branch, and with uncanny composure, "crossed her legs, and smiled down" at him.[25]

After his humiliating defeat the boy is left alone, feeling "ashamed" and "lost." But more than this, he is left with a ravenous hunger, which he appeases by stealing tomatoes from a nearby garden and gorging upon them until he becomes ill. Behind this child's distress and frustration with the mother figure, one may see an even more urgent need that has been denied him. From the greedy nature of the boy's hunger, and the implication that he is not stealing but deserves the tomatoes with which he "surfeited" himself, it is likely that what he really craves, and what he has been hunting for all along, is not the deceitful mother-turkey, but the deceitful mother's love.

It is evident from this story that the "pleasure" derived from the game of deception is not, as Robinson suspects, sufficient to fill the inner emptiness that the boy feels. What he feels is hunger, and having attempted, unsuccessfully, to obtain his desired maternal object—first by sweetly luring it and then by trying to outsmart it—he resorts to stealing. A child's lying and stealing are commonly understood as pleas for love and attention. According to D. W. Winnicott, when a child steals "a lump of sugar out of the cupboard," it is an indication that the child is acting under a compulsion: The child "is not looking for the object that he takes. He is looking for a person. He is looking for his own mother, only he does not know this."[26] The unconscious logic of the child is that he is stealing from someone "from whom he has a right to steal." Repeated behavior of this sort, Winnicott believes, points to the fact that the "thief" feels an ongoing need to re-establish his relation, not only to the mother, but to the world at large. He continually attempts to re-find the person who is willing to understand him and adequately adapt to his needs.

In addition, if the mother comes down too hard on the child, or demands a confession from him, "the child will certainly start lying as well as thieving" (164). In view of the relationship between mother and child as it exists in Twain's memory of his own childhood, and as it is depicted in his fiction, it would seem an unlikely possibility that the son would feel either safe or comfortable overtly expressing, or even consciously allowing himself to feel, love for his mother. That leaves stealing, and as Winnicott suggests, unaware of his true motive for stealing, the child would have no recourse but to lie about his behavior when confronted. The original sense of resentment, grief, and loss, however, would remain active, though deeply buried, in the child's unconscious.

In March of 1897, Twain jotted down a dream in his notebook that keenly and explicitly revealed the connection in his mind between the delinquency Winnicott speaks of and the yearning for maternal love:

I dreamed I caught a beautiful slender white fish 14 inches and thought what a fine meal it would make. I was very hungry. Then came the feeling of disappointment and sorrow; it was Sunday, and I could not take the fish home, for it would deeply grieve Livy to know that I had been fishing on the Sabbath. Then it occurred to me to catch a fish for *her,* and *that* would disarm her. (*Notebook,* 325)

This dream, Twain notes in his journal, "is a perfect reflection of my character and [Livy's], down to that last detail—there it suddenly breaks down. But in the dream it seemed quite natural that her religious loyalty should be bought for a fish" (325). It is significant that the only part of the dream which does not conform to Twain's conscious thought is the impulse to deceive his wife. However, it is an impulse to which he would readily have succumbed were it the Mother/Aunt Polly figure with whom the miscreant was dealing. In this dream we once again see all of the symptoms of mother-loss and maternal betrayal: the desire to assert spontaneously one's nature without impediment, the "hungering" for maternal love, the circuitous means of expressing filial love, and the realization that the only way to fulfill these desires is through the "disarming" mechanism of deception. The final message it imparts is that the "truth" of love, in Mark Twain's imagination, can be communicated only through acts of falsehood. Only a few months after he had this dream Twain recorded the following axiom in his notebook: "When you fish for love, bait with your heart, not your brain."[27] As might be expected, Twain gives no indication that, in framing this universal adage, he was consciously calling upon the metaphors of his recent dream.

At the root of all childhood delinquency, particularly lying and stealing, then, is a feeling of emotional deprivation, the sense that something good, once possessed (primarily the mother's unqualified love), has now been lost. In Mark Twain's image of boyhood, love is given and received obliquely, through an array of antagonistic words and acts. In *The*

Autobiography of Mark Twain, as in *The Adventures of Tom Sawyer,*
mother and son function as both comforter and tormentor for one
another; and "cuffs and kisses" are never doled out except in combination (*Tom Sawyer,* 141). If one can assume, as the evidence suggests, that
the young male protagonist of Twain's autobiographical and fictional
imagination is typical of the delinquent child, then one can also be
fairly certain that his boy hero's, as well as his own, misbehavior is
unconsciously intended to *provoke* punishment, although it is a fact of
which he is entirely unaware.

Once this domestic pattern has been established in a family, the
mother also often becomes dependent upon the operations of crime and
punishment as a means of expressing her maternal feelings and receiving
her child's love.[28] Ironically, almost any kind of disciplinary action on
the part of the mother—which indirectly reflects a form of care, concern, and love—can be better tolerated by the child than weakness or
inconsistent behavior, which signify indifference and loss to the child.[29]
Only firmness and consistent behavior will assure the child that he or
she can take risks and explore the world, knowing that there is a stable,
loving, and protective force at its center.

It so happens that weakness of resolution and inconsistency in following through on threatened punishment are two of the most noticeable
character traits of Twain's mother figures, and of Jane Clemens herself.
The most prevalent feature in Twain's fictional illustrations of his own
boyhood mischief is his mother's erratic manner of administering justice.
One of the most striking examples of this is the incident of the watermelon, in *The Autobiography of Mark Twain.* As the story goes, when
Sam was working for Mr. Ament at the printing shop he dropped a
large watermelon onto unsuspecting Henry's head. In retaliation, Henry
"landed a cobblestone" on the side of Sam's head, which, Twain lightly
explains, "raised a bump there so large that I had to wear two hats for a
time" (93). As a "just" reprisal for this "unjust" act, he continues, "I
carried this crime to my mother, for I was always anxious to get Henry
into trouble with her and could never succeed. I thought that I had a
sure case this time when she should come to see that murderous bump."
But contrary to Sam's expectations, his mother's reaction was not only
unsympathetic, but entirely devoid of emotional understanding: "I
showed it to her but she said it was no matter. She didn't need to inquire
into the circumstances. She knew I had deserved it . . ." (93).

The permanent effects of Twain's sibling rivalry with his brother

Henry will be discussed at length in the following chapter. For the moment it is sufficient to note that the difference between the two brothers was that Henry, being "a much finer and better boy than ever Sid was" in *The Adventures of Tom Sawyer,* conformed, as Sam did not, to Mrs. Clemens's idea of how a "good" and moral boy should behave.[30] Hence, Henry was able to receive direct love and admiration from her. Sam, on the other hand, as we have already seen, learned at an early age that he had little chance of competing with Henry's superior moral "goodness" for his mother's approval. Knowing that he could never compete with his morally perfect brother, it is likely that Sam Clemens, like Tom Sawyer (in relation to his impeccably behaved brother Sid), came to the realization that either his humorous falsehoods and deceptive antics would earn him the prize of his mother's love, or nothing would. As Erikson has suggested, an adolescent would "rather be *nobody* or *somebody bad . . . than be not-quite somebody*" (*Identity,* 143). Consequently, Twain appears to have adopted a "negative," or "bad boy," identity in relation to his brother, which, when combined with his innate excitability and his natural talent for entertaining, served extremely well as a means of commanding his mother's attention and winning her love.[31] As Tom Sawyer resolves, his:

mind was made up now. He was gloomy and desperate. He was a forsaken, friendless boy, he said; nobody loved him; when they found out what they had driven him to, perhaps they would be sorry; he had tried to do right and get along, but they would not let him; since nothing would do them but to be rid of him, let it be so; and let them blame *him* for the consequences—why shouldn't they? What right had the friendless to complain? Yes, they had forced him to it at last: he would lead a life of crime. There was no choice. (88)

If Sam, in *The Autobiography of Mark Twain,* did happen to behave "correctly" (which, as in the case of the watermelon ambush, usually only occurred by accident), his mother punished him anyway, "as an advance payment for something which I hadn't yet done" (33). Understandably, this taught him a lesson that was to stay with him all his life; namely, that any spontaneous or planned constructive moral efforts on his part were likely to be rendered futile. Consequently, the boy's sense of "self-esteem," in addition to his sense of morality, was seriously undermined, so that his moral ideas of "good" and "bad," and "right" and "wrong," eventually failed to coincide with the meanings of these concepts held by others.[32] It is possible that Sam Clemens came to believe, paradoxically, that he could do the "good" and "right" thing only by acting "bad," and communicate the "truth" only by way of falsehood. The conflicting relationship between Mark Twain's personal sense of morality, and the morality of his society and culture, as I will soon argue, had a profound impact on his fiction, on his career as a humorist, and on the development of his adult, pessimistic *Weltan-schauung.*

In a letter written in 1885 to the *Christian Union,* voicing his opinion of a story about a pair of incompetent parents that had recently appeared in the journal, Twain expressed his belief that the fault for a child's unruliness and disobedience lies with the child's parents. Because of the parents' inability to deal out proper justice to their potentially sweet, but now wicked, boy, "the child grew stubborn, and stood out against reasoning and affection."[33] Twain might have been referring to his own domestic situation when he exclaims in his letter:

The spectacle of that treacherously-reared boy, and that wordy, namby-pamby father, and that weak, namby-pamby mother, is enough to make one ashamed of his species. And if I could cry, I would cry for the fate of that poor little boy — a fate which has cruelly placed him in the hands and at the mercy of a pair of grown up children, to have his disposition ruined, to come up ungoverned, and be a nuisance to himself and everybody about him . . . (*Life As I Find It,* 211)

It is likely that Twain recognized the "fate" of this "poor little boy" who had his "disposition ruined" and became a "nuisance to himself and everybody about him" as his own. But even more importantly, Twain revealed, through his empathy with this boy, that he could not express his pain and grief openly. As he realized after his stage debut—as the assistant to a fraudulent traveling mesmerist—he could only "shed tears on the inside" (*The Autobiography,* 53).

Twain's ideas on raising children were again examined at length in the uncompleted story, "Which Was the Dream?" (1895).[34] In this autobiographical account, the description of the good mother is unmistakably drawn from Twain's image of his wife, Livy; and the emotional force contained in Twain's critical tone, and the keen resemblance between the corrective behavior of the "bad" mother in the story and his own mother's "extempory punishments" (*The Autobiography,* 35), give strong support to the supposition that Twain was speaking from his own childhood experiences. About Bessie, the child in the story, Twain writes:

Nobody but the mother can govern her. She does it by love, by inalterable firmness, by perfect fairness, by perfect justice. While she was still in the cradle

Bessie learned that her mother's word could always be depended upon; and that whatever promise her mother made her—whether of punishment, or a holiday, or a gratification, or a benevolence—would be kept, to the letter. . . . The mother who coaxes or hires her child to obey, is providing unhappiness for it; and for herself as well. And particularly because the mother who coaxes and hires does not always coax and hire, but is in all cases a weak creature, an ill-balanced creature, who now and then delivers herself up to autocratic exhibitions of authority, wherein she uses compulsion—usually in a hot and insulting temper—and so the child never knows just how to take her. ("Which Was the Dream?" 43–44)

In Twain's autobiographical and fictional illustrations of his boyhood, he was "unjustly used" (*The Autobiography*, 33) by his mother when he manifested, through lying and delinquent behavior,[35] his childhood feelings of privation and grief that must surely have accompanied his experiences; yet he belied his true feelings through his lighthearted story-telling voice. The full force of the grief Twain suffered from the emotional blows his mother delivered upon him, however, lived on in his fiction. In *The Adventures of Tom Sawyer*, Twain explicitly attempted to resolve one of these distressing incidents of unjust punishment through a fictional act of wish-fulfillment. Twain accomplished this by entering Aunt Polly's mind: "Then her conscience reproached her, and she yearned to say something kind and loving; but she judged that this would be construed into a confession that she had been in the wrong, and discipline forbade that. So she kept silence, and went about her affairs with a troubled heart" (26). In this episode, Twain actualized the longed-for guilty response of the mother figure. Tom is now satisfied with the outcome of the situation because he knows that "in her heart his aunt was on her knees to him" (26). But the deep-seated grief that Tom feels in response to Aunt Polly's imagined withholding of love and remorse surfaces again in his thoughts about suicide. Soon after, Tom imagines himself "lying sick unto death and his aunt bending over him beseeching one little forgiving word, but he would turn his face to the wall, and die with that word unsaid. Ah, how would she feel then? . . . he would lie there cold and white and make no sign—a poor little sufferer, whose griefs were at an end" (27).

Suicidal thoughts in children, Charles Wahl explains, are often used as "magical acts" through which they attempt to repair an exigent conflict with fantasy and illusory thinking.[36] They are motivated by the wish to punish the person whom they feel has deprived or abandoned them by infusing them with painful, guilty feelings. In Tom's reasoning about suicide one may recognize the early childhood confusion between love and aggression that appears to stem from a frustration with the disappointing caretaker.

It is also significant, with regard to suicide, that, as Winnicott suggests, it is not only the mother but the entire world that the child feels rejected by. Similarly, for Tom, disappointment becomes equivalent to the grief of separation and abandonment, and it is not just his latest crime but his very being in the world that he feels is worthless and undesirable. Thus, he no longer projects his sense of emptiness and rejection onto Aunt Polly alone, but onto a now "unfeeling world" (*Tom Sawyer*, 114). Life itself has become meaningless for Tom, and so he wanders off, seeking "desolate places that were in harmony with his spirit" (55). He feels that it is not only his aunt who has turned "coldly away," but "all the hollow world." The unconscious connection, in Twain's mind, between deprivation in love, existential despair, and the use of suicidal thoughts (as a delusional way to expiate guilt, by projecting it onto the persecuting figure), reappears in his uncompleted sketch, "Boy's Manuscript."[37] In this short fictional narrative, Twain presents a lengthy internal monologue of a boy who, like Tom, has been scorned in love: "I said the world was a mean, sad place, and had nothing for me to love or care for in it—and life, life was only misery. It was then that it first came into my head to take my life. I don't know why I wanted to do that, except that I thought that it would make her feel sorry" (De Voto, *Mark Twain at Work*, 34). Later, in *The Adventures of Tom Sawyer*, when Tom is snubbed by Becky Thatcher in the schoolyard, he similarly experiences the rejection as all-encompassing. In Tom's mind, it is not only Becky who has denied him love, but "nobody loved him"; he is universally "a forsaken, friendless boy" (114). The connection between Becky and Tom's Aunt Polly is again obliquely established when Tom, forgetting that his misery has resulted from the isolated incident with Becky, plans to run away and become a pirate in order to escape from what he describes as "hard usage and lack of sympathy at home" (114).

Thus far in my analysis of Mark Twain's real and fictional childhoods, I have attempted to establish the importance of the roles played by deception, maternal deprivation, and the desire for punishment, in his early relationship with his mother and siblings. I have also begun to suggest the part played by Mark Twain's unique gift of humor in his adaptation to his adversarial domestic environment. Humor is the central means by which Tom Sawyer, and perhaps young Sam Clemens as well, successfully deferred the expected punishment for his antics. As Aunt Polly tellingly remarks, "he knows if he can make out to put me off for a minute or make me laugh, it's all down again and I can't hit him a lick" (40). Timing is critical to the humorist, and Twain, like Tom Sawyer, was an expert in this regard. As Aunt Polly says, "He 'pears to know just how long he can torment me before I get my dander up."

Twain's sister, Pamela, reported that once, after Sam had humored Mrs. Clemens into not scolding him for some impertinence, and wholly transformed their mother's anger into mirth, she asked her mother, "Why do you always let him get the best of you?" Her mother replied, "Because Sam Clemens is the funniest boy I ever talked to, Mela" (Varble, 222–23). Hence, one may add the gift of humor and entertainment to the love-deception-aggression equation. Sam Clemens perhaps discovered that if he could not be good and truthful, like his younger brother, Henry, he could at least be bad and disobedient, but, at the same time, entertaining. In *The Autobiography of Mark Twain*, Twain writes:

My mother had a good deal of trouble with me but I think she enjoyed it. She had none at all with my brother Henry, who was two years younger than I, and I think that the unbroken monotony of his goodness and truthfulness and obedience would have been a burden to her but for the relief and variety which I furnished in the other direction. I was a tonic. I was valuable to her. I never thought of it before but now I see it. (33)

It is this ability to be entertaining that enabled Twain's boy heroes to "put off" maternal anger and retaliation, and to relieve guilt by alleviating emotional hurt. The unpleasurable, aggressive impulses on the part of both the "bad boy"-teller and the mother-hearer are effectively disguised by the pleasurable effects of humor.

As Coleman O. Parsons suspects, Mark Twain discovered at an early age "that a smart jest turneth away wrath, that a pun can placate the strong and protect the weak."[38] Indeed, it appears that Sam Clemens's "career" as a humorist began in his earliest infancy. Throughout most of his childhood, however, it is likely that Twain was aware of his talent primarily insofar as it was useful to him as a weapon against his mother, and as a means of competing for her love and attention with his "exasperatingly good" brother, Henry.

Because, in his fiction, Twain makes light of the guilt and emotional pain he claims to have suffered as a child at the hands of his mother, it is easy to forget the profound sadness that the young Sam Clemens might have felt before he came to recognize that his "badness" was in fact something useful and "good." As a child, Mark Twain must have suffered acute guilt for his "crimes," in addition to a deep sense of abandonment and frustration. Undoubtedly, he truly believed, as he so often said, that at any moment, during those frequent "nights of despair," a malevolent God might sweep his wicked soul away and bury it in the deepest chambers of hell (*The Autobiography*, 42).

When Samuel Clemens was approximately fifteen years old,[39] an event occurred in his life on a stage in Hannibal, Missouri, that marked the moment when he at last discovered (or perhaps merely stumbled upon), the full implications of his talent as a teller of tall tales, as a master performer in the art of deception, and as a humorist. Phyllis Greenacre, in her insightful studies of the childhoods of famous artists and thinkers, refers to that exultant moment of "great-relief" in the young artist's life when what he had once believed to be an isolating and quirky personal attribute—one that had marked him as different from, and inferior to, those around him—is transformed in a way that seems miraculous to him into a special "gift," an enviable endowment of superior capabilities.[40]

As Twain recalls in *The Autobiography*, for nearly a fortnight Sam Clemens astonished and delighted a small, local audience, as the assistant to a traveling "mesmerizer"/"professor," by pretending to be completely under the influence of "suggestion" (50–51).[41] In playing this deceitful role Sam acted like a shy girl at one moment, and like a monkey the next. He called forth every village rumor and old story he could remember in order to astound the audience with the "mind-reading" powers bestowed upon him by the "professor," and forced himself not to flinch even a fraction when the "professor" pretended to put him under the "influence," sticking real pins into his allegedly "insensible" body (50–51).

When the first performance had ended, he wrote, he "returned to the platform a hero and happier than I have ever been in this world since" (53). Perhaps young Sam's wild elation was a result of the fact that, for the first time in his life (on such a grand scale), he had achieved complete and conscious mastery in his efforts to conquer an audience by deception. All of his allegedly "wicked" moral habits—defiance, fraudulence, mendacity, demonstrativeness—in the space of an evening, had become assets, talents, and a source of pride. It was a momentous night in Sam Clemens's life, and an epic one in terms of his career as a humorist.

However, given his long-practiced games of deception within his domestic sphere, it actually represented only a short step in the evolution of his character. He had merely enacted a transference from his mother as audience, to his village as audience.

The moral that Sam learned from this experience was one that he had already ascertained from innumerable interactions with his mother: "Success to crime!" From this moment on, Twain adds, "I made it a point to succeed . . . let the cost be what it might, physically or morally" (*The Autobiography*, 52). The Presbyterian labels that Sam's mother had so often used in her attempts to "reform" him—"bad," "sinful," "impious," "hell-bent"—lost much of their negative impact now that he was a "hero" in the eyes of an admiring public. His transference from his mother, as an ambivalent audience for his talents, to a much larger and more powerful assembly of grateful recipients, allowed him to be free of the guilt that had, in the past, invariably accompanied the assertion of his "negative" identity. As Tom Sawyer was also to discover, after his great debut as a public prankster in *The Adventures of Tom Sawyer*—love now lay elsewhere. As a consequence of Tom's successful hoax, in which he strategically reappeared in the midst of his own funeral sermon in front of a paralyzed St. Petersburg audience, he became a "hero"—the darling of every mother and the envy of every schoolboy. But one thought in particular pleased Tom the most: "Tom decided that he could be independent of Becky Thatcher now. Glory was sufficient. He would live for glory. Now that he was distinguished, maybe she would be wanting to 'make up.' Well, let her—she should see that he could be as indifferent as some other people" (145–46). Although Tom would have liked to believe that he could so easily replace this needed love from Becky, as from his Aunt Polly, with the adoration of the public, it was clear not only that he was deceiving himself, but also that he valued his public success, in large part, because it furnished him with ammunition against his disappointing love object. Similarly, it is probable that Sam Clemens's public fame neither served as a substitute for his mother's love (and hence failed to dispel his lingering grief in relation to her), nor did it in any way resolve his problematic love/hate relationship with his mother. It simply enabled him to act out his hostility, repressed grief, and desires on a public stage. As the narrator of *The Prince and the Pauper* says of Tom Canty, "he was become a hero to all who knew him except his own family—these, only, saw nothing in him."[42]

Sam's short career as a mesmerist's assistant also reinforced another significant moral lesson that he had first gleaned from his relationship with his mother: the falsity, hypocrisy, and gullibility of those who called themselves his superiors. After the success of his stage performance, Sam realized that his whole village seemed to express the same preference for being entertained, and a similar disregard for objective reality and moral truth, as his mother had so often displayed.[43]

Even more important to his future career as a humorist was Sam's newly acquired belief that he was the only person in the town of Hannibal who could see through the world's shams and pharisaical insincerities. This aspect of social reality was also one that he had already been introduced to in his domestic life. Sam's experience as a mesmerist's assistant substantiated for him once and for all that "I should never come across a 'proof' which wasn't thin and cheap and probably had a fraud like me behind it" (*The Autobiography*, 56). The pessimism and cynicism that pervade Mark Twain's fictions, particularly his later works, can be traced to this one statement. "The Mysterious Stranger" (1898) is perhaps among the most pessimistic and hostile of any of Twain's writings. It carries to culmination the projection of self-despair, inner emptiness, and rage at the world which the voice of Tom Sawyer, in its contained innocence, merely touched upon. According to Satan in the story, "our race lived a life of continuous and uninterrupted self-deception. It duped itself from cradle to grave with shams and delusions which it mistook for realities, and this made its entire life a sham" (247).

It is also possible that Sam Clemens's two-week career as a magician's sidekick transformed the "negative" self-identity he had acquired as a child through his relationship with his mother into a morally superior one. In a lecture Twain delivered to The New Vagabonds Club of London, in July 1899, in which he confessed how he came to be the most perfect living moral specimen, one can see the mechanisms of projection and transference through which he exchanged his own negative childhood identity with that of the world's, and thus fashioned for himself a supreme moral posture: "Commit all the crimes," he instructed, "familiarize yourself with all sins . . . commit two or three every day, and by-and-by you will be proof against them."[44] In this way, he concluded, you can become "the glory and the grandeur and majesty of a perfected morality such as you see before you." Twain reasoned that because he was the most wicked, sinful, and fraudulent of men, he could see through all the hypocrisy of the "thin and cheap" world.

In the process of enacting a transference from his mother to the world at large, Mark Twain seems to have projected his mother's inconsistency, insincerity, and moral weakness onto social institutions, God, and the human race—a psychic enactment that enabled him to preserve his own personal integrity, and to establish a superior moral position in relation to a persecuting and hypocritical world. It might be Twain's own mother, and not a hypocritical God, of whom his Satan persona speaks, in "The Mysterious Stranger," when he laments that God is one "who could make good children as easily as bad, yet preferred to make bad ones"; who "mouths justice and invented hell—mouths mercy and invented hell—mouths Golden Rules, and forgiveness multiplied by seventy times seven, and invented hell; who mouths morals to other people and has none himself . . ." (252–53). Twain's merging of the mother image with God again becomes apparent in *Letters from the Earth*, in which Twain condemns God because: "He has one code of morals for himself, and quite another for his children."[45] God, like Twain's own mother, consistently violates every statute that he sets down in his laws for his "children" to follow.[46]

Although the extremity of Twain's pessimistic worldview, which only deepened over the years, represents an unrealistic assessment of social reality and human nature, his condemnation of civilization's hypocrisy and wickedness struck a chord with his American and continental audiences. In making a transference from his mother to the human race, Sam Clemens apparently projected his own "negative" identity—his "badness"—onto the world around him. Instead of rejecting himself, he rejected the world, and in his inflexible adherence to this rebellious stance, Twain became the representative rebellious adolescent for an entire culture. By laughing *with* him, Twain's audience could participate in the pleasurable adolescent feeling of defying people, institutions, and ideas which claimed authoritative power over them, without having to acknowledge the malevolence disguised within his humor.

Humor—to express oneself in a joking or non-serious way—is a fundamentally adolescent means of showing hostility without overtly inflicting harm.[47] Twain managed to escape condemnation for his own aggressive urges by strategically using his gift of humor, which Erikson would have described as a culturally approved interpersonal technique, to incorporate his fixation on adolescent rebelliousness, mischievousness, and deviance into an acceptable cultural pattern of behavior. Through his inordinately successful capability at mastering this form of adaptation,

Twain transformed his prolonged adolescence into an asset. As Erikson says of Martin Luther, Twain "made a virtue out of what his superiors had considered a vice in him" (*Luther,* 212).

In an age when few artists were able to reach conscious realization of their own greatness, Twain was fortunate enough to catch a glimpse of his own notoriety as a moralist. When Twain was working in Nevada for the *Morning Call,* he mentions having read an article, in the New York *Sun,* which enabled him "to locate" himself within American culture.[48] The article spoke of the "limitless rottenness of our great insurance companies," and of "the exposures of conscienceless graft," from one end of America to the other (*The Autobiography,* 120–21). The growing hypocrisy and corruption that grew out of America's rapid economic expansion in the "Gilded Age" validated Twain's projection of personal moral evil onto the world around him. For Twain, society itself was a sham, and like a true rebellious adolescent, he, like his young fictional hero, Huckleberry Finn, intractably stood for an ethic that categorically refused all false solutions.

Mark Twain epitomized the type of rebelliousness and antisocial behavior that characterizes the adolescent phase of development; but as is true for all delinquent behavior, at the root of his defiance and antagonism was a profound sense of grief and emotional deprivation. If Twain was going to play the role of the adolescent hero, he would also have to endure the isolation and alienation that accompanied this distinction.[49] Through his adolescent refusal to accept false solutions, and his longing to feel real in an "unreal" world, Twain came to believe that he was the only honest creature in the "damned human race," without exception, while everyone else in the world became the liars and deceivers, which, unfortunately, left Twain in the very same emotional situation in which he began as an infant in relation to his poor mirroring mother: "lonely enough in this lofty solitude."[50]

Twain's opportunity to transfer his ongoing childhood and adolescent conflicts from the private to the public sphere, which was made possible by Sam Clemens's performance as a mesmerist's assistant, provided him with one further critical lesson. His very first act of that eleven-day performance, and in fact the maneuver that launched him into stardom, was to grab a rusty old revolver that was lying on the "professor's" table and lunge after the village "bully," who, just a few days earlier, had humiliated him in the schoolyard. This frightened the poor boy half to death and sent him fleeing out of the theater, much to the astonishment of a now completely "paralyzed" audience. Not only did Sam manage to get revenge on his persecutor, but he also succeeded in deposing Simmons Hicks, his arch rival for the role of the mesmerist's assistant. Sam Clemens's ability to be entertaining, as it had so many times in his relationship with his mother, enabled him to fulfill a pressing, aggressive fantasy. It may also have been one of the first times he realized that in the public sphere, as well as in a domestic one, crime *does* pay: "Hicks was a thing of the past, a fallen hero, a broken idol, and I knew it and was glad . . ." (*The Autobiography*, 52).

Through his remarkable powers of adaptation and defense, Sam Clemens thus determined, a short time before Freud, that humor allows the teller to express the most primitive of aggressive wishes in a socially acceptable way: that it diverts even the most severe retaliatory response.[51] Humorous fiction provided Twain with a means of relating a moral truth in a way that spared the reader or listener from having to acknowledge the raw emotions that accompanied it. Twain knew, as Freud later perceived, that it "is a most pleasant thing to find that what you thought would inflict a hurt . . . has not done it."[52] Freud in fact, who had once seen Mark Twain on stage, used several examples of Mark Twain's humor to prove his point—or perhaps to formulate the point—that humor dissipates unpleasurable emotional responses in the hearer, and diverts them into something of "secondary importance," relative, that is, to the content of the joke (*Jokes*, 233).

At times, Mark Twain revealed that his passionate feelings of hostility toward the human race were too strong to allow him to disguise his thoughts comically. In a letter to William Dean Howells, written in January 1879, Twain complains about this irrepressible rage:

I wish I *could* give those sharp satires on European life which you mention, but of course a man can't write successful satire except he be in a calm judicial good-humor—whereas I *hate* travel, & I *hate* hotels, & I *hate* the opera, & I *hate* the Old Masters—in truth I don't ever seem to be in a good enough humor with ANYthing to *satirize* it; no, I want to stand up before it & *curse* it, & foam at the mouth,—or take a (club & beat it) club & pound it to rags & pulp.[53]

Perhaps because he felt he had earned, through his success, the right to criticize the world without the protective disguise of humor, during the last decade of his life, Mark Twain was a great deal more straightforward about expressing his acrimonious sentiments toward the world, sometimes raging for an hour at a time about some handy subject that happened to displease him. Shortly after the death of his daughter Susy, in 1896, Twain wrote in a letter: "I have *hated* life before . . . but I was not indifferent to it . . . I rage until I get a sort of relief."[54] Twain's statement in a letter to his mother, that before he died he was going to gather his things in order and then "kill all the people I don't like," epitomizes the restrained, raw aggression that gives his humor its unique quality of pleasurable tension.[55]

Whether Mark Twain, the "entertainer," was, at one moment, wishing to annihilate his audience, or, the next moment, bewailing his own victimization as the recipient of the world's persecution, the one rule that must never be broken was to let his audience know that it had been deceived.[56] The key to lying, as Twain announced in his sketch, "Advice to Youth" (1882), was to be "sure" never "to get caught" (*Speeches*, 105). Deception is the secret to humor as an "art," Twain wrote in his essay "How to Tell a Story" (1894); and only a master can tell a story gravely, so as to divert the listeners' attention away from the humorous possibility of the story until he is ready to spring it on them. He also claimed in this essay, that this kind of humor—humor based on deception—is an American "art": It "was created in America, and has remained at home," and, since it is "strictly a work of art . . . only an artist can tell it" (*Mark Twain's Short Stories*, 666).

Mark Twain's position within the tradition of American humor is a subject that has received a significant amount of scholarly attention. The question that this attention has not adequately addressed is why Twain thought that this particular form of mendacity-based humor was so supremely suited to an American audience. The answer, I believe, can be found in Twain's self-inclusive claim, made in an interview with the New York *World* in October 1900, that the "trouble with us in America is that we haven't learned to speak the truth" (*Life As I Find It*, 340). Specifically, Twain believed that Americans were incapable of receiving censure or social criticism of any kind. In an unpublished section of *Life on the Mississippi*, called "Reception of Captain Basil Hall's Book in the United States," Twain wrote that Americans display an "exquisite sensitiveness and soreness respecting everything said or written concerning them."[57] This, he added, was "one of the most remarkable traits in the national character of the Americans" (369). Not surprisingly, it was also one of the most salient traits of Mark Twain's mother.

In 1859, Twain wrote the following advice in a letter to his brother, Orion:

Above all things (between you and me) never tell Ma any of your troubles; she never slept a wink the night your last letter came, and she looks distressed yet. Write only cheerful news to her. You know that she will not be satisfied so long as she thinks anything is going on that she is ignorant of and she makes a little fuss about it when her suspicions are awakened; but that makes no difference—I know that it is better that she be kept in the dark concerning all things of an unpleasant nature. She upbraids me occasionally for giving her only the bright side of my affairs (but unfortunately for her she has to put up with it), for I know that troubles that I curse awhile and forget, would disturb her slumbers for some time. . . . Tell her the good news and me the bad. (*Letters,* 42–43)

It has already been suggested that it was critical for Sam Clemens, in his dealings with his mother, as it was for Tom Sawyer, when confronting his Aunt Polly, to defer the insult and hurt that would result from a direct lie by reporting whatever falsehood the situation inspired in an entertaining manner. What Twain calls "high art" in America is "to speak the truth so that the object does not object—does not become offended"; or, as he also phrased it, so that the other person can "listen to it without—getting mad."[58] Again, we see the mother-son dynamic at work, in which the teller has as much of a need to keep his own aggression from inflicting hurt as he does in circumventing the hostility of the hearer. Thus, in protecting America, as in protecting his mother, Twain was also protecting himself.

In Twain's defense of Captain Hall's book he reveals a keen insight into the narcissistic nature of the American character. He argues that so "deep is the conviction of this singular people that they cannot be seen without being admired, that they will not admit the possibility that any one should honestly and sincerely find aught to disprove in them or their country" (*Life on the Mississippi,* Appendix C, 370). Perhaps Twain came out so strongly in defense of poor Captain Hall because he sensed that America demanded of the social critic the same repression of true opinions, and the need to disguise and temper authentic self-expression, that Mrs. Clemens demanded of her son. Twain was, by *necessity,* a purveyor of "fictional" humor, I believe, because he felt compelled, as he recognized that Captain Hall did, to "spare[s] the Americans the bitterness which a detail of the circumstances would have produced" (371). This explains why Twain believed, as he stated in an interview with the New York *Herald,* in 1900, that he had "been forced by *fate* to adopt fiction as a medium of truth . . . If any man can do that, and finds that he can disseminate facts through the medium of falsehood, he should never speak the truth—and I don't" (*Life As I Find It,* 334).

Sam Clemens learned, first from his mother, then from the population of Hannibal, and finally from his American audience, that the only way to communicate the truth—whether that truth be of a moral, emotional, or political nature—was through the humorous "art" of deception. Looking back on the mesmerist episode in his boyhood, Twain remarked on the unfortunate consequences of the performance by stating, in *The Autobiography*, that: "The glory which is built upon a lie soon becomes a most unpleasant incumbrance" (56). The nature of this "incumbrance" was already observed in Mrs. Clemens's steadfast refusal ever to acknowledge that Sam was telling the truth—even when he was. After his performance as an impostor on the Hannibal stage, Twain commented that it is easy "to make people believe a lie," but "how hard it is to undo that work again!" (57). Although Twain's mother was among the "paralyzed" audience during his two wildly successful weeks, he apparently did not, at the time, let her in on his scam with the "professor." Nevertheless, thirty-five years later, when he confessed the truth, she, typically, refused to believe him. In a confessional gesture that harks back to his very first remembered act of deception—the fictional infant's lie about the diaper pin to win its mother's attentions—he disclosed to his mother about himself and the professor, confessing on his "honor," that "a pin was never stuck into me without causing me cruel pain" (58). Mrs. Clemens's response, as Twain remembered it, was poignantly ironic. She replied that Sam was "only a child then" and could never "dissemble the hurt." Her response is revealing in its lack of true understanding, not only about her son's character, but also about his exceptional creative talent. The full emotional and psychological impact of this interview on Twain is apparent in his final comment on the subject: "I realized with shame and with impotent vexation that I was defeated all along the line."

Twain's conversation with his mother reveals that his life had somewhere along the way got out of his control. It had become, like the frustrating exchanges with his mother, "a grotesque and unthinkable situation"; and it is possible that he realized, at that moment, the tragic and absurd implications of his drive for mastery, success, and love, through deceptive humor (*The Autobiography*, 57–58). The paradox of Twain's identity could not be expressed any better than in his concluding statement on the issue: "Dear, dear . . . a confessed swindler convicted of honesty and condemned to acquittal by circumstantial evidence furnished by the swindled!" (58). Here lies what I believe to be the tragic paradox of Mark Twain's life and career, which he became conscious of, albeit only vaguely, in the last decade of his life. In 1900, he made the following confession to an interviewer for the New York *Herald:* "Now, I have lied so much, in a genial, good-natured way, of course, that people won't believe me when I speak the truth. I may add that I have stopped speaking the truth. It is no longer appreciated—in me" (*Life As I Find It*, 333). Mark Twain was fully aware of his deployment of humor as a means of "laying a tragedy-trap" on his readers;[59] but he was sadly unaware of the "tragedy-trap" in which he, himself, had become ensnared as a humorist. Twain was a "tragic" humorist because he was locked within a give-and-take, master-slave, game with his American audience. He was as much a slave to the game as his "victim," the audience, was a slave to his humorous manner.

One can now see that long before Sam Clemens became "Mark Twain" he "stopped speaking the truth," because it was "no longer appreciated" in him. This is what Twain was referring to when he remarked, in the same interview, that: "Fate has its revenge on the humorist." It is critical to point out, however, that it is likely that Twain rarely actually withheld his true opinions throughout his life, but that he *felt* he did because he believed he could express them only indirectly, through the tempering and entertaining manner of humorous devices. In view of the key role that Twain's mother played in the adoption of his identity as the humorist, Mark Twain, it is ironic that Mrs. Clemens commented, indignantly, after reading one of the first letters in which Twain signed his name as "Mark Twain": "I've got no son named Mark. Your father and I raised four boys named Orion and Benjamin and Samuel Langhorne and Henry" (Varble, 269).

In both *The Prince and the Pauper* and *Pudd'nhead Wilson*, Twain reversed his mother's denial of her son as "Mark Twain," by having Tom Canty and Tom Driscoll refuse to acknowledge that they are indeed their mothers' sons. When Mrs. Canty, in *The Prince and the Pauper*, shouts out from the crowd to her son, the false prince, "O, my child, my darling!" he cruelly rejects her with the words: "I do not know you, woman!" (305). Inside, however, Tom Canty's abusive words "smote him to the heart," and he longed to relinquish his identity as an impostor and openly embrace the mother who was lost to him: "His grandeurs were stricken valueless; they seemed to fall away from him like rotten rags" (305). Although, through his false identity, Tom could win the love and adoration of all the world, he sacrificed, in return, the love of his mother; and in his moment of remorse he wished to himself: "Would God I were free of my captivity!" (305). For Roxy, in *Pudd'nhead Wilson,* it is herself, the mother, who wishes to uphold the masquerade that her son is not the lowly son of a black slave, but rather the noble, and white, "Master Tom Driscoll." Here, the mother sacrifices the love of her son in order to enable him to claim a fraudulent highborn title. At first, Roxy's maternal pride outweighs her maternal sorrow, and she willingly allows her son to become "her darling, her master, and her deity all in one, and in her worship of him she forgot who she was and what he had been" (*Pudd'nhead,* 77). Later, however, when her son's cruelty "hurt to the heart . . . her breast began to heave, and tears came," soon "the fires of her old wrongs flamed up in her breast and began to burn fiercely," and she felt the urge to expose him as a fraud— for the impostor whom, ironically, her own love, as well as her arrogance and pride, had created (106–7). Roxy's charlatan son had become "her master"—a "fiction created by herself" (77). But Tom Driscoll, who possessed only a small fraction of the conscience with which young Tom Canty, in *The Prince and the Pauper,* was endowed, would perform any evil deed required to deny his mother's claim upon him, in exchange for his powerful and respectable name and fortune.

Van Wyck Brooks believed that Twain's recurring dream of appearing before a lecture audience in his nightshirt with nothing prepared to speak about was an indication that his career as a humorist—his respectable name and fortune—was a betrayal of his true artistic nature, a sacrifice which he had made to indulge his mother's demand that he pursue materialistic goals in life. Justin Kaplan believed that this dream, and another of Twain's recurring dreams, in which he is piloting a steamboat toward a black spot in the river, were about the destruction of identity, in that they reflected a repressed anxiety over the fear that no one would believe that Twain truly was whom he claimed to be; he feared the extreme "possibility of never having existed at all."[60] My hypothesis, that Sam Clemens developed an adaptive, humorous persona that was first employed in response to an early elemental disappointment with his mother's poor mirroring of him as a self object, embraces the divergent theories of both Brooks and Kaplan. It also provides an explanation for Bernard De Voto's elusive insight that Mark Twain was a man "who either betrayed something sacred, or was betrayed by something vile" (*Mark Twain's America,* 298). Indeed, Twain's sense of early maternal abandonment, which possibly occurred well before he could even remember, and which perhaps caused his real, spontaneous self to shut down, or withdraw, was the "vile" force that "betrayed" him; and by pursuing approval and glory—the secondary gains of his false-self personality—over candid expression of his truthful, moral, and emotional nature, Twain betrayed the integrity of his own "sacred" real self.

Twain devoted a great deal of effort, in *The Autobiography*, to convincing the reader that he was dead. At this point in our discussion we can almost predict the reason which he gives for this repeated, yet enigmatic, claim. So trapped within the persona of the deceptive humorist, "Mark Twain," had Sam Clemens become, that in order to speak the truth directly, as he wished to do in *The Autobiography*, he must be not-himself—a non-person—dead. "The very reason that I speak from the grave," he tells us, "is that I want the satisfaction of sometimes saying everything that is in me instead of bottling the pleasantest of it up for home consumption" (248). Although Twain insisted that his motive in lying was to prevent others from experiencing pain, his additional claim, that he was merely attempting, through his mendacious and deceptive style of humor, "to spare myself the personal pain of inflicting" shock and hurt to others (249), suggests that, again, the aggression that was being denied was primarily his own. In 1904, shortly after executing his will, Twain recorded the following three maxims in his notebook:

"None but the dead have free speech."
"None but the dead are permitted to speak the truth."
"In America—as elsewhere—free speech is confined to the dead." (*Notebook*, 393)

In these three attempts to formulate an aphorism, Twain seemed unable to hit upon the exact phrasing he was looking for. However, it is interesting to note that the experimental versions of the adage conform to the type of reasoning that is appropriate to the three levels of Sam Clemens's development: childhood, adolescence, and adulthood. In each aphorism he seemed to be seeking justification for his own inner feeling of having had to censor his true opinions, or what we might call his "real" self. The first version is phrased as if the denial of free expression is an intrinsic quality of the world, and it reflects the immediate subjective "thinking" of a pre-verbal infant. In the second version, the sense of denial becomes an injunction that appears to be inflicted from some higher authority, and hence mirrors the intellectual ego-reasoning of an older child. The third version suggests that a projective identification onto Twain's cultural environment has taken place, so that the censoring, or superego, agency is identified as America at large. In these three short statements, then, we can observe the movement from id to ego to cultural superego of Twain's original disillusionment with his mother-object as someone who discouraged, rather than validated, his spontaneous expression of self.

In Twain's sketch, "The Czar's Soliloquy" (1905), the Czar stands naked in front of his mirror, pondering his unadorned condition, and comes to the conclusion that the titles and clothes that define his identity are mere artificialities: that "clothes do not merely make the man, the clothes are the man; that without them he is a cipher, a vacancy, a nobody, a nothing."[61] The universality of Twain's plight—being "forced by fate to adopt fiction as a medium for truth"—is, in this context, undeniable. He speaks for all of humankind when he laments that one only has "free speech," or rather, freedom from the encumbrance of a false persona, when one is dead. Similarly, one of the predominant themes that runs throughout Twain's novel *Pudd'nhead Wilson*, as Malcolm Bradbury writes, is "a deep sense that in America imposture *is* identity; that values are not beliefs but the product of occasions; and that social identity is virtually an arbitrary matter, depending not on character nor on appearance but on the chance definition of one's nature or colour."[62]

In his last years, Twain came to view himself as possessing a separate "spiritualized self" and a bodily self, the former state being the one which we fully surrender to only when asleep (*Notebook*, 349–50). So close to a dissociative position did Twain come at this time in his life that he believed that this spiritualized "partner in duality" was a "wholly independent personage who resides in me—and whom I will call Watson, for I don't know his name, although he most certainly has one, and signs it in a hand which has no resemblance to mine . . ." (439). Twain refers to the story, "The Recent Carnival of Crime in Connecticut," which he wrote many years before, and which he now explains, "was an attempt to account for our seeming *duality*—the presence in us of another *person;* not a slave of ours, but free and independent, and with a character distinctly its own" (348).[63] As John Bowlby points out, in his study of loss and pathological mourning, in cases where the individual has suffered an experience of emotional loss or deprivation during childhood—particularly in relation to the mother—after a period of "anxiously pretending to be an independent person," he or she comes to feel that there are " 'two me's,' the real me . . . petrified to reveal itself," which "hated the other me," the one that "complied with social demands." [64] As Bowlby describes one such case: "The real me, he said, would sometimes emerge briefly, for example when he felt empathy for someone in the same situation as himself. There had been occasions, he wrote, when he felt he might be inspired 'to undertake some great mission to reform mankind from a loveless miserable world.' " Ironically, Sam Clemens, from behind the protective mask of his second "me," whom he called "Mark Twain," undertook the monumental, and personally transcendent, "mission" of his "real me": to "reform mankind from a loveless miserable world." He did this by holding a mirror of humor and fiction up to the world's foibles and tragedies, thus making its inhabitants laugh at themselves until tears came, hoping, perhaps, that he, too, might be able to shed vicarious tears for the sad fate of all the loveless world.

In the story "What Is Man?" (1906), Twain attempted to explain the seeming duality of human beings by dividing the forces within him between the "head" and the "heart"; or the speaking or "mental" part of man, and the "feeling" part, each of which act wholly independently of one another. [65] Hence, while the mind was merely a "machine," whose contents were purely fictional, and whose workings were hopelessly outside of his control, only the feelings experienced in dreams seemed to be profoundly "real." It is understandable, therefore, that for most of his life Twain, indeed, believed that: "Truth is stranger than fiction" (*Notebook*, 240, 347). [66]

"[A]ll men are liars," Twain remarked in his notebook in 1885: "When a merely honest man appears he is a comet—his fame is eternal— needs no genius, no talent—mere honesty—Luther, Christ, etc." (*Notebook*, 181). Joan of Arc provided the ideal of undisguised truth that Twain aspired to in fantasy. In the fictional Translator's Preface to this novel, Joan of Arc is described by Twain, in the same way as he viewed himself: "honorable in an age which had forgotten what honor was," and "unfailingly true in an age that was false to the core" (xii). Joan was his ideal, I believe, not because she was honest (for he, himself, claimed to be "the only truly honest man" in a corrupt universe), but because she could be unfailingly true to her own impeccable character, and speak the truth directly and without adornment. It was not her truthfulness, but the directness with which it was delivered, and the complete absence of intimidation from a disapproving audience, that Twain found so extraordinary. As Twain saw it, Joan of Arc fulfilled Polonius's maxim, which he found sacred, and which he repeatedly made reference to in his poetry, speeches, and journals: "UNTO THYSELF BE THOU TRUE!" [67]

The likelihood that Samuel Clemens first used humor as a means of earning love and attention from his mother, and then maintained this inter-relational dynamic throughout his adult years as the humorist Mark Twain, implies that his adult personality structure was, by definition, "immature," in that it was a consequence of an arrested, or prolonged, childhood and adolescent development. Mark Twain's developmental arrest was grounded in an unresolved and perpetually unsatisfied feeling of loss and grief in relation to the maternal object. Humor and the telling of humorous stories were the ways that Sam Clemens attempted to repair his feelings of disappointment and privation. By its very nature, however, humor demands the repression of negative and depressing emotions, and so Mark Twain made death and grief the subjects of his humorous fictions. However, because Twain's humorous narrative extracted the terror, hostility, and sorrow from these subjects, his fiction was never able to serve for him the cathartic function that open grieving and mourning can provide. The repressed grief always returned, therefore; it became chronic, and Twain's humorous fictions about death, loneliness, terror, and grief became memorials to the grief that he, himself, could never fully work through.

According to studies of grief and mourning, when a person has never adequately separated himself or herself emotionally from the mother, all subsequent experiences of loss become extremely difficult to recover from. [68] Even in individuals who have managed to work through a period of mourning for the first lost object—the mother—later experiences of loss and separation often bring a resurgence of the anxiety and grief that accompanied their infantile experience of maternal separation. In the next chapter, I will deal more directly with the themes of death and grief in Mark Twain's life and fiction. By the age of twenty-two, Twain had witnessed the deaths of four members of his immediate family—two brothers, one sister, and his father. We have seen, in the semi-autobiographical episodes of Mark Twain's childhood, that his siblings—particularly his well-behaved younger brother, Henry—through their competition for the mother's love, exacerbated his experience of maternal deprivation. Not only did Henry displace Sam as the baby in the family when Sam was at the particularly needy age of two years old, but also, unlike Sam, Henry was the most sweet and compliant child in the Clemens family—his mother's darling. While Sam Clemens undoubtedly adored his brothers and sisters (Twain frequently, in later life, expressed his deep love for Henry), his anxious attachment to his mother would certainly have fostered intense feelings of rivalry toward his siblings. The effects of Twain's feelings of guilt and aggression toward his siblings will be shown, in the chapter that follows, to have interfered with his ability to mourn when three of them died during his childhood.

In addition to Sam's difficulty in dealing with loss, and his tendency to repress his negative emotions by displacing them onto his humor, was his mother's own tendency toward repressed grief and pathological mourning, and the influence that her distorted response to death had upon him. All of these factors, in combination with Sam's ambivalence toward his siblings, resulted in an obsession with death, ghosts, the supernatural, a nostalgia for childhood, and other displaced, and therefore pathological, manifestations of chronic grief and unworked-through mourning. The next chapter will also look at Mark Twain's ambivalent relationship with his father, whose death, when Twain was twelve years old, not only inspired his already grief-distracted son to deny the reality of John Marshall Clemens's death, but the experience of living in a father-absent family led Twain to idealize the image of the father, which made it that much more difficult for him to complete his development toward masculine maturity. Finally, while it may be argued that it was not uncommon, in the nineteenth century, for a family to lose several of its young and adult members to disease and death, this fact should encourage the survivors to accept their losses in a healthy way. That Samuel Clemens, as will be seen, had such enormous difficulty mourning, and putting the dead to rest, suggests that there was indeed a strong pathological element in his response to loss and grief.

3. "Blessed are they that mourn, for they— they—": Repressed Grief and Pathological Mourning in Mark Twain's Fiction

It is one of the mysteries of our nature that a man, all unprepared, can receive a thunder-stroke like that and live. There is but one reasonable explanation of it. The intellect is stunned by the shock and but groping gathers the meaning of the words. The power to realize their full import is mercifully wanting. The mind has a dumb sense of vast loss—that is all. It will take mind and memory months and possibly years to gather the details and thus learn and know the whole extent of the loss.

—Mark Twain, *The Autobiography of Mark Twain*

". . . Blessed are the poor in spirit, for *theirs* is the kingdom of heaven. Blessed are they that mourn, for they—they—"
"Sh—"
"For they—a—"
"S, H, A—"
"For they S, H—Oh, I don't know what it is!"
"*Shall!*"
"Oh, *shall!* for they shall—for they shall—a—a—shall mourn—a—a— blessed are they that shall—they that—a—they that shall mourn, for they shall—a—shall *what?* Why don't you tell me, Mary?—what do you want to be so mean, for?"

—Mark Twain, *The Adventures of Tom Sawyer*

Mark Twain once wrote to William Dean Howells, about one of his dream stories: "I think I can carry the reader a long way before he suspects that I am laying a tragedy-trap."[1] The infusion of tragedy into Mark Twain's humor is something that has long perplexed those readers and admirers who are familiar with his work. In order to understand this somewhat unusual admixture in Twain's comic formula, it is first necessary to decipher what he meant by "tragedy"—what, in other words, was the definition of "tragic" that life had taught Sam Clemens? An answer has already been provided, in part, through our investigation of

Mark Twain's childhood, in which the tragedy of deprivation, or the withholding of love, was shown to have colored his response to life, as well as to his professional posture as a writer of humorous fiction. A strikingly similar answer to this question is suggested by a rather strange recurring dream that he claimed to have had first at the age of seventeen, and about every two years afterwards, until the end of his life. In this dream, which he referred to as his "platonic sweetheart" dream, he was in the company of a lovely girl of fifteen.[2] After a long period of heavenly, platonic bliss with this girl she would suddenly and unexpectedly disappear. In one of the dreams she got up and walked through the door of a cottage, closing it behind her. Twain's dream-self waited frantically for her to return. When he could stand it no longer he passed through the door after her, only to find himself standing, as he said, "in a strange sort of cemetery, a city of innumerable tombs and monuments stretching far and wide on every hand . . ." (290). In each experience of the dream, his sweetheart "dies" or disappears in a similarly traumatic and unexpected way. In every case, Twain would awaken at the moment he reached a degree of panic over her death or disappearance that he could no longer tolerate. The feeling he had upon waking was always one of terrible longing and grief. On one occasion, Twain wrote, the "wave of grief that swept through me woke me up" (294).

As is dramatized in this dream, in Twain's mind, the greatest tragedy one can endure is the loss of a loved one. When a friend once informed Twain that a young girl of his acquaintance had fallen in love and was soon to marry, Twain offered his sincere condolences, for surely one of the lovers was destined to die before the other, and so his sympathy was not, as he told his friend, "for the one that shall go first, but for the one that is fated to be left behind."[3] The feeling of grief from being "left behind" is what Mark Twain called "the supreme tragedy of life" (*Letters*, 416). Indeed, the number of close personal losses that Sam Clemens suffered in his life was excessive. In the course of his lifetime, Twain lived through the tragic deaths of two brothers, one sister, a father, a mother, an infant son, two daughters, and his wife, as well as numerous close friends, whose deaths all affected him deeply.

When Sam was four years old, his nine-year-old sister, Margaret, died from bilious fever, and by that time he had also heard of the infant death of his younger brother, Pleasants Hannibal, whom he had never known. Three years later, when Sam was seven, his older brother, Ben, died at ten years old, also from river fever; and four years after that, Sam's father died from pneumonia. I believe that the later deaths of Twain's wife and daughter were so devastating to him because of an early disturbed reaction to the deaths of his siblings, which established a pattern of repressed grief and pathological mourning, and instilled a deep-seated, elemental incapacity to acknowledge the permanence of death, and thereby, to put his dead to rest. According to John Bowlby, when the death of a loved one is not adequately mourned for, the survivor's feelings toward the deceased live on indefinitely in his or her intrapsychic world, there to be unconsciously projected onto the surrounding world.[4] Only if grief and mourning are repressed does death linger on in the psyche, there to "thematically" infect every aspect of the survivor's life.[5] If Twain's hostility and bitterness toward life increased in his later years, it was perhaps because his long pent-up grief concerning his numerous childhood losses was never released. Sorrow had been denied access to the heart, and the heart had calcified, leaving only anger, melancholia, and a bewildering sense of life's injustice.

In an attempt to explain Twain's apparent obsession with death throughout his life and fiction, most biographers have focused on the death of Sam's younger brother, Henry, in a steamboat explosion, when Sam was twenty-two, and on the death of his daughter, Susy, from meningitis, in 1896. However, it was the loss of his siblings when Sam was only a young boy that, psychologists would tell us, formed the groundwork for his inability to accept and grieve in a healthy way any permanent loss.[6] If an understanding of Mark Twain's personal attitude toward death, and his fictional use of dying and murder, is to be reached, it is necessary, I believe, first to understand Sam Clemens's relationship with those individuals, both in his early and later life, who died—particularly his siblings, whose premature deaths in Sam's early childhood were the first real, emotionally charged experiences of loss to which he was exposed. It will be discovered, in fact, that Mark Twain's fictional treatment of death and loss conforms with remarkable accuracy to the symptomology of pathological mourning and unresolved grief.

The infinitely resourceful human mind has contrived a fascinating variety of ways to temper, or even eradicate, the pain of grief that comes from the experience of being left behind. Perhaps the survivor will pretend that the person has not died but only gone away, and so pines away indefinitely, hoping and waiting for the loved one to return. It may be that the survivor will fall in love with, or begin to idolize, someone who reminds him or her of the lost person. In even more extreme cases, the survivor might begin to take an interest in psychic phenomenon, visit mediums, attend seances, and even have hallucinations of ghostly visitations at his or her bedside. Alternatively, the un-worked-through grief might take a morbid turn, evoking a fascination for other people's funerals, for life-in-death stories of ghouls, mortuaries, autopsies, and walking skeletons.

All of these symptoms of pathological mourning should begin to sound a familiar chord to readers of Mark Twain's fiction and biography. One might recall the old man in "The Californian's Tale" (1893), who, on the same day every year for nineteen years, prepares his house with flowers and trimmings for the expected return of his wife, who was murdered nineteen years before on a short visit to her family—an almost clinically perfect example of what, in psychoanalysis, is called an "anniversary reaction." One could also mention "The Undertaker's Chat" (1870), in which a living corpse complains about the ill-planning of his own funeral; and "A Dying Man's Confession" (1883), in which a "corpse" reawakens on its mortuary slab; to say nothing of the ghosts and spirits that haunt the imagination of Twain's boy heroes, Huckleberry Finn and Tom Sawyer.

But, on a much broader scale, the mechanism that Twain seems to have employed to deny and erase the pain of loss and grief that plagued his psychic life was the one suggested by his platonic sweetheart dream. While the immediate effects of the dream were devastating to Twain, they were not permanent, for the one aspect of this experience of loss that Twain could always count on was that he would see his platonic sweetheart again in his next dream. Through the power of fantasy he would be able to conjure her up again and reunite with her; she would still be fifteen, just as beautiful, magical, and vital as she was when last he saw her.

Twain discovered from this dream that he could cancel out his feelings of grief by returning, in his imagination, to an ideal time and place before his losses occurred. He accomplished this simply by falling back to sleep and recovering his previously lost experience of innocence, contentment, and untainted love. In his life, Twain accomplished the same end on a sweeping scale by imaginatively recreating and entering the fantasy world of his own boyhood fiction. Through a nostalgic return to an ideal past, Twain was able to circumvent both the grief, and the work of mourning, for his life's losses and disappointments. However, just as it is fair to suggest about his dream that the pleasurable innocence of the first half occurs primarily for the reason that it is meant to be disrupted and the grief consciously realized, and perhaps then worked through, it is also likely that behind Twain's humorous narratives lay the desire to lay a "tragedy trap," not only for the reader, but for himself—a tragedy trap that would enable him to bring to the surface of his imagination, and so realize and work through, the repressed grief at the core of his creative impulse.

A child's inability to grieve can, in most cases, be traced to similar pathological mourning behavior in the child's parent. It will be discovered that Jane Lampton Clemens did, indeed, suffer from pathological mourning resulting from an inability to grieve over the deaths of her loved ones, and that this pathology was passed on to, and adopted by, her son Samuel, who lived through many of these deaths with her.[7] Mark Twain's pattern of pathological mourning and denial of grief can be further explored in connection to Sam Clemens's response to his father's death, in 1847, when he was twelve years old. The new psychological element that emerged in Twain's fictional and biographical attempts to deal with his problematic father-son relationship was the family-romance fantasy, through which he endeavored to circumvent the actual death of his own disappointing father by continuing to search for an ideal father in the external world, attaching himself, finally, through identification, with successful financial figures such as Andrew Carnegie and Henry H. Rogers. Twain's adoption of a family romance fantasy was, therefore, merely another manifestation of pathological mourning, as it strategically allowed for the repression of grief, and for a denial of the reality of death.

Nostalgia is the final manifestation of repressed grief that will be identified in Mark Twain's work, since it encompasses the experience of sibling death and loss with which he dealt as a child, focuses the discussion once again on the issue of preoedipal separation-anxiety and longing for the mother, and most importantly, provides a comprehensive understanding of Twain's motive and identity as a writer of fiction about boyhood. The nostalgic's insistent yearnings for a lost past have, in fact, been traced specifically to a disappointment and frustration with the mother in the early stages of development, and to the related experience of sibling rivalry, particularly the experience of guilt that a child suffers after losing a sibling through death. Nostalgia provided Twain with the ultimate stratagem for avoiding grief, as it allowed him to recapture imaginatively an Edenic time and place that lay safely beyond the bounds of death, disillusion, and sorrow.

For an adult, and even more so for a child, to be "left behind" by a loved one as a result of death is an experience that is fraught with anger and guilt—intensely negative and frightening feelings that a child dare not allow full expression in his or her consciousness. The guilt that a child suffers as the survivor of a sibling's, or parent's, death comes from the spontaneous suspicion that he or she has done something to drive the person away, particularly if, as in the case of the notorious family troublemaker, Sam Clemens, he had been mean, mischievous, or hurtful to the sibling.

Years after the untimely deaths of his sister and brothers, Twain expressed a tremendous complicitous guilt in his letters, journals, and fiction, as if he, personally, had been responsible for their deaths. Undoubtedly, what the young Sam was feeling was unatoned-for remorse for what he perceived as his own cruel acts toward his siblings while they were alive. After the deaths of Twain's siblings he was compelled to repress not only his grief, but his long-held feelings of rivalry-based hostility toward them. The variants of pathological mourning that surface in his works are thus largely the result of Twain's ambivalent feelings of rivalry toward those siblings and friends who died during his childhood.

The premise behind all manifestations of pathological mourning is that while death ends a life it does not always end a relationship. As the "bad boy" in the Clemens family, Sam was placed in opposition not only to the "angel" Henry, but to the obedient and eager to please Orion, compliant Pamela, and the sweet Ben, who was idealized by his mother even more after his death.[8] Between the ages of four and twenty-two, Sam Clemens lived through the deaths of one sister and two brothers. As a surviving sibling entrapped in his ambivalence, Sam would perhaps have felt that he too should have died along with them, or that he should have died instead of his siblings. Typically, he would have mulled over his own bad behavior and cruel acts toward his siblings, which would presumably have resulted in even greater feelings of guilt.[9] Included among the "crimes" which the half-man, half-child "Conscience" dwarf reminds the narrator of in "The Facts Concerning the Recent Carnival of Crime in Connecticut" (1876), is his past cruelty to his siblings, who "died thinking of those injuries, maybe, and grieving over them."[10]

The first sibling death during Sam's lifetime was that of his nine-year-old sister, Margaret, in 1839, who died from river fever when Sam was four years old. Child psychologists have suggested that children under five generally do not have an understanding of the finality of death. They view it as a sleep, a departure, or a separation, all of which are temporary, and which must be waited out until the "death" is eventually reversed.[11]

The attitude of a four-year-old child toward death cannot be better dramatized than Twain does through the persona of the dog in the sketch "A Dog's Tale" (1903). This story was composed only a few months before the final attack of illness that proved fatal to Twain's wife, Livy, early in 1904, and it is possible that his helplessness in the face of her impending death, and his anticipation of unbearable grief, reactivated the deep, natural feelings of grief over Margaret's death which his sibling rivalry had impeded when he was four years old. In the story, Twain poignantly depicts the mute helplessness of the mother dog, who watches while her cruelly murdered puppy is buried beneath the great elm in the garden. In her limited understanding, she knows only that "the puppy was out of its pain now, because it was asleep"; and she assumes that the footman was merely "planting" the puppy in the hole which he dug, and that it would soon spring up like a budding flower.[12] The dog's vigil, of course, proves futile:

I have watched two whole weeks, and he doesn't come up! This last week a fright has been stealing upon me. I think there is something terrible about this. I do not know what it is, but the fear makes me sick, and I cannot eat, though the servants bring me the best of food; and they pet me so, . . . and all this terrifies me the more, and makes me sure something has happened. . . . And within this hour the servants, looking toward the sun where it was sinking out of sight and the night chill coming on, said things I could not understand, but they carried something cold to my heart. (554)

Perhaps the most deliberately pathetic of all Twain's tales, the story offers no moral or thematic resolution, and ends with the implied death of the mother dog from overwhelming grief. The story can hardly be called a tragedy, since the dog died with no understanding of what had happened, either to her puppy, or to herself. It does, however, accurately mirror the point of view of a young child who is confronted with the mysterious permanence of death; and even though Twain was sixty-five years of age when he composed the story, it was perhaps inspired by the return of a repressed grief response of the four-year-old Sam to the death of his sister Margaret—a death that his rivalrous wishes prevented him from feeling true, filial sorrow over at the time. As it is, the story is an unconsciously built monument, not only to those whom Twain had lost, but to his own inability to express his grief overtly.

As his sister had before him, Benjamin Clemens died suddenly from a river fever at the age of ten. Sam, by this time, was almost seven years old, the age after which he once claimed life was never the same. Although Sam did not consciously blame himself for Margaret's death, he did, many years later, describe the event of Ben's death as a "case of memorable treachery."[13] It has been determined that, by the age of seven or eight, a child has a more logical view of death. Commonly, by this stage a child will interpret the word "death" as meaning enclosed in a box without air, rotting, or being eaten by bugs (Dunton, 357). The child is primarily concerned not with dying, but with being murdered, and with the fear of retaliation for his own aggression (Cain et al., 743). This is, in fact, the most common response to death acted out in Twain's fiction by his bad-boy characters, who feel the presence of ghosts and savage avengers in the night air, or expect to be struck dead by a vengeful God at any moment.

A child's fear of ghosts, and the occurrence of nightmares, while not necessarily indicative of pathology, are among the most common manifestations of repressed grief. The guilt born of sibling rivalry, which Sam Clemens seems to have felt after the deaths of his brother and sister, and which interfered with his ability to grieve their loss, may well have manifested itself in his psyche as a fear of ghosts, who had been sent back from the "other world" to punish him for his psychological "crimes."

Ghosts, nightmares, sleeplessness, and a preoccupation with ghouls and living corpses usually reveal that a lost object, about which the survivor had felt ambivalence when the person was alive, still retains a strong presence in the intrapsychic world of the bereaved, thus suggesting either an overt or covert denial of the irreversibility of the loss.[14] As Freud explained, the pathological mourner experiences something like a splitting of the ego. While part of the mourner is fully conscious that the person in question has died, another part disavows the death by acting as if it has not occurred. Therefore, it is possible that while one part of young Sam Clemens acknowledged the actual deaths of his siblings, another part held on to the object in the form of a sense of supernatural persecution.

Twain stated that as a child he often felt the presence of ghosts in his dark room at his Uncle John Quarle's farm, where he spent many of his summers; and similarly, Huck Finn and Tom Sawyer took for granted the fact that ghosts wandered at night in graveyards and "haunted" houses. Twain's short fiction, as has so frequently been noted, is also replete with ghosts and other supernatural elements suggestive of repressed grief. "A Curious Dream" (1870) presents the reader with a living skeleton who is dissatisfied with the deteriorated condition of the graveyard in which he is buried. "The Invalid's Story" (1882) contains a foul and reeking corpse in a simply constructed coffin, which the narrator had been led to believe was actually a box containing guns that he was transporting by train. The connection between a child's aggression, symbolized by the box of guns, and the image of an unburied, and ungrieved for corpse, is overtly demonstrated in this short story. The occurrence of a living corpse that refuses to stay dead is seen in the bizarre and ghoulish tale of revenge, "A Dying Man's Confession" (1883), in which a murderer, who is supposed to be dead, suddenly revives in the "death-house," only to die again at the hands of the father of the children he had murdered years before.

In the story "The Undertaker's Chat" (1870), Twain tells of the corpse who objects to the ill-planning of his own funeral, and who attempts to sing at his own memorial service, but is astonished to discover that this is impossible. In all these tales and autobiographical episodes one can see repeated the situation in which the dead cannot "die" because of a general sense of unrest, a feeling that there is something left to do which they have not yet done, whether it is atonement for their own sins, or revenge for crimes committed by others upon them.

Nightmares are also manifestations of repressed aggressive impulses which have gotten out of control, and they represent the child's need to control those impulses. In *Life on the Mississippi*, and in *The Autobiography of Mark Twain*, Twain relates how, after the violent deaths of the autobiographically based fictional characters Injun Joe, the Calaboose tramp, Dutchy, Lem, an innocent slave, and the young California emigrant who was stabbed with a bowie knife, Sam was up all night with obsessive fears and nightmares. After each episode, he writes, "I went home to dream and was not disappointed." [15]

According to Albert C. Cain and his colleagues, a surviving sibling will also often engage in a series of accident-prone, and risk-taking behaviors, in order to test his immunity to the similar fate of death.

Twain often boasted about the number of times he had tempted fate by going swimming without knowing how, and being pulled out just short of death. Who knows how many of those episodes were an unconscious attempt to prove to himself, once and for all, that it was not merely a mistake on the part of the powers that be that his siblings were meant to die, and not he. But the fact that Twain continued to "hold a grudge" against his rescuers indicates that his "lucky" close calls were not convincing enough proof of his innocence in his conspiratorial designs on his siblings' deaths (*The Autobiography*, 72). Instead of gaining reassurance from his miraculous close calls, the young Sam undoubtedly interpreted the results as proof of his mother's often repeated proverb that: "People who are born to be hanged are safe in water."[16]

According to Cain, the surviving sibling will frequently experience "anniversary" hysterical symptoms, through which he comes to believe that he will die at the same age, or in the same way, that his sibling died. Ben died of fever when he was ten, and Margaret also died when she was almost ten years old. According to Twain's memory, as recorded in *The Autobiography*, it was during the summer of 1845, when he was ten years old, that he voluntarily contracted the measles from his afflicted friend, Will Bowen. It was "dead summertime," he wrote, and "I grew very tired of the suspense I suffered on account of being continually under the threat of death. I remember that I got so weary of it and so anxious to have the matter settled one way or the other, and promptly, that this anxiety spoiled my days and my nights" (77).[17] While this rather bizarre death-defying behavior has presented a great puzzle to Twain's readers, it represents a logical, though pathological, symptomatic response to sibling death.

It can only be suggested, however, that Sam's decision to contract the measles when he did was a pathological variant of mourning in the form of an anniversary reaction to his brother's, and perhaps also to his sister's, death; however, in one of Twain's short stories, there appears one of the most clinically accurate examples of an anniversary reaction. While prospecting in the lonesome Stanislaus territory, the narrator in "The Californian's Tale" (1893) wanders across a middle-aged man living in a cozy little cottage that everywhere reflected the loving and cared for look of "a woman's hand" (*Mark Twain's Short Stories*, 311). When the narrator inquires after the whereabouts of the man's wife, he is told that she has gone away for two weeks, but is due to return that day. His host implores him to stay a while until she arrives. When a day or so passes and there is still no sign of the woman, the narrator begins to suspect that something is amiss; nevertheless, he is startled to receive the news from a visiting neighbor that the man's wife has been dead for nineteen years. His host apparently lost his mind nineteen years before, when his wife, on her return from her trip, was captured by Indians, and was never heard from since. But as the neighbor explains:

He only gets bad when that time of the year comes around. Then we begin to drop in here, three days before she's due, to encourage him up, and ask if he's heard from her, and Saturday we all come and fix up the house with flowers, and get everything ready for a dance. We've done it every year for nineteen years. . . . We drug him to sleep, or he would go wild; then he's all right for another year—thinks she's with him till the last three or four days come around; then he begins to look for her, and gets out his poor old letter, and we come and ask him to read it to us. Lord, she was a darling! (*Short Stories*, 316)

In Twain's later life, the anniversaries of his daughter Susy's death, and of his wife's death, became a conscious source of anguish for him. On June 11, 1898, Twain made the following entry in his notebook:

Clara's birthday three days ago. Not a reference to it has been made by any member of the family in my hearing; no presents, no congratulations, no celebrations. Up to a year and ten months ago all our birthdays from the beginning of the family life were annually celebrated. . . . Then Susy died. All anniversaries of whatever sort perished with her. As we pass them now they are only gravestones. We cannot keep from seeing them as we go by but we can keep silent about them and look the other way and put them out of memory as they sink out of sight behind us. [18]

Birthdays, like death anniversaries, must remain taboo when the level of guilt associated with death makes positive grieving impossible. It hardly matters that Twain focuses on birthdays, rather than the actual day of death, as a reminder of his bereavement; in his mind the two events are closely equated. Guilt taints love and grief, and can reach such an intensity of negative feelings that any positive feelings are all but canceled out.

If Sam was not consciously exhibiting the pathological mourning symptom of life-threatening, risk-taking, behavior by swimming in Bear Creek, where, he wrote, in *Life on the Mississippi*, he "used to get drowned . . . every summer regularly" (324), he was certainly aware of the likelihood of contracting a disease from the swimming hole, that was known by all to be "a famous breeder of chills and fever" (324). When a sibling dies of an illness, during which time the mother devotes her full love and care toward the dying child, the surviving sibling may come to view illness as the only route to the mother (Cain et al., 750). The solicitous nature of Twain's fictional mothers with regard to illness and dying is repeatedly illustrated in his works. "Experience of the McWilliamses with Membranous Croup" (1875), for example, is a story that is wholly devoted to Twain's conviction that illness is the only route to the mother. The tale begins with Mrs. McWilliams in a frantic state of panic at the thought that her little girl, Penelope, is dying from the croup. The child, who is usually cared for by the nurse, now qualifies for the personal attentions of her mother. Mrs. McWilliams, terrified that the baby also will catch the disease, removes its crib from the nursery and places it next to her own pillow. She concludes that Providence is punishing her for her sins by arranging for the doctor to be unavailable at this critical moment.

When the doctor is eventually dragged from his sick bed to the house, and it is discovered that the child is "not dying," but is suffering only from "some trifling irritation or other in the throat," the mother is not relieved, as might normally be expected, but furious. The doctor's "good" news made her "as mad as if he had offered her a personal affront" (*Mark Twain's Short Stories*, 126). In a moment, she had dropped all concern for her children, and "turned away in disdain and left the room." Despite the comic effect of the story, which is produced primarily through the neurotic response of Mrs. McWilliams, the moral comes across clearly: only when the mother fears that the child is dying will she display her full and unfeigned maternal love. Perhaps Twain learned this moral from his own mother's response toward her dying children, and it is this reaction that he counted upon, and was gratified to receive, when he himself tested her by contracting the measles.

If there was any question in Twain's mind regarding his responsibility for Ben's death, there was absolutely no question in his mind that he was directly responsible for Henry's death by scalding, in 1858, when the boilers blew up on the steamship *Pennsylvania*. Sam, who was twenty-two years old by this time, was apparently so distraught after the accident that his mother and sister feared he was losing his mind. The two women spent a great deal of effort trying to dispel Sam's overwhelming feeling of guilt, not only for surviving, but as he later admitted, for allowing an inexperienced doctor to administer an overdose of morphine to his ailing brother, which he believed was the true cause of Henry's death.[19]

When the identity of two siblings is fused, the loss of one is particularly crucial to the self-identity of the surviving sibling (Bank and Kahn, 271). It has already been pointed out that Henry and Sam took on complementary roles in the Clemens family; Sam positioned himself as a troublemaker relative to Henry, who was his mother's angel. Like Edward Mills, in Twain's story, "Edward Mills and George Benton: A Tale," Henry was "an increasing comfort," while Sam, the "George Benton" of the Clemens family, was "an increasing solicitude" (*Short Stories*, 179). It is possible that Sam viewed Henry as the "good" boy whom he felt he, himself, was on the inside, but which he was never able to express because of his fixed identity within his family as the difficult child. Sam was the unwanted "pauper" who was denied the recognition of his inner "princely" nature, and who, as Tom Sawyer also admits, was forced by want and need (of the mother's love) to lead a miscreant's life of deception and thievery. Together, they were Chambers and Tom Driscoll, forced to exchange their rightful inheritance, and opposite moral stature, to social and familial forces beyond their control.

Although Henry and Sam were as distinct as Cattaraugus and Catiline, in Twain's "A Cat-Tale"—the one "white" with "high impulses and a pure heart," the other "black" with "base motives" and "a self-seeking nature"—they functioned as a single, integral unit, which, when separated, as in Twain's story, comprised only "half" of a story.[20] The fused identities of these two brother cats, as with Sam and Henry, is implied in Twain's drawing of a cat for his daughters, in "A Cat-Tale," which shows one half of the cat "lying" and the other half standing up (or to slightly re-phrase the description, up-standing), with only a dotted line to separate the two.

Siblings who share this "mixed pattern" identity often develop "frozen" images of each other, especially after death. When the "good" sibling dies, the surviving child often exalts his or her "frozen misunderstanding" of the sibling to levels of exaggerated idealization, sometimes raising the image of the dead child in his or her eyes, and in the estimation of the parents, to a position of sainthood (Bank, 277). In the case of the good brother's death, the "wicked" survivor unconsciously longs to "become his brother," as he unconsciously longed to usurp his brother's positive place in the family when he was alive, and believes that he will always fall short of the angelic role once occupied by his dead sibling. Although we cannot be certain that this dynamic occurred in the Clemens family, in view of Twain's fictional presentation of brother-pairs, it offers a remarkably accurate description of what might have happened between them.[21] Had Henry not died when he did, it is more than likely that he would never have become the zenith star to which Twain aspired all his life, and relative to which he always fell short.

Furthermore, when sibling identity has been fused during life, Stephen Bank explains, death is likely to make the survivor a "psychological amputee."[22] The surviving child unconsciously feels that a part of himself has been lost, and continues to look for this "phantom sibling" in the external world, such as in works of art, or in heroic public figures. This confusion of identities, and rightful ownership of identity roles, between brothers, suggestive of the "psychological amputee" syndrome that Bank speaks of, can be seen throughout Twain's fiction, some of the most obvious examples being Tom Canty and the Prince, and Miles and Hugh Hendon, both in *The Prince and the Pauper* (1882), Tom Driscoll and Valet de Chambers, in *Pudd'nhead Wilson* (1893), and "those extraordinary twins," Luigi and Angelo.

In a lesser-known story about himself, presumably told to a reporter in an interview, Twain bemoans a fictitious twin brother who, he says, died as a baby. In response to the reporter's surprise that this forgotten incident should still move him to tears, Mark Twain goes on to explain that one morning, while he and his identical twin brother were taking their bath together, his little brother drowned. Then, after some time, while everyone was mourning him, it was discovered that it was not his brother, after all, but he, himself, who had drowned.

In view of the unbearable remorse over unforgivable and unforgiven acts of cruelty to his dead siblings and friends that seemed to occupy Twain's creative mind, one of the wish-fulfillment fantasies embedded in the story "The Mysterious Stranger" may be understood as the granting of a young boy's second chance to make amends to an injured friend *before* his friend dies. As was true after the deaths of Henry, Twain's boyhood friends, and perhaps even Ben, the narrator in the story, knowing that his friend Nikolaus was going to die, upbraided himself for the "little, shabby wrongs" that he had done to him over the years, "with a pain much sharper than one feels when the wrongs have been done to the living."[23] This feeling of guilt and remorse is again described by Twain, in *The Prince and the Pauper*, when he writes of how "the strokes of a funeral bell smite upon the soul of a surviving friend when they remind him of secret treacheries suffered at his hands by him that is gone" (185). Through the fantasy of returning back through time, in "The Mysterious Stranger," it is possible that Twain indulged in the comforting feelings that one gets when given the opportunity to take back one's past sinful acts to a loved one, and hence, to grieve openly without the impediment of guilt. This episode is, in many respects, the deeply human center of what is otherwise a cold and philosophical tale. The eleven days that the narrator spent with the dying Nik were "beautiful" to him, for they were, he says,

days of companionship with one's sacred dead, and I have known no comradeship that was so close or so precious. We clung to the hours and the minutes, counting them as they wasted away, and parting with them with that pain and bereavement which a miser feels who sees his hoard filched from him coin by coin by robbers and is helpless to prevent it. (222)

By being allowed to return to a time before his friend died, and to express openly the love and kindness that he truly felt for his comrade, the narrator is freed from the remorse and guilt he otherwise would have felt when his friend died suddenly and accidentally. Here we see what numerous clinical studies of bereavement have discovered: true grief can be expressed only when feelings of guilt toward the deceased have been overcome. The Mosaic Law, which stuck in the throat of Tom Sawyer, is here, through the help of creative fantasy, fully realized by Twain: "Blessed are they that mourn, for they shall be *comforted.*"

The belief expressed by Mark Twain's critics that death seemed to follow him throughout his life, and that he spent his whole life trying to discover the crime he had committed that would explain his persisting sense of guilt, becomes increasingly comprehensible when placed within the context, not only of Twain's sibling rivalry, but of the superstitious fears and guilty concerns that plagued the maternal conscience of Twain's mother, Jane Lampton Clemens.[24] The widespread occurrence of pathological mourning symptoms in Twain fiction supports the hypothesis that Sam inherited his mother's inability to grieve for the death of a loved one, as well as her reluctance to bury the image of the dead person along with his or her body. If Twain's fiction is haunted by ghosts and guilty terrors concerning the imminent possibility that the dead might suddenly return to life, it is, I propose, a consequence of his imitation of the mourning pathology that his mother habitually exhibited in her daily life.

A close look at the story of Jane Clemens's life reveals numerous illustrations of her repressed grief for the deaths of her loved ones, and her sublimation of that grief, particularly into pathological caretaking behavior. In accordance with John Bowlby's claims, there is a high probability that the variant manifestations of repressed mourning, which characterized Twain's mother's manner of dealing with death, infected her son's ability to accept and deal with the loss of his siblings.

According to Rachel Varble, one of the most outstanding behavioral characteristics of Peggy Lampton, (Jane's mother), when she, herself, was a child, was an attraction to all helpless creatures, including sick mules and even plants and flowers.[25] Bowlby has determined that this kind of compulsive caring for others, when it is motivated by feelings of guilt, is a common pathological response among children who feel that they have been neglected and unloved. From what we know about Jane Lampton Clemens's emotionally impoverished relationship with her mother, it is likely that her own over-zealous caring was a result of her identification with these similarly neglected creatures.[26]

After Jane's mother died, in 1817, her father, Benjamin Lampton, was adamant about not allowing his daughters, Jane and Patsy, to visit their mother's grave; nor was he ever known to have visited the grave himself. Rarely was their mother even spoken of in the household after her death. After the funeral, Benjamin Lampton encouraged his daughters to attend social events, and "would not hear of" their wearing the customary crepe bands of mourning. Varble suggests that "it was from her father that Jane learned how to depreciate a time of mourning and get through a death with the least possible pain and devastation. An achievement that would cause wonder in the years ahead, and no little criticism" (46–47).

It is evident that, at an early age, Jane Lampton developed a pathological pattern of denying the reality of death; she refused to engage in the mourning process, and thus was unable to dispel the intrapsychic image of the lost loved one. Instead, as her mother had before her, she compulsively cared for substitute objects.

Jane Clemens's strange behavior following the death of her sister, Patsy, in 1850, was observed by both Orion and Pamela. Although she exhibited no overt signs of grief—an absence that greatly surprised Orion—she began to take long, aimless walks, as she had after the death of Benjamin. According to Pamela, Jane came home one day soon after Patsy's death, hand in hand with a little neighborhood girl named Edith, who was ten years old, and who had apparently also recently lost a sister (Varble, 198–99). She insisted on keeping the girl near her, arranging tea parties for her in the afternoons. It is safe to presume that Jane's repressed grief was once again channeled into the same kind of compulsive caretaking behavior that her mother had exhibited. Through an act of projective identification, the little Smith girl became both replacement child and replacement sister, an embodiment of Jane's love, grief, and yearning for her own un-grieved for lost loved ones.[27]

Furthermore, after Ben's death, Jane's already elaborate manner of expressing excessive concern for her children and all helpless creatures, and of taking unnecessary precautions against their getting hurt or catching diseases, became even more extreme.[28] According to Varble, Sam's mother, like Tom Sawyer's Aunt Polly, frantically responded to "every symptom of fever, cold, or rash" (Varble, 153). Jane Clemens's anxiety over the fear of loss suggests that she felt guilty and responsible for her children's death. As Bowlby has demonstrated, when a child dies, overprotective behavior in a parent, especially with regard to illness, can be interpreted as evidence of guilty self-reproach, and of the mother's fear that her remaining children will also be snatched by death. It may be recalled that Twain claims to have become frantic when, only a few years after Ben's death from river fever, in May 1842, an epidemic of measles swept through Hannibal, taking with it over forty people, most of whom were children.[29] When, as he wrote in *The Autobiography of Mark Twain*, he "got tired of the suspense" over whether he was to be the next victim, perhaps what he actually meant was that he was tired of living with his mother's suspense over his, and his siblings', ever-impending death.[30]

Soon after Ben's death, Jane Clemens made the decision to become a practicing Christian. Her actions undoubtedly were prompted by her fear that the Almighty had taken Ben as punishment for her sins, and that unless she reformed, her other children might be taken from her as well. As her biographer explains, "for the theory had come to her ears that the deaths of her children seemed her special punishment for neglecting religion. If this were true, her other children also might be taken, one by one, until she was humbled" (Varble, 153). Rachel Varble suggests that one of the reasons Jane Clemens felt compelled to become a Christian after the death of Benjamin was that it provided a solace to her, as it did to the many other women she knew in Hannibal who had lost their children. Her guilty concern was, to some degree, relieved knowing that her dead child had a happy and comfortable existence in heaven. Twain's own often admitted fear of being struck dead, and his compelling impulse to repent his wicked ways, which, as he recalled, beset him immediately following the death by drowning of his boyhood pals, mirrors his mother's pathological mourning response to her children's deaths.

The religious guilt and self-absorption that Jane Clemens seems to have chronically suffered after the deaths of her children is likely to have severely interfered with her ability to grieve. This religious guilt, which impeded his mother's ability to mourn, was adopted by Sam and transformed into a distorted sense of morality and divine justice. Mark Twain frequently relates, in *The Autobiography of Mark Twain,* as well as in his fiction, letters, and speeches, the story of Henry's death, and the deaths of his boyhood friends, Lem Hackett (a fictitious name used by Twain) and Dutchy, when Twain was a young boy.[31] According to Twain's fictional interpretations of these episodes, dying an early death, particularly death by drowning, was clearly a form of retribution enacted by God to punish the wicked—a "case of special judgment" that was usually accompanied by a "ferocious thunderstorm."[32] There is little doubt that the young Sam Clemens inherited this notion from his mother's Presbyterian training, with its strict and uncompromising belief in an angry and vengeful God.

As Twain relates the story of these deaths in *Life on the Mississippi,* when Lem Hackett, who was a boy "loaded with sin" (313), drowned one Sunday, Sam determined that such an episode was a "right and proper" end for the wicked boy; and, being equally, if not more, "loaded with sin" as Lem, Sam "sat up in bed quaking and shuddering, waiting for the destruction of the world," and hoping that he would not be the next recreant to be detected by the angels in heaven, whose "celestial interest" (314) had now been turned upon his "beggarly little village." All concern and sadness over the loss of his friend were eclipsed by his own guilt and remorse "for sins which I knew I had committed, and for others which I was not certain about," and by his persistent resolve to "lead a high and blameless life forever after" (314–15).

While this experience, as Twain remembered it in *Life on the Mississippi,* was the "most distressful one I ever spent," an even more disturbing event was to occur three weeks later, not because it was more terrifying, but because it was utterly "unaccountable" to him; in fact, he wrote, it was "the most unaccountable one . . . that I had ever experienced" (317). His friend, Dutchy, drowned in Bear Creek while playing a game with the other boys in which each boy tried to hold his breath the longest under water. The difficulty here, for Sam, was that Dutchy was not a wicked boy like Lem and himself, but like Willie Mufferson in

The Adventures of Tom Sawyer, was the Model Boy of the village, and an "exasperatingly good" boy. With this incident, Sam's Presbyterian reasoning was seriously undermined. He concluded that "if Dutchy, with all his perfections, was not a delight, it would be vain for me to turn over a new leaf, for I must infallibly fall hopelessly short of that boy, no matter how hard I might try" (318). For Sam, this incident belied the Presbyterian maxim that the good are rewarded and the bad are punished.

Similarly, when Henry died in the explosion on the steamboat, *Pennsylvania,* Sam was as much overwhelmed by God's injustice in punishing the innocent as he was by the loss of his beloved brother. In a letter to his mother and sister informing them of the disaster he wrote:

Hardened, hopeless, — aye, lost—lost—lost and ruined sinner as I am—I, even I, have humbled myself to the ground and prayed as never man prayed before, that the great God might let this cup pass from me—that he would strike me to the earth, but spare my brother—that he would pour out the fullness of his just wrath upon my wicked head, but have mercy, mercy, mercy upon that unoffending boy.[33]

In two of his earliest sketches, "The Story of the Bad Little Boy" (1865), and "The Story of the Good Little Boy" (1870), Twain again illustrated his outrage and irreconcilable confusion over the discrepancy between theoretical, Presbyterian justice, and the way things *really* happen in life. In the first story, the protagonist, Jim, is a "sinful," "vulgar" bully and a "bad, neglected boy" (*Short Stories,* 9). Nevertheless, he *didn't* get torn apart by the neighbor's dog when he stole apples, he *didn't* get whipped by his teacher for stealing, and "strangest" of all, he "didn't get drowned" or "get struck by lightning" when he went fishing on the Sabbath (8). The narrator is baffled by this example of "improbable justice," because, he says, "you might look, and look, all through the Sunday-school books from now till next Christmas, and you would never come across anything like this. . . . How Jim ever escaped is a mystery to me" (9).

In Twain's companion story about the "good little boy," Jacob Blivens was his mother's darling. He never told a lie and read every one of his Sunday school books in order to live a blameless and God-fearing life. As a result, Jacob *did* break his arm trying to prevent Jim Blake from stealing apples, and he *did* get sick from falling in the river when he attempted to warn the bad boys not to go sailing on Sunday. His case, the narrator concludes, was again "truly remarkable," and "will probably never be accounted for" (*Mark Twain's Short Stories*, 77). Although fictional, these incidents conform exactly to Twain's philosophical beliefs, in works such as *Letters from the Earth*, where he writes at length about the cruelties and injustices enacted by God and his "earthly" offspring, man (24).

In her last years, Jane Clemens is reported to have become senile, often engaging in hallucinatory fantasies, which allowed for the uncensored expression of her lingering, unspent grief, or chronic mourning. She would often visit mediums and attend seances in the hope of making contact with her dead sister, which was not unusual in the mid-nineteenth century; however, she also claimed several times to have seen her sister and her deceased sweetheart, Richard Barret, in the street or at a dance, and frequently reported to Sam that she felt the "spirit" of Patsy around her, or as she said, that the spirits of the dead were "trying to get through to me" (Varble, 335).

Despite Twain's overt skepticism toward his mother's delusions, he, himself, admitted several times that he and his wife, Livy, had visited mediums in the hope of communicating with their dead daughter, Susy. Twain also held a strong belief in "Mental Telegraphy," or the notion that the mind unconsciously received messages about future events; and he was firmly convinced that dreams can predict the future.[34] Shortly before Henry's death, Jane claimed to have witnessed strange omens of disaster, one of which was Henry's favorite picture mysteriously falling off the wall. Twain, himself, remembers having a dream the evening before Henry died, in which he saw his brother's corpse lying in a metallic coffin, dressed in a suit of Twain's clothes (*The Autobiography*, 99–100).

It has often been noted that Twain's obsession with the funerals of others, especially those of famous public figures who were honored with magnificent, elaborate ceremonies, was inherited from his mother, who apparently never missed a funeral. Like his mother, Twain also made a habit of jotting down in his notebook every detail of other people's funeral rituals; the bigger and more flashy, the more fascinated he was. While it might be assumed that this desire to attend funerals reflected a willingness to grieve openly, it should be remembered that Jane Clemens avoided the funeral rituals of her own children; yet she would prepare days in advance for the funerals of others.

Doris Webster, a longtime friend of Jane's, reported, in 1925, that Jane "had no use for anything morbid . . . low and solemn"; she did, however, "adore" celebrations and social gatherings.[35] It should also be remembered that in the rural town of Tennessee where Jane grew up, a man's funeral was often the main social event of his "life." When there was a death, the body would be buried right away, with no ceremony, but the bereaved would then have to wait until there were enough corpses in their small town to make a visit from the travelling minister worthwhile. When he would arrive, sometimes many months later, a funeral ceremony would be performed with an accompanying celebration that was attended by the whole town. Thus, it was perhaps the celebratory aspect of these funeral rituals to which Twain and his mother were most especially drawn, as it allowed them the opportunity to repress the emotional pain of their grief experience. On the other hand, a concern with the deaths and funerals of others also suggests that Jane, and her son, both of whom were unable to express fully their grief for a lost loved one (and therefore still retained a strong internal identification with the lost object), were unconsciously attempting to work through their lingering mourning and put the dead to rest, not realizing, of course, that it was their own dead for whom they needed to grieve.

Both Twain and his mother also adhered to a Presbyterian tradition that encouraged the bereaved to repress feelings of grief after a death, and to view it as an exalted event—a time to celebrate the release from care and pain of the suffering loved one. Thomas Beecher, the minister of the Park Church in Elmira, with whom Twain and his family socialized for many decades, was noted to be excessive in his insistence on celebrating death and denying one's grief. The day after Susy died, in August, 1896, Twain took his second daughter, Jean, to New York for a ferry ride, in the hope of cheering her up. By distracting Jean as he did, Twain denied her the opportunity to mourn in the same way that his mother had denied him, and Jane's father had denied her. It is likely that Twain's emphasis on the celebratory aspect of death represented merely another attempt to evade and transcend his grief.

Twain's career as a fiction writer and storyteller exemplifies how an early experience of death and loss can become integrated into one's self-identity and view of the external world. Twain's fictions about boyhood represent his life-saving efforts to recapture a time before the fall—before loss, death, and grief. His nostalgic boyhood fantasies were a death-defying attempt to re-live the youthful past, and replace grief with a fictional gesture of sweeping denial. The inability to grieve over the loss, or death, of one's loved ones, which Mark Twain partly inherited

from his mother, resulted in a lifetime of distorted manifestations of un-
worked through grief and, through time, became an integral part not
only of his creative impulse, but of his innermost self.

The events surrounding the death of John Marshall Clemens, in 1847,
were something of a horror to his bereaved family, particularly to the
sensitive son, Sam. As payment for medical services, Mrs. Clemens
allowed Dr. Meredith to perform an autopsy on her husband. Based on
Twain's brief sketch, "The Autopsy," and on a later journal note in
which he stated: "1847: witnessed post mortem of my *uncle* (my italics)
through key hole," Twain's biographers feel fairly certain that he had
seen enough of the postmortem for it to have made a strong impression
on his unconscious memory.[36] There is little question that Orion saw the
autopsy since he included several passages about it in his autobiography.[37] Even the idea of a post mortem would undoubtedly have added
an element of the macabre to Sam's experience of death, and haunting
thoughts about undead corpses are certainly likely to have interfered
with his ability to grieve properly over the loss of his father.

But there was no need for Sam Clemens to put his father to rest
permanently. When John Marshall Clemens died, the event represented
a two-fold loss in the boy's life; not only had his father departed, but
also gone were his father's hopes for achieving personal success, and the
fulfillment of his father's dream of seeing his cherished 100,000 acres of
Tennessee Land (the only financial holding left to his impoverished
family) reap the enormous profit that he had literally "banked on" for
well over a decade. When in Twain's novel, *The Gilded Age,* Sellers's
partner, Father Hawkins, dies, Twain gives us what certainly must have
been an elaboration of his own father's dying words:

I am leaving you in cruel poverty. I have been—so foolish—so short-sighted.
But courage! A better day is—coming. Never lose sight of the Tennessee Land!
Be wary. There is wealth stored up for you there—wealth that is boundless! The
children shall hold up their heads with the best in the land, yet.[38]

In *The Autobiography,* Twain made no mention of his father's death
itself, but he did go on at length about his father's legacy of the Tennessee Land. He mentioned, in particular, John Clemens's dying words, in
which he assured his family that the land would soon make them all rich
and happy. "We straightway turned our waiting eyes upon Tennessee,"
Twain wrote, "but nothing ever came of it."[39] Forty years later they had
"managed it all away except 10,000 acres and gotten nothing to remem-

ber the sales by." The land, however, did serve as a sure way for Sam to remember his father. John Clemens "lived" on after death, in the mind of Sam Clemens and his family, as "the curse of prospective wealth" that he had placed upon them, and in the form of the son's hopes for the eventual fulfillment of the father-ideal, which was, like the land itself, a "faith that rises and falls but never dies" (*The Autobiography*, 24–25).

In the story "The $30,000 Bequest" (1904), Twain was able to express, in fantasy, his feelings of revenge and resentment toward his father for falsely promising his family that they would, in Father Hawkins's words, "live like princes of the earth." In this tale, a promised inheritance, by degrees, wholly perverts the minds of an entire family, transforming their once pleasant, though poor, life into a nightmare of "castle-building" and "day-dreaming."[40] In their final, devastating disappointment, upon discovering that the inheritance itself was imaginary—a vicious and revengeful plot perpetrated by their now deceased uncle—the family suffers from what Twain describes, in *The Autobiography*, as the "heavy curse" of prospective wealth that his father had placed upon his own family when he bought the Tennessee Land.

There must have been a part of Sam Clemens that nurtured a secret hope that his father's Tennessee Land would "come through" with his father's promised millions—that his father would prove to be the idealized figure that he must often have cherished. Twain, in fact, did find a way to make good on the Tennessee Land, thereby, to some extent, reinstating the heroic image of his father, and preserving his father's perpetually un-dead status in his own mind. Through an act of wish-fulfilling rationalization, Twain explained, in *The Autobiography*, how he did, in fact, eventually profit from the land: "It furnished me a field for Sellers and a book. Out of my half of the book I got $15,000 or $20,000; out of the play I got $75,000 or $80,000—just about a dollar an acre" (24). Here, Twain was conscious of the direct correlation that he was making between his father's Tennessee Land and the revenue he received from his career as a fiction-writer; but his persistent desire to make good on his father's dreams for the land did not end here, although his awareness of his efforts to do so apparently did. Twain spent a great deal of energy in his later life trying to get a "perpetual copyright" law passed that would establish books as property, so that an author would be assured of continued profit from his or her books, even after death. The argument that Twain gave, in *The Autobiography*, defending the concept of books as ideas, and words as real estate, bears a singular resemblance to John Marshall Clemens's original idea that, with special foresight, a man might attain great wealth by speculating in property.[41] Twain offered the illustration of one especially "bright" man who was "equipped with ideas, a far-seeing man" who would be able to "perceive that at some distant day" the land would be enormously valuable. Indeed, Twain might have been speaking through the voice of Sellers/John Marshall Clemens when he proceeded to argue that this man might "go home and lay the deeds away for the eventual vast profit of his children" (283). If Twain could prove that an author's ideas are as tangible as his father's Tennessee Land—that a book is property—then not only might he actualize his father's financial plan through his own chosen form of profiting from his America, he might also be able to reinstate his father as the son's fantasy ideal, father figure.

"Our heroes," Twain wrote, in *The Autobiography*, "are the men who do things which we recognize with regret and sometimes with a secret shame that we cannot do" (263). One might add to this adolescent thought the observation that a boy's paternal hero is a man who can do what his father can do, or what he wishes his father could do. In a short sketch on Theodore Roosevelt written in 1908, Twain predicted that the republic of America was destined to become a monarchy. His primary reason for believing this, he wrote, was that: "It is the nature of man to want a definite something to love, honor, reverently look up to, and obey."[42] John Marshall Clemens was sadly unable to fulfill this idealized role for his son. What Twain's father, in particular, could *not* do was see into America's future, to see the ubiquitous budding financial opportunities that seemed to be waiting to be grasped in nineteenth-century America. For Twain, Henry H. Rogers and Andrew Carnegie represented the ideal paternal hero image. Rogers, in the early 1890s, performed the heroic deed of preventing Twain's copyrights from falling into the hands of his publisher. In utter amazement and disbelief at Rogers's financial foresight, Twain commented, in *The Autobiography*, on this man's most extraordinary gift: "How could he look into the future and see all that, when the men whose trade and training it was to exercise that technical vision were forecast blind and saw no vestige of it?" (262). Unlike his own father, who time and again proved himself "forecast blind," Rogers and Carnegie were able, as Twain pointed out, to increase immensely their "fortunes steadily and successfully against obstructions that would have defeated almost any other human being similarly placed . . ." ("Carnegie," in *Mark Twain in Eruption*, 37).

The ambivalence that the young Sam Clemens felt toward his father's "prospective" success, and toward his very real financial failures, was later transferred to his attitude toward the land, and toward his own hopes for material success. Mrs. Clemens's plea to Sam, on her husband's death bed, that he "promise to be a better boy," and to be honest, a "faithful and industrious man, and upright like his father," further encouraged the transference of expected success from father to son.[43] The proposition that the boy was forced to adopt is clear: if he achieved his own success and fulfilled the father's dream, he would also have to deal with the guilt that accompanied the realization that not only had he surpassed his father in life, as he had surpassed his three deceased siblings, Margaret, Ben, and Henry, but he had surpassed him in fame and worldly success as well. As any son might, Sam could be expected both to desire and to feel enormous guilt over such personal accomplishment.

Mark Twain earned what amounted to a fortune from his writing, but he was never able to hold on to his capital; he lived in a perpetual state of worry over his debts and expenses. From numerous clinical studies, David Kreuger has determined that a parent's attitude toward money and success is frequently imitated by the child, and integrated into his or her own self-definition.[44] When money is used symbolically and transferentially, the inner conflicts that are being acted out become evident in the person's inappropriate use of funds, such as through compulsive spending, revenge spending, or excessive risk-taking (Kreuger, 211). Twain's financial habits show an indulgence in all of these inappropriate uses of money. If Twain earned forty thousand dollars on a book, he would lose forty-two thousand on a patent. The list is extensive. He lost five thousand dollars on a steam engine, then thirty-two thousand on a steam pulley, and twenty-three thousand on an insurance company that failed (*The Autobiography*, 229). At one point, when he earned twenty-three thousand dollars on an investment, he immediately lost it again on another risky venture.

Twain's difficulties in acquiring money, following through with his inventions and investments, and taking financial risks, might all be the result of what Kreuger describes as the son's fear of getting "caught" with money, and his desire to hide his success from his less successful father, thereby circumventing the "imagined consequences" (Kreuger, 220).[45] When it came to money matters, Twain, apparently, was stymied by his unresolved feelings of ambivalence toward his father, and could not seem to allow himself to surpass John Marshall Clemens's status as a business failure. Instead, he tenaciously clung to his adolescent fantasy, acted out through his incessant investments in patent rights, which contained the wish, not the reality, of actualizing the father-ideal. He was one of those who, as Otto Fenichel describes, attempts to "keep hope alive by not succeeding quite completely—not taking the final step across the finish line, so that the illusion is never confronted" (Qtd. in Kreuger, 212).

In the end, John Marshall Clemens's promise to make his son a "prince" was never realized, and Sam must always have felt he was somehow cheated out of his noble birthright. The dreams of unimaginable wealth, and of being restored to the nobility of the Lampton line that his mother so often boasted of were, however, repeatedly fulfilled in fantasy by Twain through his fiction. Like young Tom Canty, in *The Prince and the Pauper*, Sam Clemens must often have seen himself as a poverty-stricken boy who was, nevertheless, the "Prince of Poverty," and who harbored secret dreams of some day winning his crown.

At the same time, Twain's family-romance desire to attain his noble birthright was infiltrated by a contrary, rebellious, wish to dethrone his kingly ambition. Although the Lampton side of the family was descended from nobility, Sam preferred to align himself with the Clemens line, particularly with Geoffrey Clement, who helped to sentence King Charles to death. Twain partook of his ancestor's regicide without knowing quite why, except for the fact that it felt to him like "a strong and persistent and irradicable instinct." "My instincts have persuaded me," he further confessed, in *The Autobiography*, that "I did help Charles out of his troubles, by ancestral proxy" (16). Having psychically situated himself in an ironic oedipal position, Sam Clemens could now side with his father against his Lampton mother and still claim the victorious status of parricide.[46]

Twain's imagination, it seems, was possessed by a topsy-turvy family romance, leaving him highly conflicted over the issue of taking the place of the father. But it was an ambivalence that he adroitly depicted in his fiction, in which his heroes, like Tom Canty or Hank Morgan, never occupied a titled position without turning around to use that power to expose the fraud and hypocrisy of those born with this noble status. Like Twain's American claimant, or the barkeeper, in *Captain Stormfield's Visit to Heaven*, his heroes wore moral crowns, not golden ones. As the usurped uncle, in *The American Claimant* (1892), says about his bogus usurper, "morally the American *is* the rightful earl of Rossmore; legally he has no more right than his dog."[47]

It is understandable, then, why, in Twain's imagination, the son would have to surrender his noble title in order to become a man. Thus, the Earl's son, in *The American Claimant,* comes to the inevitable conclusion that he must relinquish his noble birthright: "I wish to retire from what to me is a false existence, a false position, and begin my life over again—begin it right—begin it on the level of mere manhood, unassisted by factitious aids, and succeed or fail by pure merit or the want of it" (6). The confusion in Twain's mind was this: how could the son give up his claim to the father's title in order to attain manhood, when his psychological "instinct" was to follow the path of his regicide ancestors and usurp the place of the father.[48]

Thus, Twain's heroes are always motivated by a desire to undermine the power they, themselves, seek to attain. While a part of Twain wished to erect a monarchy so as to have "someone to look up to," another part of him simultaneously believed that the "first gospel of all monarchies should be Rebellion; the second should be Rebellion; and the third and all gospels and the only gospel in any monarchy should be Rebellion . . ."[49] Mark Twain's fictional son's family-romance dilemma could not be better or more concisely expressed than it is by Sellers, in his contradictory pronouncement to Hawkins: "Oh, mourn with me, my friend, mourn for my desolate house; death has smitten my last kinsman, and I am Earl of Rossmore—congratulate me!" (*American Claimant,* 35).

Twain's psychological predicament consisted of a lifetime of repressed grief and unresolved ambivalence in relation to his father; consequently, he was fixated at an adolescent stage of development that was characterized by a desire to rebel against, and at the same time conform to, patriarchal authority. In the chapter that follows, we will see how this conflict becomes a central issue in Huck Finn's problematic initiation journey into manhood. Like Huck, Twain was unable to work through his guilt and grief, which would have allowed him to let go of his perpetual feelings of loss and deprivation. He found a satisfactory solution—though by no means a resolution—to his lingering anxiety through the nostalgic fantasy of returning to an idyllic time in his childhood before any unpleasant experiences of loss and death had occurred.

Mark Twain, of course, spent a large part of his adult life writing about boyhood. Without question, the manifestation of pathological mourning that was the most brilliantly adapted by Twain in his career as a creative artist was his nostalgic yearning for a lost past. Jack Kleiner has suggested that nostalgics may be characterized by their insatiable yearning for lost objects, and by their unwillingness, or inability, to undertake the work of mourning.[50] Studies of these individuals reveal that the aetiological factors behind their nostalgic yearnings have to do, specifically, with a sense of having been denied the mother's love and attention, particularly as this feeling arose from, or was exacerbated by, sibling rivalry, the loss of a sibling thorough death, or some other equally traumatic disturbance in the security and reliability of the mother-child relation. Not only did these factors play an important role in Sam Clemens's early life, but, as the present analysis of his life and fiction has revealed, they also comprised a significant share of his psychological concerns as a young boy.

If his fictions of boyhood are steeped in death, loneliness, and murder, it is because, for Twain, as for the nostalgic, it cannot be otherwise. These stories are not merely fictions of boyhood, but nostalgic recreations of an ideal state of being that has been lost, and therefore, behind every verbal gesture or image of pleasure and joy there lies the absent presence of sadness, grief, and disappointment. Furthermore, just as in the idyllic fantasies of the nostalgic, there is no overt grief in Twain's fiction; the fantasy exists in a world before loss and disappointment have occurred, and only in the present does life seem dead, empty, and lost.

When the Twain-narrator first returns to Hannibal, in the chapter "My Boyhood's Home" of *Life on the Mississippi*, the nostalgic's "unreal" present can be seen to dissolve mysteriously into the nothingness that his life had become following that borderline moment when he realized his boyhood dreams were irremediably lost: "I stepped ashore with the feeling of one who returns out of a dead-and-gone generation. . . . The things about me and before me made me feel like a boy again—convinced me that I was a boy again, and that I had simply been dreaming an unusually long dream" (307–8).

Twain's fictions, in which he told and retold the story of boyhood, are themselves manifestations of nostalgic mourning. On a more obvious level, they represent a mourning for a former state of the self, namely, childhood, and, as is true for all nostalgic fantasies, the past was, for Twain, a golden age, an idealized existence. Every element of which Twain's boyhood fantasies are comprised—even the murders, deaths, and crimes—is untouched by real unhappiness and disappointment. It has been called Twain's "Happy Valley," his "Boy's Paradise"; a place of dreams that in every way resembles man's true state before the fall.[51] But as we know, this nostalgic Paradise is dependent for its very existence on the fact that the "fall" has already occurred. This place of boyhood dreams is, in its every detail, infected with the unconscious feelings of grief, disappointment, and loss, which are liable to intrude at any moment into the nostalgic's precarious illusion of a life untainted by painful emotions.

Perhaps the strangest and most uncanny piece of confessional writing Twain ever produced is the previously mentioned story, "My Platonic Sweetheart" (1912), in which he tells of a recurring dream he has had. In the dream, he is suddenly joined by a girl of fifteen. She is likely to have any color hair, and any one of several names in any one dream, but invariably she will be bonded to him in her affections in an almost indescribably beautiful and satisfying way. It is not the attachment of brother to sister, Twain tries to explain, it is not "the love of sweethearts, for there is no fire in it"; but is somehow closer than these, "more clinging, more endearing, more reverent" (289). Judging by the nature of Twain's description of his relationship with this girl, it is in several important ways a resurrection of the child's feeling of blissful symbiosis with the nurturing, pregenital mother: "It was somewhere between the two, and was finer than either, and more exquisite, more profoundly contenting. We often experience this strange and gracious thing in our dreams-loves; and we remember it as a feature of our childhood-loves, too" (289). This dream, however, is half "golden fantasy" and half nightmare, for, inevitably, after a long time of heavenly "oneness" with this girl, she will suddenly and unexpectedly disappear. In each dream his sweetheart "dies" or disappears in some traumatic and unexpected way, and he awakens in a state of overwhelming grief and unsatisfied yearning for his lost love: "Then I woke, in deep distress over my loss, and was in my bed . . ." (290).

There is an uncanny resemblance between Twain's description of his feelings of euphoria in the first part of his "platonic sweetheart" dreams, and that of his experience of being "within a shade of death's door" when he was "dying that time" of the measles, and claimed that he "no longer felt any interest in anything, but, on the contrary, felt a total absence of interest—which was most placid and tranquil and sweet and delightful and enchanting" (*The Autobiography*, 76). In his essay, "The 'Uncanny,' " Freud concludes that an uncanny experience occurs "when infantile complexes which have been repressed are once more revived by some impression." At one point Freud makes a specific connection between nostalgia and the mother's body, or genitals:

This *unheimlich* place, however, is the entrance to the former *Heim* [home] of all human beings, to the place where each one of us lived once upon a time and in the beginning. There is a joking saying that "Love is home-sickness"; and whenever a man dreams of a place or a country and says to himself, while he is still dreaming: "this place is familiar to me, I've been here before", we may interpret the place as being his mother's genitals or her body.[52]

Madelon Sprengnether further elaborates the correlation among the death-drive, the return of the repressed, and the preoedipal mother in Freud's hypothesis of the uncanny, in *The Spectral Mother*, where she writes: "One thread of speculation that runs through 'The "Uncanny" ' relates it not only to this perception but also to Freud's later elaboration of the concepts of repetition compulsion and the death instinct—all of which posit the mother as a focus of longing."[53] Otto Fenichel believes that nostalgic fantasies repeat a wish to return to the fantasy symbiotic mother; N. Fodor goes even further in suggesting that it expresses the desire to return to a prenatal state in the mother's womb. Fodor compares it to a state of timelessness, liberation from concern, and a feeling of flotation as in water.[54] One has only to turn to Susan Harris's study, *Mark Twain's Escape from Time*, to verify the presence of these infantile images and impulses in Twain's fiction. In this critical work, Harris extensively catalogues the varied images of timelessness, unity, water, spiritual freedom, and transcendence of space that occur throughout Twain's works.[55]

Appropriately, in one of Twain's "platonic sweetheart" dreams, he explains: "We were living in a simple and natural and beautiful world where everything that happened was natural and right, and was not perplexed with the unexpected or with any forms of surprise, and so there was no occasion for explanations and no interest attaching to such things" (294). It is difficult to mistake in these descriptions the fusion in Twain's mind between the annihilation of the ego that, in his view, death brings, and the same pleasurable obliteration of care in his regressive fantasy of union with the symbiotic mother. Twain's description of death hints at the belief that, in death, one is able to reunite with the original object of desire—the lost, fantasy symbiotic mother who magically provided for every need and soothed all grief. In *The Autobiography of Mark Twain*, Twain compared death to that state one "lives" in before being born into this care-worn life. In both there is a: "peace, a serenity, an absence of care, grief, perplexity; and the presence of a deep content and unbroken satisfaction . . . which I look back upon with a tender longing and with a grateful desire to resume, when the opportunity comes" (178).

Twain was always impressed by the expression on the face of a person who had died, which always seemed to him so peaceful and full of youth. Implicit in Twain's creative impulse, no matter what the subject matter, is this nostalgic mother/death reunion fantasy. Twain rediscovered this mirror of the lost mother's face in his wife Livy. Livy was, as Twain described her in his autobiographical story, "Which Was the Dream?" as both a girl and a woman, which allowed him to be an adult without having to relinquish his happier hold on himself as "Youth" (Livy's pet name for her husband).[56] In *The Autobiography,* he described his relationship with Livy in symbiotic terms, explaining that it was "a strange combination which wrought into one indeed, so to speak, by marriage—her disposition and mine" (185). As the narrator of this dream-story says about his relationship to his wife: "We two were one. For all functions but the physical, one heart would have answered for us both" ("Which Was the Dream?" 38). The Twain/narrator's life with his wife was in every way a reenactment of Twain's very own "platonic sweetheart" dream, including the ever-impending sense of doom: "Every morning one or the other of us laughed and said, 'Another day gone, and it isn't a dream yet!' For we had the same thought, and it was a natural one: that the night might rob us, some time or another, and we should wake bereaved" ("Which Was the Dream?" 40). Twain never finished writing this dream story, perhaps because he was unable to reenact consciously its fated conclusion, but in his real dreamlife his dream-self never escaped without experiencing the final tragedy of loss.

The unified structure of Twain's nostalgic "platonic sweetheart" dream is such that the blissful union never occurred without the final and inevitable disappointment, loss, and grief. In Twain's fictions of boyhood, as in his "platonic sweetheart" dreams, there was no comedy without the tragedy, and no Boy's Paradise without the fall and its implicit grief and disappointment. It is, therefore, understandable why Twain believed that to be the editor of a humorous magazine might be the "saddest of all occupations" (*The Autobiography,* 266). It would create an emotional imbalance and deny the unconsciously grieving half of himself. "If I should undertake it," he wrote, "I should have to add to it the occupation of undertaker, to relieve it in some degree of its cheerfulness" (266).

One might also say about Twain's "platonic sweetheart" dreams that the grief he inevitably experienced at their conclusion was *trying* to wake up the dreamer, and that the purpose of these dreams in their entirety was to accomplish this end. In writing his nostalgic, fantasy fictions of boyhood, Twain was attempting, as De Voto believes, "to hold his grief at arm's length."[57] But, in this dream, Twain was perhaps at the same time attempting both to deny *and* to acknowledge—and thereby work through—his life's losses, beginning, we might assume, with his very first experience of loss and frustration with the archaic, nurturing mother. Nostalgia, in fact, has been called by some "mother-mourning," and while Twain's impulse toward fiction-making might appear on the surface to have been inspired by a nostalgic yearning for childhood, its symbolic prototype, if not its actual origin, lay in the tranquil state of infantile symbiosis.

The lesson imparted by Twain's recurring "platonic sweetheart" dreams, it might be conjectured, is not only, as might first be thought, that all joys are destined to disintegrate (although this is certainly an implicit moral of his dream-stories), but also that things change. In many ways, Twain's dreams in the story "My Platonic Sweetheart" could not have been more obvious in their message. During one of the dreams, the young girl tries to point out to Twain's dream-self the inevitability of the transience of all things. She gives him a kitten, which instantly, in front of his eyes, becomes a tarantula, which, in turn, becomes a star-fish. As he remembers, she even explains to him that "it was not worth while to try to keep things; there was no stability about them. I suggested rocks; but she said a rock was like the rest; it wouldn't stay" (298). But if it could not stay, that is not to say it could not be made to come back in fantasy—or in fiction.

Twain's career as a fiction writer and storyteller exemplified, in Winnicott's words, "how the sense of loss itself can become a way of integrating one's self-experience."[58] Twain's fictions about boyhood represented his life-saving efforts to recapture a time before the fall—before loss, death, and grief. His nostalgic fantasies were a death-defying attempt to re-live the youthful past, and replace grief with a fictional gesture of sweeping denial. Whatever actual losses Twain may have suffered in his early life, his inability to grieve at the time, which resulted in a lifetime of distorted manifestations of un-worked through grief, became an integral part of his core personality, and hence, of his creative impulse.

Wright Morris believes that, in writing, Mark Twain was tightly bound in the "grip of passion for what has escaped him," and that these emotions surrounding his experience of loss and disappointment are what compelled Twain to process "memory into art."[59] Twain's *Life on the Mississippi* (1883) has been described as a monument of grief and mourning to the "death" of his childish romantic illusions about the river, which were tragically deposed when he became a riverboat pilot.[60] The tedious, repetitive lessons, and the pragmatic, empirical observations of the river that he was daily forced to make as a pilot, drained his idyllic illusions of the river's magic charm, until finally, "the romance and the beauty were all gone from the river" (*Life on the Mississippi*, 63). Wright Morris believes that by ruminating on the river, by "brooding on the very experience that deprived him of his early dew-dappled enchantment, Twain was able to regain the Paradise that he had given up for lost" (275).

In accomplishing this, however, Twain locked himself into that "stifling" place where grief cannot reach, where mourning is held in abeyance, and death infects everything that he touched like a King Midas of the nightmare world. As psychoanalysis tells us, without the ability to mourn, change cannot be accepted; the result is entrapment within a dead and stale nostalgic dream, just as Tom Sawyer, in moments of insight into his own grief, finds the air "dead," "stifling," and "suffocating" (*Tom Sawyer*, 81, 87). Freud, for the most part, spoke of mourning as a process that "comes to a spontaneous end" when the lost object is once and for all renounced, and the libido is "once more free . . . to replace the lost objects by fresh ones equally or still more precious."[61] In the same essay, Freud uses the example of a flower in bloom that is doomed to die, to illustrate his theory of "transience," by which an object becomes more valuable and pleasurable for the very reason that it is destined to be lost. The nostalgic, however, who is unable to mourn, is fated to yearn indefinitely for that one lost flower to which he had become attached.

For Mark Twain, Huckleberry Finn and Tom Sawyer *cannot* grow up. They are part of Twain's nostalgic world of lost objects that evolved out of the energy of repressed grief and denied disappointment. It makes little difference whether Twain envisioned Tom Sawyer grown up as a lying judge or a crooked politician; to step out of the magic mirror of

Twain's nostalgic Boy's Paradise is instantaneously to become infected with the reality of time and change, and hence with the sadness of grief and disappointment. For the nostalgic, the past and present cannot mingle; there is no fathomable way to bridge the gap, short of going back to the moment of loss, acknowledging one's repressed grief, and working through the full process of mourning, which Twain was clearly either unable, or unwilling, to do.

Huckleberry Finn, like Tom Sawyer, is also trapped inside Twain's nostalgic mirror, but of all Twain's characters he is willing to look through it to the tragic, terrifying, and grief-filled world on the outside. Huck is drawn to the edge of Twain's boyhood Paradise again and again. He senses the grief that is just on the other side, and he even weeps a few tears as if expecting the sorrow to follow, but he can never quite cross over into the world of mature, and consciously examined, human emotions. Like Twain himself, Huck is deeply ambivalent about whether he chooses to conform to patriarchal society (and in doing so claim for himself a masculine identity), or rebel against the hypocrisy of adult civilization. Huck is also the narrator of an allegedly entertaining and humorous story of childhood adventure, which, as we have seen in the previous chapter, makes it difficult, if not impossible, for him to bring to the surface of his narrative the terror, hostility, and grief that he is experiencing. Huck is a true American orphan-hero who has cut himself off from his past—from both mother and father; and while, on the one hand, Huck is jubilant about his rebellious freedom, on the other hand he is beset by a profound loneliness and feelings of emotional isolation and privation. Because he has defiantly rejected his parents, Huck is forced to repress his grief over the loss of them, over the loss of emotional connectedness, and over his own incapacity to establish lasting intimate and loving relationships. In this respect, Huck is in sympathy with Melville's Ishmael, and like the conflicted narrator of Melville's novel, Huck is trapped in a rapprochement crisis in which he continually alternates between clinging and distancing behavior, particularly in relation to the lost good mother, who is represented in Twain's novel by the character of Jim. Unfortunately, Twain, like Melville, was unable to resolve this crisis in his young hero's life, and leaves him, at the end of his adventures, suspended between refuge and flight, dependency and independence, maturity and immaturity.

4. Huckleberry Finn's Anti-Oedipus Complex: Father-Loss and Mother-Hunger in the Great American Novel

Peter: "I'm youth, I'm joy, I'm a little bird that has broken out of the egg."
Wendy: "Ran away, why?"
Peter: "Because I heard Father and Mother talking of what I was to be when I became a man. I want always to be a little boy and have fun."

—J. M. Barrie, *Peter Pan*

As with every important loss we need to mourn—we need to mourn our childhood's end—before we can be emotionally free to commit to love and work in the human community. . . . Mourning for our lost childhood is another—a central task—of adolescence. There are various ways to evade or accomplish that task.

—Judith Viorst, *Necessary Losses*

In all of American literature there is perhaps no adolescent male protagonist who is more endearing and more representative of the American orphan-hero than Mark Twain's Huckleberry Finn. Like Melville's Pierre, Huck seeks to free himself from parental bondage, and yet, once this adolescent rebellion is undertaken, he suffers deeply from an almost unbearable loneliness and isolation. However, whereas Pierre copes with his grief from loss by philosophizing about it and identifying with such heroic sufferers as Hamlet and Dante, Huck lacks the intellectual resources that might allow him to cope with his emotional pain. As T. S. Eliot observed, of all the "permanent symbolic figures of fiction" from Ulysses to Hamlet, Huckleberry Finn is the most alone: "there is no more solitary character in fiction."[1] As the voice of Mark Twain, however, Huck's task as narrator is to be humorous and entertaining; he is therefore, during moments of deepest distress, apt to censor his feelings, cut them off short, or make light of them in one way or another. Nevertheless, Huck's emotional neediness is readily apparent in his dependency on Jim and his longing for the comradeship of Tom Sawyer, just as Pierre clings first to Isabel and then to Lucy for strength, and emotional sustenance. In many ways Huck may be compared to the mythical figure of Oedipus, albeit with the significant difference that Oedipus was separated from his parents by fate, while Huck, lacking a real mother from the start, defiantly rejects both his surrogate mothers and his biological father. Furthermore, whereas Oedipus, as viewed by Freud, represents the completion of the initiation into adulthood by taking the place of the father, Huck rejects both patriarchal civilization and the idea of the nuclear family. He is a perpetual adolescent whose compulsion to wander represents an act of mourning for the lost parents for whom he refuses to grieve. Like Ishmael, lacking any permanent or reliable source of emotional support, Huck lives perpetually on the edge of self-annihilation and emotional suicide. As long as he continues to search and wander, Huck can keep the conscious awareness of the grief that motivates his search at arm's length. Nevertheless, death, loneliness, and grief will follow him wherever he goes, and infect his precarious paradise of freedom, just as they infected the landscape of Twain's boyhood adventures.

Unlike Oedipus, who is guilty of parricide, Huck has merely run away from his parents: a symbolic act of parricide for which Huck refuses to take responsibility. He is in flight from his own guilt and aggression, but, like his grief, his repressed murderous impulses return again and again. However, they return in displaced form, and it seems that the violence of death, murder, and killing confronts him everywhere he goes. Hence, while Huck's adolescent journey is dominated by the elements appropriate to the classical oedipal drama and masculine initiation—murder, death, killing, funerals, and mourning—unlike Oedipus, Huck fails to accept conscious emotional responsibility for his own symbolic murders, or for those murders he sees acted out around him. Throughout the novel he speaks of loneliness, mournfulness, and tears, yet like Ishmael, and so many of Hemingway's male protagonists, such as Nick Adams and Frederic Henry, Huck's voice is devoid of the emotional impact these words represent. There is something wholly unconscious and mute about the emotional core of his experience that appears to be integrally bound up with the nostalgic authorial impulse that controls him. In his retreat from conscious awareness of his own aggressive impulses, from patriarchal identification, and from language itself, and in his refusal (or inability) to confront his oedipal conflicts and experience grief and mourning over his lost and disappointing parental objects, Huck embodies the archetype of the perpetual adolescent in America.

Huck's motherless and fatherless condition deprives him of an oedipal family situation through which he might otherwise act out his initiation drama. His loneliness and fear of abandonment—which he experiences externally, in his anxiety about ghosts and the afterlife—are indicative of pathological mourning and suggest his ongoing, unresolved feelings of ambivalence toward his parent objects. As is symptomatic of this denial, Huck feels compelled to flee from the controlling and smothering "bad" mother, and to escape from his own feared identification with the dangerous, oedipal father. Although, ostensibly, he is fleeing from his parents, his compulsion for wandering or escape to adventure represents an unconscious search for the "good," or ideal, lost parents. Despite Huck's numerous attempts to find an ideal, heroic father and to establish a lasting bond with the "good mother" (who, as we will see, is played by Jim in the novel), he arrives at the end of his adventures in the same psychic situation as he began them: alone and in a state of loss, pursued eternally by the return of his repressed grief.

Because Huck seems only to wish to extend indefinitely his journey through boyhood, he neither attains, nor seems desirous of attaining, his manhood. Here, it is worth mentioning that one of the most decisive functions of the male initiation ceremony, as sociologists have determined, is that it "insures conformity by involving the candidate in an intense co-operation with men in the symbolic process."[2] In order for Huck, as the archetypal adolescent boy, "to pass from the childhood phase of female dominance into the second phase of male dominance and control the boy must experience a psychological, symbolic rebirth into the world of men, severing all his attachments to the mother."[3] Huckleberry Finn, however, is under the control of a nostalgic authorial voice whose predominant impulse is to long for the lost childhood that Huck represents. Twain also imagined Huck's character in such a way that his predominant psychological concern is with non-conformity and a refusal to "co-operate with men in the symbolic process." His regressive urge to return repeatedly to the comforting maternal company of Jim and the river hopelessly conflicts with his need to establish identification with a patriarchal and symbolic masculine world. He cannot engage in masculine self-interpretation unless he acknowledges the greater truthfulness and genuine morality of patriarchal, linguistic concepts, and this Twain apparently refused to allow him to do—not only because the "real" world outside the raft is at bottom false, cruel, divisive, and emotionally unsatisfying, but also because the regressive, nostalgic impulse which pervades Huck's, and perhaps Twain's, very being drives him continually into the "back country"[4] of inarticulate maternal harmony, feminine feelings, and ultimately, silence.

It will be discovered, however, that while "regression" technically implies a return to infantile dependency, it was also the only means that Twain could conceive of that allows Huck to escape from the falsity and hypocrisy of masculine civilization and to fulfill his overriding impulses toward a morality based on relational and interpersonal experience—a moral incentive that is judged, within the frame of patriarchal culture, to be gendered female. Only by rejecting a masculine identity can Huck perceive the flaws of civilized, masculine culture—the most notable of which, in the novel, is slavery—and discern the greater wisdom of a morality based on "feminine" feelings. Gestalt psychology refers to regression as a "destructuring" of socialized behavior and ego identity, and it is precisely the destructuring or deconstructive powers which Twain assigned to Huck that permit his protagonist to criticize the fundamental, corrupt moral standards of patriarchal civilization.[5]

When we first encounter Huck, in Chapter I, he is described by the Widow as "a poor lost lamb" (2), and he has what Twain described, in his introduction to "The Raftsmen Passage," as a "persecuting father" who is temporarily absent from his life, and an all too present "persecuting good widow" as a surrogate mother.[6] His maternal situation is divided, as Jim psychically speculates from the "magic" hair ball: "Dey's two gals flyin' 'bout you in yo' life. One uv 'em's light en t'other one is dark" (22).[7] While Miss Watson is continually badgering and scolding Huck, the Widow is always intervening on his behalf with her kindness and pity. Yet what Huck feels from both of them most of the time is "persecution." Miss Watson's continual "pecking" at Huck is "tiresome and lonesome," "so lonesome" in fact, that in Huck's words, "I most wished I was dead" (4). Despite their good intentions, the Widow Douglas and Miss Watson are smothering and, hence, disappointing to Huck as replacement mothers. Their allegiance to religious ethics and strict codes of behavior situate them within the restricting social boundaries of patriarchal civilization. And although little mention is made of Huck's biological mother, one may surmise that her dying was perceived as a form of abandonment or rejection, about which Huck could be expected to feel a certain amount of guilt and resentment. Overall, Huck's experiences with the maternal figures that he has known have been fraught with tyranny and disappointment, and tainted by a sense of abandonment and loss. However, it is possible that the "light" good mother of whom Jim speaks is the kind and nurturing "good" mother whom Huck lost in infancy, and who now presumably exists only in Huck's imagination.

In Chapter II it becomes apparent, as well, that Huck, for the most part, "hasn't got a father," since, as Tom Sawyer explains, "you can't never find him" and "he hain't been seen in these parts for a year or more" (10). He is believed to have drowned, or "so people said" (14). Huck, alone, suspects that the body found floating on its back "warn't pap but a woman dressed up in a man's clothes," and this, he admits, made him extremely "uncomfortable." The father-son conflict that Twain imagined between Huck and Pap is largely oedipal in nature, centering on Pap's obsessive anger at his son's attempt to surpass him morally, socially, and financially. By rights of patrimony Huck should be unswervingly "low-down and ornery," as his father is.[8] Huck, however, longs to escape his patrimony entirely. Nor, in fact, does he want to be reformed by the Widow and conform to her idea of how a civilized boy should behave. Neither Pap nor Miss Watson serves as "good enough" parents for Huck, and although he will alternately settle in comfortably to his life with both of these figures, his overall adolescent impulse is to escape from the oppressive and stifling identities he assumes when he is with them—to get "so far away that the old man nor the widow couldn't ever find me any more" (32).

Not only did Huck apparently not mourn his father's "death," but in his statement that he "didn't want to see him no more" (14), Huck, in effect, is confessing that he wished his father was indeed dead. However, although he admits no sadness over his father's death or disappearance, his morbid, supernatural thoughts attest to his deeply-felt sense of loneliness and desertion.[9] Sitting by the window in the Widow Douglas's house, Huck tries "to think of something cheerful, but it wern't no use" (4). His thoughts gravitate to eerie reflections on death and fantasies of wandering spirits:

The stars were shining, and the leaves rustled in the woods ever so mournful; and I heard an owl, away off, who-whooping about somebody that was dead, and a whippowill and a dog crying about somebody that was going to die; and the wind was trying to whisper something to me and I couldn't make out what it was, and so it made the cold shivers run over me. Then away out in the woods I heard that kind of a sound that a ghost makes when it wants to tell about something that's on its mind and can't make itself understood, and so can't rest easy in its grave and has to go about that way every night grieving. (4)

Huck's fear of ghosts and spirits conceivably may represent his own repressed, projected aggressive wishes toward both his mother and his father. This fear of supernatural visitations is a variant symptom of pathological mourning, which impairs Huck's ability to mourn over his losses and to accept that his parents are really gone. Such projective fantasies also suggest that Huck has failed to establish internal good objects and lacks the object constancy that would enable him to hold on to a secure sense of reality.[10] Instead, Huck's reality is defined by fear and superstition. In particular, his fantasy world is a predominantly dangerous place, infected by oedipal anxieties concerning the destructive, castrating father.

As it is, Huck's "unreal" hallucinatory fantasies seem more "real" to him than objective reality. His world is peopled with lost objects and colored by anxious expectations of their return. It is likely, therefore, that the ghost that "can't rest easy in its grave" and who comes back to haunt Huck is his father's "ghost." His ominous sense of his father's impending return turns out to be well founded, as Pap appears the very next night in Huck's room. Huck's emphasis on the colorless, "fish-belly" whiteness of his father's face and hands, which, as he says, was enough "to make a body's flesh crawl" (23), is a reminder that Huck's hallucinatory fantasies are predominant in his mind and that he is still not certain whether his father has returned alive or dead.

That Huck is distraught and troubled over his isolation as an orphan who has been left abandoned in the world is revealed as early as the first page of the novel, when the Widow Douglas chooses to tell Huck the story of "Moses and the Bulrushers," which the boy seems "in a sweat to find out all about" (2). Like Huck, Moses represents the archetypal orphan whose story, Huck might well expect, could perhaps tell him something about his own "motherless and fatherless" condition. Even more importantly, Moses, as a prototypical figure in the myth of the birth of the hero, epitomizes the transition from the mother-cult of ancient Egypt to the father-cult of monotheistic religion.[11] He also manifests the adolescent's separation-individuation struggle through which a boy must sever his dependency ties to the mother and establish identification with a patriarchal, masculine world.

Perhaps the best case that can be made in favor of the assumption that Huck has never established good parental objects in his psychic life, and consequently, is compelled to search for them in the external world, is his inability to be alone with himself. "I did wish I had some company" (4), he says to himself when he is scared and alone in his room, and later that night, when Tom insists on playing tricks on Jim, Huck is alone for only a few moments before he is again overcome with loneliness. For Huck, to be so lonesome that he "wished" he "were dead" (4) suggests that he is so dependent upon external verification of love, basic trust, and object constancy that he experiences the loss of these psychic functions as nothing less than total self-annihilation.

Huck's predicament in relation to his absent and disappointing parents is perhaps best described by the fact that, unlike his pals, Huck has no "family or somebody to kill" in the fantasy initiation game that they play together (10). Some time later in the novel, when debating whether to turn Jim over to the authorities, Huck reveals his awareness of the early deprivation he has suffered in relation to his absent and disappointing parents by confessing that "it warn't no use for me to try to learn to do right; a body that don't get *started* right when he's little ain't got no show—" (127). Ironically, it is not the oedipal images of violent, bloody murder that drive Huck to the verge of tears, but the thought that he would be refused membership in the secret band of boys because he is an orphan. Furthermore, for a boy who has an instinctive aversion to "learning" (24) and formal education, Huck, significantly, admits to having "read considerable" in the book "Pilgrim's Progress," which, he says, is "about a man that left his family it didn't say why" (137). In the course of the novel, Twain allows Huck to re-enact the murder of his disappointing parents, both through the stories that Huck tells about himself, and through his witnessing the deaths and murders that afflict the families that he encounters during his journey. With every murderous act, however, Huck re-experiences the return of his repressed grief and mute sense of mourning for his own parent figures.

After presenting, in the first few chapters, Huck's grief-filled relationship with Pap and his various mother figures, Twain begins the narrative of Huck's flight to freedom, starting with his escape from Pap's cabin— by killing a pig and leaving the spilled blood as evidence of his own "murder" by intruders. While some critics have interpreted Huck's killing of the pig as a symbolic act of parricide, others have suggested that the slaying of the pig represents Huck's own death wishes.[12] These views are not contradictory, however, in view of the fact that, in Twain's mind, suicide and parricide are one and the same. For Huck to kill off his civilized identity as the ward of the Widow and Miss Watson—an identity that is fundamentally a "fiction of law and custom"—is a symbolic form of suicide. For Twain this repudiation of one's socially defined identity is an act of sanity by which the insane or spurious world is left behind.[13]

In Pap's cabin Huck is continually under the threat of death at the hands of his father. Twain makes light of what is actually a terrifying experience for Huck by describing Pap's stumbling, drunken behavior, in which Pap believes that Huck is the "Angel of death," and hollers about how snakes are, as he screeches, "biting me on the neck!" (35). Huck's first few hours of freedom are filled with fear and loneliness. It was "dead quiet" (42) in the middle of the night, and only moments after Huck feels "pretty well satisfied," smoking by his campfire, he begins, once again, to get "sort of lonesome" (48). The only way to "get over it," he says, is to keep moving, and so he "went exploring around down through the island" (48). Such inertia is deadly and stifling for Huck, and in moments of fear he finds himself in danger of losing his breath to the point of annihilation and suffocation. He feels as though "a person had cut one of my breaths in two and I only got half," or as though "somebody had me by the neck" (50). Although Huck is physically free, his anxiety in relation to his father and the smothering Miss Watson pursues him in his imagination. Understandably, he "was ever so glad to see Jim" on Jackson's Island, and as soon as he does he "warn't lonesome" any more (51).

Chapter IX, "The House of Death Floats By," marks Huck's first episode with Jim. Here, Huck stumbles across the corpse of his father, who has been shot in the back, but the identity of the dead man is withheld from Huck by a kindly Jim, who evades Huck's persistent questioning, and exercises his maternal solicitude with the words: "Never you mind, honey, never you mind" (63). It is merely a detail, however, that Huck's father is now really dead. Having run away and avoided a real confrontation and a working-through of his hostility in relation to his father, Huck continues to feel haunted by him. As Jim says, "a man that warn't buried was more likely to go a-ha'nting around than one that was planted and comfortable" (63). In the very next chapter Twain devised a more obvious symbolic suicide/parricide for Huck, through the narrative of the woman who tells him the story of his own death at the hands of his father.

In terms of Huck's archetypal initiation journey, having symbolically killed off both his "civilized" identity through "suicide," and his "oedipal" father through "parricide," Huck would be free to unite with his libidinal, or oedipal, "wife" figure. Twain, however, did not impel Huck toward this next, traditionally Freudian, step in the boy's initiation into maturity, but instead, moved him closer toward what might at first appear to be infantile regression. Huck does not confront the oedipal conflict that patriarchal psychoanalysis would claim is so critical to his progress toward maturity. Instead, he escapes from it toward a prolongation of what Western culture might call his childish dependency, but what Twain would certainly describe as his morally superior, emotionally honest, childhood experience.

Huck's apparent regression to the pleasurable, exclusive mother/child dyad with Jim is a psychoanalytically plausible development of Twain's, and Huck's, nostalgic fantasy, which, according to Phyllis Greenacre, is motivated by "the hankering of growing children for a return to the real or fancied" time when "the child shared the special privileges and unconditional love without special efforts being demanded."[14] Huck's flight with Jim also fulfills the boy's suicidal longing to be rescued by the all-providing mother—the prototype of the infant's rescuer from feelings of disappointment and abandonment.[15]

Jim has been viewed by many of Twain's critics as Huck's "true" or "spiritual" father; others, most notably Leslie Fiedler, have argued in favor of a libidinal interpretation of Huck and Jim's relationship by describing it as a homoerotic "Sacred Marriage of Males."[16] In supporting their claims, however, Twain's critics have intuitively emphasized the preoedipal aspects of Huck's relationship with Jim, and inadvertently cast Jim in the role of Huck's imagined "good" mother imago.[17] They claim that the bond between them is "inscrutable," like the river itself, that it resembles a divine, timeless, boy's paradise, an Eden before corruption and the fall, and that Huck and Jim lovingly take care of one another—all of which suggest the blissful experience of pre-verbal oneness with the fantasized symbiotic mother.[18] The endearments of "honey" and "chile" that Jim uses when addressing Huck further reinforce the unspoken assumption that mother-Jim will go to any lengths to care for, nurture, and protect the loveless boy.

Significant evidence for the interpretation of Jim as the preoedipal mother/rescuer and comforter can be found in the subtext of the critical thoughts of Leslie Fiedler. The descriptive phrasing that Fiedler uses evokes many more preoedipal, maternal images than erotic ones. In describing Jim, Fiedler speaks of our "dark-skinned beloved," who "will take us in and forgive us," "fold us in his arms," and "comfort us." Fiedler describes the relationship between Huck and Jim as "physical" yet "somehow ultimately innocent," and adds: "There lies between the lovers no naked sword but a childlike ignorance, as if the possibility of a fall to the carnal had not yet been discovered" (416). What Fiedler observes here is the preoedipal "love" relationship between a mother and her child that indeed existed before "the possibility of a fall to the carnal." As is true for the fantasy symbiotic mother, Jim is someone who can respond directly to Huck's unconscious as if it were his own. Like the mother/infant dyad, they share a common ego, and, as Jim confirms, if "one un us got los' en 'tother one was jis' as good as los' " (103).

Supporting the interpretation of Jim as a pregenital mother, rather than an ideal "father," or an oedipal wife, is Daniel Hoffman's critical observation that, "Jim's powers have their mysterious source in the river" ("Black Magic," 327). Huck and Jim's finest moments are the days and nights when the two are left alone, lying naked on the raft, in sublime, symbiotic peace. These are the times when, in Huck's words, "we'd have that whole river all to ourselves for the longest time" (158). Here, Huck and Jim know no "doing," but only "being." In these seemingly paradoxical " 'moments of eternity' . . . within concrete time," as Susan Harris describes them, time does not exist, and, as Huck observes, the days "swam by, they slid along so quiet and smooth and lovely" (156).[19] The maternal comfort that Huck derives from Jim, who so satisfactorily mirrors Huck's emotionally honest and spontaneous self, merges indistinguishably in his experience with the comforting maternal serenity of the river itself.

In *A Tramp Abroad*, Twain provided a description of the sensation of floating on a raft that unmistakably evokes the experience of oceanic bliss with the fantasy symbiotic mother:

The motion of the raft . . . is gentle, and gliding, and smooth, and noiseless; it calms down all feverish activities, it soothes to sleep all nervous hurry and impatience; under its restful influence all the troubles and vexations and sorrows that harass the mind vanish away, and existence becomes a dream, a charm, a deep and tranquil ecstasy.[20]

Twain infused Huck with an undefiled, infantile sense of trust and familiarity with the nurturing mother that he himself seems to have felt while rafting on the river. Indeed, he used precisely this analogy in his sketch, "Is Shakespeare Dead?": "I knew every inch of the Mississippi—thirteen hundred miles—in the dark and in the day—as well as a baby knows the way to its mother's paps day or night."[21] Both Jim and the river thus embody Huck's "symbiotic-like oneness fantasy" in which he is able to regain a fantasized image of a lost perfect state of being, and regressively repair whatever separation anxiety he might have originally experienced with his real parents.[22] It is with Jim and the river that Huck is able to play out his heroic, archetypal struggle to break free from "civilization" and escape into his maternal past.[23]

Fodor's suggestion that nostalgia represents "the desire to return to the mother's womb" explains "why some individuals experience ecstasy when floating in water."[24] Huck's fascination with Jim and the river demonstrates the same predisposition to an archaic identity "from which Paradise myths spring."[25] Life with Jim and the river represents Huck's "paradise regained," and the loss of them each time he goes ashore alone to expose himself to the potential dangers of "civilization" predictably feels to him, as well as to Jim and the reader, like "the Fall."

Huck and Jim's river adventures include an encounter with the wrecked steamboat, the *Walter Scott,* and an evening spent in philosophical discussions about the dubious wisdom of Solomon, until, finally, the raft approaches the town of Cairo, and Huck, who has gone ahead in the canoe, is separated from his companion in the fog. At this point, near the end of Chapter XV, Twain put the Huckleberry Finn manuscript aside (in 1876) and did not return to it in full force for seven years. Bernard De Voto, who conducted a careful study of Twain's notes and manuscripts during this period, has suggested that Twain quit writing because his creative " 'tank ran dry' " and he simply did not know which way the plot of the novel should go at this point.[26] Certainly, it would appear that Twain's indecision about what to do next in the novel is mirrored in the narrative itself, in Huck's frustrated attempts to maneuver his canoe through the fog toward the faint "whoops" coming from Jim on the raft. Huck admits to himself, despairingly, that he "hadn't no more idea which way I was going than a dead man," and the next time Jim's "whoop" is heard: "I see I warn't heading for it, but heading away to the right of it. And the next time, I was heading away to the left of it—and not gaining on it much, either, for I was flying around, this way and that and 'tother . . ." (100).

However, it is difficult to believe, as De Voto implies, that Twain's imagination merely gave out on him at this point. It is more likely that Twain suddenly recognized, perhaps unconsciously, an intrinsic problem in his conception of Huck Finn's initiation journey. Huck's psychological composition as an arrested adolescent precludes him from entering the structured world of adulthood and civilization. Unlike Oedipus, he has no predetermined goal or motive in his adventurous journey. "When one writes a novel about grown people," Twain explained in the conclusion to *The Adventures of Tom Sawyer*, "he knows exactly where to stop—that is, with a marriage; but when he writes of juveniles, he must stop where he best can."[27] If the plots of Twain's fictions about boyhood, especially *Adventures of Huckleberry Finn*, seem to progress randomly through time and across the southern landscape, without thematic purpose or structure, it is because he was deeply ambivalent about guiding his young protagonists toward psychological maturity; consequently, they are prisoners trapped within their boyhood paradises. Huck must keep moving at all times; he must find a way to "put in the time," or else be annihilated by a smothering and engulfing sense of isolation and loneliness.

For Twain's boy heroes, who are lost in the fog of a prolonged childhood, to be in perpetual motion, or to be arrested in motion, are one and the same thing. This state of psychic entrapment within the nostalgic fantasy world of childhood transformed Twain's boyhood paradise into a nightmare world that was infected by death, stifling isolation, and ego annihilation. Huck inadvertently describes his own paradoxical psychic situation, in Chapter XV, when he thinks to himself: "I was floating along, of course, four or five miles an hour; but you don't ever think of that. No, you *feel* like you are laying dead still on the water" (100).

An additional reason why Twain found it so difficult to continue the novel past Chapter XV is that this point marked a disruption in the blissful relationship that he had established between Huck and Jim. In this chapter, Huck plays a disturbing prank on Jim, allowing his friend to think that he has been drowned in the "monstrous big river" during the fog. When Huck lies to Jim about having never left the raft during the fog, he violates the relationship of basic trust that he had established with his mother surrogate. In Jim's words,

When I got all wore out wid work, en wid de callin' for you, en went to sleep, my heart wuz mos' broke bekase you wuz los', en I didn' k'yer no mo' what become er me en de raf'. En when I wake up en fine you back again', all safe en soun', de tears come en I could a got down on my knees en kiss' yo foot I's so thankful. En all you wuz thinkin' 'bout wuz how you could make a fool uv ole Jim wid a lie. Dat truck dah is *trash;* en trash is what people is dat puts dirt on de head er dey fren's en makes 'em ashamed. (105)

After discovering how deeply he had hurt Jim by deceiving him, Huck realizes that feelings—to make Jim "feel that way" (105)—are a more worthwhile determinant of actions than either fun or humor. Huck does not maintain his distance from Jim or try to defend his verbal trickery. He backs down completely and returns with a loving and contrite heart to Jim in the wigwam. Huck's actions, he says, "made me feel so mean I could almost kissed *his* foot to get him to take it back" (105). His inability to detach himself from Jim may at first seem to indicate his own, as well as Twain's, refusal to renounce his regressive, childish dependency on the mother. But in this regression Twain enacted an important gesture of affirmation in favor of feminine feelings, and against the patriarchal institution of slavery.

Furthermore, by vowing that he will never again "lie" or play "mean tricks" (105) on Jim, Huck effectively cuts himself off from the humorous voice which Twain's narrative thrives on. With this in mind, it becomes even more understandable why Twain felt unable to proceed with his story. According to Otto Rank, there is no "native language" for "feminine," or preoedipal feelings (243); and as Richard Poirier perceptively claims, there is "no publicly accredited vocabulary which allows Huck to reveal his inner self to others."[28] Twain's difficulty in continuing the novel beyond Chapter XV can thus be explained in terms of the collapsed humorous narrative in which Huck vows never to deceive or play jokes on Jim again. With this promised cessation of Huck's deceptive, humorous voice in favor of an emotionally direct narrative, Twain's humorous mode of "mendacity based" storytelling was temporarily disabled. For Twain, the undisguised communication of "truth," and his type of mendacity based humor, were fundamentally incompatible. To begin writing his humorous fiction once again, Twain would have to surrender Huck's inexpressible, emotional truth to the "lying" or deceptive tactics of humor that, earlier in the novel, were embodied in his young hero's narrative voice. While it is impossible to say exactly how Twain's mendacity-based humorous voice became reinvigorated, it is evident that by July of 1883, as he wrote to his family, to complete the manuscript of "Huckleberry Finn's autobiography" was "no more trouble to me to write than it is to lie."[29] Apparently Twain was as unwilling to take responsibility for Jim's freedom and for Huck's moral honesty as he was reluctant to accept the full implications of "freeing" his own emotionally repressed self from enslavement to the tempering, protective manner of disguising his feelings behind the humorous method of storytelling.

With his adoption by the Grangerford family in Chapter XVII, Huck's initiation drama enters a phase in which he repeatedly attempts to establish identification with an ideal masculine figure. From this moment through Chapter XXXII, the reader is presented with a series of back and forth movements, from civilization to the raft, and back again. Huck takes on and then sheds numerous identities in these episodes, never quite sure whether he prefers to lead the life of an impostor and belong to civilization, or remain true to himself and live a life of moral honesty with Jim. In his ambivalence, Huck claims, during his stay at the Grangerfords', that "nothing couldn't be better" (141), but only a short time later he finds himself agreeing with Jim that "there warn't no home like a raft, after all. Other places do seem so cramped up and smothery, but a raft don't. You feel mighty free and easy and comfortable on a raft" (155).

The desire for identification with the ideal father in these episodes battles, in Huck's mind, with his alternative longing to return to a strife-free state of narcissistic omnipotence with his ideal nurturing mother, Jim. What Huck seems to be involved in, throughout these chapters, is a classical family-romance struggle which, according to Greenacre, is motivated by an ambivalence toward the parents that reflects an unresolved oedipal conflict ("Family Romance," 32). In this contest, the growing child seeks for a masculine ego-ideal through identification with an heroic father figure in the external world. For Huck, Colonel Grangerford, Colonel Sherburn, and the "King" and "Duke," at first appear to be excellent models for a family-romance choice of a father ideal; but Huck discovers that they are all something other than what they first appear to be. Colonel Grangerford was "a gentleman all over," Huck observes, "well-born," and "as kind as he could be—you could feel that, you know, and so you had confidence" (142). But Huck soon loses "confidence" in the Colonel as a protective and admirable father, for, as he later learns, three of the Colonel's sons were brutally murdered as a result of this man's stubbornness and perverted values. Concerning the "King" and the "Duke," Huck says, it "didn't take me long to make up my mind that these liars warn't no kings and dukes at all, but just low-down humbugs and frauds" (165). Colonel Sherburn, who, like Colonel Grangerford, at first appears to possess qualities of fatherly power, leadership, and breeding, is similarly transformed, in front of Huck's eyes, into the cold-blooded murderer of a defenseless and innocent man.

Huck also discovers from his encounters with the Grangerfords, the Wilks, and the "King" and "Duke," that the purpose of language in a patriarchal world is to deceive and control others, particularly those who are helpless, honest, and loving. Colonel Sherburn employs some fancy rhetoric to deter a mob from taking just revenge for his murder of an innocent man; and the function of language, as far as the "King" and the "Duke" are concerned, is to increase the size of their purse. Toward this end they resort to fraud, false advertising, and bogus dramatics. The feud between the Grangerfords and the Shepherdsons, which is perpetuated by a hostility based on name alone, perhaps represents the most perverted use of language that Huck has encountered thus far in his adventures. The lesson which Huck learns from his participation in these family dramas is one that Twain was keenly aware of: language means deception, and deception is hopelessly at odds with the expression of true feelings. So Huck is once again thrust into his original position of adolescent ambivalence, struggling to feel real or true to himself in what he perceives as an unreal, deceitful, and dangerous world.

Huck's experiments with family-romance fantasies, and his forays into the world of masculine identification, have proved disappointing; this is because what the boy who pursues a family-romance fantasy is really "hankering" for in his apparent search for an ideal masculine identity, as Greenacre explains, is a return to a state of infantile narcissistic omnipotence experienced with the all-giving *mother* ("Family Romance," 10). Huck's attempts to find an ideal father end in tragedy and disillusionment, and after each episode he becomes conscious once again of his more profound, nostalgic wish to return to Jim and the river—the only true source that he had found, as Greenacre claimed, for "unconditional love without special effort being demanded." Huck, therefore, does not wait around to be "castrated" by these murderous father figures, but "lights out" for Jim and the raft as quickly as he can manage.

It is significant that Huck, who usually avoids any direct confrontation with his own, as well as others', deep emotions, admits that he "cried a little when I was covering up Buck's face, for he was mighty good to me" (154). Saddened and sickened by the deaths he has witnessed, Huck, as he says, "got away as quick as I could." When, at last, he hears Jim's voice he confesses with relief that "nothing ever sounded so good before" (154). Huck's happiness at his reunion with Jim is matched by Jim's loving, and more expressive, jubilation: "Laws bless you, child, I 'uz right down sho' you's dead agin. . . . Lawsy, I's mighty glad to git you back agin, honey" (154).

Huck is horrified by the hypocrisy, violence, and internal strife of the symbolically based, binary, and hopelessly "feuding," civilized world. By clinging to Jim, however, he retreats from what he perceives to be a corrupt masculine identity to the arms of mother-Jim, a retreat which enables him to avoid the oedipal conflict that confronts him. But once again, this act of repudiation represents a positive step for Huck's, and Twain's, chosen form of selfhood. The individuating child's alternative between masculine identity or maternal attachment, as presented by Freud, is based on the either/or choices available to a boy in a patriarchal culture. According to feminist psychoanalysis, the Oedipus complex can be taken as a symbolic tale about patriarchy in which children are confronted with the opportunity to take over the "law of the father," and as the stage at which the child begins to accept the patriarchal notion of the nuclear family as an organized unit.[30] Huck's aversion to the name-of-the-father, and to the oedipal family unit (no doubt inspired by Twain's own inclinations), prevents him from submitting to these developmental stages of maturity.

Instead, Huck is motivated by the adolescent desire to be true to his inner spontaneous feelings, to exist in a state of *being* rather than *doing*, which is fluid, transcendent of time, and wholly Dionysian in nature. At the same time, he feels the necessity of finding a stable, apollonian, false-self identity through which he can relate to the world—a state of symbolic identity that will enable him, as he so frequently states, to "put in the time" (48). In this state of ambivalence Huck feels endlessly compelled to choose first one identity and then another—regardless of the content of that identity—wishing throughout that he could exist without any of them. He is trying, as Julia Kristeva metaphorically states, to achieve some reconciliation between "flesh and law."[31] Through Huck's involvement with Jim, Twain envisioned, but could not seem to fully commit to, an alternative, phallic/feminine or masculine/maternal adult identity that was morally superior to the phallic/masculine identity that Twain associated with a corrupt and dishonest patriarchal culture.

Huck's two modes of living—the Grangerfords or the raft, the Wilks or Jim—also contain their respective dangers. The bogus world of masculine, adult identification, despite its offer of stability and structure, is restrictive and stagnating. Huck is "lonesome" when playing an identity role in society because he is fundamentally in a state of alienation from his real, emotional self; from Eros, and from his honest, loving, and trustworthy Jim. On the other hand, to retreat to the refuge of self-annihilating oneness with the nurturing, preoedipal mother is also a form of death and suffocating engulfment. Understandably then, while Huck treasures the serenity and bliss of his life alone with Jim and the river, the landscape often appears to him as "solid lonesomeness" (157). In this seemingly timeless world, he is repeatedly confronted with the ever-impending problem of "doing," finding direction, and "putting in the time" (48). Like Melville's Ishmael, who simultaneously values and repudiates both the "slavish shore" *and* the gaping infinite of the "open sea," Huck appears to be fixated in an unresolved rapprochement-phase conflict, in which both freedom and smothering connectedness—lonely isolation and dependency—seem equally suffocating and annihilating.

In his position of ambivalence, Huck is also in a perpetual state of mourning. He is either mourning the loss of mother-love and narcissistic omnipotence with Jim, or the loss of self-identity—the feeling of belonging to the "masculine" community. Huck moves repeatedly from the possession of a fictional identity to the violence of self-murder, and in doing so alternates from mourning the "death" of his socially determined patriarchal identity to mourning his separation from the nurturing mother.[32] The themes of death, separation, and perpetual mourning are thus inescapable in the novel, given Huck's psychic state of oedipal/preoedipal ambivalence. While the predominance of funerals, mourning sermons, violent murder, and death may seem out of place in this boy's idyllic journey, as a tale about a boy's ambivalence over the ongoing, yet frustrated, process of initiation from childhood into the symbolic certainty of adulthood, the repeated motif of loss is both consistent with the unresolved psychological issues in the novel and appropriately unrelenting in its insistent recurrence.

Huck "kills off" his parents numerous times in the course of the novel. He first tells the story that his "father and mother was dead" to the country woman, in Chapter XI, from whom he heard the gossip about the "murder of Huckleberry Finn" in St. Petersburg. He gives a similar account of his "tragic" past to the Grangerfords, but this time he apparently has only a father, who eventually wasted away and died from his "troubles." To the "King" and "Duke," he confesses that his mother "died off" along with the rest of his "folks," leaving him with his four-year-old brother, Ike, and his father, both of whom died soon after under the wheel of a steamboat. Each of these fantasy "oedipal" murders enacts a return of Huck's repressed and unresolved grief and mourning for his own desired, and yet discarded, parent figures.

Chronically missing from Huck's narrative of recurring family-romance "murders," however, are both his anger and his sorrow; for, indeed, these fantasy deaths represent a re-play of his biological family predicament and orphan status. Unlike Sophocles, in his depiction of Oedipus's adolescent initiation, Twain does not allow Huck to experience self-consciously either the aggression or the grief that should necessarily accompany his psychic position. The expression of true grief is entirely absent from the narrative, except perhaps for Twain's periodic burlesques on the lachrymose sentimentality of his fictional mourners. Huck gives a lengthy and detailed explanation of the pictures of black-veiled women in mourning, dead birds, and sorrowful faces drawn by the death-obsessed Grangerford girl who died at age fifteen, and he offers to the reader the complete mourning poem she once wrote for a young "boy by the name of Stephen Dowling Bots that fell down a well and was drownded" (139). Huck humorously notes about the eternally sad and sickeningly sentimental girl: "I reckoned that with her disposition she was having a better time in the graveyard" (138).

Like Twain, who was careful never to remove the buffer of humor that he placed between real and mock grief, Huck keeps himself at a safe emotional distance from the dead girl's paintings and poems. They "was all nice pictures," he admits, "but I didn't somehow seem to take to them, because if ever I was down a little they always give me the fan-tods" (138). Huck's significant curtailment of interest in the deaths, murders, and funerals he witnesses at the Grangerfords and the Wilks serves to contain Twain's humorous narrative safely within the fantasy world of childhood, and protect it from infiltration by the punitive, serious, and somber adult superego. Although Huck admits it made his "heart ache" (234) to see the Wilks girls "getting fooled and lied to" (234), and it "made me down sick to see" them carrying on and crying, his game of deception with the "King" and "Duke," like Twain's deceptive, humorous narrative, prevents him from openly expressing his pain and grief, and hence from receiving comfort from an honest and direct emotional intimacy with the people he seems to care for so deeply. And yet, Huck relates in full Emmeline Grangerford's "Ode to Stephen Dowling Bots, Dec'd," which tells of how the boy died a lonely death without the consolation of having been grieved over by loved ones:

And did young Stephen sicken,
    And did young Stephen die?
And did the sad hearts thicken,
    And did the mourners cry?
No; such was not the fate of
    Young Stephen Dowling Bots; (139)

The reader cannot help but feel a strong sympathy for Huck when he runs past Mary Jane Wilks's bedroom window and his "heart swelled up sudden, like to burst" (258). Huck is compelled to keep moving on, even if it means losing someone who truly cares for him, and whom he, too, loves sincerely. "She *was* the best girl I ever see, and had the most sand" (258), he says to himself about the kindly Mary Jane; and when he parts from her, only to run into the contemptible "King" and "Duke," it is no wonder that Huck concludes, "it was all I could do to keep from crying" (260). Huck's compulsion to wander prevents him from realizing that the object of his search is not only the love that was denied him by his parents, but his own capacity to love. Typically, when Huck returns to the raft and finds Jim gone, his emotions are swiftly sublimated into his compulsion to keep moving: "Then I set down and cried; I couldn't help it. But I couldn't set still long. Pretty soon I went out on the road, trying to think what I better do" (267).

The preacher in the little town church that Huck stumbles upon with the "King" and "Duke" might well be addressing Huck's own burden of guilt and grief in relation to his parents, when he preaches:

"Oh, come to the mourners' bench! come, black with sin! *(amen!)* come, sick and sore! *(amen!)* come, lame and halt, and blind! *(amen!)* come, pore and needy, sunk in shame! *(a-a-men!)* come all that's worn, and soiled, and suffering!—come with a broken spirit! come with a contrite heart! come in your rags and sin and dirt! the waters that cleanse is free, the door of heaven stands open— oh, enter in and be at rest" *(a-a-men! glory, glory hallelujah!)* (172)

Like Stephen Dowling Bots, Huck has no one to mourn for him; and he watches with great interest as the crowd rushes up "to the mourner's bench, with the tears running down their faces" (172). It is surely no coincidence that when Huck first meets the Wilks family they are in the midst of a funeral, and are mourning deeply over the recent death of the family patriarch, Peter Wilks. But, as the "King" says, in his impromptu speech to the family of the deceased, it is not the dead man but the "poor little lambs that he loved and sheltered, and that's left fatherless and motherless," who are the real sufferers on this sad occasion (216).

When he hears the murderously insane Shepherdsons shouting "Kill them, kill them!" and sees his friend, Buck, fall dead into the water beneath him, Huck is as close to a real, adult grief response as he is to get in the novel. His need to censor his own anguish at this moment reaches its highest level of critical intensity: "It made me so sick I most fell out of the tree. I ain't a-going to tell *all* that happened—it would make me sick again if I was to do that. I wished I hadn't ever come ashore that night to see such things. I ain't ever going to get shut of them—lots of times I dream about them" (153).

The origin of Twain's denial of grief in the surface of the text perhaps lay in the psyche of the book's author. It is possible that Twain (like Huck), was never able "to get shut of" the traumatic deaths and separations he experienced at an age when his immature mind was unable to assimilate his losses and properly grieve over them. It may be conjectured that Twain sublimated his own grief and guilt over the real and fancied deaths of his parents and siblings into his creative fiction, for it is certainly the return of Huck's, and perhaps Twain's, repressed and chronic grief that seems to have determined not only the tonal underside of the novel but also the exterior sequence and subject matter of the plot.[33]

In light of what have been determined to be his ongoing feelings of ambivalence toward patriarchal identification, the most challenging dilemma Huck has had to face in the novel thus far is the decision, in Chapter XXXI, of whether or not to return Jim to slavery. The crisis confronting Huck at this point in the book is not an isolated one, as critics have believed, for once again he is engaged in a struggle between the pull toward the maternal past and the satisfaction of asserting his autonomy from the mother and conforming to a symbolically based social reality.

At first Huck tries to "pray" away the guilt he anticipates he will feel if he turns Jim over to the authorities, but he soon discovers that "my heart warn't right," and "You can't pray a lie" (269). In this episode, Huck once again finds himself in what he would call "a tight place," for if he is to acknowledge that his emotional truths actually represent the "right" and "moral" thing to do, his whole fictional pose or identity would be in danger of dissolving. Faced with a similar dilemma, in Chapter XXVIII, as to whether he should, in effect, "blow his cover," and "tell the truth" to the honest and good Mary Jane Wilks, Huck "reckons" that "a body that ups and tells the truth when he is in a tight place, is taking considerable many resks; though I ain't had no experience, and can't say for certain" (239). To tell the truth without the disguise of mendacity-based humor seems "most like setting down on a kag of powder and touching it off, just to see where you'll to go" (239).

At these moments when true feelings run up against the boundaries of humorous fiction, Twain's narrative turns in upon itself in a kind of fictional, moral paradox. Unbeknownst to himself, Huck, indeed, does the "right" thing by choosing to "*go to hell*" (271). He has made an emotionally moral decision but a symbolically or ideologically immoral one. As Twain wrote in his essay "The Damned Human Race," about mankind's duplicitous relationship with God: It "is our acts that betray us, not our words. Our words are all compliments, and they deceive Him . . . we imagine that all He cares for is words—noise; that if we make the words pretty enough they will blind Him to the acts that give them the lie." [34] Clearly Twain had his own idea of who or what God is, and "He" is decidedly more of a "feminine" than a "masculine" deity. His own God, he once wrote in his notebook, "would value no love but the love born of kindness conferred; not that born of benevolence contracted for." [35] What makes Huck finally decide *not* to write the letter to Miss Watson and betray Jim is indeed his "love born of kindness conferred"—his yearnings for Eros—although he never acknowledges to himself the possibility that his ethics of attachment is more "right" than turning Jim in. His "feminine" motives are as repressed as Twain's moral truth was repressed and disguised by his humorous, storytelling narrative.

By choosing Jim over "salvation," Huck has become "entirely shut of" civilization (275). He has made the regressive, nostalgic choice of his maternal past over separation and masculine individuation, and is resolved, in effect, to head "for the back country" (274). Huck has not entirely negated himself, as James Cox believes, but has negated only his traditionally "masculine" or "civilized" identity, which would demand that he enforce the social and political statute of slavery. Both in the author's indirect condemnation of slavery, and in Huck's choice to "regress" toward a continuation of the maternal relationship, Twain asserted with full conviction the moral superiority of his hero's "feminine" impulses.[36]

Without Jim's actual physical presence, however, Huck is in a radically alienated and marginal position relative to the external world around him. As he always has been, Jim is, for Huck, an external good object; Huck has no internal good parental objects but only a longing, a lack, and a self-annihilating loss. Therefore, when Huck arrives alone at the Phelps's farm, in Chapter XXXII, he is carrying a double unconscious burden: the guilt of parricide (he is now "entirely shut" of civilization, having refused identification with the military father, the royal father, and the Father in Heaven), and his depressive separation anxiety at once again having lost or been abandoned by his good external object—Jim. As a result of fully re-enacting the loss of both of his parents, Huck is beset, in this chapter, by a more profound loneliness than he has previously experienced in the novel:

> When I got there it was all still and Sunday-like, and hot and sunshiny—the hands was gone to the fields; and there was them kind of faint dronings of bugs and flies in the air that makes it seem so lonesome and like everybody's dead and gone; and if a breeze fans along and quivers the leaves, it makes you feel mournful, because you feel like it's spirits whispering—spirits that's been dead ever so many years—and you always think they're talking about *you*. As a general thing, it makes a body wish *he* was dead, too, and done with it all. (276)

The silence, loneliness, and threat of extinction that Huck seems to feel are inescapable and unbearable. Yet there is a solution, though one that is, in many ways, deeply disappointing to the reader, given Huck's longstanding emotional investment in Jim. For it is here, within a matter of moments, that Huckleberry Finn becomes "Tom Sawyer."

Twain's critics have suggested that both Huck and his creator need Tom to provide Huck's character with a voice, a fictional "form," if the story is to continue.[37] With this in mind, it is surprising that Twain's readers and critics find Huck's return to imposturing so disappointing, since, in terms of his ongoing initiation struggle, it represents merely the boy's reluctant movement toward separation-individuation: the relinquishment of a non-verbal, preoedipal existence based on feelings, for a symbolic mastery of the external, temporal world. It is, after all, man's "great cultural achievement" that provides him with a self-identity through which he can relate to others.[38] On the other hand, what the reader experiences in this development toward the boy's masculine maturation is a legitimate and very real sense of nostalgia for his or her own lost childhood and emotional integrity.

Perhaps what the reader is responding to at this moment in the text is Twain's own resistance to repressing the adolescent's emotionally honest, and therefore morally superior, self, and replacing it with a fraudulent impostured existence. If this last section of the novel has previously been thought of as the weakest part of the book, in terms of reader response and the reader's emotional involvement with the moral and psychological issues which the novel portrays, it is without question one of the strongest moments in *Adventures of Huckleberry Finn*. It is the instant at which the reader partakes of the loss of desire and the ever-recurring homesickness that underlie the fictional authority of the entire novel. The sense of nostalgia and loss that the reader is forced to feel drives home the elements of disappointment, grief, and mourning that are essential, not only for the successful resolution of the separation-individuation process, but also for the attainment of male maturity in Western culture. The reader's sad feeling that something magical and emotionally satisfying has come to an end at this moment on the Phelps's farm is an empathetic response to Huck's bidding a tragic farewell to the blissful innocence of his childhood, and the reader is abruptly forced to recognize the sacrificial nature of patriarchal identification, and the impoverishment of a life devoid of feminine sympathies.

If the ending to Huck's story is psychologically unsatisfying, it is, I believe, primarily due to the fact that he fails finally to commit himself in any direction whatsoever. Although he was indeed relieved "to find out who I was" (282), his assumption of Tom Sawyer's name was designed by Twain as a passive act of mistaken identity. Huck fails to commit himself, either by approving of Tom's deceptive fictions, or by taking responsibility for his true-self, emotionally honest, impulses and, thereby, severing himself once and for all from Tom's world. He is again trapped on the middle ground, between a preoedipal Scylla and oedipal Charybdis, both of whom meant for Twain, and consequently for Huck, a life of alienation, loneliness, and death. As it is, he must perpetually bear the burden of loss from his comforting Jim/mother refuge, *and* from the sense of belonging that Tom/civilization might provide. Thus, at the end of the novel, as he is so many times during his adventures, Huck is merely on the edge of maturity, on the border of puberty—a perpetual adolescent.

The motive for Huck's surrendering to a bogus, deceptive, and humorous identity may have arisen, once again, from Twain's inability to reconcile Huck's grief and abandonment depression with his own humorous narrative devices, and therefore with fiction itself. Through an act of splitting, Twain simply avoided further conflict in Huck's separation-individuation struggle, and in his own creative process, by delegating the actively fraudulent role in the novel to Tom, and placing Huck in the somewhat shadowy role of the silent and defeated moral, true self.

Nevertheless, of some consolation to the reader is the fact that Twain does not abandon Huck's primary true-self goal of freeing Jim in these last chapters of the novel, but rather, strategically arranges for it to be acted out in the external world through the imposturing mode of the novel that is now embodied not *within* an internally warring Huck, but in the character of Tom Sawyer. It is appropriate, then, that the principal difference between Huck and Tom in this section is that, for Huck, the end justifies the means, while, for Tom, the reverse is true. In Tom's view, things must be done "morally" and "right," which means "by the book." Huck, on the other hand, cares only that what his inner self tells him to do is done: "When I start in to steal a nigger, or a watermelon, or a Sunday school book, I ain't no ways particular how it's done, so it's done" (307).

The overwhelming consensus among readers of the novel is that this last section is disappointing and inferior to the earlier sections of the book. This decline in the story was confirmed by Ernest Hemingway, who advised the reader to "stop where the Nigger Jim is stolen from the boys. That is the real end. The rest is just cheating."[39] The only thing that comes to an "end" at this point in the text, I believe, is Huck's feminine subjective narrative. The Huck that we have come to know so well and to empathize with is lost to us forever. For the reader, the sudden dissolving of Huck's "core" self, and the loss of Huck's emotionally honest voice, is what makes him or her feel deprived and cheated.[40]

The deceptive and contrived—or "cheating"—nature of Tom Sawyer's pursuit of Huck's "feminine" moral impulse to free Jim in this section is, in some ways, similar to Mark Twain's own indirect, or deceptive, manner of communicating his inner, moral thoughts to the world. It is perhaps for this reason that Twain felt that to complete the work "is no more trouble to me to write than it is to lie." It was "easy and comfortable" for Huck to be Tom Sawyer, not only for Huck, but for Twain as well; whereas to be Huck Finn and suffer unendurable loss and abandonment depression had gotten too much for either of them to bear. But, while Twain, like Huck, "went along" with Tom's plan, it is likely that in his "secret heart" he "didn't like it much" (295).

Jim's enslavement at the end of the story is ironic, not only because he has already been freed by Miss Watson in her will, but also because he remains emotionally free and true to himself, whereas Huck has become a prisoner of Tom's absurd and fraudulent game of fiction. The "mournful inscription" that Tom contrives for Jim's "escape" is a remarkable document of Huck's position of emotional self-alienation in the latter section of the novel, and might well have been written by his now "imprisoned" and repressed emotionally true self:

1. Here a captive heart busted.
2. Here a poor prisoner, forsook by the world and friends, fretted out his sorrowful life.
3. Here a lonely heart broke, and a worn spirit went to its rest, after thirty-seven years of solitary captivity.
4. Here, homeless and friendless, after thirty-seven years of bitter captivity, perished a noble stranger, natural son of Louis XIV. (322)

Tragically, however, as Twain's critics have noted, the "comfort" that Huck now feels from having gained an identity, albeit an impostured one, has been won at the expense of Jim's freedom.

Adventures of Huckleberry Finn is not, finally, a novel of male initiation, but of an aborted initiation; and while, in terms of Western, patriarchal culture, Huck's failure to reach "maturity" may be deemed as one of the novel's shortcomings, his indecision and persistent tendency to regress to childhood dependency are also responsible for the novel's greatest moral and cultural insights. Within a framework of traditional masculine development, the novel's apparent limitations are perhaps at times experienced by the reader as disappointing for the reason that these limitations are the author's own. Mark Twain, T. S. Eliot wrote in his introduction to the novel, "was a man who . . . never became in all respects mature" (330). Like Thomas Wolfe, Twain was a perpetual adolescent in an adult world, who was neither able to achieve maturity, nor quite recapture a secure childhood.[41] If Huck was so irremediably locked within an oedipal struggle it was perhaps because Mark Twain was as well.

It is also possible that, like Huck, Twain occupied a regressive, nostalgic position with regard to his own separation-individuation struggle; and possibly, also like Huck, was therefore never able to establish his own good internal objects. Guy Cardwell makes the observation that throughout his life Mark Twain always "felt himself to be emotionally alone," just as Huck did.[42] Twain was possessed, Van Wyck Brooks confirms, with a "frequently noted fear of solitude, that dread of being alone with himself."[43] Also like Huck, it is possible that, while Twain denied his need for external manifestations of his own real or imagined "lost" parental objects, he continued his incessant search for them in his fictions of boyhood.[44]

At the same time that Twain was motivated by his lack of maturity, he also appears to have sought in the external world, and in his fiction, a way to act out his rebellion against patriarchal culture, manifested and made possible in the novel through Huck's unresolved adolescent conflicts. Nostalgic regression was the specific psychological mechanism Twain employed to avoid adolescent oedipal confrontation, circumvent the experience of grief, and give expression to his moral, true-self impulses that were at odds with traditional masculine selfhood. In *Adventures of Huckleberry Finn*, Mark Twain draws upon the dominant psychological issues that, as I have demonstrated in the previous two chapters, he struggled with throughout his life: his resentment toward his mother, or toward what he later in life referred to as "fate," for having to disguise and alienate himself from his true or emotional self through the humorous and entertaining manner of telling stories; his pattern of repressing or displacing his grief over loss and death; and finally, his attempt to repair his deep-seated disappointment in the mother through the repeated nostalgic retreat, in his fiction, to a fantasy world that exists prior to any and all experiences of disillusionment and loss.

Wright Morris suggests that Twain continually used his "craft" to recover a serene past, to "regain the Paradise that he had given up for lost" ("Available Past," 276). In his fictional recreations of childhood, Twain found what Kenneth Lynn describes as "a haven of refuge against the corruptions of the new era" (*Southwestern Humor*, 187). But even more psychologically pressing, Twain found an escape from what T. S. Eliot identified as "his hatred of himself for allowing society to tempt and corrupt him and give him what he wanted" ("Introduction," 330). Immersed in his own nostalgic fictional fantasies, Mark Twain was able to enter "that Happy Valley" of the "magic circle of youth" (Lynn, 187): that "common ground" of childhood, as Twain called it, in his speech in honor of General U. S. Grant, where a person is innocent of all the iniquity and wrongdoing that sullies his later accomplishments and successes.[45]

The irony that defined the conflict Twain faced was that he, like Huck, was dependent upon language and the deceptions of humor and storytelling to recapture his youth, so that once there, he could then give outlet to his honest, spontaneous, and primary process feelings. Lee Clark Mitchell is correct, therefore, when he senses that the ending of Twain's novel drives home the inevitable truth that feelings are indeed dependent upon language.[46] As the novel suggests, Twain was equally committed to his inner, true self *and* to his surface, humorous, or false, self. His way of voicing his true, moral, and emotional impulses was through the deceptive devices of humor, language, and fiction, which from his uncorrupted true-self, or Huckleberry-Finn, perspective, were viewed as nothing but self-betraying "lies," which he simultaneously wished to be "entirely shut of" (275).

This ambivalence in Twain's fictional voice and creative process accounts for Harold Beaver's observation that Mark Twain, like Huck, both "loved . . . and despised" Tom Sawyer (144). He loved Tom in the same way that he loved fiction-making itself—as a means for expressing his true moral self and regaining the blissful freedom of innocent childhood.[47] Like Huck, and Melville's Ishmael, Twain may be viewed as a kind of self-willed orphan, whose fate it was, as Roy Harvey Pearce claims, "to seek a freedom beyond the limits of any civilization," but whose search, nevertheless, depended on that civilization to give it voice and life.[48] Twain's impulse, like Melville's, and Huck's, was symbolic suicide; but he recognized the psychological truth that, in Karen Horney's words, to "kill the hated self he must at the same time kill the glorious self, as Dorian Gray did."[49] To use Twain's own analogies, to kill half a dog or hang one of "those extraordinary twins" was to deprive them not of half but of "all their energy and . . . interest in life."[50] Thus, for Huck and Tom, as Twain said about the twins Luigi and Angelo: "Their story was one story";[51] and when Twain imagined Huck's and Tom's death it was inevitable, as he said, that they would "die together."[52] The problem of adolescence as Huck experiences it, which mirrors Twain's dilemma as a fiction writer, is not whether to choose between feelings or humorous fiction, but more integrally, as the "Duke" presents the problem at hand: "To be or not to be; that is the bare bodkin / That makes calamity of so long life" (*Huckleberry Finn*, 179).

If the Oedipus myth is about the conscious realization of one's own intolerable psychic crimes and desires, *Adventures of Huckleberry Finn* is wholly a myth about the circumvention and transcendence of mature psychological awareness. The conflicts that govern the surface action of Sophocles' drama are equally dominant in Twain's novel, but under the American author's control the conflict has become subliminal, and consequently the themes of grief and aggression appear only in repressed form. Feminine, emotional, and psychological truth continually runs up against the limitations of nostalgia and deceptive American humor in Huck's story, but undeniably, from out of this tension comes the radiant power of Twain's novel.

The telling of a joke, Freud suggests, involves a fusion of the first and third person, of id and superego. While the content of the joke engages the hearer in the challenge of a taboo through the exposure of forbidden impulses, the complicitous laughter that follows restores the superego's power of repression.[53] Twain's humorous narrative relies on the same dynamic as Freud's tendentious joke in that it simultaneously exposes and conceals the grief, aggression, and loss, that is taboo, both to Twain and to his American audience. If *Adventures of Huckleberry Finn* is considered to be Twain's greatest work, it is perhaps because he was able to enact in it a perfect amalgamation of the return of the repressed and the return of repression. Twain's style of humor, like the processes of a joke, adroitly defuses both the hostile response of the hearer and the hidden aggression in the teller, and it is likely that in protecting America from self-conscious psychological truth and feminine identification, Twain was also protecting himself. The enduring popularity of *Adventures of Huckleberry Finn*, then, speaks not only for Twain's extraordinary competence in telling a humorous story, but for his uncanny ability to disguise the truths of violence, grief, and loss within a humorous lie— to release his audience's repressed psychic energy and at the same time contain it.

Ernest Hemingway, perhaps even more so than Twain, exerted a pressure on language to simultaneously repress and reveal the aggression, grief, and emotional neediness that accompany the young American male's development from adolescence to adulthood. Whereas Melville and Twain fought against the surfacing of grief and aggression in their texts, and consequently these repressed emotions returned again and again in displaced form throughout their fiction, Hemingway was keenly aware of the power of repression to create emotional tension and pathos in his fictional narratives. However, while Hemingway used the repression of grief and loss to his advantage in his creative process, in his personal life, he was no more able than Twain or Melville to work through his inner conflicts and surmount, or control, the deep sense of grief and disappointment that followed him throughout his life. The plight of the American adolescent male who is torn between his dependency needs and his desire to assert his masculine autonomy through an identification with an heroic paternal ideal finds expression in the early short fiction of Ernest Hemingway. But if Hemingway, both in his life and in his fiction, transformed the self-reliant, emotionally invulnerable tough guy into a modern American icon, he also confirmed the fact that at the heart of the American male experience lies a profound sense of father-hunger and mother-loss which neither the repression of loss and grief, nor the pursuit of an abstract image of tough masculinity, can eradicate or transcend.

5. The Shaping of Hemingway's Art of Repressed Grief: Mother-Loss and Father-Hunger from *In Our Time* to *Winner Take Nothing*

This plant would like to grow
And yet be embryo;
Increase, and yet escape
The doom of taking shape . . .

—Richard Wilbur, "Seed Leaves"

Growing up means letting go of the dearest megalomaniacal dreams of our childhood. Growing up means knowing they can't be fulfilled. Growing up means gaining the wisdom and skills to get what we want within the limitations imposed by reality—a reality which consists of diminished powers, restricted freedoms and, with the people we love, imperfect connections.

—Judith Viorst, *Necessary Losses*

Ernest Hemingway's commitment to the taboo against grief was perhaps the most dedicated, artistically refined, and ultimately self-devastating of any figure in American literature. About Hemingway as a young man, Gregory Clark, features editor of the *Toronto Star Weekly,* once observed that "a more weird combination of quivering sensitiveness and preoccupation with violence surely never walked this earth."[1] Clark's insight into the nature of Hemingway's character captures the paradoxical qualities of this complex American writer's life and fiction. It implies Hemingway's need to disguise his emotional vulnerability behind a facade of strength and control, which again brings to mind Mark Twain's use of humor as a buffer against hostility and grief, and Herman Melville's deployment of objective cytological narrative in *Moby-Dick* to protect him during his courageous deep-diving into the potentially engulfing chaotic depths of the unconscious. In his most powerful works of fiction, as in his life, Hemingway, like Melville and Twain before him, mastered a stylistic technique through which he repeatedly found ways to insulate himself from loss, grief, and emotional pain.

The combination of grandiosity and feelings of insecurity that may also be inferred from Clark's statement is symptomatic of the kind of manic-depression that some psycho-biographers have proposed lies at the heart of Hemingway's lifelong inner conflict.[2] After extensive interviews with people who knew or had met Ernest Hemingway, Denis Brian was most struck by the dual quality of Hemingway's self-image; of the contrasting images of kind and cruel, sensitive and thick-skinned, exultant and morose that he showed to others.[3] Yet, the relationship between these polar states of the self clearly seems to have been one of defensiveness. As Earl Rovit assesses Hemingway's character, he was "a defensive-aggressive person, or an aggressive-defensive, however you want to put it."[4] Similarly, concerning Hemingway's alcoholism it might be said that he drank defensively, seeking to transform his depressive lows into highs, at least temporarily. However, he could never fully admit to himself (until perhaps the last few years of his life), that drinking was in fact one of the methods upon which he most heavily relied in order to defend against—to act as a totem against—his sense of loss in relation to himself, or in other words, his emotional vulnerability. Hemingway's taboo against grief, as Tom Dardis says about alcoholism, "is characterized as a disease of denial."[5] Hemingway organized his life around "self-delusion," Brian concludes, because he needed to believe he was great; even more, he needed to *be* great in reality, "in order to survive" (321). For Hemingway, therefore, as for Melville and Twain, greatness depends not merely on one's vulnerability to loss, disappointment, and grief, but on one's strategic ability to repress, or more accurately, to disguise, one's emotional vulnerability.

What the manic-depression theory by itself does not adequately explain is why Hemingway was so desperately ashamed of his weakness, even those normal weaknesses, self-doubts, and emotional dependencies that define one as human. Nor does it explain why Hemingway's inner conflict between manic behavior (violence, autonomy, and aggressiveness) and depressive behavior (sensitivity, dependency, and passivity) also manifested itself as a gender-identity struggle between the incompatible extremes of masculine and feminine behavior.[6] Furthermore, the physiological inclination toward manic behavior cannot entirely account for Hemingway's indefatigable urge to achieve fame, and to live up to his own inner-constructed grandiose self-image, both as a man and as a writer. The significance of this urge is revealed in the reminiscences of Hemingway's younger brother, Leicester, who states that as early as he could remember, Hemingway wanted to be "Superman's older brother" (Brian, 22); he wanted to be larger than life, always the center of attention. Although it is reasonable to view Hemingway's delusions of grandeur as an adult, particularly in his later life, as symptomatic of a manic high, his desire for greatness, and the extremely high heroic expectations that he had erected as his ego ideal from childhood through middle age, do not suggest delusional thinking so much as the kind of elevated idealism that is usually associated with adolescence. Hemingway's youthful arrogance, which is so often spoken of by those who knew him as a young man, reflects an innocent hopefulness for the fulfillment of an ideal self-image that in his youth undoubtedly served to subdue any encroaching periods of depression. The greatest challenge he had to confront in his early years, I believe, was not so much depression as disillusionment; or in other words, narcissistic injury and ego-ideal deflation.

Hemingway's biographers and critics commonly argue that the four most traumatic episodes in Hemingway's early life were his wounding during the war, his experience of being jilted in love by the nurse Agnes von Kurowsky, his being thrown out of home at age twenty-one by his mother and his puritanical father, and his father's suicide in 1928. These injuries, though they may also have resulted in depression, represented devastating blows of disillusionment and disappointment to Hemingway's adolescent ego. He learned from them, respectively, that he was not immortal,[7] that love means loss, and that love was not unconditional.[8] His wallowing in depression for a long period of time after these events occurred may have indicated a genetic proclivity toward depression, but his sense of grief and disappointment was commensurate with his previously held impervious and inflated adolescent heroic self-image or ego ideal.

In the same way that alcohol for Hemingway, as for many manic-depressives, mimicked and exaggerated the manic highs and the depressive lows, his early compulsion toward the fulfillment of an inflated ego ideal fueled and exacerbated his alternating feelings of grandiosity and low self-esteem. In either case (and there is good reason to believe that both cases may have existed simultaneously), loss—primarily the grief from loss that results in disappointment and disillusionment—was the demon of life that affected Hemingway most intensely. Clinical studies of loss and mourning indicate that an early experience of loss, disillusionment, or emotional deprivation can contribute to depressive disorders by adding to the risk that the disorder will develop, by increasing one's sensitivity or vulnerability to loss, and by affecting the severity of the depressive disorder later in life.[9] As John Bowlby points out, "genetic influences never operate in a vacuum";[10] and as clinical evidence now shows, traumatic experiences of loss and the resulting disappointment and depression bring about neuroendocrinological changes that permanently prolong or intensify a genetically stimulated depressive reaction.[11] Therefore, if Hemingway did indeed invite disappointment and loss upon himself by consistently setting unrealistically high or inflexible ego ideals (or conversely engaged in idealistic fantasies to counterbalance his tendency toward depression and ego deflation), then his ego-ideal pathology would have significantly added to the severity of his developing depression.[12] To oscillate between feelings of inviolable greatness and low self-esteem, then, is typical, not only of manic-depression, but also of an ego-ideal pathology in which the individual attempts (with only periodic success) to live up to an exaggerated self-image acquired through an identification with an abstract and impossible-to-attain heroic ego ideal.

While Hemingway's depressive disorder has for the most part been confirmed, the role that the simultaneous presence of an emerging ego-ideal disorder played in his life and art has not yet been fully explored.[13] To do so, for one, would be to suggest an explanation as to why and how he drove himself in such a compulsive way to achieve fame and recognition. Why, in other words, did he become one of the most popular and notable American literary figures in the twentieth century, rather than merely another statistic in the study of chronic or manic depression? A consideration of his chronic self-esteem problem would also explain Hemingway's obsession, throughout his early and late fiction, with paternal disappointment, repudiated maternal dependency (or feminine identification), and his need to formulate a transcendent heroic paternal ideal. Finally, such an approach would also provide an explanation for Hemingway's growing interest as a writer in finding ways to deflect from conscious awareness the pain of loss and disappointment, particularly with regard to adolescent narcissistic injury, vulnerable masculinity, and the loss of self-esteem.

The possibility that Hemingway suffered from a characterological self-image, or ego-ideal, conflict, in which he perpetually agonized over the discrepancy between who he was and who he would like to have been, carries vital import for the aims of this study, as it ties together the theme of repressed grief, or denied emotional vulnerability, and the fixation of Hemingway's male heroes at the adolescent stage of emotional development. As will be demonstrated in this chapter, in Hemingway's life and fictional texts, the fixated belief in a grandiose ego ideal not only predisposes one to the disavowal of disappointment, disillusionment, and loss, (and therefore the disavowal of grief itself), but allows the individuating male to transcend both an identification with the disappointing or biological father, thus eliminating the need to engage in sexual, or oedipal, competition with the paternal figure, and the process of reality-testing, both of which are critical to the development of a mature masculine identity.[14]

My purpose in the present chapter, therefore, is to re-evaluate some of Hemingway's best early works of fiction, composed between the years 1920 and 1935, in terms of his young male protagonists'—and, in many ways, his own—ego-ideal crisis and failed separation-individuation struggle. This separation-individuation conflict is characterized by a boy's inability to make a clean break with the mother, and to move beyond the stage of adolescent idealism by coming to accept the limitations and compromises of a disappointing reality. Stylistically, in the early works to be discussed in this chapter, Hemingway experiments with the different ways that language can be used to repress emotions, and to defend his characters from conscious recognition of the loss and grief that necessarily accompany the separations and disillusionments that are a natural part of growing up. The defensive ways in which Hemingway's adolescent heroes protect against a deflation in self-esteem indicate that the specific nature of the separation-individuation conflict in Hemingway's early fiction has primarily to do with the development of an age-appropriate and reality-based ego ideal.[15] *In Our Time* (1925), *The Sun Also Rises* (1926), and *A Farewell to Arms* (1929) for the most part clearly fall into this developmental category, while in his last two collections of stories, *Men Without Women* (1927) and *Winner Take Nothing* (1933), Hemingway begins to dramatize his awareness of the sacrifices, and the increasing psychological danger, that result from the denial and repression of grief. In my study of his early fiction in this chapter, I shall demonstrate that the best stories are crafted from the same defensive repression of grief in the text that Hemingway may himself have employed in early life.[16]

Loraine Thompson, who knew Hemingway from Key West, made the comment that one of his "philosophies, which he used always to say to me . . . was that you shouldn't become too fond of anything in this world because something's going to happen to it and you're going to be hurt" (Brian, 78). In this sense Hemingway's attitude toward loss is remarkably similar to Twain's, who, if we remember, defined love as a tragedy in the making, since it inevitably means that one of the lovers "is fated to be left behind" when, through some twist of fate, the beloved other is permanently lost to him.[17] In the story "In Another Country," Hemingway reiterates this guiding philosophy through the voice of the Major, who pronounces to Nick Adams that a man "should not place himself in a position to lose. He should find things he cannot lose."[18] Like the Major, Hemingway could not "resign" (38) himself to loss. It is likely that Hemingway's manic zest for living life to the extremes of pleasure—for always pushing himself to the front line of exhilarating experience—along with his drive to fulfill and embrace his elevated, heroic, and ideal image of himself, would not have allowed him to rest content with a compromised life of mediocrity and resignation to loss. Instead, like his early fictional heroes, Hemingway may have defended himself against loss, disappointment, and depression not by denying the losses themselves, but, even more perilously, by denying the very fact of his vulnerability to loss. If it is true, as his brother Leicester said, that Hemingway was an intensely "oversensitive" person, then it follows that his defenses had to be as solid and impenetrable as his emotional sensitivity was soft and susceptible to hurt, his manic highs as elevated as his depressions were low, and his alcoholic rushes as fortifying as his hangovers were excruciating. Hemingway's work—his writing—may have provided him with a catharsis for pain, but failing this, his other defenses—drinking, sexual affairs, denial, rationalizations, and exaggerated tales of his own heroism—offered a temporary "opium"[19] or anesthetic that served as a totem to ward off the infiltration of grief that threatened to overrun and annihilate his vulnerable, depressed, and fragile ego. However, because Hemingway, like Twain and Melville before him, sought above all to deny his vulnerability to grief by repressing it from consciousness, ironically, grief, or the fear of loss, became the one thing that was never lost to him. Furthermore, the open expression of grief and mourning is a way of adapting to the losses and disappointments one experiences in life, and when this mourning process is interrupted psychic development is impaired and emotional growth stagnates. When the grief that is denied has to do specifically with the disillusionments a child or adolescent must accept as a natural part of growing up and confronting the contingencies of reality, psychic development can become defensively fixated at the stage of adolescent idealism. In a letter to Hemingway, General Charles Lanham refers to Hemingway and himself as "ever-blooming adolescents."[20] To become fixated at the adolescent stage of development, like Hemingway's young heroes of *In Our Time*, is to remain vulnerable to a defensive regression to primary narcissism, to reject the fallible real father, and to strive eternally to find an heroic paternal ideal with which one can identify, and on which one can rely for one's self-esteem. It is to live always on the verge of narcissistic injury and the resulting regressive fantasy of infantile omnipotence and maternal dependency. Through his writing, then, the young Hemingway found a way to transcend his own personal sense of adolescent disillusionment and loss by universalizing the conflicted and ambivalent plight of the perpetual adolescent in his fiction.[21]

In Hemingway's early short stories, his heroes find ever new ways to repress the pain of disillusionment and disappointment that must be acknowledged, grieved over, and worked through in order to temper the immature omnipotence of adolescence and childhood, and transform it into a mature acceptance of life's compromises and limitations. The inability of Hemingway's characters to achieve this state of acceptance and compromise sentences them to lives of perpetual adolescence and prolonged suffering, in which they either regress or in some other way block out and disavow their emotional pain and disillusionment. In Hemingway's own life, this intractable need to enforce a taboo against grief seems to have been encouraged by a depressive disorder combined with a compulsive desire to inure, and in effect inoculate, himself against the pain of disappointment, separation, and loss.

As a group, the stories of Hemingway's *In Our Time* reveal the son's denied dependency on the mother, or on women in general, and his denial of the grief inspired by his willful separation from her. Further, they demonstrate how the boy, who has suffered disappointment in relation to his father, attempts to use an idealized image of the father as a defense—or totem—against his lingering emotional dependency upon the mother, and as a way of achieving male individuation and a masculine self-identity structure. The real, or biological, father in these stories is circumvented by the boy's identification with a grandiose father image, which in turn results in added feelings of grief, arising from the inevitable loss of real emotional intimacy with the father.[22] This developmental dynamic, in fact, bears a close resemblance to Hemingway's own childhood and adolescent experience growing up in the Hemingway family in the Oak Park suburbs of Chicago.

The family member who figures most prominently in many of the biographical accounts of Ernest Hemingway's early childhood is his strong-willed and ambitious mother, Grace. Recent biographers, such as Kenneth Lynn and Bernice Kert, consistently evoke a portrait of the great hunter and *code hero*-to-be as an infant in a girl's dress who devotedly calls his mother "fweetee," and who for the first six months of his life slept snuggled up to his buxom mother "contented to sleep with Mama" and "lunch[es] all night" at her breast.[23] Many of the reports on Hemingway's early relationship with his mother point to her persistent tendency to control her children's lives, to mold them to her expectations and desires, rather than allow them to express and pursue their own likes and dislikes.[24] Madelaine Hemingway, in her biography of her brother, writes: "Though Mother loved all her children, she had very high standards of conduct and achievement that she wanted us to live up to. While we all did much that she wanted done, it sometimes seemed as if we could never really satisfy her. Her criticisms and disappointment could show unexpectedly—and sometimes we thought unfairly."[25] According to Kenneth Lynn, Grace "took early action to assert her authority over even the sexuality of her son" by dressing Ernie and Marcelline in the same sex clothing and then maintaining the "elaborate pretense that little Ernest and his sister were twins of the same sex" (*Hemingway*, 40). As an intensely ambitious woman who gave up her professional singing career to become a wife and mother, it is possible that Grace pushed her children to achieve the recognition that would make up for her own lost feeling of importance. For whatever reason, Grace Hemingway appears to be what D. W. Winnicott would call a poor "mirroring mother" to her children, fostering a power-play between herself and them within the Hemingway family.[26] Her excessive involvement in Ernest's life resulted in his developing what Lynn calls an "intimate dependency" on her, or in Kert's words, a "delicious dependency," which certainly would have made it exceptionally difficult for the young Hemingway to separate himself fully from her emotionally.

Understandably, therefore, the story of Hemingway's adolescence is consistently one of a rather anxious boy striving with desperate and exaggerated effort to prove himself to be what he *thinks* is a "man."

Young Ernie's frustrated masculine development reached a breaking point one day, however, when he shouted out to his mother: "I not a Dutch dolly, I Pawnee Bill. Bang—I shoot Fweetee" (Lynn, *Hemingway*, 44). As Lynn rhetorically asks: "Caught between his mother's wish to conceal his masculinity and his eagerness to encourage it, was it any wonder that he was anxious and insecure?" (45).

During his early years, Ernest looked to his father for a much needed model of manly behavior. From Clarence, Ernest learned to hunt, fish, camp out, and dissect insects. But Ernest's idealization of his father was short-lived. According to Michael Reynolds, "when Ernest entered puberty and most needed his father, the Doctor began to succumb to a nervous condition, which Ernest, in his teens, could not understand . . . after 1912, the Doctor lost interest. He still loved the woods and the lake, but increasingly he loved them alone, shutting out his son."[27] Clarence Hemingway suffered from angina, diabetes, weak nerves, and severe bouts of depression (Reynolds, *Hemingway*, 608–9). Although Ernest was later to blame his mother for destroying his father, and therefore for depriving him of his adolescent, male ego ideal, he admitted to Malcolm Cowley that "the first big psychic wound of his life had come when he discovered that his father was a coward."[28] It is perhaps closer to the truth, however, that Hemingway's father was not a coward as much as he was, simply, a fallible human being, and that his mother was guilty, in Max Westbrook's words, only "of having the strength that Clarence lacked."[29] Nonetheless, Ernest sought a father figure whom he could idealize and who possessed the grandiose, heroic attributes that his demanding and ambitious mother expected him to have. Perhaps he saw this paternal ideal in his grandfather, Ernest Hall, a Civil War hero, who in his mother's estimation was "the finest purest noblest man I have ever known" (Lynn, *Hemingway*, 30). Mainly, however, Ernest Hemingway found his courageous, honorable, skillful, and most importantly, supermasculine ego ideal within his own adolescent imagination. The Hemingway *code* of manly behavior that began to emerge in his earliest works of short fiction became a model of the ideal American male, not only for himself to follow, but also for thousands of his male readers, and it was a narcissistic self-image that Hemingway spent the rest of his own life trying to live up to.[30]

As is typical of the adolescent's fantasy ideal, however, Hemingway's *code hero* was an abstract concept of idealized parental perfection impossible to attain in reality. In Leonard Kriegel's words, "not even Hemingway can be Hemingway."[31] And yet, many men, including Hemingway himself, never gave up trying. Hemingway provided, says Wright Morris, "the formula for the public-private sectors of American life, the tough exteriors, the sensitive, brooding interiors, spawning the macho-tough fiction and the Bogart movies."[32]

Above all else it is the self-aggrandizing quality of the ideal self-object and the unrealistic search for concrete perfection that characterize the ego ideal of adolescence. Unless a more realistic father figure comes into a boy's life to assist in compelling him to compromise his grandiose expectations of himself and of the world, his reality testing will be permanently impaired, and his ego ideal is in danger of remaining "an immature, self-idealizing, wish-fulfilling agency."[33] As a consequence of retaining an immature ego ideal and self-image, the prolonged adolescent is susceptible to severe bouts of depression and poor self-esteem as an adult as a result of repeatedly experiencing futile attempts to live up to his own grandiose self-image.

Through personal fame and the immense popularity of his fiction during his lifetime, Hemingway managed to make a virtue of the arrested adolescent's ego-ideal pathology. Yet, personally, he paid a price for his exaggerated efforts at self-esteem regulation. As John Raeburn observes, the "persona" of the super-masculine *code hero* that Hemingway created for himself developed "a life of its own, and he had to sustain it so that it could sustain him."[34] In the long run, however, Hemingway's persona did not sustain him, and in the chapters that follow I will explore the ways in which Hemingway's ego-ideal crisis in later life, exacerbated by depression and alcoholism, took its toll on him both personally and as a creative writer. It will become evident, as Leonard Kriegel remarks, that Ernest Hemingway eventually became a "prisoner of his past" who knew, but could never admit, the true "terror of being a man, of not measuring up" (429–30).

Orpen: A Psychoanalytic Model for Hemingway's Early Fiction

A short-story fragment about a young soldier named Orpen, which Hemingway probably wrote sometime in the late 1920s or early 1930s, serves well as a model for identifying the separation-individuation conflicts in Hemingway's fiction.[35] Although both Kenneth Lynn and Peter Griffin were sufficiently struck by the openly confessional quality of this tale to include it in their biographical accounts of Hemingway's early years, they failed to recognize or draw out the richly significant insights into Hemingway's life and identity as a writer that the story has to offer. Not only does the story foreshadow the separation anxiety, search for an heroic paternal ideal, and vulnerability to infantile regression that appears throughout the stories of *In Our Time*, it also anticipates Hemingway's disillusionment with the masculine ideal of military heroism that will become a primary theme of *A Farewell to Arms, For Whom the Bell Tolls,* and *Across the River and Into the Trees.*

The narrative begins with Orpen guarding a bridge against enemy attack. As the Germans approach Orpen shoots down a gray-coated enemy soldier who is riding a bicycle across the bridge. He is surprised at the ease with which he is able to take the life of another human being. "The life was gone. The machine went on. You pressed the trigger, some one died and somehow you didn't feel bad about it." Orpen's only answer: "Ether in the brain." He is apparently so fatigued from days of marching without sleep that he would rather die than get up on his feet again. After the shooting Orpen begins to daydream about the "digital dexterity" of a machine gunner, which resembles that of a piano player's: "Fingers to skip over the keys. Ears to hear the music." Apparently Orpen had once hoped to become a concert pianist, and he recalls how his mother used to encourage and direct his practicing when he was a boy. When the shells begin to rain down on him he hears only a "crescendo whine, a vibration in the air, a crash, a sound like a thousand jew-harps [sic] twanging at once, then quiet." He also listens, as if from a distance, to his sergeant's machine gun, which "went tac-tac-tac like a typewriter." Face down in the dirt the smell of the earth reminds him of: "Spring mornings three years ago—dreaming of being old enough to get in it and be a hero. Now he was in it."

Suddenly Orpen himself is hit in the leg by an exploding shell and either from shock, fatigue, or both, mistakes the exploding shells for "a symphony for drums," while the soldiers are transformed in his imagination into the musicians bobbing up and down on their seats in the orchestra. Although Orpen can still hear the noises of battle around him, he moves in and out of consciousness, imagining in his periods of hallucination that he has gone to heaven, or rather to a "higher plane" than heaven, a place called Valhalla, where he finds himself in the company of numerous famous war heroes—Lord Nelson, Horatius, Eric the Red, Alexander the Great, Hannibal, Davy Crockett, General Custer, Napoleon Bonaparte, and others—all members of his dreamland "Hall of Heroes." He soon discovers that these supposedly great men are fighting and "bickering" among themselves like children, running each other through with swords and bayonets, but without actually wounding or hurting each other. As Orpen remarks, "you fight for the fun of it." Orpen also bleakly observes that everyone around him was "hacking and chopping . . . chopping and hewing . . . chopping blindly."

As Orpen's hallucinatory dream continues, he delivers a groin wound to the father of his country, George Washington, and in turn receives a chest wound from the great man. With this, Orpen decides that this war play is a "hateful game," a farce. "You had to pretend to like it." "Why did he go on playing" he asks himself: "Really he hated it all. . . . Somehow he wished he hadn't died a hero's death. Now he could never be anything else but a hero—and they chopped at each other all day long here." Believing that "no one would understand" that "he wanted to get out," Orpen sneaks away from Valhalla via a staircase that, to his surprise, leads to a small road in his home town. Here it is warm, with "the soft sounds of waves and a glowing in the half dark." To Orpen's astonishment he sees Horatio Nelson courting a woman on a country lane, and notices Eric the Red fishing in a stream. He too "seemed to know his way without hesitation," and turning to see a doorway he enters through it only to find his mother waiting for him with the words "I knew you'd get here, son."

Orpen is delighted to see that his "notebooks" and "pen and ink" were waiting for him just as he had left them. He begins to boast to his mother about his exciting battle exploits with George Washington and the others, explaining to her: "We fight because it is the greatest joy of man. To cut—and slice." But before long he is struck by a growing suspicion that his mother does not believe a word he is saying. "She smiled at him like the mother of all wisdom," and suddenly, "before he knew it, he was on his knees before her and she was holding his head." He tearfully admits that the war was not "wonderful": "It was horrible. Nothing but fighting, mother. I wanted to stay and do my music mother—I don't want to be in Valhalla!" His mother strokes his head and he begins to feel at peace: "It was like being a boy again." She assures him that all the heroes in Valhalla are at home now with their mothers. They hate fighting as much as he does and come down from Valhalla to Heaven to "do the things they like to do." They only fight for show, she tells him, when a new hero—of which there have been many recently as a result of the world war—makes his appearance in heaven. Orpen is overjoyed at this news and with delight makes "great high leaps in grace-note form" all around the room, until suddenly he is struck with a pain from the wound in his chest. At that moment he awakens in a hospital room. "Tell 'em I don't want to go back to Valhalla" he whispers to the nurse, who assures him, as his mother had in his dream, that he will never have to go back.

In the most general terms this story is a tale about the effects of an early experience of parental deprivation on a boy who consequently has come to view himself as an "orp[h]en," and who engages in a fantasy of belated emotional fulfillment. More specifically, without any reference to biographical data, the Orpen story represents a superb example of an adolescent wish-fulfillment dream, in which the protagonist enacts and then regressively attempts to repair a narcissistic injury. As a result of the injury he experiences a reawakened feeling of infantile separation anxiety, but resolves the internal conflict by way of a regressive restoration of primitive narcissism through a fusion with the omnipotent "mother of all wisdom."

From the nature of the wound that Orpen receives later in the story it can be surmised that his watchful task at the bridge is one of ego maintenance; he must carefully guard the "bridge" that holds together his ego and his heroic, ideal self-image, acquired through an identification with the abstract figures of great war heroes such as Bonaparte and Sherman. The significant absence of Orpen's biological father from his drama suggests that he did not take his father as an ideal, and so no adolescent integration of the real father has taken place, further suggesting that Orpen has circumvented the negative oedipus complex and with it the taboo against incest and regressive fusion with the mother. Consequently, Orpen still harbors a secret fear of castration, as well as the repressed knowledge that his grandiose, heroic ego ideal is a hollow pretense.[36]

The wound that Orpen receives is therefore a narcissistic one, a blow to his tentatively held grandiose ego ideal. Like the endangered bridge, his wound symbolizes the breakdown between ego and ego ideal. The result is a feeling of castration (an injury to Orpen's masculine identity), that in turn signals a reawakening of separation anxiety from the mother, with whom a restored unity might supply much needed narcissistic gratification.[37] As is true for Nick Adams in *In Our Time*, Orpen's aggression toward the father (Washington) is oedipal in nature, and so he deliberately chooses to thrust his bayonet into the father's groin. Yet the wound the father delivers to Orpen is emotional, symbolized by Washington's stab close to the boy's heart. Although Orpen consciously hopes that his war "game" and abstract heroic ideal father together could serve as an authentic replacement for the more real narcissistic gratification he received from his music and his mother, he comes to the realization that they cannot. Not surprisingly, therefore, in the remainder of the story Orpen attempts to work his way back to the comforting embrace of the good mother, which his wounding and resulting delirium cleverly allow him to do via his dream.

One of the most interesting aspects of this story, and one that brings to the fore some intriguing questions about Hemingway's creative process, is the connection Orpen makes between the primitive narcissistic gratification he receives from his mother, and the pleasure and self-esteem he derives from his art. However, although Orpen's "art" takes the form of his musical compositions, in his dream the specific mentioning of his "notebook," his "pen and ink," and the typewriter imagery he uses in his descriptions of war, clearly imply a correlation, in Hemingway's imagination, between music and the composing of fiction. In his conscious reveries Orpen makes the connection between being a machine gunner (an inadequate form of narcissistic gratification that he later recognizes as a "game" of imposture) and writing, or playing the piano (a more satisfying narcissistic activity associated with the mother's love and approval). Orpen's dream allows him to act out his regressive wish to return from his "Hall of Heroes" to "Albert Hall," or from the ego-ideal, fantasy world of Valhalla, to "heaven," his true "home" with his mother, where it is as warm, serene, and comforting as the oceanic womb. In the midst of this regressive transformation the battle noises slowly dissolve into the sound of symphony drums, and the soldiers merge with the musicians in the orchestra.

The murderous "cutting," "slashing," and "hacking" of war of which Orpen speaks again and again as an important part of the pretense maintained by his masculine heroes bring to mind the controlling activity of editing and styling for which Hemingway's writing is so celebrated. The implication is that the masculine-gendered actions of "editing" and "cutting" are secondary-process functions in Hemingway's art, which he uses defensively in an attempt to control and contain the "feminine," or primary-process, free-flow of the creative imagination. It is also impossible to avoid recognizing in Hemingway's story the importance of the mother's influence on his identity as an artist. But the feminine identification with the mother, which Hemingway himself must have been loath to admit, is defended against by the masculine appropriation, or control, of the artistic impulse through his skillful hacking and slashing. As Orpen defensively protests to his mother, to "cut—and slice" is "the greatest joy of man."

Death, or more accurately, the pain of loss, is the central fear with which Orpen is concerned in his war experience. His defense against it, as he says, is "ether in the brain," an apt metaphor for the numbness of repression, the anesthesia of denial that is the end result of the precision cuts and slashes of Hemingway's editing. Hence, Orpen's insight into how to cope with intolerable fear and disappointment foreshadows Hemingway's own realization that death, grief, and emotional pain are the things which make one feel life most deeply and powerfully, and that, as Freud believed, great art consists essentially in veiling, or in some other way disguising, the unconscious. For Hemingway, what constitutes the unconscious in his art, as in his life, is that aspect of human life that in Western culture is gendered female; specifically, emotions, vulnerability, irrationality, dependency, and the chaos of non-meaning and death.[38] The act of writing, for Hemingway, therefore was a sexualized activity in which art, like manhood, was designed with the purpose of veiling or occluding femaleness.[39]

Hemingway's Orpen story is particularly valuable as a psychoanalytic model of his early works of fiction because it clearly outlines both the essential components of a boy's ambivalent separation-individuation conflict, and Hemingway's use of emotional repression through cutting and editing in the formulation of his fictional style. It also points to Hemingway's belief that to have acquired an identity as a hero was as much of a burden and a loss as it was a victory, since he could now, as Orpen says, "never be anything else but a hero," and was fated to live up to an abstract and fundamentally fraudulent role. In the Orpen story, the young man's regressive desire for the mother and his dissatisfaction with the ideal father are undisguised. Perhaps this weakly subliminatory aspect of the piece is what led Hemingway to abandon it as an inferior work of fiction. Hemingway also may have deemed the work unpublishable because of its shamelessly confessional quality, particularly the acknowledgment of his mother as an invaluable positive influence on his professional identity as a writer. Furthermore, because the emotions associated with the boy's separation-individuation conflict appear so openly in the dialogue and narrative of Orpen's tale, his story lacks the profound psychological tension that serves to energize Hemingway's more successful fiction. Nevertheless, it functions extremely well as a turn-key that allows the psychoanalytic critic access into some of Hemingway's best stories. In particular, it points to the repression of loss and grief from father-hunger and mother-loss as a critical component in Hemingway's early fiction-making process.

In Our Time: *Male Separation Anxiety*

Taken as a whole, the stories of *In Our Time* may be seen as a study in the adolescent conflict of male separation anxiety, or the struggle of a young boy to establish masculine identification against the powerful pull of regressive maternal dependency. Particularly in "Indian Camp," "The Three-Day Blow," "Soldier's Home," "My Old Man," and "The Doctor and the Doctor's Wife," Hemingway imaginatively invests his young protagonists with a pressing urge to establish an ideal masculine father image in order to repair an early experience of deprivation, to deny dependency needs on the mother or woman, and to transcend his disappointment with the biological father. However, the defensive use of the ideal father breaks down continually in these stories because the boy's initial separation from the mother is never fully accomplished, and because his self-identity, like Orpen's, is based on an abstract and hollow ideal father image. The grief and disillusionment from mother-loss and father-hunger that accompany the separation-individuation process pervade these stories, but in every case it is the discrepancy (carefully orchestrated by Hemingway) between the reader's recognition of these painful emotions and the young boy's repression of them that produces the tremendous affective and psychological narrative force.

The central idea in the story "The Doctor and the Doctor's Wife" is that of the father's passivity relative to the manipulative passive-aggressiveness of Nick's dominating mother. Nick's father lacks resolve in dealing with both his wife and Dick Boulton, and any strength that he might derive from his professional standing as a doctor is eclipsed by his wife's contradictory belief in Christian Science. After his humiliating defeat in the contest of wills with the half-breed, the doctor retreats into his room to console himself, playing with his rifle and brooding upon his homicidal and perhaps suicidal thoughts.

Whether or not Nick overhears his mother's badgering conversation with his father, it is clear that he shares his father's resentment toward her, as well as his hatred of her dominating role in the family. By refusing to acquiesce to his mother's request that he "come and see her" in her suffocating room "with the blinds drawn," and choosing instead to go off into the woods with his father, Nick preserves the heroic image of the father by defying his mother in a way that the doctor is incapable of doing himself.[40] Not only must Nick block out his father's failings as a part of his identification process with the ideal paternal figure, but he must also deny the sense of loss and anger that accompanies the repudiation of his own maternal dependency.

Hemingway does not allow Nick to recognize consciously his hatred toward his mother, or more accurately, his anger over his own lingering emotional dependency on her. Nor does Hemingway permit Nick to realize his sense of loss in relation to his disappointing father. Instead, squirrel hunting represents Nick's grief and hostility in displaced form, just as Dr. Adams's loading and cleaning of his gun provides an outlet for his displaced anger toward his wife, as well as the disappointment and emotional distance that undeniably characterize his relationship with her. Through these displacements, and through the psychological tension that they evoke in the reader, Hemingway reveals an early stylistic mastery of the use of repressed emotions to transform plot into art. This technique allows the reader to experience what might be described as a mourning response to the unmourned-for and un-grieved-for losses, disappointments, and grief that Hemingway's characters are themselves unable to feel. Therefore it may be suggested that Hemingway's willfully erected taboo against grief and loss—his fear of vulnerability and his desire to anesthetize himself against it—provides the motivational impulse behind his artistic style.

Although "My Old Man" is viewed as one of the weaker stories in Hemingway's collection, partly because he was accused of basing it too closely on a story already written by Sherwood Anderson, it is still one of the finest fictional representations of a boy's disillusionment with the heroic father ideal. Perhaps it is for this reason that Hemingway was originally drawn so strongly to Anderson's story. This one thematic aspect of the boy's separation-individuation struggle works so well in this story, as in all the Nick Adams stories, because it is a normal and age-appropriate response to be experiencing feelings of denial and repression as a defense against narcissistic disappointment. However, when this same type of disavowal and denial is exhibited by Hemingway's older protagonists, such as Richard Cantwell, Robert Jordan, and Thomas Hudson, it is a symptom, not of healthy adolescent narcissism, but of ego-ideal pathology.

Throughout "My Old Man," young Joe has many opportunities to temper the completeness with which he idolizes his father. After all, Butler was never a particularly successful jockey; he was overweight and a cheat; and there is a hint that he had to leave the States because of some illegal dealings with the racing commission. But while these imperfections are obvious to the reader, they are not acknowledged by Joe, making Joe's repression of loss, grief, and shame the emotional center of his adolescent experience. Joe is unable to think badly of his father. Even the discovery of the part his father played in fixing Kzar's race is not consciously assimilated by Joe; instead he displaces his anger toward his father onto the magnificent horse's jockey, George Gardner. In turn, Joe's intense wish for a heroic father ideal is transferred to the magnificent horse. All he is able to recognize when Kzar loses is that he feels "all trembly and funny inside," since to acknowledge even a partial, small flaw in one's perfect ideal object is to destroy the integrity of the whole. Understandably, then, the final, unavoidable recognition of his father's dishonesty compels Joe to conclude: "Seems like when they get started they don't leave a guy nothing" (129). However, the fact that Hemingway does not allow Joe to admit any doubt about his father's greatness until the very end of the story deprives it of the tension of repression and the need to keep grief at arm's length that gives so many of the stories in *In Our Time* their psychological power.

The child's defensive response to an experience of disillusionment with the overvalued father ideal is also the theme of "Indian Camp." In this story, however, the boy reacts to the narcissistic injury that results from the ideal object being exposed as flawed by suffering a severe disturbance of the ego. Here the attempt at self-esteem regulation dependent upon the maintenance of his ego ideal is interrupted by severe trauma. When the story begins it is evident that young Nick looks up to his father, the important Doctor Adams; and his father's ongoing narrative to his son, whom he calls his "interne" (17), about what he is doing during the operation suggests that he encourages such an identification. This father-son dynamic indicates that Nick's self-esteem, at this point in his life, is narcissistically dependent upon an elevated image of his father.

The central event of the story is the trauma experienced by Nick when he is forced to witness the Indian woman's Cesarean section. Compounding Nick's traumatic ordeal is the awful sight of the woman's dead and bloody husband lying in the upper bunk. Not only is the grotesque scene too much for Nick's young ego to assimilate, but the explicit sexuality of the operation must also have been overwhelming. It is unlikely that a young boy's normal defenses could shield him from these experiences, in the way that Joe's denial in "My Old Man" protected him from a less extreme anxiety. Instead, Nick becomes numb, and "looking away," he closes down his senses: "His curiosity had been gone for a long time" (17).

The final blow to Nick's adolescent ego, which has been invested in his father's grandiose image, occurs when the doctor so drastically miscalculates the husband's responses to his wife's ordeal, first announcing—"Ought to have a look at the proud father"—and then pulling back the blanket to see the Indian's throat "cut from ear to ear" (18). Disillusionment, finally accepted by Joe in Hemingway's later story, is strangely absent from "Indian Camp." As Nick rides back across the lake, he seems closer than ever to his father, and asks him, "Is dying hard, Daddy?" (19). Even then, the boy's anxiety about death seems to disappear like the ripples from the wake of the boat, and, ironically, sitting quietly in the stern while his father rows them both home, Nick "felt quite sure that he would never die" (19).

It is likely that the trauma Nick experiences causes a cathexis of his young ego through which his psychic interest is withdrawn from his ideal object to what Annie Reich would call his "endangered self."[41] Nick's ego is in fact doubly "endangered." First, the once steadfast paternal ego ideal on which his self-esteem depended has been severely and suddenly deflated. Second, Nick is prompted by his father to witness what must have appeared to the boy as a violent molestation of the Indian woman, and this at a time when Nick himself had probably not yet fully overcome the anxiety of his own oedipal contest with his powerful father. If Nick's ego has indeed responded defensively to his ordeal by regressing to a state of infantile dependency, then it is likely that his regression is accompanied by a feminine identification with the Indian woman, transforming her bloody surgery into what he might well have perceived as his own castration at the hands of his father. This temporary regression, however, also enables Nick to experience a renewed feeling of primitive narcissistic omnipotence, which serves to protect him from his castration anxiety. Thus, he can magically sustain his father's ideal strength and deny his own castration fears—both of which are linked through his ego's investment in a grandiose masculine ego ideal—and genuinely believe in the compensating narcissistic fantasy that he "would never die." Whereas in "The Doctor and the Doctor's Wife" the artful psychological tension of the story is created through a displacement of Nick's anger and disappointment, in "Indian Camp" the greater intensity of Nick's terror is brilliantly matched by Hemingway with a far more pathological manifestation of repression in the form of complete denial and hallucinatory fantasy.

In "The Three-Day Blow," the dialogue between Nick Adams and his friend Bill reveals the drama of a boy's strained attempt to find a male role model or ego ideal that will allow him to sever his emotional dependency on the woman/mother, who, in this story, is the absent figure of Nick's ex-girlfriend, Marjorie.[42] In the first part of the story Nick and Bill discuss their favorite books. The boys seem far more interested in the male authors of these books, however, and their conversation periodically returns to thoughts about their fathers, both of whom are something of a disappointment to the boys. Nick thinks Bill's father is "a swell guy," a manly man who drinks liquor and allows his son to drink, whereas Nick's own father has "never taken a drink in his life," and, in Nick's estimation, has "missed a lot." On the other hand, Bill's father, according to his son, "gets a little wild sometimes," suggesting that perhaps he drinks a bit too much. Although Bill defends his father by explaining to Nick that his dad has "had a tough time," his disappointment comes through in his pronouncement to Nick: "Everything's got its compensations" (44).

The underlying emotional and psychological power of the conversation between the two boys issues from the disappointment and sense of loss that they feel in relation to their respective fathers, and yet this grief is never spoken of directly. For Hemingway, the silence of repression— the masculine, heroic refusal to acknowledge the emotional pain that one is feeling—again becomes the vehicle for artistic expression that fundamentally parallels the individuating male's use of an exaggerated masculinity to guard against emotional vulnerability and to defend against lingering dependency needs and a feared identification with the maternal/feminine traits of passivity, weakness, and sentimentality. To speak directly of their grief is taboo for the boys, just as it is taboo to speak about baseball, which has also been compromised in their eyes, because they know it is fixed. Instead, the boys fantasize about their favorite male authors, Walpole and Chesterton, imagining them as substitute fathers whom they can look up to and with whom they can go fishing. "I wish he was here now," Nick confesses longingly about Walpole. "I wonder if he'd like to go fishing," Bill adds. "Sure," Nick says. "He must be about the best guy there is" (43). Realizing, finally, that their hope for an ideal father figure is just an illusion, the boys decide to "get drunk," seeking a different form of escape from their grief.

It is not until the story is half completed and the "Marge business" (46) is brought up that one begins to sense the real reason why Nick, and perhaps Bill as well, are so desperately in need of a strong masculine role model with whom to identify. Beneath all of Nick's talk about being a big man who can be "practical" (45) and "hold his liquor" (44), he harbors a secret dependency on Marge, with whom he has recently broken up. It becomes clear that his repressed grief over her loss is the focal point of Hemingway's story. As soon as her name is mentioned Nick can think of nothing else: "He wasn't sitting in front of the fire or going fishing tomorrow with Bill and his dad or anything. . . . All he knew was that he had once had Marjorie and that he had lost her. She was gone and he had sent her away. That was all that mattered" (47). In order to forget about Marge and disavow his experience of loss, Nick tries to get even more drunk, but it does not work.

A study of the preceding story, "The End of Something," which tells of the break-up between Nick and Marjorie, reveals that it was Nick's fear of intimacy with his sisterly Marge, who had grown into a narcissistic mirror of himself, and his inability to accept his feelings, that originally drove him to send Marge away. Nick is only able to say weakly to Marjorie in explanation for his actions that love "isn't fun any more" (34). It is more likely, however, that because Marjorie and Nick had been seeing each other for so long, and had gotten to "know everything" (34) about each other, the growing intimacy between them, and therefore Nick's own emotional dependency on her, had become too intense for him to handle. Lacking a secure sense of his own masculinity, in large part due to the absence of a strong father figure with whom to identify, Nick experiences intimacy as smothering—a threat to his masculine independence. But, unable to acknowledge or confront his fears, Nick feels an inner need to withdraw completely from the threatening relationship. "I don't know why it was," Nick says to Bill. "I couldn't help it. Just like when the three-day blows come now and rip all the leaves off the trees" (47).

The image of the "three-day blow" is an especially appropriate symbol for Hemingway to employ since it brings to mind both loss—through the metaphor of the changing seasons—and the ether wind of repression that blows that loss away, albeit only for a time. Merely having repressed his dependency needs, Nick's anxiety is not permanently "blown away," but surfaces again when his defenses are down, which is precisely what happens when he starts drinking with Bill.

Like getting drunk, finding male companionship, and the three-day blow, refusing to "talk about" his feelings fails to dispel Nick's grief about Marge and his father, but only buries it beneath a thin surface of repression. By having the boys employ one defensive maneuver after another in an attempt to either distance or anesthetize themselves against grief and disappointment, Hemingway draws out the psychological tension that he maintains throughout the course of the story. Nick, at the end of the story, now confronted by a renewed need to re-repress his grief from loss—a need reawakened in him by his remembrance of Marjorie—discovers that an even better way to repair the pain of loss is to think of it as temporary. By entertaining the possibility that he "might get back into" his relationship again, Nick feels better. He willfully reinstates his repression of loss and grief by choosing to believe that: "There was not anything that was irrevocable. . . . He felt happy. Nothing was finished. Nothing was ever lost" (48). In a manner akin to Nick's disavowal in "Indian Camp," Hemingway creates an artistic textual product by using Nick's repressive denial of loss as a reaction-formation that, temporarily at least, postpones the painful recognition of grief from loss. As usual, the reader's reaction to the disavowal of grief is predominantly a mourning response to the losses for which Nick himself is unable to mourn—a cathartic experience that Hemingway's male character is himself denied.

Even if Nick were to "get back" (48) with Marjorie, however, there is a strong possibility that the same pattern of feared intimacy, break-up, and repressed longing would occur again. For without a secure, individuated masculine identity and a fully worked-through oedipus complex, there can be no satisfactory emotional separation from the mother/woman. Hence, in a manner reminiscent of Ishmael's rapprochement-phase crisis, Nick will always feel ambivalent toward Marjorie, one moment wishing to be with her always, and the next wanting to escape from the emotional engulfment aroused by the intimacy between them. As Bill cautions Nick, getting back with Marjorie is as much of a "danger" (48) and a source of anxiety as it is a relief from anxiety. And of course, as Bill says, the commitment of marriage is the worst trap of all: "Once a man's married he's absolutely bitched" (46). Nick's anxiety does not result from entrapment, however, but from his own repression, and from his refusal to confront his ongoing separation anxiety and insecure masculinity.

As in so many of Hemingway's stories, "The Three-Day Blow" has no women, only male characters engaged in, or talking about, super-masculine activities such as hunting, fishing, baseball, or drinking. To the man, or boy, who fears the complex of emotional intimacy and his own dependency needs, women are incompatible with a masculine self-image. Nick cannot "go" with Marjorie and at the same time be a real man with Bill. As Bill says, if Nick had not been "wise" and broken off with Marjorie, he "would be back home working," he "wouldn't even be going fishing tomorrow" (46–47). Yet, the mother/woman, in the guise of the repressed and longed-for girlfriend, is omnipresent in the story, and the emotional and psychological brilliance of Hemingway's male-male dramas is contained in the fictional space of her absence—her loss, and the man's repressed mourning for her loss.

Like most of Hemingway's young protagonists, Krebs, in "Soldier's Home," suffers the torments of a frustrated separation-individuation process. In the case of Krebs, as in the story of Orpen, it is the absent father who features most prominently in the boy's psychic life. The physical absence of Krebs's father symbolizes the more significant emotional absence of the father in relation to the son. As a result, Krebs is forced to act out his struggles with his father indirectly, through his mother. One morning, when Krebs's mother informs him that his father has decided to allow him the use of the car in the evenings, Krebs seems pleased, but he is doubtful that the idea came from his father and not from his mother. It is as if any direct interest in him shown by his father is too foreign an idea for him to accept. Krebs is accustomed to his father being "non-committal" toward him (70). Later, however, when it comes time to go to his father's office to speak to him in person about the car, Krebs refuses to go, indicating that his feelings toward his father are ambivalent, alternating between a longing to repair the sense of loss he feels, and a wish to act out his resentment.[43]

Whenever Krebs's mother speaks to him his reaction is to feel "embarrassed and resentful as always" (75). Like Nick Adams, Krebs has been unable to develop positively in relation to his father, and so instead has developed negatively against his mother, and against women in general.

Also like Nick, Krebs's antagonism toward the woman/mother is a consequence of his failure to develop, with the help of the father, a secure masculine identity, leaving him open to the danger of emotional engulfment by the smothering mother. With a lack of emotional distance separating the boy from his mother, it is a short step for Krebs to regress to an infantile relationship with her. Consequently, when he realizes he has hurt her, he calls her "Mummy," pretends to pray with her, and childishly consoles her by promising to "try and be a good boy for you" (76). Still imprisoned in his identification with the mother, the son fears the feminine side of his own personality. It is, therefore, not only the actual mother that Krebs rejects but his entire emotional self. Hence, when his mother asks him: "Don't you love your mother, dear boy?" and Krebs hurtfully replies, "No," he defends himself and tries to soothe her by explaining, "I don't love anybody" (76).

Furthermore, Krebs wants a girlfriend, but he does not want the complicated emotional involvement of a relationship. Seeing the cute girls around town, Krebs says to himself that: "He did not want them themselves really. They were too complicated. . . . He did not want to get into the intrigue and the politics" (71). Instead, Krebs convinces himself that one does not "need a girl unless you thought about them" (72). Krebs, however, thinks about girls all the time, and his stubborn denial fools no one but himself. One cannot help but feel Krebs's pain and psychological discomfort when reading Hemingway's story; but what the reader feels above all else is the frustration of Krebs's lack of insight into his inner conflicts (as was the case with Nick Adams). Hence, the reader is compelled to mourn the fact that Krebs is likely never to work through the issues that trouble him so deeply. While the reader may glean an important lesson from Krebs's pain, Krebs himself is the sacrificial victim of Hemingway's art of repression, and so must bear the burden of an unconscious unilluminated by understanding.

What Krebs is really lacking in his life is the self-confidence and self-esteem that would enable him to talk to a girl—to do the kind of "work" required to "get her" (71).[44] The discord between Krebs's experience of self and his desired self-image is the central psychological tension evoked by Hemingway in "Soldier's Home," surfacing in the narrative through Krebs's chronic lying about his war experiences. Krebs has set too high an ego ideal for himself, and in order to live up to it he is compelled to lie: "Krebs found that to be listened to at all he had to lie," and soon a "distaste for everything that had happened to him in the war set in because of the lies he had told" (69).[45] Lacking a personalized father figure, it is likely that Krebs's father ideal took on mythic, heroic proportions, as it did for Nick, Joe, and Orpen. The great war heroes who populate Orpen's "Hall of Heroes," and who appear in the history books about war that Krebs likes to read, have undoubtedly become the ideal objects on which Krebs bases his masculine self-identity and self-esteem. This perfect and exotic image of the father presents an impossible ideal for Krebs's ego to measure itself against.

Krebs's suspicion that his mother "made" his father agree to give him the car, along with her assumptions about how "weak men are" (75), suggest that Krebs's mother is the more dominating of his two parents. The poor reality-testing skills that result when a boy lacks a strong father figure fuel Krebs's narcissistic inflation by allowing him to persist in his belief in a grandiose father ideal and in a related concept of self, untempered by the compromises and disappointments of reality. Hence, the most apparent manifestation of Krebs's prolonged immaturity and low self-esteem is his inability to face inner and outer reality. Consequently, Krebs's primary concern is "to keep his life from being complicated" (76): "He wanted his life to go smoothly" (77). He therefore does not try to go out and meet a girl, and he will not meet with his father at the office. "He would miss that one" (77). Instead, he chooses to immerse himself in the childish world of his younger sister. "You're my girl now" (74), he tells her at breakfast: Seeking to escape from his adult responsibilities, he resolves to run away to Kansas City and "get a job" as soon as he can, but for the present, he "would go over to the schoolyard to watch Helen play indoor baseball" (77). Regression, even if it carries incestuous implications of brother-sister love, is easier for Krebs than is confronting the pain of loss and disillusionment, both in relation to his past war experiences, and to his present smothering and aimless existence.

As he entered his twenties, Hemingway used his exceptional psychological acumen to understand and evaluate the grief, emotional pain, and losses he experienced during the war and in his early relationship with his family. In his early life and art, Hemingway possessed an intense, courageous unwillingness to buckle under the onslaught of his griefs and losses. This unwillingness is transformed, in his art, into a fundamental inability on the part of his characters to recognize consciously and, hence, work through, the disappointments and disillusionments of growing up. Hemingway meticulously designs his narrative text as an artistic totem to enforce his private taboo against grief, disillusionment, and his own feminine sensibilities. In *Death in the Afternoon* Hemingway describes his typical story as an "iceberg," in which a part is used to stand for the whole. In a similar way, in his early stories, action and behavior uninformed by self-analysis, psychological insight, and understanding—behavior that reflects a displacement, disavowal, projection, or rationalization of repressed painful feelings—are used by Hemingway as a replacement for the emotions that motivate and infuse the behavior of his fictional heroes.

The Sun Also Rises: *The Code Hero and the Phallic Mother/Woman*

In *The Sun Also Rises,* Hemingway's first attempt at novel-writing, both his taboo against grief and loss, and his masculine defense against feminine identification, are brought forward into the plot and textual surface of the fictional narrative from the repressed unconscious of his characters. The loss and disappointment, as well as the endangered masculine identity, that are repressed or packed down into the unconscious of Hemingway's younger protagonists in *In Our Time,* are manifested in corporeal form in *The Sun Also Rises* through the groin wound that Jake Barnes received during the war. In addition, drinking, in Hemingway's novel, becomes the "ether," or anesthetic, that allows his characters, as Orpen explained, "somehow" not to "feel bad" about the sense of loss that pervades their post-war experience. The ritualized art of bullfighting provides them with a means of controlling and mastering both the chaos of non-meaning and the threat of painful emotions that the narrative of repression provides for Hemingway's characters in his short fiction. The psychological tension that, in the short stories, is produced by Hemingway through his characters' inability to confront grief, loss, and disappointment is evoked in the narrative surface of his novel primarily through Jake's ongoing attempts to come to terms with his physical loss, emotional pain, and vulnerable masculinity.

Bullfighting is the behavioral *code* in Hemingway's novel that replaces the stylistic *code* of repressed emotions that he employed so successfully in his short stories to guard against both grief and an insecure masculine identity. The *code* of controlled and ritualized behavior in sports and war that Hemingway begins to formulate in *The Sun Also Rises* complements the *code* of repressed emotions demonstrated in his short stories.

Both were embraced equally by a male American culture that sought justification and support for the exaggerated masculine behavior that incorporates, and depends upon, the repression of feelings, the lack of overt emotional expression, and the repudiation of inner feminine sensibilities.

Furthermore, in *The Sun Also Rises,* it is not the symbiotic, or nurturing, mother but the phallic mother who holds sway over Hemingway's artistic psyche.[46] A brief look at Hemingway's life between the early and mid-1920s reveals a psychoanalytically plausible explanation for the change in emphasis from the nurturing to the phallic mother in his fiction over this short span of years. There is little question that Grace Hemingway had strong phallic components in relation to all of her children, as well as to her husband. It has often been suggested, in fact (as Hemingway covertly reveals in his Orpen story), that he derived much of his artistic talent, ambition, and creative sensibilities from his mother, whose dominating and contentious personality was otherwise a source of great anguish to him, particularly as it rendered problematic his masculine identification with his father. Grace's gesture of defiance in kicking Hemingway out of the house in 1920 was merely the culmination of his heated conflictual relationship with this phallic maternal figure.

Through the company of the expatriates he sought out when he arrived in Paris in 1922, Hemingway came to associate creative and artistic potency with promiscuity, gender-crossing, and, particularly, the phallic woman or butch lesbian—the most prominent of whom, in the next few years of his life, was Gertrude Stein. Stein, according to Peter Griffin, "was Paris to Hemingway."[47] More than a social and professional acquaintance, in Hemingway's eyes Stein personified the progressive thinking about writing and art that the young author thought he had been striving for. As fate, and psychological destiny, would have it, Hemingway found in Stein the phallic/creative mother whom he could envy and with whom he could identify.[48] Hemingway's association with Gertrude Stein thus enabled him to play out his own phallic contest with his mother, Grace Hemingway, whose musical talents made her, if we recall from the autobiographical Orpen story, young Hemingway's first source of artistic envy and inspiration.[49] Stein tutored and encouraged Hemingway in his writing, and he, in turn, freely partook of her phallic, creative powers.

In late adolescence, a boy experiences an increase in genital libido and a decrease in pregenitality. If, as is the case with Hemingway's male protagonists, and perhaps with Hemingway himself, he enters this genital phase with a persisting fixation on, or infantile need for oneness with, the archaic mother, he is likely to suffer an especially strong castration anxiety in relation to the phallic mother, or to women in general.[50] This additional anxiety aggravates the normal feelings of enfeebled masculinity, homosexual fears, and gender-identity confusion that beset a boy during this phase in his development. As a defense against the castrating mother/woman, the boy often seeks the "protective and reassuring peership" of an idealized father figure. If the actual father is absent, or in the boy's eyes, too weak or disappointing to play this role, he will pursue, as Orpen and Nick Adams do, a cultural or abstract image of strong, masculine heroism and narcissistically share in its ideal "paternal power and superiority" (Blos, "Genealogy," 57).

Through the psychological dynamic linking the threat from the phallic, castrating woman to the defensive desire for an aggrandized, masculine heroic ideal, it becomes possible to understand the connection in Hemingway's creative unconscious between Jake's insecure masculinity and the Hemingway *code hero,* who makes his first real appearance in *The Sun Also Rises.* Jake's impotence symbolically situates him in the role of the adolescent who manifests a feeble masculine component, and who both pines after and feels threatened by the manly Brett, his maternal-phallic rival. Brett embodies the phallic power that the emasculated Jake longs to possess for himself. He craves the irresistible sexuality that Brett seems to exude, and yet, the closer he gets to her the more he is reminded of his own lack of phallic potency.

Mark Spilka sees Brett, and all of Hemingway's masculine women, as embodying an ideal androgynous state of being to which Hemingway unconsciously aspired. Jake's wounded condition, Spilka believes, renders him half female, and therefore androgynous.[51] Androgyny is far from an ideal gender state for either Jake or Hemingway, however. It is merely a symbolic representation of the adolescent's unavoidably ambivalent position. Gender-identity confusion is a usual symptom of late male adolescence. Therefore, it is not Brett's androgyny that makes her so appealing to Jake—and to Hemingway—but her flagrantly displayed masculinity. According to gender psychologists, the "mannish" woman reinforces, rather than challenges, patriarchal sex-role and gender categories because she reasserts the male-dominant stance that the wish to be a man, or as like a man as possible, is normal.[52] As a representative of this type of woman, Brett strengthens Jake's masculine defense against feminine identification insofar as she truly strives to be a "gent"—just one of the "chaps."[53]

Through the bullfighter, Pedro Romero, Hemingway found a way to valorize the fearless, physically competent bullfighter, or *code hero*, and his observer counterpart, the *aficionado*, thereby separating masculinity and femininity, and asserting the superior position of the man. Hemingway imaginatively subdues the phallic quality of Brett by pairing her romantically with the virile and irresistible Romero—the ideal man. Through his identification as an *aficionado* with Romero, Jake attains the "protective and reassuring peership" of a "real" man, sharing with him "the idealized paternal power and superiority" that he himself is lacking (Blos, "Genealogy," 57).

Men Without Women: *Denial of Loss and the Sacrifice of the Emotional Self*

The theme of the young male's separation from the maternal/feminine, and his individuation toward masculine selfhood, appears periodically in Hemingway's 1927 collection of stories, *Men Without Women*. The repression of grief and the denial of loss permeate these stories, particularly insofar as these gestures of repudiation serve as defensive strategies used by the male to guard against emotional vulnerability and feminine identification. In "Fifty Grand," Jack grows tired of the great effort it takes to sustain his victorious masculine role, and he openly admits that all he wants is to return home to his wife and family. Bill Campbell, in "A Pursuit Race," refuses altogether to engage in competition for women or sport by hiding under his bedsheets, choosing instead to "kiss" his bedsheets—in effect falling in love with his own defensive tactic of denial and repudiation.[54]

The pain that young Nick Adams suffers in "Ten Indians," when he discovers from his father that "his girl" (98), Prudence Mitchell, was seen "having quite a time" in the woods with Frank Washburn, similarly isolates him from the world around him. Insensitive to the depth of his son's anguish, Dr. Adams foolishly, and perhaps sadistically, offers Nick the "opium," or consolation, of "another piece" of pie to heal his wounded heart (101). Rather than remain silent about what Nick is feeling, as Hemingway often does in his stories, this time he distances Nick from his feelings through ignorance, implying that this is the boy's first experience of loss in love. "My heart's broken," Nick thinks. "If I feel this way my heart must be broken" (102). Hemingway allows Nick to receive temporary solace from his grief not through repression but through sleep. Surely there is no reader who does not empathically recognize the peace of oblivion that sleep represents to the bereaved, nor that devastating moment of lost bliss when Nick awakens the next morning and suddenly "remembered that his heart was broken" (102). One partakes of Hemingway's taboo against grief by wishing that Nick could simply have forgotten forever, (or in terms of Hemingway's craft, repressed indefinitely), the painful emotional wound that he has received. In this story, as in so many of Hemingway's best stories, the author is aware of the fact that art depends on loss—on a veiling of the painful contents of the unconscious—and on the agonizing release of tension when the grief that before was unconscious suddenly becomes conscious, and as such, demands that a new strategy of repression become implemented and enforced.

In "A Canary for One," "Cat in the Rain," and "Hills Like White Elephants," the narrative tension is produced not from the discrepancy between the conscious and the unconscious, but between the two separate conscious minds of a man and a woman. What is lost in these stories is the happiness that would, in a perfect world, result from a communion of separately directed minds, and from an intimacy of shared sensibilities. In these stories the characters' grief results from their awareness of this unbridgeable gap, and from their inability to restore their lost intimacy as a couple. Hemingway carefully crafts these stories of "gender miscommunication" [55] by pointing to that which is missing, or lost, from the dialogue between the man and the woman, just as in *In Our Time*, he points to the painful emotions that are repressed by the hero into the realm of the unconscious.

Of all the stories in the 1927 collection *Men Without Women*, "In Another Country" presents most perfectly a man's willful attempt to protect himself against the grief of loss. As in the Orpen story, the crippling wounds that the soldiers receive in the exaggerated masculine activity of war merge symbolically with the deep-seated psychic wounds that result from the loss of a woman's love. The men who come to the hospital for rehabilitation are led to believe that the machines will enable their mutilated bodies to be "completely restored" (38), but the experienced and cynical Major knows that these artificial contrivances will never repair the physical and mental losses that he has suffered. If, for

Hemingway, the physical wound is a corporeal symbol of emotional pain and loss, his message in this story is that no artificial contrivances or prosthetic devices can repair or permanently eradicate loss—neither machines, the ether of repression, drinking, nor the "opiums" of religion, money, patriotism, or music, as suggested in the later story "The Gambler, the Nun, and the Radio."

The Major can neither "resign" himself to the loss of his wife, nor is he able to work through it by giving himself up to grief. Instead, his grief is displaced onto his anger and repudiation. "A man must not marry," he says angrily to Nick: "He should not place himself in a position to lose. He should find things he cannot lose" (37). No statement describes more succinctly Hemingway's task as a writer throughout the 1920s and 1930s. Rather than acknowledging and dealing with one's early experiences of loss and disillusionment in love, a man should avoid all inner psychic conflicts with women by physically and emotionally isolating himself, immersing himself in wholly masculine—that is, what he believes to be non-feminine—activities, such as fishing, hunting, writing, or war. Even if he does manage to distance himself emotionally from women, his denial and avoidance cannot eradicate or repair loss and grief but only repress them, and at the center of the young male's unconscious experience, as in the central courtyard of the Milan hospital, there will always be a silent funeral sermon in process. As Hemingway demonstrates in this story, loss kills something in the soul; it numbs the heart permanently against future pain. The "country" of the wounded heart, where one is always irrevocably "a little detached" from the fullness of life, is the "other" world of grief and mourning that Hemingway juxtaposes with the world outside the hospital that is filled with people who have not yet been "crippled" by life's losses and disappointments, and who therefore "did not understand" (35)—who, indeed, *could* not understand—those who struggle for renewed life within.

In the last story in the collection, "Now I Lay Me," Nick uses pleasant and emotionally neutral memories as a totem to ward off his grief from the losses he suffered during the war, as well as the grief from disappointment in his mother and father. The free association of his memories, however, typically leads him to remember precisely those painful issues that he wishes to forget; namely, his father's passivity in relation to his mother's dominant role in the family. But, given Nick's lack of insight and understanding about the failures of his parents' marriage, he cannot quite make sense of why the thought of being married could never, as John tries to convince him, "fix up everything" that troubles him, thereby allowing him to fall asleep without fear (137). "Now I Lay Me" is a parable of Hemingway's artistic style in that it is about the desperate need to master the contents of the conscious mind so that loss and grief are denied entry into this precariously and defensively controlled domain of the psyche. Once again, Hemingway adroitly allows the reader to gain the greater and more lasting satisfaction or control of chaotic experience that he deliberately refuses to grant to his characters.

A Farewell to Arms: *Disillusionment and the Flight from the Heroic Self-Image*

Nick Adams's traumatic war experience foreshadows Hemingway's own growing disillusionment in the years that followed 1929, not only with the masculine ideal of war, but with his own grandiose heroic self-image, as can be seen in the early Orpen story. Hemingway's 1929 novel, *A Farewell to Arms*, bears a close resemblance to Hemingway's story fragment about the disillusioned and narcissistically wounded soldier Orpen, who chooses to escape from his own fear of death and his growing disillusionment with war by returning to the comforting embraces of his mother. From the early chapters of the book, Lieutenant Frederic Henry is unable to identify himself with the manly activity of war. He is drawn to spend his leave whoring in Milan rather than hunting in the mountains, and upon his return makes the observation that "it did not matter whether I was there or not"—that the war "seemed to run better while I was away."[56] Frederic Henry feels the war "did not have anything to do with me" (37), and finds the idea of carrying a pistol ridiculous. Furthermore, he has no desire to go to Carpathians where the fighting is. For Frederic Henry, as for Orpen, there is something unreal and distant about war. To be in the midst of the war seems to Frederic to be like acting in a movie. To echo Orpen's words about war: "You had to pretend to like it."

The fact that Frederic Henry needed little incentive to lose confidence in the ideal of war, and the ease with which he comes to view his abstract heroic ideal as a pretense and a fake, suggests that he, like Orpen, initially possessed an abstract conception of idealized heroism, and so has failed to establish a secure identification with a realistic paternal figure. As such, like Orpen, he is vulnerable to the regressive fantasy of falling in love with, or being sexually drawn to, a woman who doubles as the narcissistically gratifying maternal object, thus enabling him to recapture, as Orpen does, his infantile lost paradise.

Like Orpen, to lie wounded and helpless in his hospital bed makes Frederic "feel very young," like "being put to bed after early supper" (68). By physically wounding his hero, Hemingway again repairs in fantasy the adolescent's narcissistic wound, which signifies a blow to the masculine ego, and results in a breakdown between the ego and the paternal ego ideal. This in turn motivates a renewed need for narcissistic gratification that may be fulfilled by a regressive fusion with the good, nurturing mother. Wounding facilitates the Hemingway hero's regressive fantasy for unconditional love. It is not the wound itself, therefore, but this unconscious desire for love that may be identified as the repressed, which continually returns in Hemingway's fiction.

Catherine's desire for Frederic mirrors his own fear of loss and separation. Her sexual promiscuity is motivated by the loss of her fiance to whom, as she now regrets, she had denied sex before he went off to war, where he was later killed. As she explains to Frederic, "I thought perhaps he couldn't stand it and then of course he was killed and that was the end of it" (19). Thus, both Catherine and Frederic are searching to regain a love object that this time cannot be lost, which implies a wish for total self-annihilation through mutual love.

More conscious of her narcissistic desires than Frederic is of his, Catherine longs for complete fusion with him—to feel "our hearts beating" (92) as one—and for the assurance that he has "never belonged to any one else" (105) but her. Like the perfect nurturing mother, she tells him during their lovemaking that she will "do anything you want. . . . There isn't any me any more" (106). Physically she makes him "all clean inside and out" (104), symbolically restoring him to a state of infantile purity; and after his wounding, like the good-mother nurse in Hemingway's Orpen story, she embodies his unconscious hope of never having to return to war again.

Frederic Henry's "corruption," or regression to infantile fusion, is made complete with his desertion from the army. Hemingway plays out Frederic's symbolic rebirth through his escape from the Germans into a river from which he finally "crawled out, pushed on through the willows and onto the bank" (227). With this gesture his allegiance to patriarchal society "was washed away in the river along with any obligation. . . . I was through. . . . That life was over" (232–33). Having surrendered to his regressive desires for the nurturing mother, Frederic's infantile needs rise to the surface: "I was not made to think. I was made to eat. My God, yes. Eat and drink and sleep with Catherine" (233). The moral implicit in Frederic Henry's actions is one that corroborates both contemporary studies of gender identity and the most ancient Indo-European folklore; namely, that in a patriarchal civilization love is incompatible with patriarchal social structures, and "peace"—meaning the blissful peace of regressive infantile fusion—can only be won at the expense of the sacrifice of a man's masculine identity and autonomy.[57] To achieve a permanent union with Catherine feels to Frederic as if he had at last "come home," and he confesses: "We could feel alone when we were together, alone against the others" (249).[58] As Freud and others have proposed, however, the lovers may feel entirely "together," but only by maintaining an opposite stance "against the others." This isolation from the world thus represents merely another kind of loss that Frederic Henry embraces in exchange for his feelings of loss and disillusionment about war.

Later, therefore, when secreted in a small Italian hotel with Catherine, and occupied with nothing but the primal activities of eating, sleeping, and lovemaking, Frederic Henry begins to show signs of restlessness and boredom. He avoids reading the paper, which reminds him of his desertion and separation from the outside world; and it begins to dawn on him what the "stakes" (31) of his self-willed narcissistic engulfment in the sexual, maternal female really are. Not only does he "feel like a criminal" (251), but after experiencing a taste of his old masculine autonomy by spending an afternoon fishing with the barman, he confesses to Catherine: "My life used to be full of everything. . . . Now if you aren't with me I haven't a thing in the world" (257).

After the lovers escape across the lake to Switzerland, the symptoms of Frederic's isolation begin to worsen, so that now Catherine too senses his restlessness. "I should think sometimes you would want to see other people besides me" (297), she says to him anxiously. Although he denies his emptiness, the narcissistic Catherine, who seeks to merge her identity with Frederic's, still feels threatened and redoubles her hold on him by attempting to persuade him to let his hair grow long like hers so that "we'd both be alike. . . . I want us to be all mixed up. I don't want you to go away" (299–300). Despite her wish that they both "go to sleep at exactly the same moment" (301), Frederic does not go to sleep, but lies awake in his bed, contemplating his growing feeling of entrapment.

Through the character of Frederic Henry, in *A Farewell to Arms,* Hemingway explores the ambivalence between the desire to indulge in narcissistic and regressive patterns of behavior in order to escape from his feelings of grief, and his awareness of the dangers of such behavior.

It is impossible to say for certain what led to Hemingway's final decision to kill off Catherine and her baby during childbirth, thereby setting Frederic Henry free from what was originally his refuge from the burden of military heroism. Perhaps it was his own unconscious struggle to assert his masculine autonomy against the marvelous but dangerous comforts of narcissistic, or regressive, maternal fusion and sexual indulgence; or perhaps it was a fictional act of revenge on the procreative-phallic woman and her latest offspring.[59] On a much more fundamental level, however, it is also possible that as a staunch and defensive champion of patriarchal civilization, Hemingway simply could not envision an alternative scenario within the possibilities allowed by Western culture that would enable Frederic and Catherine to live contentedly in isolation from, in Freud's words, "the surrounding world." Hemingway also may have realized that love and sex, particularly regressive, narcissistically based love, do not provide a permanent catharsis for grief; that like gambling, patriotism, drinking, and not-thinking, they are merely temporary anesthetics against disillusionment and loss, and so in time must be given up, albeit reluctantly.

A number of Hemingway's critics have suggested that the rain outside the hospital, through which Frederic Henry walks at the end of the novel, symbolizes his unvoiced feelings about Catherine's death. I would alter this interpretation slightly by proposing that the falling rain represents the tears of grief that Frederic Henry is *unable* to shed himself. In what has been called the omitted "religious" ending to the novel, Hemingway writes: "Blessed are the dead that rain falls on, I thought. Why was that?"[60] Hemingway's phrasing calls to mind the Mosaic Law, which Twain employs more directly in *The Adventures of Tom Sawyer* as a metaphor for his own taboo against grief: "Blessed are those who mourn, for they shall be comforted." Perhaps what Hemingway had in mind in his alternative construction of Frederic's thoughts was this: blessed are those who, like the rain, can cry tears of grief, for they, through their open expression of mourning, can find meaning in death, and thereby find comfort for their loss.

In both the published version of the novel's ending, and a number of the unpublished versions, Frederic finds saying good-bye to the dead

Catherine to be "like saying good-by *[sic]* to a statue" (332). In one of the omitted endings in which this sentence occurs, Frederic returns to Catherine's death-bed one last time to see if he could find an emotion to fill the void that he feels; but, as he admits in the published ending, "it wasn't any good" (332). Because Frederic Henry cannot openly express or acknowledge his grief, he must suffer the more devastating loss to the self that results from repressing one's emotions, and mourn eternally, not only for the beloved whom he has lost, but for the *nada* of his own inner emotional emptiness.

Winner Take Nothing: *Creeping Disillusionment and the Increasing Hazards of Repressed Grief*

Hemingway's obsession with loss, grief, annihilation, and spiritual in-completeness in his 1933 collection of stories, *Winner Take Nothing,* as the title suggests, reveals his growing awareness, first explored in *A Farewell to Arms,* of the price of increased loneliness and depression that must be paid when one attempts to escape or anesthetize oneself against grief and loss, and, in doing so, to exclude "feminine" emotions from one's experience of life.[61] The overt concern with death, departures, divorce, spiritual emptiness, and mutilation in these stories indicates that Hemingway was becoming increasingly self-conscious about the elegiac nature of his fictional technique of tabooed and repressed grief.

"The Mother of a Queen" is one of the most provocative stories in the collection, due to the connection that is made between the man's denial of grief, his emotional untouchability, and his inability to separate from the mother. To bury one's dead mother for only five years, as the bullfighter does, and to refuse to pay for her continued burial care, suggests a pathological inability to accept that she is dead and so perma-nently lost. By not burying his mother, the matador is able to retain his psychic connection with her by imagining, as he tells his manager, that "she is all about me in the air, like the birds and the flowers. Now she will always be with me" (64). His inability to make an initial separation from his mother and break his early feminine identification has had a profound impact upon his adult life. Not only is his continuing feminine identification manifested in his active, adult homosexuality, but he also shows an intolerance for loss, separation, and grief of any kind.

Therefore, just as the bullfighter uses the flimsy excuse of poverty to keep his mother "alive" and close to him, he keeps his nurturing manager from leaving him by withholding the money and emotional concern that his friend deserves. "Why don't you pay me the money you owe me so I can leave?" his manager asks him. "I want you here," the matador replies, "and I will pay you. But now I need the money" (65). As in Hemingway's earlier stories, the repressed grief and longing for love that lie behind that grief are displaced, this time onto money, thus evoking a narrative tension through the matador's unwillingness to connect his displaced thoughts and actions to their disavowed motivating emotions; namely, the disavowed feelings of deprivation and loss. When the manager, in disgust, insults the bullfighter with the accusation that he "never had a mother" (67), the matador denies all his emotional ties to his mother, and along with them his grief over her death, with the rationalization that she died before he was old enough to grow to love her. This seems an odd statement considering the fact that the adult matador's mother died only five years earlier. One can only speculate, therefore, that some disturbance in the mother-child relationship resulted in an insecure attachment from which the matador never fully recovered. In this somewhat parodic story of the omission of feelings and the denial of feminine identification in the face of gross evidence to the contrary, the reader is led to conclude that it is not only the matador but the majority of Hemingway's male protagonists about whom the manager speaks when he dismally concludes about "queens": "You can't touch them. Nothing, nothing can touch them." (67).

"God Rest You Merry, Gentlemen" and "A Day's Wait" are relatively inferior stories insofar as they depend for their psychological tension on delusion rather than on defenses erected by the characters to enforce their own, and Hemingway's, taboo against grief. The young boy in "A Day's Wait" is merely under a misconception about the difference between Fahrenheit and Centigrade as measures of temperature; and the boy who begs the doctors to castrate him in "God Rest You Merry, Gentlemen" naively believes that, by doing so, the doctors could put an end to his "sinful" lust. The latter story is redeemed, however, by the psychological complexity of the Jewish Dr. Fisher's unspoken yet implied problematic relationship with the mythical Christian concepts of hell, damnation, and salvation.

In contrast to these two stories is the more successful "A Clean, Well-Lighted Place," which in technique and theme is a companion piece to the earlier story "Now I Lay Me." Like the post-war Nick Adams, the old waiter fears oblivion, chaos, the dark, and lack of control; or in other words: death, meaninglessness, and "nada." Like Nick, the old waiter may indeed have insight into the nature of his grief and fear, but he is unwilling, or unable, to admit to himself the real emotional cause of his discomfort, instead choosing to believe that "it is probably only insomnia" (17) that prevents him from resting peacefully until daylight comes. The ritual of work, like Nick's ritual of reciting from memory the names of rivers and people, acts as a charm against the infiltration of the mind by negative thoughts and fears. There is a clear correlation between Nick Adams or the old waiter, and Huck Finn, who is perpetually attempting to keep busy and moving, to "put in the time," in order to ward off loneliness and depression. In the same way that Huck refuses to think about things that are too terrifying or violent, Nick and the old man, as well as many of Hemingway's other fictional heroes, discover that by not thinking they can avoid the emotional pain associated with those thoughts.

As in "Big Two-Hearted River," Hemingway projects onto the old waiter's landscape—the cafe—the internal conflict that afflicts him. The well-lit cafe that exudes "a certain cleanness and order" (17) parallels his defensive psychological bulwark against darkness, night, and the grief of having nowhere else to go, just as the swamp and the warmth and security of Nick's campsite represent for him the overwhelming sense of loss, and the protective safety of ritual and control, respectively. Without work the old waiter's life is utterly defined by a feeling of loss; yet the artificially enforced distance that he creates between himself and his grief signifies for the reader what is perhaps a more tragic sense of loss and grief.

In "Fathers and Sons," the story that concludes the collection, Hemingway resumes the saga of Nick Adams for one last time. Through the voice of the adult Nick, Hemingway confesses that he "had gotten rid of many things by writing them," and although he says "it was still too early" to write about the life and death of his father, this story is Nick's first attempt to deal with his grief-filled relationship with his father (154). Nick's love and respect for his father as a hunter and a model of masculine behavior are rendered equivocal by his father's inability to teach his son what he needed, and wanted, to know about sex. Dr. Adams was "as sound on" fishing and shooting as he "was unsound on sex" (153). Nick says that as a boy he loved and idolized his father, but he also reveals that there was little emotional intimacy between them. Mr. Adams undoubtedly kept his "hands off" his son the same way that he believed one should "keep your hands off of people" in general, whether for love or lust (154).

This lack of true emotional understanding between father and son takes its final toll on Nick when his father takes his own life. On the face of the corpse Nick must have read a certain grief and despair that he could not fully understand; yet in retrospect, Nick now sees that it was a face that "had been making itself and being made for a long time" (154). Like a ghost who cannot rest in peace, Nick's father "came back to him in the fall of the year, or in the early spring when there had been jacksnipe on the prairie, or when he saw shocks of corn, or when he saw a lake" (159). Perhaps Nick could not bury the image of his father and achieve catharsis through grieving because of the ambivalence he felt toward him, which he had never attempted, until now, to work through.

As was also true for Hemingway, after Nick "was fifteen he had shared nothing" with his father (159). Since, as a boy, Nick repressed his grief over having been something of a lost son with an absent father, he still unconsciously mourns the fact of never really having come to know his father. Hemingway brilliantly captures the repressed grief in the father-son relationship in the episode that Nick remembers about how he felt "sick" (159) when he was forced to wear his father's old smelly longjohns. He buried them under some stones in the creek, and when he told his father that he had lost them he was whipped for lying. His father did not ask his son, nor was Nick able to confess to him, what had really happened. Nick had no idea why his father's smell disgusted him; nor did he understand why he found himself sitting "inside the woodshed with the door open, his shotgun loaded and cocked, looking across at his father sitting on the screen porch reading the paper, and thought, 'I can blow him to hell. I can kill him' " (159). One hardly needs the help of psychoanalytic theory to infer from this episode that Nick perhaps felt as guilty as if he had pulled the trigger himself when his father finally shot himself many years later, and that it was this guilt that rendered grieving for his father's death difficult if not impossible. It is not only Nick's guilt, however, that Hemingway draws out in the story "Fathers and Sons," but also the son's grief over the lack of intimacy, and the loss of love, in his relationship with his father.

Most disturbing in this story is the shadowy presence of Nick's own young son who, throughout most of the narrative, sleeps on the seat of the car at his father's side. The adult Nick is still so preoccupied with his own adolescent relationship with his father that he all but ignores the real presence of his own son who, when he awakens finally, repeatedly insists that he someday be allowed "to pray at the tomb of my grandfather" (162). Like Nick in relation to Dr. Adams, Nick's son idolizes his father, and cannot believe that his grandfather could possibly have ever been "a better shot" than Nick. Yet the son's persistent interest in his grandfather suggests that something is lacking in his relationship with his own father. "I hope we won't live somewhere so that I can never go to pray at your tomb when you are dead," the boy says to Nick (162). Nick's relationship with his son clearly is at a crossroads, whereby the son's idealization of the heroic image of the father can be replaced by real lasting intimacy, or take the same route that leads to loss and grief that Nick's father-son relationship had taken before him.

After Hemingway's death, his son Gregory, although he loved and respected his father, confessed that he "felt profound relief when they lowered my father's body into the ground and I realized that he was really dead, that I couldn't disappoint him, couldn't hurt him anymore."[62] In the story "Fathers and Sons," Nick realizes that he was *forced* to disappoint his father by fornicating and masturbating, and by not keeping his hands off of people; and therefore that it was his father who had disappointed him by insisting that such behavior is weak and sinful. Perhaps Gregory felt he could not live up to his father's impossible expectations to shoot well, to be athletic and heroic, and yet perhaps he sensed that only by doing so could he earn his father's love.[63]

Hemingway's high expectations of his sons invited disappointment, just as Mr. Adams's puritanical ideals did for Nick. One can expect that unless the cycle of unresolved ambivalence toward the ideal father is finally broken, the sons, out of anger and guilt, will continue to live in "another country" of repressed grief where they cannot, and will not, "go to pray at the tomb" of the father. Perhaps in this story Nick, and Hemingway, come to terms with the father's fallibility, realizing at last that the heroic ideal father who was lost through disappointment can be replaced by a disappointing yet human father whom the son can forgive, embrace, and finally grieve over. As Nick concludes about his son's request to visit the tomb of his grandfather: "We'll have to go. . . . I can see we'll have to go" (162). As I suggest in the chapter that follows, *Death in the Afternoon*, which overlapped with the writing of "Fathers and Sons," represents Hemingway's continuing struggle with the ambivalence he felt in relation to his father's suicide. It is not until *For Whom the Bell Tolls*, in the late 1930s, however, that Hemingway to some degree comes to terms with his grief over his father's death, and with his ego-ideal identification with the grandiose yet hollow and abstract notion of his own grandfather's heroism.

Many of the stories in Hemingway's *Winner Take Nothing*, as I have pointed out, foreshadow his increasing disillusionment with the efficacy of the taboo against grief—of the repression of emotions—in fortifying himself against depression and despair. Hemingway's developing realization of both the futility and the very real physical and mental hazards of anesthetizing oneself against emotional pain through alcohol and numbing disavowal begins with the stories "After the Storm," and "A Natural History of the Dead," in the collection *Winner Take Nothing*, and reaches an epiphany-like culmination in his 1936 story "The Snows of Kilimanjaro." All three of these stories will be looked at more closely in the next chapter. From that moment of recognition on, Hemingway's craft was no longer entirely a product of the repression and displacement of grief and loss, but of his obsession with grief and loss as the consciously acknowledged subject matter of his art. Through the use of nostalgic memories in his later fiction Hemingway will confront the fact of disillusionment and loss, but at the same time will attempt to deflect the pain of these experiences by indulging in nostalgic fantasies, thereby once again denying the painful consequences of a disappointing reality, and enforcing in a new adaptive way his indefatigable taboo against grief.

6. "Ether in the Brain": Blunting the Edges of Perception in Hemingway's Middle Period

Peter: "To die will be an awfully big adventure."
In a sort of way Peter understands why he must not be touched, but in most sorts of ways he doesn't. It has something to do with the riddle of his being. If he could get the hand of the thing his cry might become "To live would be an awfully big adventure!"

—J. M. Barrie, *Peter Pan*

But as she has grown, her smile has widened with a touch of fear and her glance has taken on depth. Now she is aware of some of the losses you incur by being here—the extraordinary rent you have to pay as long as you stay.

—Annie Dillard, *Pilgrim at Tinker Creek*

Hemingway's attitude toward his previously valorized defenses against loss and grief underwent a metamorphosis during the period between 1934 and 1936—the years that according to Tom Dardis marked "a watershed in the transformation that came over Hemingway, what some have seen as a profound personal change."[1] By the mid-1930s Hemingway began to realize that his taboo against grief, or more specifically, the defenses he used to arm himself against loss and grief, represented another, and perhaps a more personally devastating, kind of loss. The first suggestions of this change appear in the stories "After the Storm" (1932), and, even more so, "A Natural History of the Dead" (1932), with their pictorial dramatizations of the consequences of a sensibility that is altogether devoid of human emotional response. Through the narrators' objective, or "naturalistic," mode of observation concerning the horrors of violent death, these two stories derive their psychological effect from another kind of horror—the horror of repression itself. The impersonal tone of the opportunistic diver, in "After the Storm," emotionally distances him from the real atrocities of the scene that he sees under the water; his human emotional response is as inaccessible to him as the gold ring on the hand of the woman who "floated in the water through the glass."[2] He speaks, without passion, of "those pieces that came out" of the ship after the explosion, just as the narrator, in "A Natural History of the Dead," impersonally informs the reader that in war, "the dead are usually the male of the human species" (98). The thoroughgoing taboo against grief in these two stories transforms them into eerie tales of the grotesque that are, paradoxically, not "naturalistic," but rather, super-natural. In claiming to relate "a few rational and interesting facts about the dead" (97), the narrator in "A Natural History," with intended irony on the part of Hemingway, challenges the reader to regard as "rational" that which is anything but rational—death, disfigurement, and war itself.

Scientific objectivity and greed—like patriotism, drinking, not-thinking, writing, and emotional pain—Hemingway seems to be saying, can numb the human brain to such an extent that even the most grotesque and hideous experiences no longer touch the heart. Some losses are so potentially overwhelming and devastating that the human heart is incapable of grieving over them, and so the heart must be closed off completely, the emotions shut down. All that remains is the cold eye of the "naturalist" observer (97). However, as the reader of Hemingway's stories discovers—indeed, the theme that Hemingway is evoking—is that there exists no horror more lamentable than the denial of grief carried to its extreme. The alleviation of suffering that comes with the repression of painful emotions is not worth the cost of one's humanity, for it is by experiencing pain, specifically emotional pain, that we feel, and, by feeling, live. In "A Natural History of the Dead" and "After the Storm," therefore, it is not only the bloated bodies lying, floating, in halves and pieces, that are dead, but also the narrators of these tales, whose hearts and souls have calcified and died within their still-living bodies.

For Hemingway, therefore, permanent numbing of emotional pain is a form of death-in-life, while those who only temporarily anesthetize themselves to pain are, like Hemingway himself, the true, suffering heroes of his fiction. Among these temporary "opiums" against pain and despair, as Hemingway dramatizes them in "The Gambler, the Nun, and the Radio" (1933), are religion, music, money, patriotism, gambling, sex, and the "sovereign opium," the "giant killer"—liquor. Revolution is "catharsis," Hemingway states in this story, but it cannot be prolonged indefinitely. At the conclusion of the story, Mr. Frazer opts for the opiums of drink and music. He will "play the radio so that you could hardly hear it" (148). The "it" that Frazer speaks of here is not only the radio but also the despair and grief in his head, and in his heart, that he hopes, in effect, to tune-out.

In "The Snows of Kilimanjaro" (1936), Harry recognizes that the anesthetic against pain that he had counted upon to save his body, his mind, and his art—drinking, money, and self-control—were numbing him, destroying the life-force within him, and hence, destroying his talent. While there is reason to question whether Harry does, in fact, meet his death at the end of the story, there is no question that, in this story, the writer confronts face-to-face his disillusionment with an idealistic notion of death; and for Hemingway, disillusionment with the possibility that one can die nobly or well inevitably brought with it an unraveling of his justification for his art, and for life itself. As I proposed in my discussion of Ernest Hemingway and his early fiction, emotional pain and grief, which he often portrays metaphorically as physical pain, are the central subjects of his fiction; they are what, in his estimation, make a person feel and experience life most deeply and profoundly. But, at the same time, emotional pain and grief are those which, in the surface of the text, as in the surface of the mind, must be disavowed, displaced, and set back from conscious awareness, in order to be transformed into art. The grief that enriches Hemingway's early fiction is located in the unconscious of his characters, and the methods used to insure that this grief remains safely in the realm of the unconscious provide the compelling psychological tension of some of his best stories from this period.

The epiphany that Harry experiences, in "The Snows of Kilimanjaro," is also a monumental one in terms of Hemingway's career as a writer, for he realized that that which he believed his survival depended upon— the repression of grief and pain, his attempts to numb the pain, to anesthetize it, his "opium" against debilitating despair—was actually that which had been destroying him all along. The story begins with this sudden, startling revelation when Harry announces to his wife: "The marvelous thing is that it's painless. . . . That's how you know when it starts."[3] Harry's wife, voicing the defensive code against emotional and physical vulnerability that is usually voiced by Hemingway's male heroes, advises, "You can't die if you don't give up" (4). For the informed Hemingway reader, Harry's reply explodes with irony. "Where did you read that?" he snaps back at her. "You're such a bloody fool" (4). It is, of course, toward Hemingway himself that Harry's accusation is directed.

Within the story, Harry's wife is anything but a "bitch," as he calls her. She is, as he also admits, "always thoughtful" (10), a "damned nice woman too" (13), who loves him passionately and sincerely, and who has only wanted to do what he has wanted to do. Nevertheless, Harry cannot reconcile himself to his own fundamental ambivalence about himself in relation to his wife. He has wanted the comfort which she, with her money and her personal devotion to him, has been able to provide for him; yet, as an anesthetic against pain, her money and all the comfort that she has offered him has made her a "destroyer of his talent" (11). He has voluntarily "traded away what remained of his old life . . . for security, for comfort too, there was no denying that" (13). But, like his drinking, and like the whores whom he has used "to kill his loneliness," the opiums of money and love have "only made it worse" (15). These things "blunted the edge of his perception" and in doing so "had destroyed his talent" (11). As Harry thinks to himself: "Since the gangrene started in his right leg he had no pain and with the pain the horror had gone and all he felt now was a great tiredness and anger that this was the end of it" (5). Although the pain inspires in him a feeling of "horror," Harry realizes that the end of the pain is something much more terrifying. The absence of feeling about death, not the pain and fear of death, Harry learns, is apparently what *real* death is all about. For Hemingway, as for Harry, the pain of a death wound confirms life, whereas the repression of pain, his defense against it, kills the life force within him. This is the irony of the leg wound that Harry has received; as he concludes to himself, "it was probably using that weak carbolic solution when the other antiseptics ran out that paralyzed the minute blood vessels and started the gangrene" (6). Like the antiseptic that turned out to be the cause, not the cure, of Harry's present suffering, the measures he has taken to guard against pain and grief—to soothe and comfort his despair—have in the end numbed him and, hence, destroyed his artistic talent.

Through Harry's disillusionment in the face of real death, Hemingway confessed his own belief that he "could beat anything . . . because no thing could hurt him if he did not care" (23). He would try not to care about death the way that he had always tried to "not care" about all those people that he "had loved too much" because he was afraid of losing them. His defense against loss and grief had been to destroy his relationship with the people he loves, so that he would not have to suffer the pain of losing them. Like Krebs, who was terrified, above all else, of his own vulnerability and dependency on the love of his mother, Harry cruelly replies to his wife when she asks, "Don't you love me?" "No . . . I don't think so. I never have" (6), he says, adding finally, "Love is a dunghill" (8).

Real death, not the abstract conception of it that energizes the life force, Harry now realizes, is not a gain but the loss of everything. His brutality toward his wife—his efforts to convince himself that he does not care—are merely his attempts to harden himself against loss, and against his vulnerability. "It's trying to kill to keep yourself alive, I imagine," Harry admits to her (9). In the same way, Hemingway kills off Thomas Hudson's sons and first wife, in *Islands in the Stream,* because he sensed that Hudson, like himself, could no longer live with the pain and anxiety over the possibility of impending loss. When a thing is finally dead, is finally lost for good, one no longer needs to live with the constant fear of losing it. If you expect the worst, in other words, you will never suffer disappointment when the worst suddenly occurs. As Harry explains, "I don't like to leave anything. . . . I don't like to leave things behind" (9). Ironically, it is because Harry, like Thomas Hudson, loves *too much* that he kills the thing he loves. In the same way, it was because Hemingway felt life so deeply and intensely—so much more deeply than anyone else—just as Nick Adams's father "saw much farther and much quicker than the human eye," that he had to protect himself from these feelings, or else risk succumbing to his vulnerability and being overcome by them.[4]

Harry still truly believes that to say to his wife, "Don't pay any attention, darling, to what I say. I love you, really. You know I love you," was to give her "the familiar lie he made his bread and butter by" (9); and also that "when your affections are not too involved you give much better value for the money" (12). But Hemingway was beginning to know better. One may lie when one does not love at all, but one also lies when one loves too much, just as Harry's reveries point out that when *"there was no snow you gambled and when there was too much you gambled"* (7; emphasis in original). Harry made his "bread and butter" by defensively repressing his love for his wife; Hemingway made his by repressing pain and grief. Harry now knows that the repression itself was perhaps the bigger lie, the vulnerability he was repressing the greater truth. "If you have to go away," his wife says to him, "is it absolutely necessary to kill off everything you leave behind? I mean do you have to take away everything? Do you have to kill your horse, and your wife and burn your saddle and your armour?" (8–9). In "The Snows of Kilimanjaro," it may or may not be Harry that is killed, but either way Hemingway dealt a death-blow to his own "armour" against grief and loss, wounding his confident and assured belief in the *art of repression* as the aesthetic technique on which he based both his life and his creative style.

Hemingway, as Harry says, "had been contemptuous of those who were wrecked" (23). He had been particularly contemptuous of F. Scott Fitzgerald, whose story "The Crack-Up," which appeared shortly before Hemingway wrote "Snows," had so repulsed him. But, as Hemingway's own story reveals, his disgust was unmistakably inspired by the devastating recognition of his own vulnerability, by his realization that the belief that "no thing could hurt him if he did not care" was not true, and that it was the not-caring that was killing, not saving, him. His whoring and drinking, his not-loving, not-caring, not-thinking, were the antiseptics/anesthetics that only temporarily dulled the pain and protected him from his own vulnerability. If he thought Fitzgerald was pathetic because he believed that the rich "were a special glamorous race and when he found they weren't it wrecked him" (23), in "The Snows of Kilimanjaro" Hemingway managed to implicate himself as a pathetic and "bloody fool" for his own special brand of self-delusion.

Remembering, for Harry, was a form of writing. "I've been writing," he says to his wife after one of his long periods of day-dreaming about the war, his experiences in Paris, and the people he has known. Although he claimed (through the voice of the adult Nick Adams, in the story, "Fathers and Sons") that he "had gotten rid of many things by writing them" (154), it becomes clear in this later story that Hemingway was also beginning to see writing as a way to keep from losing his past. Harry's nostalgic internal narrative about some of the episodes in his life that "he had saved to write" (5) is an act of mourning for those things that he believes will now be lost forever. Hence, memory and writing become the defenses against grieving through which he is able to nostalgically recapture his lost past, and at the same time get "rid of" the unresolved and repressed grief that he was unwilling to grieve and work through when these incidents first occurred in his life.

Hemingway realized that the emotional pain and grief that he had once thought he was able to control through his art—the editing and cutting-out of feelings that he employed not only in his fiction but in his life—were not an indication of his strength but of his weakness, of his fear of pain and emotional susceptibility, and of his detestable, "feminine" desires for happiness, comfort, and love. Perhaps this is why whenever Harry thinks about how happy he is drinking, feeling at peace with life, and being in love with his wife, that is the moment that he feels death coming over him. When he looks at his wife "and saw her well known pleasant smile, he felt death come again" (18):

Drinking together, with no pain now except the discomfort of lying in one position, the boys lighting a fire, its shadow jumping on the tents, he could feel the return of acquiescence in this life of pleasant surrender. She *was* very good to him. He had been cruel and unjust in the afternoon. She was a fine woman, marvelous really. And just then it occurred to him that he was going to die. (14)

In terms of the development of Hemingway's career as a writer, then, "The Snows of Kilimanjaro" marks a new thematic realization: that death is not the surmountable challenge that he had once believed it was, and that his "armour" against grief and loss—his drinking, not-thinking, and not-caring—did not shield him from death but numbed him to life, and that numbing, that not-feeling, was in fact the most deadly of all.[5] Indeed, from about 1937 on, Hemingway's art was no longer the psychologically powerful repressive art in which the intense internal tension of the text results from the escaping, the disavowal, the artful dodging, of emotional pain and grief. Instead, his later fiction was directly about the loss, emotional pain, and vulnerability that, before, he had so adroitly attempted to eliminate from the surface of his narrative and his fictional plots. He could perhaps no longer justify to himself that his anesthetic art—his "ether in the brain"—protected him from his fear of death and loss, because the ether and the anesthetic—repression itself—presented the more real and devastating threat of death.

Death in the Afternoon: *Paternal Disappointment and the Justification of the Grief Taboo*

Although *Death in the Afternoon* (1932) predates "The Snows of Kilimanjaro" by three or four years, it was Hemingway's first full-length work since *The Sun Also Rises* in which loss, physical and emotional pain, and death become the overt subjects of his creative impulse. While "The Snows of Kilimanjaro" represents the fictional dramatization of the end of his ingenious and fertile love affair with the art of repression, it is possible that this sense of an ending was gestating in Hemingway's imagination as early as 1928. That year, and 1929, were years of disappointment and disillusionment for Hemingway: his father committed suicide, and he himself suffered, in rapid succession, a number of serious physical injuries that confirmed for him the message that life kills: As he tells the Old Lady in *Death in the Afternoon*, life is "a hard trade and the grave is at the end of it, and he is no true-story teller who would keep that from you."[6] Further, there "is no lonelier man in death, except the suicide, than the man who has lived many years with a good wife and then outlived her. If two people love each other there can be no happy end to it" (122). While *Death in the Afternoon* represents Hemingway's attempt to work through his ambivalence about the lonely and desolate fate of the suicide (more specifically, his father's death), and hence to attain some degree of catharsis for his pain through grieving, he will not deal at length with the grief from loss in love until *The Garden of Eden*, and, of course, in that openly nostalgic testament to lost love, *A Moveable Feast*.

Hemingway was writing *Death in the Afternoon* at about the same time that he was completing "Fathers and Sons." This autobiographical novel, I believe, was Hemingway's attempt, as Nick Adams resolves in the story, to pay a much belated visit to the tomb of his father. Both this work, and the similarly autobiographical *Green Hills of Africa* (1935), reveal a growing interest in the artistic possibilities offered by nostalgia and the power of memory to transform the past into the present, and hence, through nostalgic fantasy, wipe out the ravages of age and time, and the grief of permanent loss and death.

In the first chapter of *Death in the Afternoon*, Hemingway confesses that his goal as a writer was to "put down what really happened in action; what the actual things were which produced the emotion that you experienced," because only in this way could he record something about life "which would be as valid in a year or in ten years" (2). Writing, in other words, must somehow be made to conquer death and time, and to reproduce present reality with such verisimilitude that it is never lost. Furthermore, Hemingway asserts that, "a writer should create living people; people not characters. A *character* is a caricature" (191). What Hemingway asks of the writer is, of course, an impossibility. People who appear in the pages of a book cannot be "living people," no matter how closely they are drawn from real life. Yet, only by engaging in the fantasy of the resurrecting powers of the nostalgic writer could Hemingway gain the illusion of achieving immortality through writing.

If Hemingway is, nostalgically, to recapture the moving and complex present as it occurs, he must also somehow deal with the problem of not being able to include everything in his stories. His concept of the "ice-berg" principle in writing, which states that even those things left out are silently included by way of implied reference, offers a solution to this problem. Thus, he assures us in *Death in the Afternoon,* a writer "may omit things that he knows and the reader, if the writer is writing truly enough, will have a feeling of those things as strongly as though the writer had stated them" (192). While the "ice-berg" principle accurately describes the repression of painful emotions in the textual narratives of Hemingway's early stories, in *Death in the Afternoon* it also becomes a compromise formation for the writer's inability to transform, nostalgi-cally, past reality into the artistic present.

For Hemingway, writing had become a means of mastery and control, and the one aspect of life that makes it tragic—death—is what he deemed most in need of control. Hemingway did not choose to write about death because it is connected to bullfighting; rather, he chose to write about bullfighting because it gave him "the feeling of life and death that I was working for" (3). He confesses that he might well have written about "death by disease, or so-called natural death, or the death of a friend or some one you have loved or have hated," but these forms of death have too many "complications" (2). It is unclear what Hemingway meant by "complications," but all of these other occurrences of death (which bring to mind the recent death of his own father whom he clearly both "loved" and "hated"), far from being events which can be studied objectively, carry substantial emotional baggage; therefore, it is typical of Hemingway to wish to avoid such "complications." Significantly, albeit in an off-hand manner, Hemingway specifies among those inci-dents of death that he "had never been able to study . . . as a man might," the "death of [a man's] father" (3).

The pain and anxiety arising from the suicide of Hemingway's father were among those things that he was not yet ready to confront directly. The grown-up Nick Adams, in the story "Fathers and Sons" (1933), explicitly admits this fact to himself, when he confesses that "knowing how it had all been, even remembering the earliest times before things had gone badly was not good remembering. If he wrote it he could get rid of it. He had gotten rid of many things by writing them. But it was still too early for that" (*Winner,* 154). Bullfighting thus became a convenient subject onto which Hemingway could displace the unresolved issues about his father's suicide. In *Death in the Afternoon,* he confronted and attempted to explain this subject that had never been confronted before. Concerning his purpose in writing the book, he cryptically stated that "it is because such things have not been admitted that the bullfight has never been explained" (7). Specifically, he will attempt to prove that "doing something tragic" is somehow, in some way, "dignified" (7); that although the bull always dies in the end, he possesses the trait of "nobility" that justifies his violent and bloody death.

Speaking of the seemingly senseless death of the horses in bullfighting, Hemingway advises the spectators to "sense the meaning and end of the whole thing even when they know nothing about it; feel that this thing they do not understand is going on, the business of the horses is nothing more than an incident" (8). Further, the "aficionado, or lover of the bullfight, may be said, broadly, then, to be one who has this sense of the tragedy and ritual of the fight so that the minor aspects are not important except as they relate to the whole" (9). Both the aficionado and the writer, in other words, are faced with the same challenge: to justify and to find meaning in the minor tragedies of man's life-and-death struggle by viewing them as a necessary part of a grander theme. Bullfighting, like the death of one's father, passes quickly and so is, in a sense, "impermanent" (14), and thus requires the impossible task of "instant recording" (3). Both fleeting events need the writer to transform them into something "permanent" and, therefore, meaningful. By justifying, with respect to bullfighting, the tragic element of life—that it inevitably ends in violent and sometimes ugly death—Hemingway was able to grieve his father's tragic death without having to confront it directly. As we shall see, he also indirectly confronts his anger toward his father and his mother as a result of this tragic incident in his life.

We are thus able to identify a common motive running though both *Death in the Afternoon* and Hemingway's nostalgic impulse: to make time stand still, and to superimpose the past onto the present, so that the past is ever-new and ever-present. Yet the fact of loss is also never lost to the nostalgic dreamer. This is why compulsive nostalgic thinking is considered a manifestation of pathological or perpetual mourning; it indefinitely prolongs the mourning process, and therefore, in a sense, prevents the bereaved from working through grief, accepting loss, and optimistically moving forward with his or her life.

In a number of paragraphs throughout *Death in the Afternoon,* Hemingway's nostalgic impulse surfaces undisguised in the narrative. He speaks of how in "the old days the bulls were usually bigger than they are now; they were fiercer, more uncertain, heavier and older" (67). The matadors "were mature men" in the old days, and bullfighting was a more "exciting" sport (68). "There were always giants in those days" (183), Hemingway adds, and there "is not, in Spain to-day, one really great killer" (233). Since 1873, in fact, which was "the golden age of all golden ages," bullfighting "has always been considered by contemporary chronicles to be in a period of decadence" (240). But as is typical of the nostalgic, Hemingway makes a virtue of loss, by extolling the influence of decadence on bullfighting and bullfighters: "It is a decadent art in every way and like most decadent things it reaches its fullest flower at its rottenest point" (68). To decay, as the life of Hemingway's father decayed to the point of suicide, and as he, himself, had begun to decay, is a sign of nobility. Hemingway's hero, Belmonte, in fact, was so "decadent" that he was "almost depraved" (69). Belmonte had a "beautiful unhealthy mystery" about him, and "for seven years" he "had a golden age in spite of the fact that it was in the process of being destroyed" (69).

When one is obsessed with the inevitable fact of one's mortality, life itself becomes something that is "in the process of being destroyed." In fantasy, Hemingway compares the "impermanence" of bullfighting to painting and writing:

Suppose a painter's canvases disappeared with him and a writer's books were automatically destroyed at his death and only existed in the memory of those that had read them. That is what happens in bullfighting. The art, the method, the improvements of doing, the discoveries remain; but the individual, whose doing of them made them, who was the touchstone, the original, disappears. (99)

Hemingway's nostalgic moral is that things become more valuable by virtue of the fact that they can be lost. This is a justification not only for bullfighting and art, but for a loved one's death, and the loss of one's own omnipotence and the physical intactness of youth. By roundabout, deductive reasoning, Hemingway concludes that greatness is impossible without death and physical decay, for "a major art cannot even be judged until the unimportant physical rottenness of whoever made it is well buried" (99).

The nostalgic's taboo against grief is essentially a taboo against emotional pain. But whereas, in Hemingway's early fiction, the taboo against grief meant the repression or displacement of emotional pain, here it signifies the endurance of pain and loss consciously realized. Manera was a great man, according to Hemingway, because he refused to acknowledge the fact that he was going to die, and denied to others (which meant enduring silently) the excruciating pain from a horn wound. Like Orpen's "ether in the brain," Jake Barnes's and Nick Adams's not-thinking, and Harry's anesthetic, Belmonte's attitude toward pain is to act "*as though* it were not there" (my italics, 79). Thus, Hemingway again transforms the tragedy and pain of life into a potential virtue, valorizing the manly defenses of denial and repression.[7] Yet, as I have pointed out, by the time Hemingway wrote "The Snows of Kilimanjaro" only a few years later, he had begun to realize how fully self-destructive the repression of pain really is. The presence of the story "A Natural History of the Dead," in *Death in the Afternoon,* which—like "Snows" —contains the message that the repression of grief carried to its extreme sucks the life force out of human experience, supports the possibility that this realization was already germinating in Hemingway's mind.

The loss of the innocence of youth, Hemingway argues, is the most valuable loss of all. For the bullfighter, his loss of innocence comes with his "first severe horn wound . . . and until a matador has undergone this first severe wound you cannot tell what his permanent value will be" (166). In *Across the River and Into the Trees,* Richard Cantwell speaks of his own wounding: "No one of his other wounds had ever done to him what the first big one did. I suppose it is just the loss of the immortality, he thought. Well, in a way, that is quite a lot to lose."[8] The first "big wound" is what imbues the matador with an emotionally charged conscious awareness of his impending death—whether that time is a year or twenty years away. The courage that the matador possessed before his wounding was a blind courage. Only when consciously up against his own mortality can his true mettle as a man be tested. The loss of a man's omnipotence and immortality, therefore, is an incomparable virtue, for it allows him to achieve real greatness. With this fact clearly established, Hemingway could view the loss of his own youth, and immortality—inspired in part by his father's death—as a noble and ideal accomplishment. Thus, paradoxically, one gains from loss. Hemingway, in effect, maintains that the tragedy of life itself, which is filled with losses and with occurrences "as banal as suicide" (102), test a man's pride and honor as much, if not more so, than bullfighting.

Once again, the key to greatness in both style and behavior is loss; or rather, the opportunity that loss offers for exercising control over the pain and grief concerning that loss. Hemingway's rejection by his first true love, Agnes von Kurowsky, represented the first "wound" in affairs of the heart—the first blow to Hemingway's masculine ego—that he had ever received; and it was one from which, he and others often claimed, he never fully recovered. He also claimed that the break-up with Agnes "hardened" him, and, as Griffin insightfully proposes, this "heartbreak had brought him to the discovery of his own voice, and his writing 'style.' "[9] If Hemingway's style is based on the repression of feelings and the denial of psychological pain, it follows that the control of his emotions, particularly the repression of grief from deprivation and loss, was the yardstick by which he measured his own greatness as a writer.

There are, of course, alternatives to control as a defense against loss and grief. One of these is avoidance and escape, as the Major, in Hemingway's story, "In Another Country" (1927), suggests: a man "should not place himself in a position to lose. He should find things he cannot lose."[10] Another possibility, but one which—as Hemingway dramatizes in "Snows"—is fraught with sacrifices to one's humanity, if not one's life, is denial and emotional "deadness," which Hemingway demonstrates for the Old Lady in *Death in the Afternoon* through the embedded narrative, "A Natural History of the Dead."

As I have already pointed out, Hemingway's sardonic attack on so-called "humanists," in "A Natural History of the Dead," pushes the cold, emotionless prose of the naturalist to an extreme. The reader cannot help but be shocked at the contrast between the horrifying subject matter—men and women sprawled, dismantled, and bloated in death—and the objective terminology used by Hemingway to describe the scene. Despite his use of words such as "extraordinary," "amazing," and "horror," the absence of the narrator's emotional shock and grief over what he witnesses is disturbing, and he forces the reader to view the situation with the same "quality of unreality" that he does. The reader is more horrified by the narrator's lack of emotional response than by the horror of the scene itself. Hemingway's customary use of understatement to exclude emotions from a story is intentionally exaggerated in "A Natural History," as when the ghastly images of death are described as merely an "unpleasantness" (136); and it is precisely through this exaggeration of repression that the reader's emotional response is elicited.

The alternative ending to "A Natural History of the Dead," again points to Clarence Hemingway's suicide as Hemingway's motive for justifying violent and seemingly wasted death in *Death in the Afternoon*.

The omitted paragraph concludes as follows: "I think this is perhaps, enough about the dead. There is no need to continue and write an accurate observation on a friend dead, a dead lover or dead parent since a writer can deal at length with these in fiction rather than in natural history."[11] Until *For Whom the Bell Tolls,* however, Hemingway could not, in fiction, deal directly with his father's suicide, unless one considers the story "Fathers and Sons" as a prelude to the later novel. Instead, he dealt with it indirectly, by striving to convince himself that apparently meaningless death is not meaningless at all but is rich with significance. As Hemingway asks, rhetorically, in an omitted section of "A Natural History": "Who knows how profitable the dead may be if we live long enough? Who knows how much gold may be extracted from them?" This metaphor brings to mind the gold ring and other golden treasures that are buried, along with the dead, in the watery tomb of the sunken ship, in the story, "After the Storm."

Language is also one of Hemingway's critical defenses against the grief of loss in *Death in the Afternoon.* Through the defensive use of language Hemingway is able to defuse his son's grief over the death of one of his favorite matadors; replacing the word "died" with "umpty-umped" so many times that the grief associated with the fact of death is entirely lost (228).

The next story that Hemingway tells, in *Death in the Afternoon,* about the doctor, the lieutenant, and the man in the death-house, contains an embedded psychological tale that reveals Hemingway's anger toward his mother, and the role he believed she played in his father's suicide. It also identifies, to some degree, the nature of the fears and anxieties aroused in Hemingway by his father's death. In this story, the artillery officer is being treated for a wounded arm. The doctor, whose eyes are "red and the lids swollen, almost shut from tear gas," insists on putting a dying soldier in the death-house, which deeply upsets the lieutenant of artillery (141). They argue, and the doctor, in anger, throws iodine in the lieutenant's eyes. In a fury, the lieutenant fumbles for his pistol, but the doctor is not in the least afraid of him. "I am the boss," he tells him. "All is forgiven since you know I am the boss. You cannot kill me because I have your pistol" (143). With this, someone announces that the dying man has just died. "See, my poor lieutenant?" the doctor says, "We dispute about nothing." And he assures the officer that his "eyes will be all right" (144). As the story ends, the lieutenant again cries out to the doctor: "You have blinded me!"

In Hemingway's family, eyes played an important symbolic role. His mother gave up her singing career, she often said, because of her poor eyesight; and at one point in her youth she apparently suffered from a case of hysterical blindness.[12] Hemingway supposedly inherited his mother's weak eyes. His father, on the other hand, had exceptionally good eyesight. In the story "Fathers and Sons," Nick Adams confesses that although his father had a weak chin, his eyes, that saw "much farther and much quicker than the human eye sees," were "the great gift his father had." When Nick thinks about his father, who is now dead (supposedly a suicide), "it was always the eyes" that he "first thought about" (*Winner*, 152). Eyes had also been a subject of recent concern for Hemingway, since he injured one of them badly in December 1929, and finally, in 1931 (while writing *Death in the Afternoon*), he broke down and admitted that he needed glasses.[13] A. E. Hotchner relates that Hemingway believed at one point that he had frozen tear ducts, which could not more perfectly metaphorically describe his ultimate realization that the repression of grief and tears, whether through denial, drinking, or some other way, while it functioned so superbly as a technique in his early writing, ironically, numbed the emotional responses of the writer in a way that jeopardized his creative abilities.[14]

The members of the Hemingway family are thus transformed into the characters of Hemingway's story about the doctor and the lieutenant. While Hemingway's own father was a doctor, his mother was the "boss" in the family, and held the "pistol," or phallic power, over his weak-jawed father. Grace Hemingway was also the one who, like the doctor in the story, had the injured eye. Hemingway's recent arm injury from a car accident places him in the role of the artillery officer who is injured in the arm and almost blinded by the callous "boss" doctor. The emotional core of the story resides in the lieutenant's anger and hatred toward the doctor for abandoning the dying man, and his own fear of being blinded by him. By way of biographical parallel, one might say that the lieutenant is Hemingway, himself, who is outraged at his mother—the boss/doctor—for carrying the "pistol" in his family, and for passively standing by while his father slowly deteriorated mentally and physically to the point of suicide. If she had the power to castrate or destroy his father, Hemingway naturally fears her power to castrate (or blind) him, a fear acted out in the story through the doctor's near blinding of the lieutenant.[15]

A few pages later Hemingway tells the Old Lady another perplexing story which, when looked at psychoanalytically, possesses a theme quite similar to the earlier story. Here, one man is lured into a homosexual relationship with another man. Before he surrenders his masculinity, however, the first man runs into the hotel room next to his, which is occupied by a newspaper reporter, and frantically cries out that he "would kill himself first" before giving himself to the older man (180–81). In the end, however, he does yield to the more experienced homosexual and is himself transformed into a feminine gender role. The reporter knows that this is the case because, when he next sees the younger man, he has "had his hair hennaed" (182).

The younger man, who would rather kill himself than be emasculated, again brings to mind Hemingway's father, whom Hemingway always believed was driven to suicide by his emasculating mother. Hemingway, himself, in this story, plays the part of the child/reporter who listens at the door of his parents' bedroom to hear his mother's castrating abuse of his father and his father's pathetic protestations. As the adolescent boy who identifies with his father as a masculine ideal, the son is both disillusioned and disappointed in his father for playing such a passive role, and naturally, as a result, fears for his own possible castration by the mother/phallic woman figure.

Both these stories are tales of anger, resentment, revenge, and castration anxiety, which may represent, as the story "Now I Lay Me" more clearly represents, Hemingway's attempt to work through his conflicted relationship with his parents. If these stories are more cryptic than the earlier story, however, it may be because Hemingway's desire for resolution was more precipitously motivated and emotionally charged by his father's recent death, for which he strove to grieve unencumbered by anger and guilt. Thematically, these stories also resemble the anecdote told much earlier by Hemingway, in *Death in the Afternoon*, of the boy and girl who fulfill their revenge on the bull that killed their brother by castrating it and then eating the bull's testicles. As in *The Sun Also Rises*, the bull is the phallic mother personified. In search of symbolic revenge for destroying their brother, the children castrate the phallic bull-mother, thus redeeming the phallic power of the dead masculine figure.

The last story Hemingway tells in *Death in the Afternoon* is about his meeting with a girl in Paris who is writing a fictionalized life of El Greco. Based on the "androgenous faces and forms"—specifically, the men with women's features—that fill El Greco's paintings, Hemingway suggests that the girl depict the painter as a "maricón"—a homosexual.

But it is "too late," the girl tells him. "The book is done" (204). As an extension of this discussion with the girl, Hemingway claims that Goya should have painted bullfighting posters because he would have made all the matadors look like Christ-figures. Connected to the symbolic portrait of Christ that Hemingway evokes is his observation that the effeminate El Greco feminized Christ in his paintings. In Hemingway's nostalgic imagination, his father becomes an emasculated Christ-figure, a sainted emasculated hero like "San Sebastian." Although his father was dead, and it was "too late" to save him, it was still not too late to "redeem" his image in his son's eyes. For, despite the fact that El Greco was a "maricón," he was a great man. He was not a "prissy exhibitionistic, aunt-like, withered old maid" like Gide, or Wilde, but a magnificent painter with an exquisite eye for art. Even if "he was one," (a maricón), Hemingway argues, his great abilities as a man would "redeem" the "tribe" of all maricones from ill-repute; and so, therefore, could his father be redeemed.

Hemingway seems to have mixed feelings about suicide in *Death in the Afternoon*. While he calls the act "banal" and undignified, elsewhere he claims that the greatest dignity is "the rebellion against death which comes from its administering" (233): "But when a man is still in rebellion against death he has pleasure in taking to himself one of the Godlike attributes; that of giving it" (233). Richard Hovey calls this philosophy a "sick . . . worse than ludicrous . . . metaphysical lucubration" that borders on "criminal pathology."[16] Hemingway's metaphysics is not so "ludicrous," however, and the distinction between homicide and suicide becomes irrelevant, when one remembers that suicide involves the triple wish to "be killed, to kill, and to die."[17] When a person, especially a child, contemplates the possibility of suicide, he is attempting to take active control over an unpleasant feeling of being passively abused by life, particularly by his parents. By administering death, rather than passively being killed by another, the suicide attains the satisfaction of ego control. Whether motivated by narcissistic injury, depression, or both, *Death in the Afternoon* was Hemingway's courageous attempt to gain control over death. Hence, he identified closely with the bullfighter, feeling he must actively deal out death against the onslaught of depression and suicidal impulses or else passively succumb to them.

Hemingway's final outlook, in *Death in the Afternoon*, is both grim and mournful. He continues to grieve over the past, over the fact that "Pamplona now is changed," and that "[t]hey tore down the old Gayarre and spoiled the square" (273). But, "if your memory is good you may ride still through the forest and the Irati." Hemingway, however, may not, at this point, have been certain whether his memory was indeed good enough. As he stated earlier in the book: "Memory, of course, is never true" (100). Apathy, resignation to age—"we are older"—and "deadness," define the limits of Hemingway's slender personal victory in *Death in the Afternoon*: "I know things change now and I do not care. It's all been changed for me. Let it all change" (278). The nostalgically inspired "ice-berg" theory is still Hemingway's greatest defensive tactic against loss and grief as a writer. "Then any part you make will represent the whole if it's made truly. The thing to do is work and learn and make it" (278). If Hemingway fails to resolve his personal ambivalences in *Death in the Afternoon*, his strategies for coping with loss, disillusionment, and the inevitability of pain and death were universalized in this work through the analogy of bullfighting, and thereby transformed into permanent guidelines for noble and heroic behavior, regardless of whether the final outcome of one's actions is victory or defeat.

Green Hills of Africa: *Denial of Loss and the Resurrecting Power of Memory*

By the time Hemingway wrote his next book, *Green Hills of Africa* (1935), he had gathered his forces somewhat against his doubts about the resurrecting power of memory. Here, he put memory to work to create the illusion of wholeness and completeness, and the illusion sufficed. He, in effect, "captures" time in Africa, made it stand still, transformed the part into the whole, and invested memory with the power to make the past "true" once again.

In the Foreword to *Green Hills of Africa*, Hemingway expressly states that he is attempting to write:"an absolutely true book to see whether the shape of a country and the pattern of a month's action can, if truly presented, compete with a work of the imagination." The realities of time (a month) and place (Africa) are not, as Hemingway perhaps wishes to believe, in competition with the fictional imagination. But if nostalgic memories are to "magically" wipe out the grief of a lost past, then it follows that those memories must be invested with the power to re-evoke the "real" and the "true."

The irony, and, in a sense, the optimism, that define Hemingway's nostalgic mode of creative writing in the latter half of his life, lie in the fact that, while he writes about the grief of what can be lost, the tragedy of all life that ends in death, and his own physical decline, he attempts (with equal strength and enthusiasm) to deny these things through the *act* of writing. This ideology of compensation for loss through nostalgic memory is embedded in Hemingway's argument in *Green Hills of Africa;* namely, that it is only the art leading to the kill that matters—the "pursuit" of "happiness," not happiness itself (1, 175, 215). At this point in his life, one of Hemingway's greatest challenges was to survive, which, for him, meant to survive as a writer. Under the assault of depression, self-doubt, debilitating alcoholism, and a feared psychological and genetic identification with his father—who, despite Hemingway's protests in *Death in the Afternoon,* did in effect give up—Hemingway was deeply concerned with continuing to pursue his craft, even against increasing odds.

As Hemingway says in *Green Hills of Africa,* he, like Harry in "Snows," can perceive the hyena "racing the little nickelled death inside him," and, he adds less convincingly than Harry, "I did not take my own life seriously any more" (72). When in the present (mainly at night, after he has been drinking), Hemingway, like David Bourne in *The Garden of Eden,* feels "completely happy and quite tired," he feels "no obligation and no compulsion to write" about life, "only to live it" (55). When not "quite" so "happy," however, the power to remember and to write down his memories becomes critical in order to re-produce a time when he was indeed happy, or thought that he was.

Hemingway marvels at Tolstoy and Turgenev because they allow the reader to live in another "time" and "place," to efface the ego of the past tense and replace it with an ego of the present tense: "I had been in the family Buddenbrooks. . . . I saw all that. And it was me they did not break on the rack that time" (108).[18] Joyce was another who could completely manipulate time, not only in his novels, Hemingway says, but apparently in his life as well: "And when you saw him he would take up a conversation interrupted three years before" (71).

Through an analysis of the subject of time in *Green Hills of Africa,* Barbara Lounsberry establishes a connection between time and death in Hemingway's novel, concluding that "ultimately it is memory and its transfiguration into art which Hemingway posits against the ravages of time and space."[19] In the last paragraph of the book, Hemingway skips forward in time to the Sea of Galilee where he, P.O.M., Karl, and Karl's wife are vacationing a month later. P.O.M. is sad because she cannot remember Mr. J.P.'s face. "I think about him and think about him," she says, "and I can't see him. It's terrible" (295). Hemingway, however, is assured and confident. "I'll write you a piece some time and put him in," he tells her. Through the illusion of the perpetual present allowed him by memory and art, Hemingway believes that he will never lose Mr. J.P.'s "beautiful" face.

And yet, beneath Hemingway's confident assertions is a touch of the nostalgic's neurotic use of memory. In chapter 4, for example, soon after the safari is under way, Hemingway is already anticipating its end and the loss of his pleasant experience of time and place:"All I wanted to do now was get back to Africa. We had not left it, yet, but when I would wake in the night I would lie, listening, homesick for it already" (72). The nostalgic's neurotic vulnerability to loss compels him to experience his expected separation anxiety long before it occurs. His desire to arrest time is so intense, and his devaluation of the present is so great, that the present all but ceases to exist, and time is displaced altogether.

As Hemingway's attitude in the novel's last paragraph about Mr. J.P.'s face suggests, he is still fairly optimistic about his ability to stave off time, death, and separation with his art. Perhaps Hemingway believed that his "experiment" in testing the limits of memory in *Green Hills of Africa* was a successful one. But this would not always be the case in his later works of fiction, nor in his life ahead. The mournfulness and grief that are part of the nostalgic experience, the remorse and sense of inadequacy as an artist for never being able to "get it all" back, and the longing for a love that could never be recaptured, present an increasing challenge to Hemingway's optimism in *Across the River and Into the Trees, A Moveable Feast,* and *Islands in the Stream.*

The grief and anxiety of loss and deprivation, that the narrator so carefully manages to keep at arm's length in the autobiographical narrative of Hemingway's African novel, are cleverly displaced onto the old man, Hemingway's helpmate on the safari, who bursts forth at the end of the trip with a fear of parting that mounts to something like panic. The old man holds tightly onto the ropes of the car, refusing to let go, and shouting, "I want to go with B'wana!" (289). M'Cola and Kamau have to pry him off the car. This little episode is more than an exhibition of how loved he is by the natives. As the old man holds on to Hemingway's arm, he talks "very quietly" of his emotional pain; but significantly, as Hemingway says, the man spoke "in a language that I could not understand." Hemingway thinks that perhaps the man wants money;

but he is wrong. Again miscalculating the intensity of the old man's grief, the Hemingway narrator then removes a "penknife" from his pocket and tries to place it in the man's hand. Hemingway's symbolism is brilliant here, as the "pen" *is* his "knife" that he uses to sever himself from his own grief and loss. But the old man is not interested in Hemingway's symbolic, or displaced, emotions; he wants the real thing. "No," he says in response to Hemingway's offering. "No." Nothing more is said about the incident. But, as they begin to drive away without the old man, Hemingway "could hear him in the dark screaming, 'B'wana! I want to go with B'wana' " (289). Undoubtedly Hemingway does understand, perhaps better than anyone else ever could, the indecipherable but still loud and clear message of the native's depth of grief, for which, as Hemingway's silence ominously implies, there is no remedy.

For Whom the Bell Tolls: *Coming to Terms with the Grief of Father-Hunger and Mother-Loss*

With the publication, in 1940, of Hemingway's second major novel about war and love, his acclaim as a writer and his notoriety as a public personality had soared to the highest point it was to reach during his lifetime. The critical reviews of *For Whom the Bell Tolls* at the time of its publication were, for the most part, positive. Some believed it to be one of Hemingway's best works to date, while others, primarily Communist and Spanish critics, thought that his portrayal of Spanish culture and his sympathy with the Loyalists were mistaken and insulting.[20] I tend to agree with those who view the book as artistically inferior to Hemingway's early stories, particularly since it lacks the power of repression and the artfully enforced taboo against grief that characterizes Hemingway's unique and unsurpassed mastery of language in his best (usually short) works of fiction. When *For Whom the Bell Tolls* is viewed psychoanalytically as Hemingway's generally successful attempt to work through his hero's separation-individuation process, however, the novel is psychologically, if not artistically, strengthened and integrated—and hence, we are given new reason to judge it as a serious fictional enterprise. It is with this goal in mind that I temporarily diverge from tracing the development of Hemingway's taboo against grief in his later fiction and focus more heavily on the development of his psychological theme of masculine individuation and the fate of the arrested adolescent in his work.

Part of the unique quality of *For Whom the Bell Tolls* is Hemingway's use of colloquial Spanish, even if it more closely resembles an archaic sounding Latinate narrative than a direct translation of Spanish vernacular. Indeed, much of the recent critical attention paid toward the novel has primarily dealt with the issue of Hemingway's use of language in this book. Earl Rovit and Carole Moses agree that Hemingway's stylized prose serves to distance the reader from the novel, and that the limitations of language as a communicative tool are in fact a major subtheme of the work.[21] Perhaps this narrative technique also provided Hemingway with a means of distancing himself sufficiently from the novel to allow him to deal more objectively with many of the psychological issues that he could not resolve either in his life or in his previous works of fiction. It is precisely this narrative objectivity, however, that makes the characters in *For Whom the Bell Tolls* significantly less compelling, or, one might even say, less human, than, say, Nick Adams, or even Hemingway's minor characters, such as Marjorie in "The End of Something," and the Major in "In Another Country." On the positive side, as Earl Rovit maintains, the distance created by Hemingway's language contributes to the archetypal or universal quality of the characters and circumstances described in the novel. *For Whom the Bell Tolls* therefore lends itself to, and indeed invites, interpretation as a universal psychoanalytic narrative which, as I will demonstrate, relates the story of one man's attempt to come to terms with his personal past through a transference onto the present figures in his life. As such, this work of historical fiction earns itself a place of permanent literary merit.

For Whom the Bell Tolls at first merely appears, once again, to act out the psycho-social theme of Hemingway's earlier novel *A Farewell to Arms,* and his early Orpen fragment; namely, that love and war are incompatible. However, a close psychoanalytic reading of the novel's sequence of events and seemingly tragic conclusion reveals what may conceivably be interpreted as a working-through-in-fantasy of Hemingway's unresolved narcissistic and ego-ideal pathology, accomplished here through a long-postponed integration of the grandiose ego ideal with the tempering influence of reality.

Robert Jordan's actions in the first half of the novel cannot be understood psychoanalytically without skipping ahead to chapter 30, where Hemingway provides a more detailed explanation of Jordan's early relationship with his parents. (This delayed psychological understanding may be one reason why the novel does not pull together better as a work of art.) Through Jordan's reveries about his past it is learned that his father shot himself with Jordan's heroic grandfather's Smith and Wesson pistol, an act that, for Jordan, revealed his father's cowardice and weakness of character:

> I'll never forget how sick it made me the first time I knew he was a *cobarde*. Go on, say it in English. Coward. It's easier when you have it said *[sic]* and there is never any point in referring to a son of a bitch by some foreign term. He wasn't any son of a bitch, though. He was just a coward and that was the worst luck any man could have. Because if he wasn't a coward he would have stood up to that woman and not let her bully him. I wonder what I would have been like if he had married a different woman? That's something you'll never know, he thought, and grinned.[22]

At this point in my investigation of Hemingway's life and fiction it should become evident immediately that Robert Jordan's family situation parallels not only that of Hemingway's other adolescent male protagonists but also that of Hemingway, himself, in that it is comprised of a weak father and a dominating, castrating mother.

Predictably, Jordan's anxiety primarily has to do with his own lack of self-esteem, and with his lingering doubts about his masculinity. Not only does Jordan fear his identification with his cowardly father, but like the Hemingway/Lieutenant character in Hemingway's story of the doctor and the lieutenant in *Death in the Afternoon*, he also fears being castrated by his mother, who successfully castrated—by driving to suicide—his father. Since suicide involves a primitive wish, in relation to the dominating, over-responsive mother, to kill, be killed, and die, Jordan's anxiety about his own masculinity—his fear and aggression toward the phallic mother—is integrally related to his fear of his own suicidal impulses.

As if cowardice was something passed on from father to son through the blood, or what Jordan calls "juice" (and, as Hemingway perhaps knew or intuited by this time, his father's "weaknesses"—depression, angina, nervousness, etc. were indeed passed on "through the blood");[23] he hopes that the good "juice" that coursed through the veins of his grandfather, the Civil War hero, somehow skipped his father's generation and "only came through straight again after passing through that one" (338). It becomes clear that the psychological motive driving Jordan in his attempts to prove himself a hero in the Spanish Civil War is his desire to break, once and for all, his identification with his weak biological father and to establish a secure narcissistic identification with the grandiose, abstract paternal ideal embodied in the "military geniuses" of the American Civil War—such as Grant, Sherman, Stonewall Jackson, Jeb Stuart, and of course his own grandfather—all of whom he had learned about when he "studied the art of war" when he was "a boy" (233, 335). Referring to the important day when he is scheduled to blow up the bridge, Jordan says to himself: "Don't get to referring to the good juice and such other things until you are through tomorrow. . . . We'll see what sort of juice you have tomorrow" (339). As is true for so many of Hemingway's heroes, Jordan's psychic life is troubled by a fear of the phallic or castrating, aggressive mother, a narcissistic need to live up to an abstract, heroic masculine ego ideal, and, as a consequence of having circumvented a secure masculine identification with his real father, an unconscious yearning to regress to a state of narcissistic omnipotence by falling in love with, or merging with, a pregenital mother figure.

If we return for a moment to Hemingway's early story, "The Doctor and the Doctor's Wife," in which Nick Adams's hen-pecked father cleans and loads his rifle in the privacy of his bedroom, suggesting not only his suicidal thoughts but also his unconscious aggressive wishes against Nick's mother, it can be assumed that Jordan, too, harbors strong aggressive thoughts toward his castrating, "bullying" mother. It also may be assumed that because Jordan, as I have pointed out about Nick Adams in the story "Fathers and Sons," was so overcome by shame and guilt over his father's suicide, he was not able at the time to grieve his father's death. This unresolved grief undoubtedly added to the grief Jordan felt, as a boy, at his lack of emotional intimacy with his real father. His longing and grief in relation to his father are revealed in Jordan's yearning for genuine intimacy with his dead grandfather: "Aw hell, I wish Grandfather was here, he thought. . . . I would certainly like to talk to him. . . . I think that we would get along all right. I'd like to be able to talk to him now and get his advice. Hell, if I didn't get advice I'd just like to talk to him. It's a shame there is such a jump in time between ones like us" (338). Jordan's desire to identify with, and be close to, his grandfather is merely a displacement of his grief for his own emotionally absent father, and hence, the psychological theme underlying Jordan's heroic actions throughout the novel is his denial of grief in relation to his father's death.

Furthermore, because of Jordan's ongoing aggressive wishes toward his mother, he denies his lingering dependency on her, despite his attempts to repair his repressed grief or separation anxiety in relation to her through his symbiotic-like relationship with Maria. Therefore, a double thematic strain of the taboo against grief informs and motivates Hemingway's imagination in *For Whom the Bell Tolls*, and, it may be presumed, accounts, in part, for the elegiac implications of the novel's title.

In view of these assumptions about Jordan's psychological condition, his obsession with the theme of suicide takes on a mixed constellation of determinants. Jordan's intense fear of his own suicidal impulses suggests that, on some level, he is drawn to the possibility of taking his own life. Suicide is sometimes an act of self-punishment to expiate profound guilt feelings, and it may, therefore, hold an appeal for Jordan as a means of relieving the unresolved guilt and grief he feels in relation to his father's death.[24] Since suicide also may be a means of expressing a fantasy of returning to infancy in order to re-experience—this time positively—the disappointing relationship with the nurturing archaic mother, Jordan's indulgence in his symbiotic-like love affair with Maria provides a solution through which he can repair an early experience of disappointment and deprivation.

For the first time in any of his stories or novels, however, Hemingway hinted at a profound psychological and symbolic correlation between his own, and his male hero's, domestic situation and the thematic subject of war. As is true for World War I, but is even more obvious in the case of the Spanish Civil War, the contest of war involves the battle against fascism and despotism. The fight for the Republic in which Jordan is engaged, like the war of "Rebellion" (as Jordan's grandfather called the American Civil War), occurred when the leaders of a country became the enemies of the people. Jordan is drawn to the Spanish people and to Spain, he reasons, because never was there "a people whose leaders were as truly their enemies as this one" (163). War is thus an apt symbol for the adolescent in a state of rebellion against his disappointing leaders—his parents. Like so many of Hemingway's adolescent protagonists, Jordan is living in a state of war in relation to his parents.

The transition from the role of child to the role of soldier is explained by Hemingway through Jordan's reasoning about himself, that in "him, too, was despair from the sorrow that soldiers turn to hatred in order that they may continue to be soldiers" (447). Jordan, in effect, became a "soldier" when his leaders—his parents—became his enemies. The tragic sacrifice the child/soldier must make when he declares "war" on his parents is thus the repression of sorrow and grief, and the displacement of that grief onto hatred and aggression. Not only does the taboo against grief allow the child to occupy the aggressive role of "soldier," but the adoption of that role demands an even greater sacrifice—the denial or loss of the emotional self: "Once you saw it again as it was to others, once you got rid of your own self, the always ridding of self that you had to do in war. Where there could be no self. Where yourself is only to be lost" (447). Throughout the novel, Jordan continuously reminds himself that his success as a soldier depends upon his enforcement of the taboo against grief. In war, "you have to have very much head and be very cold in the head," he tells Pilar (21). Alcohol and women, as with all of life's pleasures, are antithetical to war because, as Jordan tells Pilar, they "interfere with my work" (91). Feelings and thoughts about feelings must be carefully avoided, for, as Pilar explains: "In war one cannot say what one feels" (301). In terms of Jordan's internal familial war, until his hostility toward his disappointing parents has been defused, and until his definition of ideal masculine heroism is softened by the compromises of the reality principle (and is therefore no longer incompatible with his split-off, emotional self), love and fornication, or what Jordan early in the novel calls "personal fallibility," will always be acts of "heresy" against the Republic and against masculine "resolution" (164). In this immature adolescent state Jordan believes that his love for Maria and his feelings of guilt and grief over both killing and being killed has, as he says, "no place in his life" (267).

If the Spanish Civil War has a symbolic parallel in Hemingway's fictional separation-individuation conflict, so too does the cause that Jordan is fighting for—democracy and self-rule. In his internal battle, Jordan is fighting for the unity of the "republic," for an end to "civil war," and therefore, in effect, for self-integration. Unlike Orpen, who was desperately concerned with keeping intact the bridge between his ego and heroic ideal, Jordan's aim is to destroy that bridge, to expose, and, he hopes, to accept, the gap between the ego and the narcissistic, paternal ideal. "As Jordan goes, so goes the bloody bridge, other way around, really," he thinks to himself (438).

Through the events that unfold in the novel, Jordan will go an important step farther than either Orpen, Frederic Henry, or young Joe in "My Old Man," all of whom merely suffered the disappointment that comes with the boy's narcissistic disillusionment in the heroic paternal ego ideal. Jordan, however, accepts and comes to terms with the fallible father, and with this critical step in the ego's integration of the reality-based superego his aggression toward the phallic mother will be defused, and he will no longer view the maternal, primal love-object, Maria, as his rescuer from narcissistic injury. In the course of the novel, Jordan will fuse both the good and bad mothers and the good and bad fathers. The final, healthy psychic outcome in store for Robert Jordan, which is clearly ironic in view of his tragic physical end, but which marks a positive development in the ego-ideal conflict of the Hemingway protagonist, is the integration of his heroic, masculine self-image and his split-off and "lost" emotional, or "feminine," self—a merging of love and war that Orpen and Frederic Henry were never able to achieve.

To achieve self-integration, however, Jordan first must work through his past internal object relationships as Hemingway lays them out for the reader in chapter 30. Hemingway makes this working-through possible by re-creating a substitute or transferential nuclear family for Jordan. What Maria says to the boy, Joaquin, might well have been said to Robert Jordan:

> "I am thy sister," Maria said. "And I love thee and thou hast a family. We are all thy family."
> "Including the *Ingles*," boomed Pilar. "Isn't it true, *Ingles?*"
> "Yes," Robert Jordan said to the boy, "We are all thy family, Joaquin." (139)

Within the first few hours of Jordan's appearance at the mountain camp he finds himself in a contest for power with the leader of the small band of loyalists, Pablo. "I am more wolf than thee," Pablo says to Jordan, and informs him that "here no one commands but me" (10). Jordan soon discovers from the other members of the group, however, that Pablo has lost his resolve in his fight against the fascists. "He was a very good man," Pilar tells Jordan, but "now he is terminated" (32). The Spanish translation of the word "terminated" is "nostalgia," which Hemingway later used in *Islands in the Stream* to describe the deteriorated and withdrawn personality of the grief-obsessed Thomas Hudson. The Spanish "nostalgia," then, as Hemingway understood it, means "used up," or "worn out." In *Islands in the Stream*, Hemingway used the word in the phrase *"Nostalgia hecha hombre,"*[25] implying that once a man is "worn out," he is on the path to death or "termination." To "give up," as Pablo has, identifies him as a potential suicide, like Jordan's own father. Pablo, Jordan is told, now cares for nothing but himself and his horses, and in Jordan's mind, this self-preoccupation is a sign of *"lâcheté"*—cowardice—and therefore of suicide. When Jordan later tries to make sense of his father's suicide he surmises that a person has "to be awfully occupied with yourself to do a thing like that" (338).

Pablo further resembles Jordan's father in that he is a man who is dominated in his private life by a strong, phallic woman. Pilar torments the weak-willed Pablo, just as Jordan's mother abused his father to the point of suicide. When Pilar asks Jordan how his father died he cryptically replies:

> "He shot himself."
> "To avoid being tortured?" the woman asked.
> "Yes," Robert Jordan said. "To avoid being tortured." (66–67)

That Pablo has, in effect, been castrated is made clear to Jordan by Anselmo, who explains to him that Pablo "is as finished and as ended as a boar that has been altered" (193). Pablo is a "boar, that is a boar no longer" (194). Primarily because of his fear of death, Pilar explains, Pablo is "dangerous" to the Loyalist cause.

The character of Anselmo was explicitly designed by Hemingway to act as a foil to Pablo, in that Anselmo is "afraid of no one": "I am an old man who will live until I die" (16). While Pablo is a brutal and ruthless man who, without conscience, slaughtered a town of fascists who were formerly his close friends, Anselmo is distinguished by the fact that he is essentially a kindly man who abhors the very idea of killing men. Yet Hemingway was careful to add that Anselmo is not a coward; as the old man says about killing, "I feel nothing against it when it is necessary. When it is for the cause" (39).

Through the characters of Anselmo and Pablo, Hemingway split his intrapsychic images of the good and bad father, thus facilitating Jordan's introjection of both of these paternal figures. It remains for Jordan, in the resolution of his separation-individuation conflict, to integrate into himself, and hence, never lose, the good father, Anselmo, and come to terms with the weak and dangerous father, Pablo.

Within Jordan's transference from his biological family to this Spanish family, Hemingway also enacted a splitting of the good and bad, or nurturing and phallic, mothers through his creation of Maria and Pilar. By the end of chapter 2, it has become evident to Jordan that Pilar is a powerful and dominating woman, yet her roles as cook, as Pablo's wife, and as the "mother" of the band, identify her as a maternal figure. In her pronouncement to Jordan that she "would have made a good man" (97), she claims the identity of a phallic woman. Her castrating powers are confirmed by Rafael, who explains that Pilar "has a tongue that scalds and that bites like a bull whip. With this tongue she takes the hide from any one. In strips. She is of an unbelievable barbarousness" (28).

Because Jordan knows that Pilar will never allow personal doubt to interfere with her "resolution" to fight for the "cause," he finds himself "trusting her instantly" (31). When she, in turn, confesses to him, "I speak to you as though I knew you for a long time," he replies: "It is like that . . . when people understand each other" (32). Because Pilar is constructed by Hemingway from the same mold as Jordan's, and his own, dominating mother, it is understandable why she and Jordan feel they have known each other "for a long time." Jordan's intimacy with Pilar points to an unacknowledged debt that Hemingway might well have paid to his own mother, as the ideal model for his own phallic or "masculine" strength of character. While Hemingway, who often referred to his mother as a "bitch," could never get beyond his intense resentment of her for "torturing" his father to death, he allows Jordan, dimly, to perceive about his own parents: "Maybe the bully in her helped to supply what was missing in the other" (339).

There is an additional reason why Jordan establishes an instant emotional and professional bond with Pilar. It may be remembered from Hemingway's Orpen story that the dominating mother who criticized and directed his musical compositions when he was a boy was the original idealized figure who inspired his budding creative, artistic impulses. Hemingway rediscovered this creative, procreative, ideal phallic mother many years later in Gertrude Stein, and without her enriching influence his career might have taken a much less dramatic turn. Despite Pilar's steadfast function as a Loyalist leader, Jordan's admiration of her becomes most animated when she serves as an inspiration for his "other" life as a writer and storyteller. Hemingway devotes several pages to Pilar's narrative of the slaughter of fascists in her small home town. When she has finally come to the end of her story Jordan thinks to himself: "God, how she could tell a story. She's better than Quevedo, he thought. He never wrote the death of any Don Faustino as well as she told it. I wish I could write well enough to write that story, he thought" (134).

Maria is a variation on a familiar theme in Hemingway's fictional imagination, playing the nurturing and good mirroring mother/woman to the regressive side of Jordan's personality. Maria is associated with food in the novel and devotes herself to caring and providing for all of

Jordan's needs. When he thinks of her he thinks of "the first time you looked at her as she came out bent over carrying that iron cooking platter" (167). The regressive nature of Jordan and Maria's relationship is recognized by Pilar, who scolds the girl by asking her: "Must you care for him as a sucking child?" (203). Thus, Maria represents a potential regressive source of narcissistic gratification and omnipotence for Jordan.

For Orpen and Frederic Henry, the yearning for symbiotic fusion with the fantasy primal object is activated by a narcissistic blow, or wound, to the boy's heroic ideal through his sudden disillusionment with the ideal war hero. Since, as early as the first chapter of the novel, Jordan finds himself wondering "what could make me feel the way those horses make Pablo feel" (16), Hemingway suggests that, already, there is something not one hundred percent about Jordan's dedication to war and to his role as a soldier. Perhaps, as is so often true in Hemingway's early stories, it is because Jordan's identification with the heroic male ideal has always been unstable, and therefore, because his regressive yearning for primary narcissistic fusion is just below the surface of repression, that he must continuously defend himself against his vulnerability to emotional expression by "not thinking," by "being cold in the head," and by extension, cold in the heart as well.

For Jordan, life meant nothing before he met Maria. "You go along your whole life and they seem as though they mean something and they always end up not meaning anything. . . . And then . . . you run into a girl like this Maria. Sure. That is what you would do. You ran into her rather late, that was all" (167). Because of the immature and vulnerable nature of Jordan's masculine ego ideal, Maria provides for him—as Catherine Barkeley provided for Frederic Henry—the narcissist's rescue fantasy. She represents the shortest route to his longed-for experience of narcissistic omnipotence. As such, she is predictably associated with Jordan's nostalgic desire for the easy and comfortable civilian life he had in Madrid and at home in the States. When he is with her he fantasizes about what it would be like to be married to her and living together as "Mr. and Mrs. Robert Jordan of Sun Valley, Idaho. Or Corpus Christi, Texas, or Butte, Montana" (164). When he thinks of Maria he no longer wants "to make a Thermopylae, nor be Horatius at any bridge, nor be the Dutch boy with his finger in that dyke. No. He would like to spend some time with Maria. That was the simplest expression of it. He would like to spend a long, long time with her" (164). Just as the perfect mirroring mother, Renata, is "everything" to Richard Cantwell, Maria will "do everything" and be everything for Robert Jordan (70). What at first only absinthe could do for Jordan, now Maria will do. "What is it for?" Pablo asks about the flask of absinthe Jordan carries with him. "For everything," Jordan replies. "It cures everything. If you have anything wrong this will cure it" (50). Maria and absinthe fuse in Jordan's mind with the "wood-smoke and the burning leaves of autumn. That must be the odor of nostalgia, the smell of the smoke from the piles of raked leaves burning in the streets in the fall in Missoula" (260).

As explained in the previous chapter, the primal origins of the nostalgic impulse, some psychoanalysts believe, reside in the desire to return to a fantasy state of blissful symbiotic fusion with the fantasized all-providing mother, who magically met all of one's needs, and before that, to a time of "peace, beauty, harmony, warmth, freedom from want and timelessness," in the intra-uterine state.[26] This is precisely the image Hemingway evokes when Jordan and Maria are snuggled together in his warm sleeping bag, with Maria "curled far down in the robe, breathing lightly and regularly, and in the dark" (74). Maria nostalgically rescues Jordan from all adult responsibility and concern, "comforting against him, abolishing loneliness against him, magically, by a simple touching of flanks" (264). As is true for the mother-infant dyad, the loss of this symbiotic relationship feels like the end of life itself, "as though she were all of life and it was being taken from him" (264).

As studies on nostalgia have suggested, also at the heart of the nostalgic impulse is a death-wish—a desire to return to the inorganic state.[27] Jordan experiences sexual union with Maria as a journey down "a dark passage which led to nowhere, then to nowhere, then again to nowhere, once again to nowhere, always and forever to nowhere, heavy on the elbows in the earth to nowhere, dark, never any end to nowhere, hung on all time always to unknowing nowhere" (159). For Hemingway, sexual intercourse was an act of regressive, nostalgic fulfillment, the goal being to repair narcissistic injury and abolish his hero's grief-filled separation anxiety. At the moment of sexual union with Maria, Jordan "knew that nothing could ever happen to the one that did not happen to the other, that no other thing could happen more than this; that this was all and always" (379).

As Hemingway was well aware, however, the symbiotic bliss that love provides is always an Eden that is destined to be lost. For Hemingway, as for the nostalgic, the people he loved and the pleasures of life that he enjoyed were valuable by virtue of the fact that they would eventually be lost to him. While Jordan hates "to leave a thing that is so good" as his relationship with Maria, and while he has "learned much about life in these four days," he suspects that "you only learn them now because you are oversensitized because of the shortness of the time" (380–81). What was fundamentally lacking in Jordan's, as in Huck's, inner experience of love, was a sense of basic trust and object constancy which would have allowed him to retain the feeling of intense love, even after the beloved object is lost. As it is, for Robert Jordan, as for so many of Hemingway's male lovers, "oneness" can only be experienced at the precise moment of sexual union, which cannot be sustained over time, and so is destined to end in tragic loss, disappointment, and separation. By the end of *For Whom the Bell Tolls*, however, Jordan will undergo an emotional transformation that will restore a primitive sense of basic trust in relation to the narcissistically chosen love-object.

Through the characters of Pablo, Anselmo, Pilar, and Maria, Hemingway re-created a complete transferential object-relations scenario for Jordan, composed of, respectively, the dangerous father, the good, emotionally accessible father, the castrating, phallic mother, and the nurturing, symbiotic-like mother. The fact that these characterizations are not simple or archetypal, but rather, were delineated by Hemingway with a greater degree of psychological complexity, will become significant in the development of Jordan's character later in the novel.

For the most part, however, Jordan is engaged in a competitive sexual triangle with these parent figures. Pilar, at one point, betrays her husband by aligning herself with her symbolic son, Jordan, over the issue of the bridge. When she announces to Pablo that she is "for the bridge," Pablo has a "betrayed look on his face and the sweat on his forehead as he turned his head" (53). Pablo, in turn, is in sexual competition with Jordan for Maria. He "has a sickness for her already," Pilar informs Jordan. "It is on him like a sickness when he sees her" (32). Pablo is further involved in a power struggle with the phallic mother and her "son," Jordan. In his resentment, Pablo confesses to Pilar that he would like to "shoot thee and the foreigner both" (55).

As is typical of the sexually competitive son, Jordan finds Pablo a threat to his life and to his status as a professional "soldier," both of which correspond to his feminine identification as a freedom fighter and an artist with the phallic mother, Pilar. Jordan's initial impulse is to eliminate Pablo by killing him; but, in terms of his oedipal-like contest

with Pablo, it "would be ideal if she [Pilar] would kill him," he thinks
(63). Agustin, whom Jordan at one point refers to as "my brother," also
admits to Jordan that he has "cared much for" Maria. "More than one is
able to imagine," he adds. "I can imagine," Jordan knowingly assures
him (290). Further complicating Jordan's competitive family triangles is
Pilar's protective love for Maria and her jealousy of Jordan. "I, too. I
care for her very much. Yes. Much," Pilar confesses to Jordan (91).

Jordan's way of dealing with the various love triangles that he is
involved in is not to confront them head on but to avoid conflict. He
defers the killing of Pablo to his regressive inclination to be rescued from
father-son confrontation by escaping, as Orpen and Frederic Henry do,
to the arms of the nurturing mother, in this case, Maria. As Raphael
accuses him: "When thou needest to kill a man and instead did what you
did? You were supposed to kill one, not make one" (79).

Jordan's avoidance of a masculine contest and his susceptibility to
indulge in his regressive rescue fantasy with Maria are both psychologically consistent with the immature or adolescent nature of his masculine
ego ideal. His persistent adolescent identification with an unrealistic,
abstract, heroic paternal ideal can be maintained only if he avoids the
tempering influence of the reality principle. As it slowly begins to dawn
on Jordan, in the course of the novel, that his heroic paternal ideal is a
hollow, fraudulent, and quixotic fantasy constructed by his adolescent
imagination, the tide of events changes radically.

Through the indirect English translation of the Spanish word "faith,"
Hemingway ironically translates Pilar's expression of "belief" in the
Loyalist cause in her statement to Jordan: "I put great illusion in the
Republic" (90). With more directness, Pablo accuses the entire band of
being "a group of illusioned people" (215). The Madrid bar, Gaylord's,
is Hemingway's symbol for Jordan's loss of innocence in relation to his
heroic ego ideal. It is at Gaylord's that Jordan first learns that the
Spanish Civil War was not led entirely by the poor masses, but also by
imported, Russian-trained military leaders. "That had been the first big
disillusion to him a few months back and he had started to be cynical to
himself about it" (229).

Whereas, earlier in the novel, Jordan "employed . . . without criticism" phrases such as "enemies of the people," "patriotism," and "revo-
lutionary," and intellectually he knew how corrupt the "whole business"
was but "had accepted it and enjoyed it" (23), it is not until he acts out
his own private "mission" with Pablo's band and the bridge that he

comes to understand *emotionally* his own personal disillusionment with his grandfather and his heroic, paternal ideal. Before Jordan attempts to blow up the bridge he senses that his "orders were impossible to carry out," but when he discovers in actuality that his trepidation was justified, he also discovers that his own heroic ego ideal in which he held such "illusion" was an impossible one for him, or for anyone, to attain.

In order to drive home the theme of ego-ideal disillusionment, Hemingway does not rely solely on the competing voices in Jordan's head, which tell him at one moment, "I get tired . . . of me and of the war and why did it have to snow now?" and at the next moment, "Cut it out and take it" (181). He also accomplishes this through Pilar's story of the purposeless sacrifice of dozens of innocent Spanish peasants, and through poor Andre's Kafkaesque journey to deliver a message to Golz. Bringing to mind Kafka's novels, as well as *The Wizard of Oz*, Andre's adventure reveals an impotent madman, Colonel Marty, at the helm of the Republic cause. Hemingway has created his hero in *For Whom the Bell Tolls* as a thoroughly competent soldier who, most likely, is capable of the kind of grand heroics Jordan imagines his grandfather might have demonstrated. In order to bring about Jordan's disappointment in the less than successful fulfillment of his order to blow up the bridge, Hemingway has Pablo steal the explosives that would have allowed Jordan to complete the task perfectly and without risk to human life. When Jordan recognizes, in chapter 35, the tremendous danger to his own safety, and, more importantly, to his self-esteem, that now faces him, his anger and resentment toward his idealized, heroic conception of his grandfather, and toward the Spanish cause, comes to a head:

Oh, muck my grandfather and muck this whole treacherous muck-faced mucking country and every mucking Spaniard in it on either side and to hell forever. . . . Muck the whole treachery-ridden country. Muck their egotism and their selfishness and their egotism and their conceit and their treachery. . . . God muck Pablo. Pablo is all of them. God pity the Spanish people. Any leader they have will muck them. One good man, Pablo Iglesias, in two thousand years and everybody else mucking them. How do we know how he would have stood up in this war? I remember when I thought Largo was O.K. Durruti was good and his own people shot him there at the Puente de los Franceses. . . . And that Pablo that just mucked off with my exploder and my box of detonators. Oh muck him to deepest hell. But no. He's mucked us instead. They always muck you instead. (370–71)

This moment in Jordan's adolescent disillusionment of his previously held heroic paternal ideal is a critical one in the individuation process of Hemingway's protagonist. Significantly, however, Jordan does not regressively escape from reality and adult responsibility, as Orpen does, by hiding in mother-Maria's embrace, and childishly pleading with her not to make him "go back" to the fighting; neither does he, like Frederic Henry, run off to Switzerland with his mother surrogate, Catherine. Nor does Jordan narcissistically view this single imperfectly executed mission as the complete downfall of his heroic ideal and like young Joe in "My Old Man," conclude that "when they get started they don't leave a guy nothing."[28] Instead, Jordan transcends his anger and proceeds with his plan as best he can under the "impossible" circumstances. "God, I'm glad I got over being angry," he says to himself. "It was like not being able to breathe in a storm" (371). Despite his disappointment he makes his final resolution: "We'll be killed but we'll blow the bridge" (371). Although Jordan can now only "believe ten percent" (233) in his heroic ideal, he accepts that ten percent as "something" rather than "nothing." Jordan has made the important realization that he can still aspire to his heroic cause and at the same time acquiesce to the limitations of reality and to his own impaired ability to fulfill his ideal:

And you, last night, thinking about how you and your grandfather were so terrific and your father was a coward. Show yourself a little confidence now. . . . She thinks you're wonderful, he thought. I think you stink. And the *gloria* and all that nonsense that you had. You had wonderful ideas, didn't you? You had this world all taped, didn't you? The hell with all of that. (386)

Whereas, in Hemingway's Orpen story, the hero's task was to guard with his life the symbolic bridge that upheld the adolescent, narcissistic illusion of the coming together of the ego and the grandiose, heroic ego ideal, here, Jordan is determined to destroy that bridge and accept the limitations of the father ideal. Jordan expects to be killed when the bridge is destroyed, but he miraculously discovers, in effect, that his ego has survived the narcissistic blow of the bridge intact; although "he still felt numb with the surprise that he had not been killed at the bridge" (452).

The acceptance of the limited father and of his own flawed ego ideal has a tremendous impact on Jordan's object relationships in the novel. For one, Jordan begins to come to terms with his long held disappointment in his biological father. When he bids an emotional farewell to Maria on his way to the bridge he suddenly "knew this had happened before" (405):

Robert Jordan had not felt this young since he had taken the train at Red Lodge to go down to Billings to get the train there to go away to school for the first time. He had been afraid to go and he did not want any one to know it and, at the station, just before the conductor picked up the box he would step up on to reach the steps of the day coach, his father had kissed him good-by and said, "May the Lord watch between thee and me while we are absent the one from the other." His father had been a very religious man and he had said it simply and sincerely. But his moustache had been moist and his eyes were damp with emotion and Robert Jordan had been so embarrassed by all of it . . . he had felt suddenly so much older than his father and sorry for him that he could hardly bear it. (405–6)

Just as Jordan was later to be "embarrassed" by his father's suicide, he is here ashamed of his father's undisguised emotional weakness. At a time when the boy needed his father to be strong, in order to help him overcome and deal with his own weakness and fear of separation, his father failed him. He resented his father because, instead of taking care of the boy, the boy had to take care of the father, and, as a result, the boy "felt much older" than the man. The father's frailty forces Jordan to be "cold in the head," and in the heart—to repress his own grief in deference to the older man's more conspicuous grief. The sadness and anxiety Jordan feels when he says good-bye to Maria allows him to identify with his father's "weakness"—a weakness he did not know he, himself, possessed until this moment—and activates something like forgiveness toward his father's human fallibility.

Jordan's final gesture of forgiveness toward his father, however, comes only after he has been severely wounded in the leg, when his big gray horse topples over on him during his escape from the blown bridge. Jordan's pain is excruciating and he finds himself, ironically, in the same situation as his father once found himself—contemplating a speedy end to his pain through suicide:

I don't want to do that business that my father did. I will do it all right but I'd much prefer not to have to. I'm against that. Don't think about that. . . . I guess I'm not awfully good at pain. Listen, if I do that now you wouldn't misunderstand, would you? *Who are you talking to?* Nobody, he said. Grandfather, I guess. . . . You're not so good at this, Jordan, he said. Not so good at this. And who is so good at this? I don't know and I don't really care right now. But you are not. That's right. You're not at all. Oh not at all, at all. I think it would be all right to do it now? (469–70)

Jordan has failed the test in which he vowed never to "do the thing" his father did. Even though he does not commit suicide, he realizes that it "would be all right" if he did. Although he knows he is going to die and that his heroic mission cannot be carried out perfectly, his meager contribution to the cause is acceptable to him.

Jordan's belief in the grandiose, heroic, paternal ideal in the past protected him against a possible confrontation with the real, castrating father, a role that is symbolically played in the novel by the potentially dangerous Pablo. When Jordan's military assignment is compromised and he comes to terms with the possibility of failure and the blow to his self-esteem that his vulnerability represents, he also, in effect, experiences his long-avoided confrontation with the limitations of reality, embodied in the dangerous and fallible father. It is at this point in the novel that Pablo becomes a benign object in Jordan's phallic contest. Although Pablo is essentially responsible for the deaths of many of his own men, the fact that he returns to help Jordan carry out his orders suggests an integration of the ego with the threatening father.[29] Symbolically, as Pilar observes, Pablo, the circumvented real father, "art back" from "a long way gone" (391). Like the dreaded and repressed castrating father and the apprehensive adolescent son, Jordan fears the worst from a long-avoided intimacy with Pablo. When "he put his hand out" to grasp the hand of Pablo, Jordan

expected that it would be like grasping something reptilian or touching a leper. He did not know what Pablo's hand would feel like. But in the dark Pablo's hand gripped his hard and pressed it frankly and he returned the grip. Pablo had a good hand in the dark and feeling it gave Robert Jordan the strangest feeling he had felt that morning. We must be allies now, he thought. (404)

But like the reserved alliance between the ego and the superego, Jordan and Pablo "always hated each other *au fond*" (404). The psychic letting-go of the grandiose father ideal also activates a re-awakening of the homosexual libido in relation to the phallic father, which Hemingway discloses through Pilar's accusation to Jordan and Pablo: "What are you two doing? Being *maricones?*" (404).

The integration of the ego, the ego ideal, and the superego in Jordan's family drama, eliminates the prior need for the split-off good father, personified in the novel by the character of Anselmo. Hence, Hemingway appropriately killed off Anselmo at the very moment that the bridge is destroyed, but not before Jordan has integrated this benevolent father's qualities into himself. Anselmo's philosophy of killing is that "there must be some form of civic penance organized that all may be cleansed from the killing or else we will never have a true and human basis for living" (196). When Jordan reads some of the letters he finds on the bodies of the young soldiers he has killed, he learns for himself the lesson of human tragedy that war has always represented for Anselmo. He realizes, as the old man so often said, that "to shoot a man gives a feeling as though one had struck one's own brother" (442). Although Jordan admires and identifies with Anselmo's benevolence and moral conscience, he is careful to keep these aspects of himself in a realistic perspective: "Anselmo does not like to [kill men] because he is a hunter, not a soldier. Don't idealize him, either. Hunters kill animals and soldiers kill men" (287).

Jordan's reconciliation (albeit a forced and superficial one), with the phallic father also carries the predictable consequence of defusing the castrating and "barbarous" nature of the phallic mother. Throughout the course of the novel, running parallel to Jordan's disillusionment with ideal heroism in war, is his growing fondness for Pilar. He has learned that beneath this woman's hard exterior is a generous and loving soul. While she would "kill" or "curse" Pablo for the sake of the cause, she would never "wound" his feelings (89), and at a moment when her humanity and feminine softness show through, Jordan opens his heart to her. "Robert Jordan put his arm on her big shoulder. 'I care for thee, too,' he said. 'I care for thee very much' " (92).

Perhaps, in terms of Hemingway's past belief in the incompatibility of love and war, the most significant consequence of Jordan's acceptance of the fallible father is the reconciliation between his masculine, heroic self-image and his split-off emotional self. Up until the hour that Jordan is supposed to blow up the bridge he believes, as Hemingway's male protagonists always have, that the woman in his life "had no place in his" work (267). The day before Jordan is scheduled to carry out his orders, he, Pablo, and the band are faced with the possibility of fighting in the mountains with an approaching cavalry of enemy soldiers. "Say that you love me," Maria says to Jordan, as he is departing for battle. "No. Not now," Jordan sharply replies:

"Not love me now?"
"*Dejamos.* Get thee back. One does not do that and love all at the same moment."
"I want to go to hold the legs of the gun and while it speaks love thee all in the same moment."
"Thou art crazy. Get thee back now."
"I am not crazy," she said. "I love thee."
"Then get thee back." (269–70)

Until this moment, love and war have had no place together in Jordan's, and Hemingway's, exclusively masculine conception of war. Hemingway has imagined Maria's character in such a way, however, that she cannot be separated from the masculine pursuit of war in which Jordan is engaged. Everything about her, even her strange beauty—her cropped head and violated sexuality—are part of the Loyalist cause for which Jordan is fighting. As he says to her: "I love thee as I love all that we have fought for. I love thee as I love liberty and dignity and the rights of all men to work and not be hungry. I love thee as I love Madrid that we have defended and as I love all my comrades that have died. . . . But I love thee as I love what I love most in the world and I love thee more" (348). Maria's character, as Hemingway conceived it, is an extension of Jordan's purpose and meaningfulness as a man. Her very being is politicized, a part of the movement; and at the precise moment his fantasy escape with her through sexual intercourse draws him away from the "cause," her personal and political past pulls him back into the reality of war. Hence, for the first and perhaps the only time in Hemingway's fiction, his male hero's regressive love for the symbiotic rescuer-mother is sublimated into his pursuit of masculine heroism. When Jordan goes off to blow up the bridge he truly believes he will never see Maria again. Afterwards, when he sees her, he comes to the extraordinary realization that the two aspects of himself that he had always kept safely at a distance from one another—the masculine and the feminine, war and love—can indeed function as an integral unit:

> He had never thought that you could know that there was a woman if there was battle; nor that any part of you could know it, or respond to it; nor that if there was a woman that she could have breasts small, round and tight against you through a shirt; nor that they, the breasts, could know about the two of them in battle. But it was true and he thought, good. That's good. I would not have believed that and he held her to him once hard, hard, but he did not look at her, and then he slapped her where he never had slapped her and said, "Mount. Mount. Get on that saddle, *guapa.*" (456)

Through the events of Robert Jordan's life as Hemingway envisaged them, his hero, in effect, and broadly speaking, integrates into himself the phallic mother, the castrating real father, the kindly superego, and the sexual woman; and successfully introjects these split-off aspects of his personality through symbolic identification with Pilar, Pablo, Anselmo, and the sexual woman, Maria. It remains for him to do the same with the nurturing, pregenital mother, also embodied in the figure of Maria.

Jordan accomplishes this last important step in the separation-individ-uation process during the final few pages of the novel, when he lies mortally wounded on the forest floor. "Thou wilt go now, rabbit," he orders Maria. "But I go with thee. As long as there is one of us there is both of us" (463). All of life, psychoanalysis tells us, is a prolonged process of separation from the satisfying, nurturing maternal object. One may mourn the loss of her as an external object and live with an unre-solved feeling of grief and separation anxiety; or, one may integrate her loving, nurturing qualities and carry within oneself the love and basic trust learned from the comforting mother-infant relationship. When the novel begins, Robert Jordan does not possess this inner sense of basic trust. He needs the actual presence of Maria, his fantasy mother surro-gate, to rescue him from his "loneliness" and vulnerability to separation from her—a departure that before signaled an end to "life itself." Here, his good maternal object at last becomes integrated into himself, and as he assures Maria: "Whichever one there is, is both" (463).

Robert Jordan's final gesture of psychic communion partakes of, and perhaps is made possible by, the spirit of Anselmo, which has also now become a part of him. It was Anselmo who, only a short time before, lay on the dirt as Jordan is lying now, but who "was not lonely nor did he feel in any way alone. He was one with the wire in his hand and one with the bridge, and one with the charges the *Ingles* had placed. He was one with the *Ingles* still working under the bridge and he was one with all of the battle and with the Republic" (443). The ability to integrate into oneself, and therefore never to lose—and never to have to grieve over the loss of—one's friends and one's enemies alike, begins with one's earliest relationships with the good and bad—strong and weak—parents. This is the "education" (381) of adult life Jordan receives in the brief three and a half days he spends in the Spanish hillsides:

I have been all my life in these hills since I have been here. Anselmo is my oldest friend. I know him better than I know Charles, than I know Chubb, than I know Guy, than I know Mike, and I know them well. Augustin with his vile mouth, is my brother, and I never had a brother. Maria is my true love and my wife. I never had a true love. I never had a wife. She is also my sister, and I never had a sister, and my daughter, and I never will have a daughter. I hate to leave a thing that is so good. (381)

The "good thing" Jordan most fears leaving in the end is indeed not entirely lost, for in *For Whom the Bell Tolls*, Hemingway tells the story Robert Jordan could not go on to tell for himself. The psychological task of separation-individuation, and the working through and integration of past internal object relationships, dramatized by Hemingway in *For Whom the Bell Tolls*, is implied in Donne's sermon, which Hemingway used in both the epigraph and title of his novel: "any man's *death* diminishes *me*, because I am involved in *Mankinde;* And therefore never send to know for whom the *bell* tolls; It tolls for *thee*" (italics in original).

Through Jordan's death, and through the eventual defeat of the Spanish Republic, Hemingway, as he so often did in his fiction (but tragically, in the end, could not do in his own life), finds "triumph in defeat." Hemingway had completed only fourteen chapters of his novel when he heard of the defeat of the Loyalists in Spain. Certainly he must have been drawn to the Spanish Civil War as a subject for his novel precisely because it served as a perfect archetypal story of the adolescent's disillusionment with the impossible to attain, heroic, paternal ego ideal. Whereas this subject had always been a source of personal anxiety and grief for Hemingway, as his early stories and novels illustrate, perhaps his great personal success as a writer during the time he wrote *For Whom the Bell Tolls* supplied him with the self-esteem and narcissistic sustenance he needed to confront the pain of his disillusionment in the grandiose ego ideal, and perhaps then to move forward toward a mature vision of ego integration and the establishment of a reality-based identity structure.

Robert Jordan's death at the end of the novel, however, is both literally and symbolically a consequence of his adolescent disillusionment in the heroic, paternal ego ideal, which re-awakens in him the threat of castration by the real, flawed, and threatening father. The fatal nature of Jordan's wound—his leg that was severed from his body at the thigh by the castrating father's big gray horse—suggests on a symbolic level that his ego does not, in fact, survive the narcissistic injury he suffers. Possibly Jordan was acting out a disguised suicide wish by refusing to escape with Maria and the others, and instead staying behind where he awaits certain death. If this is indeed the case, then one must again conclude that he has achieved a psychic reconciliation with his suicidal father. Death also provided Jordan with a way of avoiding a prolonged, and therefore realistic, commitment to his love-relationship with Maria. As in *A Farewell to Arms*, Hemingway may have been unwilling (or unable) to integrate his idealistic notion of passionate, romantic love with peacetime—and time-worn—reality. Perhaps, also, Hemingway could not envision for himself, personally, the consequences of the infiltration of the ego by the reality principle in less devastating terms than complete annihilation of the narcissistically vulnerable ego. If *For Whom the Bell Tolls* represents Hemingway's attempt in fantasy to integrate the good and bad parents into oneself, his increasingly severe bouts of depression, alcoholism, pathological nostalgia, and eventual suicide, lead to the inevitable conclusion that Hemingway, the man, could not in the end integrate his fictional fantasy into his personal experience of reality. In both its biographical and universal psychoanalytic implications, however, *For Whom the Bell Tolls,* like many of Hemingway's later novels, provided an effective outlet for his effort, as well as that of his character, Robert Jordan, to come to terms with reality, and therefore to make the reader reflect upon strategies for emotional survival that apply to all human beings.

Many of the works produced by Hemingway during his middle years, including *Winner Take Nothing,* "The Snows of Kilimanjaro," and *Death in the Afternoon,* have been re-evaluated in this chapter in terms of his increasing self-consciousness, and, one might even say, his wavering faith, in relation to his *art of repression.* One of the consequences of this disillusionment was his increased reliance on writing as a nostalgic enterprise that fights off the debilitating effects of depression and the grief of loss, and therefore allowed him to maintain a functioning degree of self-esteem equilibrium. But, just as Hemingway in his mid-years became aware of the emotional and physical hazards—as well as the numbing effects—of those defensive mechanisms such as drinking, repression, disavowal, and regression, that had once served to shield him from grief and loss, in his last works of fiction, which I will now turn to, particularly *A Moveable Feast, Across the River and Into the Trees,* and *Islands in the Stream,* Hemingway becomes aware of his excessive dependency, this time upon nostalgic fantasy, as a way of making a final stand against the overwhelming encroachment of depression, loss, and grief on his personal and professional stability.

7. Grief Hoarders and "Beat-Up Old Bastards": Hemingway's Bittersweet Taste of Nostalgia

A man is not old until regrets take the place of dreams.
    —John Barrymore, quoted in Gene Fowler, *Good Night, Sweet Prince: The Life and Times of John Barrymore*

Sorrow's crown of sorrow is remembering happier things.
                —Alfred, Lord Tennyson, "Locksley Hall"

You may my glories and my state depose,
But not my griefs; still am I king of those.

                                    —Shakespeare, *Richard II*

As I suggested in the previous chapter, in his later life and career, Hemingway became conscious of the disturbing fact that the art of repression, while it functioned brilliantly as a strategy of defense against personal loss, disappointment, and depression in the composition of his fictional narratives, had a way of taking its toll on him personally and professionally, as it did on Harry in "Snows," by augmenting rather than diminishing the physical and psychological ills that plagued him. Also, by the mid-1930s, Hemingway appeared to have begun to identify narcissistically with the grandiose paternal image of the Hemingway *code hero* that he, himself, had created. It follows that the greatest danger confronting Hemingway was again the loss of self-esteem. According to Jackson Benson, "the act of creative writing, when Hemingway became successful, was an act of self-dramatization which justified his emotional history and gave substance to a created identity."[1] In a similar vein, Carlos Baker has observed that: "To his original impulse to transform his personal past into material for art was added an ulterior and perhaps mainly subconscious determination to exploit it as a means of justifying himself and his actions in the eyes of the world."[2] In his psychoanalytic study of Hemingway, Leo Schneiderman affirmed that "Hemingway's self-centeredness made his writing an exercise in subjectivism disguised as dispassionate reporting."[3] The list of similar observations is a long one. Perhaps Joyce Carol Oates stated the situation most concisely when she proposed that once Hemingway became famous, writing became a "means to an end: the enshrinement and immortalization of Ernest Hemingway."[4] To the extent that one can responsibly hypothesize about Hemingway the man, we might say that in later life he appeared to be a depressive struggling with the neurotic use of memory and with many of the patterns associated with narcissism that are portrayed in characters like Richard Cantwell, Thomas Hudson, and the Hemingway narrators of *A Moveable Feast* and *Green Hills of Africa*.

In his late, as in his early, years, therefore, one of Hemingway's primary tasks was to live up to the ego ideal or masculine ideal object as embodied in his fictionally presented *code hero*. If Hemingway's writing increasingly became a means to his own self-glorification, it was perhaps owing to the fact that over the years his ideal object became more of a self-object than an objective fictional construct, thus leading the way to the formation of narcissistic patterns of behavior. As Michael Reynolds has suggested, it is "so easy to fall in love with one's own fictions" and "Hemingway could not resist the temptation."[5] One might say that for Hemingway, life and fiction merged into a composite source of narcissistic gratification, so that, by the 1940s, he was a "prisoner" of his own "myth."[6] Hemingway's reputation as a "hairy-chested male," courageous war hero, daring sportsman, adventurous journalist, and womanizer became larger than life, so that, as one magazine columnist wrote, he became, in the eyes of the world, "a more fabulous character than any he ever created."[7] Eventually, according to John Raeburn, it became impossible to tell whether the public reputation "squared with the 'real' personality of Hemingway" because no one, not even Hemingway, knew any more who the "real" Hemingway was.[8] In his study of Hemingway's decline as an artist, Philip Young pointed out how the "confident self-absorption" of Hemingway's early life worsened over the years into an "insecure obsession with self."[9] His need for flattery, Young added, "at times nearly determined his life" (237). Both Carlos Baker and Mary Hemingway, in their biographies of Hemingway, have also emphasized that the loss of confidence and a growth in preoccupation with self were among his more serious troubles in his last years. Yet, like his later protagonists, Robert Jordan, Richard Cantwell, and Thomas Hudson, Hemingway cannot entirely be defined by these narcissistic patterns of behavior. His insight into his own narcissistic relationship with his grandiose self image reveals that he had enough perspective to struggle to control these drives, to turn his obsession with the past, and the search for grandiosity and self-validation, to constructive purpose by sublimating them in his art, modifying them so that they had some universal application.

The devastating effects that Hemingway's excessive drinking and his proclivity toward severe depression had upon his personal life and his writing must also not be underestimated. According to Tom Dardis, in his study of alcoholism and the American writer, Hemingway's downward slide, which began sometime about 1936, after he had completed "The Snows of Kilimanjaro" and "The Short Happy Life of Francis Macomber," was largely due to his increased use of alcohol, which intensified his bouts of depression.[10] "Hemingway's ' *'fraid of nothing!'* philosophy," Dardis maintains, "extended to alcohol" as well. It was, therefore, Hemingway's ignorance of alcoholism as a disease, or perhaps his refusal to admit this fact to himself, that caused him the most harm. "It was from about this time," Dardis concludes, "that Hemingway began to escalate his all-out machismo, which would grow to become a monstrous parody of itself" (172). Ronald Fieve has postulated that Hemingway increasingly began to suffer from a genetically inherited bipolar disorder or manic-depression. Psychiatrist Philip Scharfer has speculated that Hemingway may even have begun to exhibit symptoms of "a borderline personality disorder," probably accompanied by "self-image problems."[11] These self-image problems, which are descriptively similar to, though not necessarily clinically indicative of, narcissism, will be explored more fully in my upcoming discussion of Hemingway's later life and fiction.

Throughout the 1940s and 1950s, Hemingway suffered increasingly severe periods of depression and self-doubt. Without question manic-depression and a borderline personality structure, both of which exhibit symptoms that generally resemble those of narcissism, served to magnify Hemingway's self-destructive and bipolar behavior.[12] What most disturbed not only Hemingway's third wife, Martha, but many of Hemingway's close friends and relatives was his seemingly narcissistic "need for self-glorification." As Bernice Kert observed, if "reality did not provide him with continuous triumphs, he drew on his fantasies,"[13] perpetually telling made-up tales about his heroics to his Cuban friends. Although Otto Kernberg might say that Hemingway indulged in the narcissist's need "to feel great and important in order to cancel feelings of worthlessness and devaluation" (234), it is important to note that the greater likelihood is that Hemingway was caught between the attraction to narcissistic behavior and his insightful understanding of the perils of such behavior. Therefore, if Hemingway's psychological problems gave rise to self-absorption, they also inspired a penetrating awareness of his own emotional needs, desires, and ambivalences that resulted in some of his most poignant and grief-filled later fiction.

After his mid-thirties Hemingway also no longer had the youth and physical stamina to live up to his heroic, ideal self-image, and thus to experience himself as larger-than-life; nor was he any longer the adolescent whose inflated ego could be seen as part of a boy's healthy masculine development. In middle age, Hemingway began to doubt his ability to live up to his heroic, grandiose self-image; for to do so required the superhuman physical agility and competence he no longer possessed.[14] In sum, this image demanded the "heroics" common to the fiction of many postwar writers that, as Wright Morris has observed, "excluded the possibility of growing old."[15] As early as the mid-1930s, then, it appears that life for Hemingway became a defensive attempt to deny the realization that neither his work nor his usual activities as a sportsman and journalist any longer seemed to bridge the gap between his inflated ego and his grandiose ego ideal. Like his fellow writers of the period, as his son, Gregory, surmised, Hemingway "never could develop a philosophy that would allow him to grow old gracefully."[16]

Indeed, Hemingway's physical decline was anything but graceful. He had problems with his eyes, joints, knees, liver, and skin. The hair on his head was receding and thinning, and he was fierce about not letting anyone touch his bald spots. A number of head injuries left him at one point with double vision, slowness of speech, loss of verbal memory, a tendency to write backwards, dull headaches, and a ringing in the ears.[17] Hemingway's customary response to these ailments was to downplay the physical and psychological pain that must have accompanied them; yet his awareness of the devastating effects of these losses, and the new challenges that they presented for him, led him in his later fiction to focus on the theme that in a man's limited understanding of his own human frailty he might still be able to find triumph in defeat.

In addition to using alcohol as a defense against encroaching feelings of self-doubt, in his later life and fiction Hemingway defended himself against narcissistic injury and loss primarily, as we have already begun to see, through an increasing nostalgia[18] for a lost ideal past as well as for a lost heroic self-image. The nostalgic fantasy allowed Hemingway to acknowledge the fact of loss and disappointment, but at the same time to recapture in fantasy, and through the reveries of memory, a lost ideal state of the self. From personal experience Hemingway was able to explore in his later works, especially *Death in the Afternoon, Green Hills of Africa, Islands in the Stream,* and *A Moveable Feast,* how nostalgia can be used to minimize the pain of disappointment and loss.

The nostalgic desire to re-attain something akin to an infantile experience of omnipotence is believed by some to be at the root of narcissism; but it is also, more generally, the same fantasy engaged in by those who are attempting to compensate for an early experience of deprivation.[19] This compensating regressive fantasy contains a powerful nostalgic drive—the drive to regain the perfection of one's own youth, and before that, a fantasized time of blissful symbiotic oneness with the all-giving mother who, ideally, met all one's needs as if magically, and even earlier a time of "peace, beauty, harmony, warmth, freedom from want and timelessness," when organic life was barely distinguishable from inorganic life.[20] The Greek roots from which the word "nostalgia" is derived suggest its psychological cause and function: *Nostos,* which means "return to the native land," and *Algos,* meaning "suffering or grief."[21] Johannes Hofer, the first physician to describe medically the condition of nostalgia, in 1688, called upon the German term, *Heimweh,* which denotes "grief for the lost charm of the Native Land" (373). Nostalgia, then, as David S. Werman points out, is a substitute for mourning, a defense for those who cannot seem to surmount the process of mourning for one's lost youth and ideal self-image.[22]

For Hemingway, therefore, the nostalgic impulse of protracted mourning acted as a totem in his fiction, as perhaps it also did in his own life, to enforce his taboo against the grief evoked by the loss of youth, the loss of an image of a perfect, omnipotent self, and the disappointments and disillusionments that inevitably accompany the aging process and the passage of time. It is understandable, then, given Hemingway's increasingly neurotic use of memory in later life, that the single most powerful force operating in the psychic life of his fictional protagonists was nostalgia for their personal past.[23]

Hemingway's impassioned artistic goal in the works he produced from 1932, until his death in 1961, was to re-write his past. In this sense, fiction became something of an analytical narrative for Hemingway.

Nostalgia, or fictive mourning, functioned as a compromise formation that enabled him to sublimate his own feelings of endangered self-esteem into his art. In the works that I will investigate in this chapter, Hemingway's wishful nostalgic fantasies result in what appears to be the narcissist's "pathological nostalgia" or "neurotic use of memories."[24] Remembering, in effect, became the Hemingway hero's greatest source of narcissistic gratification. The nostalgic fantasy brings the past back to life, and sometimes, merely by virtue of being lost, the past becomes an ideal and treasured experience. But remembering is also fraught with a degree of pain since the longing for the past brings with it the anguish of grief over that which is gone. The grief that underlay Hemingway's denial of the past as something that had been lost to him through time was often consciously confronted by his characters, and therefore occupied a prominent place in their nostalgic fantasies. So powerfully did these compensating nostalgic fantasies operate in the minds of his protagonists that the themes of loss, repressed grief, and the infirmities of an aging body became the primary subjects of several of Hemingway's later works.

Hemingway's obsessive concern with death and suicide (both so closely tied to the denial of one's mortality and the wishful fantasy for infantile omnipotence) also pervaded the majority of his later works. Simply stated, a concern with death is a concern with time.[25] Death, as Thomas Hudson comes to realize in *Islands in the Stream,* cannot be evaded. In the guise of the suicidal impulse, it also represents the possible dissolution of the ego that threatens to occur when the nostalgic narcissist gives up the pretense of maintaining an ideal state of the self and of his world. Depression and suicide are two of the intrapsychic dangers that the narcissist, and certainly the manic-depressive, must fight off on a daily basis. If he "does not have sufficient ego strength to tolerate" these feelings when they occur, as Kernberg has warned, "his life is in serious danger" (256).

The idea of no longer having to expend such great quantities of psychic energy on maintaining one's nostalgic fantasies also holds great relief for the narcissist. Death, or suicide, represents, in effect, the nostalgic's underlying wish to put an end to his impostured identity of perfection. Hemingway, like his protagonists, was therefore trapped in a love/hate relationship with both suicide and death.

After 1940, with the publication of *For Whom the Bell Tolls,* Hemingway was increasingly denied his two primary sources of narcissistic gratification: the ability to live up to his grandiose, heroic self-object, and unconditional literary and public popularity. His increasing impotence also put an end to the ego-sustaining love affairs that had been a major part of Hemingway's early-life experiences. The ego strength required to sustain him thus came in the form of his devotion to what he called his "duty" as a writer. Viewed as the one last thing that he could not lose, duty was integrally related to Hemingway's penchant for nostalgic remembering and his obsession with death and time. Consequently, it also played an important role in Hemingway's artistic process, and as a thematic subject within his art, occupying a particularly conspicuous role in his uncompleted novel, *Islands in the Stream.* Duty, or writing, is what allowed Hemingway to transform the past into a tangible present. It enabled him, through creative fantasy, to control time and to deny loss. Motivated by his accelerating illness and his growing preoccupation with death Hemingway began to rely more heavily than ever before on his "duty" as a writer in order to satisfy his need to discover some consoling pattern of behavior outside of his personal experience that also was greater than his own personal concerns. Duty, in effect, was the last empowered totemic resource available to Hemingway—as with Robert Jordan, Thomas Hudson, David Bourne, and Richard Cantwell—that magically enforced his private taboo against grief—even when the chief subject of his fiction was grief itself.

The Garden of Eden: *Father-Hunger and Mother-Loss Revisited (Hemingway's Nostalgia Solution)*

Although Hemingway began writing *The Garden of Eden* in 1946, and came back to it in the early 1950s, he did not venture upon a comprehensive revision of the work until 1958, at about the same time he was revising *A Moveable Feast.* *The Garden of Eden* represents something of a transition between the earlier works, *For Whom the Bell Tolls* and *Death in the Afternoon,* and the later *A Moveable Feast,* in that it deals both with loss in relation to the father—which figures largely in both *Death in the Afternoon* and *For Whom the Bell Tolls*—and with loss in love, which was to become the main focus of *A Moveable Feast.* Hemingway embarked upon all four works, however, with the nostalgic presupposition of loss and disillusionment. A reading of the original manuscript—some 1600 pages—of *The Garden of Eden* leads one to conclude, as Robert Flemming did in *"The Endings of Hemingway's*

Garden of Eden," that, in editing the manuscript for Scribner's, Tom Jenks, despite an overall admirable job, miscalculated the novel's ending by portraying it as optimistic, rather than tragic, which is clearly how Hemingway conceived the lamentable fate of the two couples, Catherine and David Bourne and Barbara and Nick Sheldon.[26]

In the unpublished version, Catherine is institutionalized for a nervous breakdown, making a questionable recovery at the end, while Barbara suffers a similar fate but goes a step farther by drowning herself in a dirty Venice canal. The Jenks ending, in which David and Marita live together in sexual and professional compatibility, belies Hemingway's overall summation of the book as being about "the happiness of the Garden that a man must lose."[27]

As in so much of Hemingway's later fiction, he acted out, in *The Garden of Eden*'s plot, the deterioration from happiness—both in sexual and parental love—to disillusionment. He thus dramatized his characters' realization of the inevitability of loss and grief, rather than, as in his early stories, their defensive denial of these tragic aspects of life. The later novels, *Across the River and Into the Trees* and *Islands in the Stream*, differ slightly from this formula in that they both begin with a male protagonist who has already experienced loss and disillusionment, and who is merely acting out an heroic struggle with the final stages of his deterioration.

The patterns of disillusionment and loss in *The Garden of Eden* resemble the emotional pain and ambivalence of a boy's separation-individuation process which, as we have seen, Hemingway presented many times before in his fiction. The end of Catherine and David's blissful and harmonious "honeymoon" on the French Riviera begins when the narcissistic Catherine cuts her hair into a boyish bob and begins to question her own, and David's, gender identity by requesting that he play the role of the woman during their lovemaking so that she might assume the figurative, and literal, phallic role of "Peter."[28] With this, everything "changes" for David. Symbolically, this breakup, paralleled in the manuscript by the similarly motivated dissolution of Barbara and Nick's marriage, signals the universal loss of the Edenic happiness of infancy that all human beings must give up. Yet, like Frederic Henry's (and Melville's) powerful ambivalence about whether they really desire dependency or autonomy, David is torn between his wish to indulge in Catherine's narcissistic fantasy of symbiotic fusion, and his impulse to heed his foreboding thoughts of the danger to his masculinity and his career as a writer that such ego-loss represents.

A reading of the complete manuscript conveys more clearly the sense that Catherine and Barbara are actually satisfying David's and Nick's secret desire to engage in escapist narcissistic behavior, but which they also know will lure them away from the purposeful pursuit of their art. As Nick, at one point, says about Barbara: "But she's destructive Dave, and I'm destroy material." Yet, not long afterwards, when Nick is asked "What about work?" he replies: "The hell with work." For a while David tries to keep things the way they were, saying to Catherine repeatedly, "You're a girl. You are a girl" (55), and pleading with her to let him wear his hair even an inch or two shorter than hers; but he realizes that he is fighting a losing battle (not only with Catherine but with himself), and surrenders to the inevitability of loss and disappointment. Now, when the pair have sex, the "hollowness" and "badness" (14) always return, and David's separation anxiety is, in effect, re-experienced each time.

Once David's early blissful relationship with Catherine is lost, his nostalgic impulse begins to play a critical role in his psychic life. He becomes aware of the "newly built up areas" in the town, which are "dull" compared to the old parts, and prefers to hang around the Prado where the buildings and walls were "very old" (44, 51). Most of all, writing his nostalgic stories about the past once again becomes of great importance, which also testifies to the positive, and compensating, consequences of autonomy and the loss of Eden. When he "started to write," David "forgot about Catherine . . . and the writing went by itself" (42). Writing serves a nostalgic purpose for David since it halts time and does away with the need to mourn over a lost past. Hence, he must "write the story which he believed he must write now or lose" (93). Writing, like the moment of sexual union, repairs both the loss and grief of separation, and the passage of time. Later in the novel, when David is able to achieve the same kind of ego-merging through sex with Marita that he once had with Catherine, his free association of thoughts makes clear the parallel nature of sex and writing as a means by which he can restore an inner sense of Edenic peace and unity:

They held each other and he could feel himself start to be whole again. He had not known just how greatly he had been divided and separated because once he started to work he wrote from an inner core which could not be split nor even marked nor scratched. He knew about this and it was his strength since all the rest of him could be riven. (183)

Writing about the past makes it "come alive" again for David (108), and past and present merge into a single "now" of fictional time. The imaginary time of David's fictional nostalgic narrative merges with the present in a way that parallels his previous narcissistic, sexual merging with Catherine, so that both he and the reader often become lost altogether in time: "At half past ten he had crossed the lakes and was well beyond them. By then he had reached the river and the great grove of fig trees where they would make their camp. . . . But the half past ten was on the watch on his wrist as he looked at it in the room where he sat at a table feeling the breeze from the sea now and the real time was evening" (139). As David's life with Catherine and Marita becomes increasingly complicated, his nostalgia seems to border on the pathological, and he "talked and listened in the unreality that reality had become . . . he was back from what he cared about into the overpopulated vacancy of madness" (193). Despite her jealousy of David's writing, Catherine is, in a sense, correct when she says to him that "the stories are just your way of escaping" (190). Drinking, of course, is an alternative way for David to expunge, or at least to compensate himself for, his grief and sadness over the loss of "Eden." He "took his remorse to the cafe" and by the time "he was finishing his second absinthe" he notices that "the remorse was gone" (68–69). Whether the choice is alcohol, nostalgic writing, or sex, once the original experience of Edenic wholeness is lost, all forms of imaginative return to Eden—and all artificial attempts to repair the grief and anxiety of separation—will prove temporary, and leave one with the same recurring feeling of "hollowness" and "emptiness."

Like the title of the book David is reading, what he, in part, seeks to attain through sex, alcohol, and writing, is a time *Far Away and Long Ago* (94). In the complete manuscript, the narrative, mostly dialogue, of both the Barnes's and the Sheldon's lovemaking, drinking, eating, and cutting and coloring of hair, goes on for page after tedious page, as though Hemingway could not get enough of this playful, hedonistic, narcissistic fantasy. In contrast, the narrative of the autobiographical story David is writing, about an elephant hunt he went on with his father during a trip to Africa, is concise, forward moving, and purposefully developed. It is equal to any of Hemingway's best early stories. Appropriately, therefore, Jenks cut only a few lines from the original sections on the elephant hunt.

The theme of David's father-son tale is the now familiar one of a boy's disillusionment with the heroic paternal ideal. Although Hemingway, like David in the story, may have viewed this story as the one that he had never before been able to write, it is, in most respects, a replay of the male individuation theme that Hemingway had told many years earlier in the Orpen story, *A Farewell to Arms*, *The Sun Also Rises*, and the stories in the collection *In Our Time*. Although David accepts the fact that his father no longer embodied his inviolable heroic masculine ideal, confessing to himself that the "elephant was his hero now as his father had been for a long time" (201), he fails to accept that his father, like life itself, can *never* be without flaws. Had this episode taught David the lesson that no one, and nothing in life, is perfect (a lesson that Robert Jordan reluctantly, though unmistakably, learns in the course of *For Whom the Bell Tolls*), he might have ultimately forgiven his father, as Robert Jordan does, and perhaps even established a greater emotional bond with him. Instead, he condemned himself to a perpetually unsatisfied father-hunger: When his father asks him, "Do you want to make peace Davey?" he replies, "All right," but only, as he thinks to himself, "because he knew this was the start of the never telling that he had decided on" (202). David will reject life's contingencies and continue to search for the heroic ideal. However, as Hemingway himself did, he will simply look elsewhere, rather than to his father, to find it. Yet, having lost his heroic ideal once without properly grieving over his loss, David's search, like Hemingway's, will always be fraught with nostalgic and tragic overtones.

What is perhaps most interesting about this repeated Hemingway theme is its placement within the larger thematic context of *The Garden of Eden*. The seemingly arbitrary placement of the embedded story within the text as a whole, which is something that has troubled critical readers of the novel, makes psychological sense when the novel is understood as highlighting the recurring anxiety of separation and loss; or in other words, as David Bourne's traumatic experience of grief and deprivation, first, through mother-loss, and second, through father-hunger. Hemingway made apparent the fact that the feeling David has when he comes to realize his father's shortcomings as a man and as a paternal ideal is the same as his feeling after sexual intercourse, after the alcohol wears off, and after he stops writing. It is a feeling of hollowness, hunger, and emptiness deep within himself. "David thought then in the night that the hollow way he felt as he remembered [the elephant] was from waking hungry. But it was not and he found that out in the next three days" (166). Psychoanalytically, of course, it is not a similar feeling but a replay of the same feeling of original grief and narcissistic loss from separation from the fully gratifying mother/woman—the Catherine of the novel's first few chapters—that returns to David after sex, drinking, and writing, as after young Davey's disappointment with the heroic paternal ideal.[29]

Within the embedded story, however, the consciously acknowledged result of David's father's shooting of the elephant is confined to the loss of the father ideal. If it is remembered that the paternal ego ideal, which the oedipal boy looks up to and aspires to imitate, to some extent intrapsychically replaces the narcissistic perfection and omnipotent gratification he previously received from the good, nurturing mother, then David's loss of his loving bond with Catherine (and with the elephant), and the disappointment with the paternal ego ideal, become one and the same psychic experience of deprivation and loss. For, as Hemingway made clear, it was not just the loss of the heroic father that David suffered in those three days in Africa, but something much more profound. It was "the beginning of the knowledge of loneliness" (201), which, in effect, is the moment at which an infant first begins to realize that he or she is a separate and autonomous being who is no longer "whole" or at one with the fantasized nurturing, all-providing mother. In terms of feminist, or revisionist, Freudian psychoanalysis, it is the moment of primary castration for David. It signals, in other words, the end of innocence, and in many ways, the end of unconditional love— the end of Eden. But at the same time, it is also, as Melville discovered, a moment of affirmation, as it signals the beginning of David's autonomy and his personal mastery as an artist.

The loss of love and basic trust brings about the beginning of something that is to stay with David for the rest of his life, and is eventually to play a critical role in his career as a creative writer. For it was "the start of the never telling" for young Davey (202): the moment at which he vowed never to speak his mind and open his heart to another again, choosing instead to erect a lifelong taboo against the open expression of both love and grief. David's father senses his son's resentment, as well as the broken bond of ideal love between them. "He knows all about it now and he will never trust me again" (182), David thinks to himself. "That's good. I don't want him to because I'll never ever tell him or anybody anything again never anything again" (182). Repression and control of his feelings will henceforth guide David in all his future interpersonal relationships, making him invulnerable to grief and emotional hurt from others, and allowing him, later in life, to view his writing as emanating from "an inner core which could not be split nor even marked nor scratched" (183). As a professional writer, David's "form," like Hemingway's art of repression, "came by what he would choose to leave out" (211). Hemingway's narrative, in *The Garden of Eden,* provides an explanation of how both David Bourne's personal psychology, and the taboo against grief that defines his writing style, resulted from the same trauma of childhood loss and deprivation. Father-hunger and mother-loss merge into a single affective experience of separation, grief, and loss that, through an affirmative gesture of personal consolation, is sublimated by the artist into his creative style and artistic process.

As Peter Griffin, Kenneth Lynn, and others have emphasized, for much of Hemingway's life his father was the one person he cared more about than anyone else. But, to use David Bourne's words, after "his change of feeling toward . . . his father," that is to say, after the "dreadful true understanding" (182) of the gap between his ego and his paternal ego ideal, he "cared about the writing more than about anything else" (211). Through his art, David, like Mark Twain, would recapture—and this time, never again lose—the happy moments of his past; and as he wrote the past would come to life again like "the champagne that was born new each time he poured a glass" (234). After Catherine destroys David's stories and he begins once again to reconstruct the past, he discovers that, through his fictional nostalgic fantasies, the power of the resurrection of Eden was forever within him: "He wrote on a while longer now and there was no sign that any of it would ever cease returning to him intact" (247). David could perpetually recall through his fiction, as *The Garden of Eden* recalled for Hemingway, the bliss of symbiotic love and the narcissistic gratification, or self-esteem, that comes with the unsullied belief in an heroic father ideal, even if his purpose in nostalgically recapturing these moments of real happiness is to re-enact the tragic loss of them again. Such is the cycle of eternal return in a universe of tabooed grief. However, in re-enacting the past through their fiction, both David and Hemingway were able to universalize, and thereby, transcend, their personal neurotic desires, ambivalences, and anxieties.

The knowledge that *The Garden of Eden* ends with the destruction of

Catherine and Barbara is critical to an understanding of the novel as it was originally conceived by Hemingway. Although these women mirror the narcissistic and hedonistic longings of David and Nick, there is a significant difference between the male and female characters. Both Barbara and Catherine are unable to step outside of their neuroses and make objective sense of their lives and anxieties, whereas David's and Nick's art not only allows them to do this, but to do it in a way that gives the narratives of their lives a larger purpose, and therefore a meaning that transcends their personal predicaments. This explains why David resists Catherine's pleas that he write the narrative of their life together. It is because Catherine believes that *life is art* that she establishes an obsessive narcissistic relationship with herself and with David that inevitably leads to a destructive self-absorption and grandiosity. Conversely, it is because David believes that *art is life* that he is able to resist his own narcissistic patterns of behavior—his obsessive nostalgic interest in his personal past—and thus, in the end, save himself. In this regard, Marita is indeed a far better companion for David. Marita includes David's art, and his objective, distanced perspective on life, within the circle of the two of them as a couple. She allows David to indulge in narcissistic behavior, particularly with regard to lovemaking, but without transforming that outlet for regressive fulfillment into a one-ended trap of unhealthy interdependency.

Across the River and Into the Trees: *A Parody of the Nostalgia Solution*

Hemingway's 1950 novel *Across the River and Into the Trees* represents a continuation of his disillusionment with the heroic, masculine ideal that began with the stories of *In Our Time,* but it goes a step farther by exploring the ways in which he and his male heroes compensate for loss, physical deterioration, and impending death. The novel reveals Hemingway's progressive attempts to understand the neurotic nostalgia and obsession with loss with which Richard Cantwell, like the later Thomas Hudson, finds himself struggling. If *Across the River and Into the Trees* has been judged a weak and even embarrassing work of fiction, perhaps it is because the novel's moral, like the moral of *For Whom the Bell Tolls*—that one may be triumphant in defeat (a theme of some of Hemingway's best, as well as his worst, fiction)—is loaded with arrogance and conceit.[30] The Colonel's hands, which have been "shot through twice," and which place him, symbolically, in the role of a sacrificial Christ-figure, do not attest to tragic seriousness but to Hemingway's self-centered approach to the loss of his own grandiose self-image.

Although actual physical death awaits the Colonel, Richard Cantwell, at the end of the novel, the attitude he expresses toward life and death throughout his last few days again reveals—as it did in "Snows"—that, for Hemingway, physical death was symbolic of a psychic form of death. Cantwell is a man who, much like Hemingway himself, has based his life and actions on pretending to be someone who is emotionally impenetrable, and invulnerable to death. *Across the River and Into the Trees* dramatizes the challenges to the stability of his ego and self-esteem that confront the Colonel when he finally gives up the illusion of his imposture. For Richard Cantwell, every day of his life has been "a new and fine illusion."[31] Whether true or not, he felt that his life was "destroyed . . . under other people's orders" (242). Although Hemingway expressed his disillusionment with "manly" heroics and war less artistically in the Orpen story than in stories such as "Now I Lay Me," and "Soldier's Home," and in the novels *A Farewell to Arms* and *For Whom the Bell Tolls,* nowhere does he state more directly than in the unpublished Orpen fragment his reasons for this disillusionment. It may be recalled that Orpen says to himself, after realizing what a farce war is: "Why did he go on playing? Really he hated it all. . . . Somehow he wished he hadn't died a hero's death. Now he could never be anything else but a hero—and they chopped at each other all day long here."[32] By dying in fantasy, Orpen is permitted, retrospectively, to condemn the lies, horror, and pretense of war; only by dying can he give up that pretense and return to the comforting arms of his mother and his artistic compositions. In *Across the River and Into the Trees,* Hemingway made the war hero's death a forgone conclusion from the start. He therefore was able to imbue the Colonel with the same objective, cynical perspective on war and love that the "dead" Orpen possessed. The novel is a monument to the loss of the self that accompanies being branded a hero, and represents Hemingway's mourning for what can happen to the war hero who was condemned never to "be anything else but a hero," even if it was himself who, as Orpen confesses, could not wait to be "old enough to get in it and be a hero."

Within Cantwell's nostalgic drama, Renata plays the role of the perfect mirroring mother/woman who, unlike Hemingway's own mother, has no extraordinary expectations of her "son" and, as a result, does not need to be lied to. In contrast to Krebs, in the story "Soldier's Home," Cantwell does not have to lie to Renata in order to prove his manhood; he can expose his true limited and crippled self to Renata without fear of rejection. It is, in fact, because he is wounded and near death that she seems to love him so deeply. Not only do Cantwell's war stories "never bore" Renata, she even makes a point of saying to him: "Nothing about fighting bores me except lies" (236). Renata plays the role of the perfect mirroring object so well that Cantwell does not even have to speak in order to communicate his thoughts and desires to her: "The Colonel told her all about it; but he did not utter it" (248). Yet, unlike Catherine Bourne, in *The Garden of Eden*, and Catherine Barkeley, in *A Farewell to Arms*, Renata defers her own desire—to engulf Cantwell within the confines of their mutual love—to his professional integrity and autonomy, even if all that is left of his professional identity is the egotistic nostalgic fantasy of a lost heroic past. By telling her the truth about his flaws and mistakes, Cantwell finds, as he says, that "I bore myself, Daughter" (240). But she justifies his life of imposturing and obedience to others by assuring him that he "would not have done something all your life if you were bored by it" (240).

As in so much of Hemingway's fiction, it is not the death of the body but the disenchantment with the heroic ideal about which the Colonel is most concerned. Gabriele d'Annunzio, the Colonel's long-time hero, wasted away from age over the years to become, finally, a "poor beat-up old boy" like himself; he is now dead and buried. To the world, d'Annunzio (like Hemingway himself) was a "writer and national hero," but the "Colonel did not believe in heroes" any longer (50–51). Cantwell defecates on the spot where he was wounded and first gave up his adolescent belief in his own "immortality" (33) thirty years before. Through this ritualistic act the Colonel embraces his imperfections as a man—his heroic "excrement"—and "relieves" himself of the mythical persona he has had to maintain all his life. This monument to loss and physical deterioration was a "poor effort," he admits, but it was more valuable than any falsified heroics because the effort was truly, as he says, "my own" (18). Where once the Colonel was able to "hold that river" (21)—Hemingway's often-used symbol for aging and change—he now gives up trying to hold back the ruinous effects of time. His retelling of old war stories with the *Gran Maestro* (which recalls Hemingway's own use of nostalgic fantasies to recapture the competent and heroic self-image he possessed in the past), no longer serves as a source of narcissistic gratification. By admitting aloud that there "aren't any such times any more," the magical power of the nostalgic's neurotic use of memories is vanquished, and the Colonel confesses that "the spell was broken" (63).

In a tone reminiscent of the aging man who has regressed to the state of boastful adolescence, the Colonel says to the *Gran Maestro:* "We must have been tough then." "We were tough then," Cantwell's friend replies: "We were bad boys then, and you were the worst of the bad boys" (121). In a parody of his former intrepid self, the Colonel insists on sitting in the corner of the dining room in order to make sure that he "had both his flanks covered" (115). He also believes he has intimidated, merely through his stare, the two young men who insult him on the street, although it is likely that a real physical confrontation with them would have resulted in a severe beating. Nevertheless, he brags to Renata like a conceited adolescent: "It is a pity they weren't ten against one . . . couldn't those badly educated youths realize what sort of animal they were dealing with?" (187). It is pitiful to hear the Colonel discuss again and again where he would like to "be buried," and what "the best way to be over-run" might be (34, 228, 104). While he preaches to himself that "No horse named Morbid ever won a race" (34), his greatest challenge, like Hemingway's, is to put into practice what he knows to be true.

Despite his efforts, Cantwell cannot seem to reconcile himself to death, not because he fears the annihilation of the self, but because it entails a greater loss than the loss of life; the loss of love. Hence, the Supreme Secret that Cantwell finally reveals to Renata is that "Love is love and fun is fun. But it is always so quiet when the gold fish dies" (271). Renata understandably begs for clarification of this cryptic secret of life and death. "What happens to people that love each other?" she asks. "I suppose they have whatever they have, and they are more fortunate than others. Then one of them gets the emptiness forever" (271). For Hemingway, in this novel, death was equivalent to the loss of love, or more accurately, the loss of love was a kind of permanent loss or death. Perhaps this is why "[l]oving and leaving" (289) always came together in Hemingway's fiction; it is also why, when Cantwell thinks of the perfect mother/woman, Renata, it dawns upon him "how close life comes to death when there is ecstasy" (219).

A Moveable Feast: *The Nostalgia Solution Hits Home*

One of the themes common to *Green Hills of Africa, The Garden of Eden,* and *Across the River and Into the Trees;* namely, that one can, to borrow Colonel Cantwell's words, be "triumphant" in loss and "defeat" (55), emerged from the later Hemingway's nostalgic wish to establish conciliatory philosophical, behavioral, and artistic patterns that would allow him to cope with the irremediable reality of grief and loss. Although his plan to write *A Moveable Feast* had probably been in his mind for many years, by the time he began writing it, in 1957, four years before his death, he seemed to have arrived at the comforting notion that the nostalgic impulse—a substitute for the act of mourning one's lost perfect past—not only was useful to him in his writing, but, even more so, was an *imperative* part of the writing process. One definition of nostalgia (though by no means the only one), which is particularly appropriate in relation to *A Moveable Feast,* is a hungering for a lost ideal state of being associated with the narcissistic omnipotence of infancy. In psychoanalytic terms, it is a hungering for the comforting and all-providing breast which has been lost. Perhaps, then, it was the intuitive, primary-process thinking to which the creative artist has special access that inspired Hemingway to draw upon the metaphor of hunger as a recurring image for nostalgia in this, his most openly autobiographical, work.

Hemingway employs hunger in a number of different ways throughout *A Moveable Feast,* but in every case it denotes both loss and the longing for reparation. Hunger, however, is unquestionably a virtue in Hemingway's view. Without hunger, Hemingway is deprived of the emotional impetus to write, for as he says: "Memory is hunger" (57). Paradoxically, hunger, or the emptiness and grief that come from loss and absence, is food for his nostalgic fiction. In *A Moveable Feast,* Hemingway no longer hungers for a lost past—for sustenance to fill the emptiness within—as much as he hungers for hunger—for the nostalgic's particular brand of manifested grief and loss that fuel his later fiction. Hemingway does not self-consciously point to the unhealthy, or neurotic, use of nostalgia in this work, as he does in "Snows," *Across the River and Into the Trees,* and *Islands in the Stream.* Perhaps this is because in *A Moveable Feast,* as a clearly stated memoir, Hemingway recognizes the past as past—or, in effect, grieves the fact that the past is past—and makes no attempt to use the past to compensate for a disappointing present. Especially near the end of the work, Hemingway mourns outright the losses he has suffered, and openly admits his emotional vulnerability to the inevitability of loss and grief.

In the opening pages of the book, Hemingway observes about himself as a writer that "away from Paris I could write about Paris as in Paris I could write about Michigan" (7).[33] More self-conscious than ever before, in *A Moveable Feast*, Hemingway recognizes the fact of loss itself as his greatest professional tool. He does not call this nostalgic impulse "remembering" (a word that carries the depressing connotation of loss, as he did in *Green Hills* and *Death in the Afternoon*), but refers to it in an objective tone as the technique of "transplanting yourself" (5). As with David Bourne, Hemingway uses the objectivity that art provides, and his insights into the creative process, to compensate for an experience of deprivation in his personal life.

As he did in *Death in the Afternoon*, Hemingway speaks again of what, in the earlier work, he had called his "ice-berg" principle. This time, in reference to his story, "Out of Season," he again explains his "theory that you could omit anything if you knew that you omitted and the omitted part would strengthen the story and make people feel something more than they understood" (75). Within the context of *A Moveable Feast*, the "ice-berg" principle may be seen as Hemingway's wish to leave the reader hungry for the same emotional feeling of loss, and the desire for something left out or missing, that he experienced before he wrote the story. Desire and grief hence become incontestable assets that bridge the gap between the pain of personal experience and the satisfaction of professional accomplishment. As in *The Garden of Eden,* the "hollowness" and "emptiness" that are the consequences of separation and the loss of love, predictably, occur after lovemaking and writing in *A Moveable Feast*, but, as Hemingway remembers them in this autobiographical work, they make him "happy" as well, because they confirm his continued professional success as a writer. "After writing a story," he says, "I was always empty and both sad and happy, as though I had made love" (6).

In *A Moveable Feast*, the lost object for which Hemingway nostalgically longs, and which, when remembered, makes him "both sad and happy"—that which he hungers for most—is his first wife, Hadley. "I loved her and I loved no one else and we had a lovely magic time while we were alone" (210–11). While Hadley may indeed, in retrospect, have been Hemingway's one true love, and therefore her loss one of the greatest tragedies to occur in his life, it is also likely that he needed to create in his remembered image of Hadley a fantasy love-object in order to intensify and to purify the quality of his nostalgic hunger and longing for her.

Hemingway's loss of Hadley, which does not take place until the last few pages of the book, informs every word from beginning to end. From the first paragraph, Hemingway's tone reveals a consciousness of the loss that is to occur at the end. When he speaks early in the book of "being in love and being married," he also parenthetically adds, "time would fix that" (15). When Hadley says to Hemingway, in an early chapter, "we'll never love anyone else but each other," and he replies, "No. Never" (38), the reader cannot help but sense that Hemingway is intentionally deceiving both himself and the reader. The foreboding of the statement, "We're always lucky" (35), uttered by Hemingway to his wife, clearly signals his awareness of impending grief and doom.

Hemingway also seems to imply that he was entirely a passive, "innocent" victim of his second wife, Pauline's, seductions, which caused the breakup between Hadley and himself. It was "wicked" Pauline's money, or "the rich" in general, that is responsible for his heart's demise. In this work, as throughout Hemingway's life, it is more likely that Hemingway's losses—of wives, people, places, and his own health—were a consequence of his acting out of an inner sense of loss, deprivation, and a depressed outlook on life that was always already there. In this sense, Hemingway, like Melville and Twain, was indeed a passive victim of an unconscious dynamic whereby a repressed feeling of grief from traumatic separation and the loss of love sought a way to surface in his life. But Hemingway is the only one of the three authors (about whom we know for sure) who had to combat serious depression in addition to early deprivation and the loss of loved ones. All of these factors, when combined, resulted in the ambivalence, grief, and cynicism with which Hemingway, like Melville and Twain, had to come to terms in later life. It is possible, in fact, that all three authors unconsciously directed their lives so as to provide an opportunity for them to re-live, and perhaps work through, an early unresolved traumatic experience of loss and separation anxiety.

Philip Young's theory, that Hemingway continually wrote about his wounding to re-live the unresolved trauma of his wounding during the war, is insightful here. However, it is not the wound in Hemingway's leg that he tried to re-live and perhaps work through, but the narcissistic wounds in love he received as a young man, first from Agnes's rejection, later from his parents' rejection, and lastly from the loss of Hadley, for which he, himself, was primarily responsible. Specifically addressing the magical, ideal love that he "remembers" having had with Hadley, Hemingway writes: "So you live day by day and enjoy what you have and do not worry. You lie and hate it and it destroys you and every day is more dangerous, but you live day to day as in a war" (210). The wound in war is a metaphor, in Hemingway's fiction, for an already existing wound in love. Initially, as the imagery in *The Garden of Eden* implies, it is a boy's separation from the comforting, symbiotic mother which brings loss, loneliness, mortality, and the end of omnipotence into the world. Hemingway may have become conscious of the losses and disillusionments that resulted from the end of his youthful feelings of immortality and omnipotence only when he was wounded in the war, but they have more primitive and originary psychic roots. Somewhere along the line, his belief in the inevitability of being wounded (emotionally and physically) in war, and the inevitability of loss in unconditional self and object love, fused within Hemingway's creative imagination.

Indeed, when he writes that he "wished I had died before I ever loved anyone but her" (210), meaning Hadley, Hemingway is wishing for something much more profound than a return to a time and place when he lived happily with his first wife. Hemingway's, like Twain's, death-wish carries within itself the primitive nostalgic fantasy-wish to return to a time of infantile omnipotence and bliss, before loss and loneliness ever entered his realm of experience. Hemingway may call this time Eden, Hadley, or Paris, but these are also metaphors for an experience of love without strife—devoid of hunger, memory, or even the need to eat. Paris may have been Hemingway's screen memory for the nostalgically desired, ever-new, and ever-perfect "moveable feast," but it is the voiceless, wordless ecstasy of a more originary "moveable feast"—the mother's breast, and, even before that, the intrauterine state—about which one may truly claim that "wherever you go for the rest of your life, it stays with you."[34]

While, for Hemingway, hunger is something to be desired, there is another aspect of writing that he desperately seeks to avoid, and that is "the death loneliness that comes at the end of every day that is wasted in your life" (165–66). Specifically, he is referring to those days in which he had failed to work on his writing, and he predicates his belief on his own, David Bourne's, and perhaps every creative artist's, compensating fantasy that art *is* life. Hemingway's life, or rather, his own past that was transfigured through nostalgic fantasy into art, was the subject about which he wrote; and his nostalgic longing—as well as the artistic product that resulted from it—was his primary source of narcissistic, ego gratification. Therefore, by not writing Hemingway deprived himself of one of his greatest sources of self-esteem. While this fact may be true for most creative artists, it was especially true for the aging Hemingway, for whom his "duty" as a writer remained a last defense against depression, grief, and the very real threat of death from suicide. Regardless of any and all losses that he may have suffered in his life, Hemingway believed he could stave off the "death loneliness" of deep depression and narcissistic injury by working on his art, itself in some ways (as his Orpen story demonstrated), a narcissistic reflection of his lost adolescent ideal self-image. As we shall see, in the novel *Islands in the Stream* Hemingway systematically forces Thomas Hudson to lose everything that Hudson holds dear, eventually stripping away all sources of ego gratification except one—his work, or what he refers to as his "duty."

Islands in the Stream: *Hitting the Wall of the Heroic Code (The Nostalgia Solution: "People did not know that you died of it")*

The posthumously published *Islands in the Stream*, like *The Garden of Eden*, was written over a period of many years, and was finally edited by Carlos Baker and Mary Hemingway for publication in 1970. Hemingway composed the "Bimini" section in 1946 and 1947; after several years' hiatus the "Cuba" portion was completed in 1950, and the "At Sea" section was finished soon after writing *The Old Man and the Sea*, in 1951. The book was a great deal more popular with the public when it was published in 1970 than was *Across the River and Into the Trees;* yet, as Jeffrey Meyers explains, the "novel was inevitably read with the knowledge that the author had killed himself," and by this time "the public was eager for Hemingway's work" (*A Biography*, 484). Critics accused Hemingway of sacrificing art for autobiography in this novel, although perhaps not as shamelessly as in *Across the River and Into the Trees*. In the character of Thomas Hudson, Hemingway created a man who (from overwhelming disappointment and personal isolation) becomes intensely fixated upon the past, but who, like David Bourne, attempts, through discipline and a devotion to his work as an artist, to establish some consoling patterns outside of his personal experience that will minimize his neurotic fear of loss. Through the events that unfold in the novel, and through Hudson's progressive deterioration as a man, it is evident that his nostalgia had become so severe that his vulnerability to loss, and his perpetual anticipation of it, nearly outweighed any grief and emotional pain he might have suffered from actual loss. In his efforts to come to terms with a disappointing reality, Hudson employs a number of strategies for emotional survival, such as drinking, not-thinking, and the adherence to a rigid work schedule, all of which, by this time, should be familiar tactics of defense against loss and grief. However, with the additional tragic losses that Hudson suffers throughout the course of the novel, he implements these strategies of survival to such an extreme degree that (as foreshadowed by the fate of Harry, in "Snows") they ultimately serve to accelerate his process of deterioration, rather than to retard it.

As with Harry, the primary adverse consequence of Hudson's attempts to anesthetize himself against emotional pain is an almost death-in-life numbing of his spontaneous emotional self, to the point of near-total withdrawal from all human loves and attachments, either past or present. As John Bowlby has said about those who are genetically prone to depression, or who have had repeated and frequent experiences of separation and loss, the more anxious and distressed they are, the more defensively hardened to grief they will become. In such cases, Bowlby maintains, the "[c]ultivation of self-sufficiency and a self protective shell, with as much disavowal as possible of all desire for love and support, are the natural sequelae"; and as Bowlby concludes, in "some persons, indeed, the shell becomes so thick that affectional relationships are attenuated to a point at which loss ceases almost to have significance. Immune to mourning they may be; but at what a price!"[35] As Hemingway was, on some level, aware, however, the self-administered inoculation against grief may eliminate the pain, but not the disease, which will silently, and at times even soothingly, eat away at body and soul, leaving only the protective shell to think to itself, tragically, that it has finally attained the blissful transcendence of pain which it has, for so long, been seeking. Yet, if Hemingway (and perhaps Thomas Hudson as well) understood all this, then, like Richard Cantwell, either he did not understand well *enough*, or, more likely, he, like Richard Cantwell, could not find within himself—whether from a failure, or an unwillingness, to look—the resources to remedy what he knew to be true.

When the novel begins, Hudson is preparing for a five-week visit from his three sons, David, Andrew, and Thomas. Only a week after their arrival, however, he is already becoming anxious about the fact that he will lose them again: "there was no good derived from any fearing of it now," he thinks, and yet he is unable to suppress that fear, and, "as he worked he felt a loneliness coming into him already."[36] The neurotic nostalgia that was only momentary in *Green Hills of Africa*, when Hemingway lay in bed and longed to "get back to Africa," even though he "had not left it, yet," has completely taken over Hudson's view of reality in *Islands in the Stream*.[37] Hudson attempts to compensate for a disappointing present by pursuing a life of nostalgic fantasy: "Now when he was lonesome for Paris he would remember Paris instead of going there. He did the same thing with all of Europe and much of Asia and of Africa" (7). Hudson's thoughts imply, as is typical of the compulsive nostalgic, that he is almost more content with a life lived in the past of his imagination and memory than he is with the present. Because those whom he has loved the most are now forever lost, he embraces the grief of loss as a present, palpable substitute for the unattainable and intangible past. As Willie says to Hudson about his friend's grief: "You might as well hoard it so as to have something" (271).

Psychoanalytically, one may almost anticipate that Hemingway will kill off Hudson's sons in the novel.[38] As Hemingway discovered in *A Moveable Feast*, nostalgia, which thrives on loss, is something that cannot itself be lost; and what is remembered can be retained in its purest and most unblemished form. The nostalgic, therefore, when faced with the inevitability of loss, and the lack of a better solution, will kill the thing he loves in order to love it more deeply and purely, and to possess it, through memory, forever. This is possibly why Hudson had to leave his first wife, and why Hemingway, in *A Moveable Feast*, could not say he loved Hadley more than life itself unless she was hopelessly lost to him. Paralleling this psychological consolation is the fact that Hudson, although he cannot figure out why, continues to burn the driftwood of which he is so especially "fond" (5).

In the opening "Bimini" section of the book, Hudson still retains the capacity "to enjoy life," but it is a life that must be carefully controlled within the "limits of the discipline that he imposed" (9).[39] By enforcing a strict regimen in his daily life—painting in the mornings and drinking in the afternoons—he is able to exorcise his grief and ward off loneliness. His obsession with "training," "rules," "customs," and "discipline" is so rigidly enforced, however, that his taboo against thinking too much about a lost, and never to be recaptured, past borders on the pathological. His paranoia about what would happen should he let down his defenses severely encroaches upon his ability to appreciate the tangible presence of his sons: "He had been happy before they came and for a long time he had learned how to live and do his work without ever being more lonely than he could bear; but the boys' coming had broken up all the protective routine of life he had built and now he was used to its being broken" (95).

Hemingway forces Thomas Hudson to confront his conflicted relationship with the past by making his sons a mouthpiece for his own, as well as for Hemingway's own, nostalgic fantasies. For several pages, Hemingway devotes the narrative to a series of thinly disguised autobiographical stories about his own personal past, allegedly motivated by the boys' curiosity about their father's past: "Tell us some more about in Paris," David asks. "Do you remember Mr. Crosby?" someone else asks him. "Who else do you remember?" "Papa, tell us some more about when you and Tommy and Tommy's mother were poor." And so on.

At a later point in the novel, Hudson thinks to himself, that there "is no way for you to get what you need and you will never have what you want again" (282). With regard to his desire "to be always healthy and to live forever and not decay in mind nor body," he confesses that "you could not have them any more than you could have the children; nor that who you loved could be alive if who you loved was dead or gone out from your life" (97). Hudson is trapped between not being able to have what he wants—"that he had [his children] always and that he was married to Tom's mother" (96)—and not being able to get what he needs—an escape from the disappointing present.

When the telegram arrives announcing "YOUR SONS DAVID AND ANDREW KILLED WITH THEIR MOTHER IN MOTOR ACCIDENT" (195), the reader must assume that Hudson is overwhelmed with grief, for Hemingway's depiction of the father's devastation is unconvincing, if not startling, in its callousness. In a narrative tone reminiscent of "After the Storm" and "A Natural History of the Dead," Hudson understates his own feeling, referring to it as "sorrow," which he knows "can be blunted or anesthetized" through his usual "remedies" of drinking and work (197). Although he vows to keep to his work "as the one thing he must not lose," there is no evidence in the remainder of the book that Hudson ever again picks up a brush to paint. With disturbing ease, and with cunning irony on the part of Hemingway, Hudson resolves about his lost wife and sons to "[g]ive them up. . . . Just remember how they were and *write* them off" (my italics, 198). With a kind of perverse satisfaction and relief, Hudson's sons can now become pure and ideal love objects whom he can possess forever in his nostalgic memory, without further fear of loss. Calling to mind the Major from "In Another Country" (but this time with unmistakable pathological implications), Hudson complains that he "should not have loved them so damn much in the first place" (199). The joy that Hudson seems to feel when he is with his sons indicates that he did indeed love them; but while they were alive, the anticipation of losing them was almost too much for him to bear.

Furthermore, by killing off Hudson's two youngest sons and his second wife, Hemingway strategically moves Hudson's reality back in time to the happier days when he had only his first wife, whom he says he truly loved, and his first son, Thomas. Richard Hovey believes that Hudson longs to "abolish the inward self" (186); and indeed, it is the conscious ego, burdened by time and place, which Hudson wishes to rid himself of. Throughout the next section of the book, Hudson becomes increasingly out of touch with his emotional self, and, consequently, with his grief, by numbing himself with pills, alcohol, and a more rigidly enforced censoring of his spontaneous thoughts. Instead, he seeks in various ways to move back into his own past, or to efface altogether his own ego, or conscious, thinking mind.

When the middle "Cuba" section opens, Hudson is living a solitary life; his only personal interaction is with his cats, particularly his favorite cat, "Boise." As part of the process of closing down, and hardening, his emotional self, he apparently displaces his love for human beings onto this one animal, onto whom he also neurotically projects all sorts of thoughts and emotions. However, he retains his vulnerability to separation and loss, even in relation to Boise, whom he fears could be killed at any time like the dead cat he sees on the road to Havana. Incredibly, Hudson's nostalgia in this section of the novel has become even stronger than it was and, as he does with his sons during their visit, he prefers most of the time to reminisce about when Boise was "a kitten playing with his reflection on the glass top of the cigar counter of the bar at Cojímar" (208). Throughout the "Cuba" section, Hudson is narcissistically preoccupied with looking at the reflection of his own past in the glass of his memory. He thinks about the princess with the "thickish ankles" (222) with whom he once had an affair, about his trip to Damascus, and his days in Marseilles. When he is not living in the past he is trying desperately to avoid thinking about the present, which means he tries not to think at all. With full neurotic force he negates the present and even negates his attempt to negate it:

It certainly had been fun not to think about the sea for the last few hours. Let's keep it up, he thought. Let's not think about the sea nor what is on it or under it, or anything connected with it. Let's not even make a list of what we will not think of about it. Let's not think of it at all. Let's just have the sea in being and leave it at that. And the other things, he thought. We won't think about them either. (235)

Only his nostalgic fantasies and his defenses against ego awareness are admissible to consciousness for Hudson in the "Cuba" section, which points to a form of self-inflicted suicide of the ego. "If you don't think about it, it doesn't exist," he reasons to himself. Employing the negative of Descartes theory — "I think ergo I am" — Hudson assumes that if he does not think, then *he* is not. He looks at Juan Gris's painting, "Guitar Player," and thinks "*Nostalgia hecha hombre*. . . . People did not know that you died of it" (237). Thomas Hudson knows full well that he is, in effect, slowly dying from his own nostalgia.

When he walks into the Floridita bar in Havana, Hudson refuses to talk about what we soon learn is the latest tragedy of his life — the death of his son, Tom, in a plane crash. Willie, the bartender, accurately pegs Hudson as a "grief hoarder" (271); indeed, by holding on to his grief over his three sons' deaths, Hudson loves them in the only way he has left. The local whore, Honest Lil, coerces Hudson into talking by encouraging him to reminisce about his past, which he does for the next several pages of the book. Now, with the last of his three sons removed from the land of the living, Hudson moves a step farther back into his past. He continues to progress farther and farther into the past through the stories he tells to Honest Lil, until she asks him, finally, to tell her about Wambimi. Here, Hudson relates one of the most impressive death and re-birth scenes in American literature.

"The river was covered with logs a long way above the town. One time I had been fishing and I wanted to cross the river and I crawled across on the logs. One rolled with me and I went into the water. When I came up it was all logs above me and I could not get through between them. It was dark under them and all I could feel with my hands was their bark. I could not spread two of them apart to get up to the air."

"What did you do?"

"I drowned."

"Oh," she said. "Don't say it. Tell me quick what you did?"

"I thought very hard and I knew I had to get through very quickly. I felt very carefully around the bottom of a log until I came to where it was pushed against another log. Then I put my two hands together and pushed up and the logs spread apart just a little. Then I got my hands through and then my forearms and elbows through and then I spread the two logs apart with my elbows until I got my head up and I had an arm over each log. I loved each log very much and I lay there like that a long time between them. That water was brown from the logs in it. The water that's like your drink was in a little stream that flowed into that river."

"I don't think I could ever have come up between the logs."

"I didn't think I could for a long time."

"How long were you underwater?"

"I don't know. I know I rested a long time with my arms on the logs before I tried to do anything else." (278)

Hemingway, undoubtedly on some level aware of the regressive nature of the thoughts he imparts to Thomas Hudson, follows the course of Hudson's intense desire for complete ego-loss, leading him downward into his past to a time of infancy—a time before loss, grief, and separation were part of a human being's experience. When Lil then asks Tom to tell her "something happy," he spontaneously launches into a story about when "young Tom was a little baby" (279); and although he consciously refers to his son Tom, it is undoubtedly no coincidence that this memory of the happy childhood of his namesake follows directly from his own fantasy re-birth into infancy. In the true spirit of the nostalgic's neurotic use of memories, Hudson remembers his son's infancy as nothing short of ideal. "He laughed all the time," Hudson tells Lil; and through what can only be labeled as a wishful nostalgic fantasy, he confesses to her: "I never heard him cry when he was a baby" (280).

Although Hudson, and certainly Hemingway as well (with his extraordinary battalion of defenses against grief), knows that at whatever the cost "you always get over your remorse" (296), he longs to place himself in such a complete state of egolessness through regression into the past, or through an avoidance of his present grief, that there will no longer be anything more to "get over" (296). At the end of the "Cuba" section, Hudson's first wife appears. He tells her, dispassionately, of Tom's death, and expels her from his life forever, in effect, "finishing off" the last person in his life whom, in the past, he had lived in fear of losing.

If, as the saying goes, "no man is an island," Hudson, in the last section of *Islands in the Stream*, "At Sea," attempts with all the psychic strength he has left to defy this aphorism. He will become emotionally isolated, tied to his crew only by the bonds of companionship in duty—the only form of love in which Hudson will now allow himself to indulge. Both literally and figuratively, Hemingway has set Hudson adrift in space and time, with nothing but the wind that "was blowing heavily and had blown now, day and night, for more than fifty days. It had become a part of the man. . . . It fortified him and gave him strength and he hoped it would never stop" (335). His pistol is "his girl" now, and even the cat, Boise, is nowhere to be found. Hudson is doing "a good job at nonthinking"; he has even given up living in the past universe of his nostalgic fantasies (384). In his waking hours he thinks about nothing but his "duty," so that "he would not think of anything but work" (445). In his sleep there is no need for nostalgia, for in his dreams he can return to a time when "his son Tom was not dead and that the other boys were all right and that the war was over" (343). He dreams of making love with his first wife and, in his dream, man and woman merge into one being, losing their individual identities. In this moment of perfect, blissful egolessness, like an infant at its mother's breast, Hudson can "lose everything and take everything too." As if seeking the final moment of non-being and ecstatic love with the fantasy symbiotic mother, he asks her to "hold me so tight it kills me" (345). Eventually, however, Hudson does wake up, and the "hollowness" overtakes him; he knows that, for him, only "[d]eath is what is really final" (449).

When Hudson is shot, and he finally comes to "realize that he was probably going to die" from "his three wounds" (perhaps symbolic of his three traumatic losses in love), a sudden, wonderful peace comes over him. At last he will find nostalgic relief from his present emotional pain—or rather from continuously having to defend, and armour himself, against pain—that he has been seeking for so long. As he begins to lose consciousness, his ego drifts away, so that even "his voice sounded strange to him" (463):

He felt far away now and there were no problems at all. He felt the ship gathering her speed and the lovely throb of her engines against his shoulder blades which rested hard against the boards. He looked up and there was the sky that he had always loved and he looked across the great lagoon that he was quite sure, now, he would never paint and he eased his position a little to lessen the pain. The engines were around three thousand now, he thought, and they came through the deck and into him. (466)

Hemingway symbolically envisioned the ultimate fulfillment of Hudson's nostalgia as a return to a prenatal state. Snuggled up in the womb against the throbbing chest of the mother, he listens to the purring of "her engines against his shoulders." Finally, he comprehends what he has desired all along—the return to the womb that lay at the heart of his perpetually unsatisfied nostalgic longing. "I think I understand, Willie," Hudson says to his friend; but with a powerful irony, enacted by Hemingway, Willie replies: "Oh Shit. . . . You never understand anybody that loves you" (466). What Hudson does not, and perhaps at this point in his life cannot, understand, is a love that does not need to be hidden, repressed, or killed for fear of the overwhelming grief that might result from the loss of that love. This is the spontaneous expression of love that flows freely from Willie, when he says to his mortally wounded friend, again with superb irony on Hemingway's part: "I love you, you son of a bitch, and *don't die*" (my italics, 466).

For the most part, critics have not had many positive things to say about *Islands in the Stream,* except to claim (and I concur in this) that a number of the descriptive scenes in the novel, for instance, David's contest with the broadbill, and many of the expository interludes on nature in the section "At Sea," contain some of Hemingway's most eloquent and inspiring prose. Gregory Sojka stands out among those who have praised the novel. While Sojka admits that Thomas Hudson attempts "to order his life against the imminent confusion of his fears," he makes the fatal mistake of valorizing Hudson's use of order, discipline, and a strict regimen in his work in order to "keep his life from falling into the debilitating disorder" of chaos and uncontrolled suffering.[40] Sojka concedes that the Hudson of the "Cuba" section is not "the stoic, hard-working artist" of the earlier section, but "an idle, self-pitying, pill-popping rummy" (273). Yet he goes on to argue that Hudson's military mission, in the final "At Sea" section, enables him to be "reborn in his command with responsibility to duty and to a crew that replaces his lost family" (275). When I say that Sojka makes a "fatal mistake" in viewing as an affirmative gesture Hudson's strict adherence to the code-like "virtues" of discipline, order, stoicism, and not-thinking, I mean just that. Hudson's thoroughgoing taboo against grief—his progressive tendency to replace life and feelings with "art" or "duty"—is indeed what kills him in the end. Furthermore, in view of the fact that Hemingway painfully knew, as few writers ever have, the dangers to one's physical and spiritual being that come with the repression of emotional pain and loss, there is little question that Hemingway also knew that Hudson's taboo against grief—for which his work, or "duty," was merely another artificial totem—was the true cause of Hudson's final demise. As Richard Hovey reminds us, citing the remark by Edith Wharton, "the trouble with always doing one's duty is that it unfits one for doing anything else."[41]

Hovey claims, as I also maintain, that Hudson's "sufferings are the most real thing in the story, an obsessive gloom from which even the amusing or lovelier passages are only momentary distractions" (175). Sojka, on the other hand, contrasts Hudson with Roger Davis, who, he says, "leads an undistinguished life of self-indulgence and emotional messiness" (266). Simply because Hudson denies his grief—arranging his daily schedule around his work and his self-indulgences (primarily his drinking), and forcing himself not to think about the devastating condition of his emotional life—does not (as any specialist in alcoholism would confirm) mean that he is not an emotional "mess" inside, and a seriously ill alcoholic. The nobility of Hemingway's *code* of ritualized behavior depends upon the endurance of a pain consciously acknowledged. Hudson, however, does not use this *code* of discipline and order to endure pain, as much as he uses it to escape from a painful reality. The difference here is a fine, but critical, one, in that it points to the life-saving distinction between coping with a recognized illness, and the refusal to recognize that one is ill and therefore in serious need of remedial physical and psychological attention.

Hemingway's own downfall, according to Tom Dardis, was that he could never admit that he was a "rummy," and this was why he could let the illness go so far that it destroyed him.[42] The distinction between the virtuous use of the Hemingway *code*, and an absurd and unhealthy co-dependency upon the *code* is that, while both uses are motivated by a taboo against grief, the former implementation of the *code* succeeds as a strategy of coping with pain and disillusionment, while the latter results in a dissociation from reality and emotional truth. Therefore, merely to recognize Hudson's use of the *code* as a strategy of coping and consolation does not automatically sound a note of affirmation in the novel. There is a point at which such strategies must be identified as self-destructive denials, and this is the point that Thomas Hudson, like Hemingway himself, reached during the final phases of his psychological and physical decline.

Furthermore, Sojka affirms Hemingway's own philosophy when he claims: "Whether in fishing, painting, or writing, discipline, the key to aesthetic enjoyment, is always preferable to emotional indulgence" (271). To grieve for the death of one's children and one's once dearly loved wife *cannot*, however, be counted as an "emotional indulgence." To be so close to the edge of falling apart that one must "write off" one's sons, by sheer will "give up" one's dead ex-wife, and further, play down the pain of that grief simply from a fear of becoming emotionally "sloppy," is irrefutably pathological, no matter how aesthetically virtuous one believes it may be to maintain "control" for the sake of one's work, or of anything else for that matter. The aesthetic of Hudson's, and Hemingway's, duty becomes but a life-destroying force—and beauty becomes a hideous distortion of the truth—when the aesthetic is used as an anesthetic to numb one to painful reality and emotional honesty. Hudson's drinking and use of sleeping pills—his "medicine"—in the "Cuba" section, indicates not only Hemingway's awareness of the fact that the repression of emotions can result in self-destructive behavior, but also his full comprehension of the horror (as he artfully portrayed this "horror" in "After the Storm" and "A Natural History of the Dead") of carrying one's taboo against grief to such an extreme that, as the manager says, in "The Mother of a Queen," "nothing can touch" the heart any more. When Hudson is shot he refuses morphine because he feels the need "to hold his pain in control," so that he can continue "to think" about his duty. In a similar way, throughout the novel, and with increasing desperation, Hudson holds his emotional "pain in control" to a point where he dies, not only in body, but in soul.

Islands in the Stream is nevertheless, I feel, a vitally important part of the developing Hemingway canon of tabooed grief for the very reason (and with the same irony as in "Snows," "After the Storm," and "A Natural History") that here Hemingway intentionally revealed, with the deepest personal pain, fortitude, and heroism, the devastating—even the absurd—price that must be paid in order to survive with even the semblance of dignity. In this novel, as in all of his fiction (regardless of artistic merit), Hemingway put all of his emotional crutches to the test. More often than not, they crumble in his fiction as they crumbled in his life. *Islands in the Stream* was Hemingway's final, brutal, and self-inflicted act of self-abuse, in which he knocked out from under himself the last remaining crutch—his art—that separated him from total collapse.

The Old Man and the Sea: *Transcending the Fear of Loss*

When *The Old Man and the Sea* was published in the early 1950s, many of Hemingway's readers who, over the past few years, had become increasingly skeptical about his ability as a writer (particularly after the dismal reception of *Across the River and Into the Trees* in 1950), viewed the novella as affirmative proof that the master had not lost his touch. James Michener, for one, who was asked by *Life* magazine to review the book, remembers having "said something about how happy writers like me were that the champ had regained the title." [43] If *The Old Man and the Sea* may indeed be considered to be one of Hemingway's best later works of fiction, it is perhaps for the paradoxical reason that in this story Hemingway envisioned a man who truly has nothing left to lose. Santiago has taken a critical step beyond Thomas Hudson, who was still possessed by the fear of losing what he loved, and so had to go on killing. Santiago, on the other hand, is resigned to the very idea of loss and grief; he is, therefore, free to love deeply and truly. It is this capacity to love that makes Santiago, and his experiences, so rich with the life force that is continually being eaten away by pessimism and disillusionment in Robert Jordan, the Hemingway narrator of *Green Hills of Africa* and *Death in the Afternoon,* David Bourne, Richard Cantwell, and Thomas Hudson. The love that Santiago feels is immune to loss and death; it is a love that does not first have to be killed in order for him to die without pain.

Hemingway attempted to create this transcendent character in *Across the River and Into the Trees,* but he could not disguise Cantwell's overriding nostalgia for the love and the life force he left behind him through death. By contrast, as Santiago says about the great fish: "You loved him when he was alive and you loved him after." [44] Therefore, when Santiago concludes that a "man can be destroyed but not defeated" (103), the reader is more fully convinced of the authentic power of love, and cannot but believe the old man's words. Thomas Hudson, on the other hand, makes too great a sacrifice in exchange for his questionable victory; and Richard Cantwell is a "beat-up old bastard," who is too full of nostalgic pride to be convincing when he boastfully claims, in sharp contrast to Santiago's humility, that one is "always triumphant in defeat." [45] Although Cantwell, like Hudson, claims to be immune to grief, he resembles the dying Harry in "Snows," when he confesses that for two people to love each other means merely that "one of them gets the emptiness forever" (271).

Across the River and Into the Trees is the story of a man who is "preparing the best way to be over-run" (104), whereas Santiago somehow cannot be over-run, either by the fish or by death. He is resigned to loss; and although life may indeed be tragic, the drama for him has already ended. In his mind he already lives in the land where the lions roam; his home the dazzling white western summit of Kilimanjaro *"called the Masi 'Ngaje Nagai,' the House of God."* [46] Even though Santiago feels that "he was beaten now finally and without remedy" (119) after having failed to bring in the big fish, no one else, not the boy Manolin, nor the proprietor of the cafe who says that there "has never been such a fish" (123), nor the fishermen who measure the skeleton of the fish that "was eighteen feet from nose to tail" (122), feel anything other than awe and respect for the old man. Santiago is perhaps the truest code hero to be found in Hemingway's fiction, not because his willingness to confront death, and to love, is a defense of willful rebellion against his fear of vulnerability to loss, death, and love—totems against a tabooed grief—but precisely because he offers no defense against them. His modesty, submissiveness, and calm acceptance of pain and death are his touchstones in life; therefore, he can lovingly say to the fish: "Come on and kill me. I do not care who kills who" (92). In *The Old Man and the Sea,* then, when Hemingway killed the thing he loved, he carried out this act primarily with the strength of love, not with the strength of fear.

The emphasis on dialogue, and the general absence of exposition in Hemingway's best fiction, point to drama as being one of the genres that (perhaps next to poetry) most resembles his creative style. Therefore, if Freud was indeed correct when he described the "psychopathological drama" as that which presents to the spectator a conflict "between a conscious impulse and a repressed one," then we have reason to proclaim Hemingway as (what many of us hardly need Freud to confirm), one of American literature's most outstanding writers of psychological fiction. [47] I have referred to Hemingway's craft as the *art of repression* numerous times throughout the last three chapters, particularly with regard to his early works of fiction, maintaining that through his exceptional mastery as an editor and stylist—or through what he called his "ice-berg" theory of composition—he created an intense psychological tension in his stories by refusing to allow his characters to admit to consciousness the painful emotional consequences of the losses and disappointment they suffered in the course of their experiences.

In Hemingway's early short stories, the painful emotional impulses which his adolescent protagonist resisted consciously recognizing usually resulted from his character's unwillingness to confront the griefs that are a natural part of the masculine process of separation-individuation. Specifically, the losses that inspired a grief response in him resulted from his recognition of the real father as flawed, from his disillusionment in the adolescent's fantasy belief in an abstract heroic paternal ideal, and from his loss of love in relation to the mother/woman, which he himself initiated because of his repudiated emotional dependency upon her. Frequently he would either project these griefs onto the landscape, displace them into anger directed against someone, or something, else, disavow them by regressing to an emotionally impervious state of infantile omnipotence, or simply refuse to think about them. However, while the level of psychological tension produced from the repression of these griefs was raised within the mind of the character, the reader, who is able to grieve for—or rather instead of—the character, experienced a pleasurable discharge of emotional tension, making the essential act of reading Hemingway's stories a cathartic experience of mourning.

It is important, as well, to remember that Hemingway never identified the repressed emotion—either for the edification of the character or for the reader—thus fulfilling Freud's primary precondition of the psychopathological "form of art," which is, that "the impulse that is struggling into consciousness, however clearly it is recognizable, is never given a definite name; so that in the spectator too the process is carried through with his attention averted, and he is in the grip of his emotions instead of taking stock of what is happening" (309). By averting his attention through the acts of repression and sublimation in his art, Hemingway achieved a catharsis in which he, like the reader, to some extent, loosened himself from the grip of painful negative emotions.

According to Freud, an additional and critical precondition for enjoying this psychological form of drama is that the reader or spectator "should himself be a neurotic" for whom "the repression is on the brink of failing; it is unstable and needs a constant renewal of expenditure" (308–9). The tremendous popularity in America of both Hemingway the man, and his work, supports the argument that the average American male shared in his "neurosis"—specifically, in his hero's developmental arrest at the idealistic, adolescent stage of the masculine individuation process. Hemingway's enforcement of the taboo against grief in his craft was coextensive with his fictional attempts to prolong the adolescent's illusion of possessing a grandiose, or heroic, ego-ideal. Through his art of repression, as well as through his own larger-than-life mythical heroic persona, Hemingway sustained for an entire society of American men the adolescent illusion of the coming together of the ego and the grandiose ideal. All those men who looked up to Hemingway's *code hero*—and to Hemingway himself as a leader—were thus able (as for a time Hemingway himself was), to by-pass in fantasy the oedipal conflict, the reality principle, and the anxiety of castration, and hence, to share in Hemingway's "bigger phallus" by projecting a common American ego ideal onto the figure of the Hemingway *hero,* and by extension onto the author himself.

At the time Hemingway began writing in the early part of the twentieth century, the American family structure was such that most nuclear families lacked a strong and present father figure; consequently, the children remained especially close to, and emotionally dependent upon, the mother. With a large population of American men suffering, in effect, from father-hunger and mother-loss, Hemingway and his *code hero* became an ideal father substitute; and, through his growing popularity, Hemingway satisfied the need of thousands upon thousands of American men to establish a personal family-romance myth. Hemingway provided for all those young men who, like himself, suffered from secret dependency needs and disturbances in self-esteem, an easy way to regress to a gratifying state of primary narcissism, by identifying with the Hemingway super-masculine hero who gave them the illusion of the union of ego and ideal.

To carry Freud's insights one step farther, for the sake of understanding the transformation in Hemingway's art and life, in the mid-1930s, and how that metamorphosis led to a general decline in the artistic quality of his work, it is significant that, as Freud submits, "the victim of a neurosis is someone into whose conflict we can gain no insight if we first meet it in a fully established state" (310). In Hemingway's best early stories, it is almost always the case that the principal character begins the story in a psychologically stable state, and then undergoes a traumatic loss (either in relation to mother-loss, father-hunger, or both), which threatens to weaken his defensive repressions and force upon him the painful recognition of the repressed impulses. Thus, thrust into a weakened state, he is required to expend a certain amount of new psychic energy, as Freud maintains, to "repeat the act of repression" (309). In "Indian Camp," young Nick's hallucinatory regressive fantasy of narcissistic omnipotence in relation to himself, and to his father, represents the reinstatement of his taboo against the grief of father-loss; just as, in "The Three-Day Blow," the adolescent Nick is able to put off the conscious recognition of his grief by believing in the compensating fantasy that "nothing was ever lost."

In Hemingway's later fiction, beginning, perhaps, with *Death in the Afternoon* in the early 1930s, the narrator's neurotic fear of loss is, from the beginning of the novel, to repeat Freud's words, "in a fully established state" (310). In *Death in the Afternoon, Across the River and Into the Trees, Green Hills of Africa,* and *Islands in the Stream,* Hemingway did not, as Freud says, "set up" the neurosis and allow the reader "to follow the development of the illness along with the sufferer" (310); instead, he presented a hero who was already in a state of disillusionment and loss—who was already, in effect, "sick"—and as Jeffrey Meyers has observed, "repeated rather than developed" his characters' thematic concerns.[48] Thus, as Freud explains, "we shall be inclined to send for the doctor (just as we do in real life) and pronounce the character inadmissible to the stage" (310). The success of Hemingway's art of repression depended upon the rise and fall, and necessary rise again, of the tabooed grief impulse. If Hemingway's later works are both psychologically and artistically inferior in this regard, it is perhaps because the pattern of repression is not wavering but flat and undeveloped, and the emotions that would have gained power, had he disguised them better, fall flat from over-exposure. Despite fleeting moments of remission and relief that ultimately lead nowhere, his later narrators, for the most part, do not go from well to sick to well—or from stable to neurotic to stable—but move along a steady neurotic decline.

The unfortunate consequence of Hemingway's ever-increasing depression and self-absorption in middle age, therefore, was that it prevented him from achieving sufficient imaginative distance from his fiction to allow him to objectively and dramatically "set up" the character's need to repress, or rather, to re-repress, painful emotional impulses. That is not to say, however, that Hemingway himself did not have an insightful, and perhaps even a full, understanding of the nature of his characters' sufferings and repressions. Nevertheless, in his later novels, Hemingway did not divert the reader's attention away from his character's suffering— from the initially repressed grief impulse—long enough, or skillfully enough, to allow the reader to participate in the character's desire to resist the conscious recognition of painful emotions. Instead, he made it all too obvious from the start that the narrator was "sick" from loss and grief, and therefore merely in need of a physician. As Freud affirms, "if we recognize the conflict, we forget that he is a sick man, just as, if he himself recognizes it, he ceases to be ill" (310). Perhaps it was because the aging Hemingway himself could not, or refused to, recognize that he was sick—that his alcoholism, delusions of grandeur, chronic depression, and physical infirmities were not manly heroic defenses against "feminine" weakness and emotional vulnerability but real illnesses—that he was no longer able to objectively, imaginatively, and artistically separate "well" from "sick" in his mind, and, therefore, could no longer dramatize the vicissitudes—the rise and fall and subsequent rise—of the neurotic need for the repression of grief. He was, in other words, too personally involved in the tragedy of what was *happening* to him to avert his own—and the reader's—attention from the grief and loss that gripped him, to envision, even in fantasy, what it meant to be "well."

Essentially, what I am describing in the Hemingway of later years is a loss of the real hope—not the *abstract* heroic conviction that one may be triumphant in defeat—that is critical to the "setting up" of an effective tragic psychological drama. Once again, Santiago, in *The Old Man and the Sea*, is somewhat of an exception here. Santiago's unconditional love for nature, the sea, the boy Manolin, and his occupation as a fisherman, and the unconditional love that he receives from them in return, envelops his work and his bruised life in an aura of hopefulness. His faith is somehow not of this world; it is spiritual not physical, and so is not destined to be brought down by mortal losses and disappointments. He has, in effect, incorporated into himself the unconditional love of that all-providing, all-forgiving mother/woman which the heroes of Hemingway's fiction, for the most part, only attain temporarily during the fleeting ecstatic moments of drinking, writing, and lovemaking, and which they must always lose and leave behind them, like Hemingway's "great bird flown." By contrast, Santiago's love is not in competition with, nor does it drain the life-force out of, the "manly" activities of war, writing, or fishing. It is no matter, as he says to the boy, Manolin, that "I am not lucky anymore" (125). Love, of the kind that exists between the boy and the old man, is more valuable and enduring than luck, and so, as the devoted boy assures his ancient friend, "I'll bring the luck with me."

Conclusion

While psycho-historical generalizations should always be posited with an appropriate degree of speculative caution, it is difficult—given our inherited national symbolism, which speaks of the *birth* of America, the *growth* of a nation, the *father* of our country, and the *founding fathers* of American democracy—not to think of American history in terms of the evolution of an emerging collective consciousness. The image of such a collective cultural figure which has been indirectly evoked throughout this study is that of the rebellious male adolescent who clings with stubborn pride to unrealistic and idealistic notions of self-control, emotional invulnerability, and personal perfection: who, in effect, invites upon himself disappointment and loss, but whose inherited cultural *Weltanschauung* lacks an internal psychological mechanism for incorporating and coming to terms with loss, disillusionment, and compromise.

Mourning, as we have learned, is essentially a means of adapting to disappointment and loss, and the grief associated with mourning, we have come to realize, is fundamentally a therapeutic process, not a state. According to current psychoanalytic theories of loss and mourning, the process of an individual's "growth and maturation can be compared to mourning work in that every step towards maturation involves some adaptation to separation, and therefore some mourning work."[1] The adolescent who persistently retains idealistic notions of self and the world, who refuses to let go of innocence and illusions, to relinquish a sense of endless options, and to accept ambivalence, seeks to prolong indefinitely what is meant to be a transitional phase of adolescence. Instead, he or she, in effect, longs perpetually for the lost utopian narcissistic omnipotence of childhood.

John Bowlby distinguishes between two fundamental forms of distorted or pathological mourning. The first is *chronic mourning*, in which sorrow is disavowed in favor of the belief that the loss is reversible.[2] Like Mark Twain and Melville's Ishmael, this individual searches and pines for a lost love object whom he or she refuses to accept is gone, often because of unresolved feelings of guilt or aggression directed toward the person before death. The American Adam—the mythical representative figure of the idealistic perpetual adolescent—similarly denies his sorrow over the disillusionments associated with a lost Edenic childhood by continuing to mourn chronically for his lost ideal past, and to yearn for an unattainable utopian future. The second form of distorted mourning identified by Bowlby is the *prolonged absence of conscious grieving*, or the extension of the mourning phase that is characterized by emotional numbing. From the stories of *In Our Time* to the uncompleted *Islands in the Stream*, we have seen that Hemingway skillfully employed the grief defense of anaesthetization in crafting his fictional narratives, just as within his fictional plots, his male heroes used this mechanism of desensitization to disavow conscious recognition of painful negative emotions.

The American spirit of hopeful optimism that defined the future outlook, first of the Puritans, later of the New Republic, and finally of the late nineteenth- and early twentieth-century proponents of the American Dream, similarly allowed for a perpetual deferment of the conscious recognition of grief. In *A Time to Mourn*, Verena Kast, reaffirming the theoretical and clinical findings of Helene Deutsch and Vamik Volkan, maintains that individuals who bypass conscious mourning will always be described as both self-assured and proud of their independence and self-control.[3] Like Hemingway, they valorize their emotional repressions, viewing their manifestations of distorted mourning—their numbness and stoicism—as bravery and fortitude. "Adults who show prolonged absence of conscious grieving," Bowlby confirms, "are commonly self-sufficient people, proud of their independence and self-control, scornful of sentiment; tears they regard as weakness."[4]

Individuals who engage in chronic mourning, the prolonged absence of conscious grieving, or both, tend to live out their lives with a vague yet persisting sense of depression and sadness; they are unable to pinpoint the root cause of their disillusionment, emotional unfulfillment, and despair. Primarily, such people live a life of feigned independence and emotional invulnerability, and appear unable to establish intimate interpersonal relationships. As Joyce Warren has pointed out, "the basic principle of American culture," refined and authenticated by the philosophy of Ralph Waldo Emerson, who advocated that every individual must be "self-dependent" and lean "solely on his own character,"[5] is that narcissistic self-sufficiency was, and remains, the highest of our nation's personal, philosophical, and political aspirations.[6] In words that fore-shadow the stoicism and emotional deadness of Hemingway's matador in the story "The Mother of a Queen," about whom the bullfighter's manager says "you can't touch" him, "nothing can touch"[7] him, Emerson writes in his essay, "The Heart": "Man is insular, and cannot be touched. Every man is an infinitely repellent orb."[8]

Although it may be stretching matters to suggest, as Warren does, that the malaise of modern American culture, specifically the loneliness, alienation, and self-absorption (as well as the emotional insularity that it fosters), is a psychological manifestation of the unraveling of the American Dream—the "coming down" from a centuries-old "high" of illusionary adolescent idealism and forced optimism—the connection Warren makes rings true. Her hypothesis is supportable not only on the level of American mass culture, but, as I have attempted to prove in this study, on the psycho-biographical level of the individual American male author, as well as within the psycho-dramas of these authors' fictional adolescent heroes, many of whom—including Melville's Ishmael, Twain's Huckleberry Finn, and Hemingway's Nick Adams—have become literary icons of American thought and culture.

Psychoanalytic and cultural theorists, such as Heinz Kohut, Christopher Lasch, R. D. Laing, James Masterson, Erich Fromm, and Robert Bly, to name just a few, have striven to draw out these connections: to label, diagnose, and etiologically decipher a distinctly American malaise, the origins of which can be traced back to the earliest religious, familial, political, and ideological foundations of American life.[9] These theorists identify the American nuclear family configuration as one of the primary causes of the malaise of the adult American male (or, in fact, of anyone of either gender who chooses to fulfill the tough and emotionally invulnerable identity structure that in Western culture is thought of as "masculine"). In this situation, the father, typically, is both physically and emotionally distant within the family, yet harbors secret dependency needs and a fear of his own weaknesses, while the mother acts as the central object around which the family's emotional needs and psychological dependencies gravitate. Voicing the opinion of many of these theorists, Nancy Chodorow explains that this "close, exclusive, preoedipal mother-child relationship first develops dependency in a son," and when "a mother 'rejects' her son or pushes him to be more independent" (or, in other words, to act in accordance with a set of behaviors defined by Western society as "masculine"), the son "carries his still powerful dependency with him, creating in him both a general need to please and conform outside of the relationship to the mother herself and a strong assertion of independence. The isolated, husband-absent mother thus helps to create in her son a pseudo-independence masking real dependence." [10]

The son, then, as Peter Blos adds, turns to the father so as to distance himself from his unworked-through dependency needs on the powerful mother. But the emotionally distant father cannot act as an outlet for the son's acquired need for intimacy, and so, throughout adulthood, the son searches unceasingly for a substitute, over-idealized father who will provide the kind of unconditional and satisfying ego gratification originally supplied by the devoted preoedipal mother. Having bypassed both oedipal competition with the father (the negative oedipus complex), and the reality-testing phase of psychic growth in which the boy comes to accept his own, and life's, limitations and imperfections, the son remains indefinitely in a state of arrested adolescence in which he seeks to recapture his lost childish omnipotence. Despite what he may "know" to be true about his own and life's inadequacies, his fixated psychological development compels him to harbor illusory fantasies of fabulous achievement for himself: fame, greatness, wealth, adventure, and excitement, in short, complete narcissistic fulfillment.

The son's narcissistic gratification originally acquired from his relationship with the mother, in other words, has been transferred to his hopes for fulfilling an abstract conception of the overvalued paternal ideal. [11] In a way, then, the American son's fantasy of grandiosity and ego overvaluation represents the psychological echoes of a more originary desire for a transcendent symbiotic fusion with greatness (or with the fantasy omnipotent preoedipal mother herself). The American male's dreams of a future utopia, and of realizing an ideal paternal self-image, enable him to transcend the reality of grief, disappointment, and loss, to avoid father-son oedipal frustration, and to retain his secret (but by now unrecognized) emotional ties to the loving and comforting mother (a disguised fulfillment of oedipal wishes), without having to relinquish his tough, independent, and inviolate "masculinity."

The perilous consequences for himself and for American culture are, however, deeply tragic and significant. As with the male authors investigated in this study, self-doubts about one's true greatness, emotional loneliness and insularity, the endlessly unfulfilled search for an ideal heroic father, an abiding sense of anxiety and fear toward women, and a potentially crippling depression and grief, await the perpetual adolescent around every corner. From the Puritans through to the twentieth century, America has been compulsively caught up in a love affair with political, philosophical, and psychological utopias that are both infantile in their essential nature, and gendered female, but which, as transcendent masculine defenses against feminine identification and emotional vulnerability, have been appropriated by patriarchal culture and transformed into visions of ideal masculinity.

If we accept these psychoanalytic assumptions about the connections between American masculine idealism, preoedipal narcissistic satisfaction, and the repression of grief, feminine identification, and the regressive nature of our most cherished "patriarchal" ideological beliefs, then the American Dream, and the whole pyramidic socio-political structure of which it is the historical apex, may conceivably be re-defined as an adolescent defense against mourning and conscious grieving. When episodic bouts of disillusionment, self-doubt, and despair should happen to occur, which according to this psychological schema they inevitably will (both in the life of the individual and in American culture at large), then active mourning and conscious grieving are reactivated, and new defenses against disillusionment and the disappointments of reality must be instituted. As part of this mourning response, the desire for primal symbiosis is reawakened, but can be appeased by finding recourse in mysticism, fusion with the Divine, total absorption in a greater whole, political and economic re-visioning, and so forth. As Judith Viorst explains in *Necessary Losses:* "Our pursuit of this connection," or, rather, this re-connection, "of the restoration of oneness" and paradise "may be an act of sickness or of health, may be a fearful retreat from the world or an effort to expand it, may be deliberate or unaware. Through sex, through religion, through nature, through art, through drugs, through meditation, even through jogging, we try to blur the boundaries that divide us. We try to escape the imprisonment of separateness. We sometimes succeed."[12] The Puritan Age, Transcendentalism, the "Gilded Age" of American industrial growth, the post-war 1920s, the rebellious 1960s, and the psychologically depressed and spiritually impoverished 1980s and 1990s, may all be characterized not only as moments of cultural progress, but also, to some extent, as periodic episodes of mass cultural disillusionment, depression, and grief.

Most of the psycho-historical issues about the evolution of American culture that I have just raised, admittedly with the most liberal indulgence in theoretical speculation, have yet to be comprehensively addressed and convincingly drawn out by specialists in the fields of sociology and cultural psychology. Yet, it is a worthy task that to some degree has already been, and hopefully will continue to be, undertaken and further evaluated within the ever-changing context of American history. I have not presumed to undertake this task directly in the main body of this book. *The Grief Taboo in American Literature* is a study of American culture only by way of implication and extrapolation. I have aimed, rather, to focus on the issues of repressed grief, prolonged male adolescent idealism, denied and displaced feminine identification, and repudiated regressive impulses in the lives and fiction of three American male authors who are, without question, viewed as representative products, and producers, of a distinctly American ideology and spirit. Certainly, many of the particular, as well as the broader, psychological themes evoked in their fiction have become common motifs in modern American culture: the fear of abandonment, a penchant for idealistic thinking, an emphasis on the self to the exclusion of others, difficulty with intimacy and with the assertion of the real self, nostalgia for a lost utopian childhood, ambivalence about whether to grow up or remain a child, and an inability to grieve openly and thereby come to terms with the losses, tragedies, and disappointments of life.

Although psychoanalysis, whether Freudian, feminist, Lacanian, or object relations, like any theoretically based methodology, is inevitably fraught with its own liberty-taking abstractions and internal controversies, I have endeavored, through my concentration on actual fictional texts and generally established biographical data, to concretize as much as possible my literary and psychoanalytic investigations of the authors under consideration. While my primary goal has been to demonstrate how and why repression—specifically the repression of grief, adolescent disillusionment, and feminine/maternal influence—in Melville, Twain, and Hemingway (combined with the unique quality of their imaginations), played a profoundly significant role in the construction of great art, in doing so I have also indirectly sought to undo that repression: to subvert the male cultural fantasies that their fiction both embodied and perpetuated, not only *without* subverting the greatness of those literary achievements, but also with the hope of understanding, and thereby further championing, their timeless brilliance.

I would like now to address directly the potentially therapeutic role of literary criticism by exploring briefly the profits that may be gained for American culture as a whole from an understanding, or undoing, of a fundamentally emotionally paralyzing and developmentally intrusive American form of repression. Throughout the foregoing chapters, a psychoanalytic tracing of the repression of, or taboo against, grief in the lives and fiction of Melville, Twain, and Hemingway has repeatedly led to an awareness of their unreconcilable ambivalence in relation to the archaic image of the mother. The alternating clinging and distancing behavior of Melville's Ishmael and Pierre emerges in *The Grief Taboo in American Literature* as a consequence of the splitting of the "good" and "bad" mother into a comforting utopia of egolessness, and a smothering and abandoning hostile force, respectively. Twain similarly projected the grief of maternal deprivation and deception onto a hostile and hypocritical external world, intrapsychically preserving the image of the lost and longed-for "good" mother in the form of his nostalgic fantasy of the innocence of a strife-free and morally honest eternal boyhood paradise. Hemingway, too, like the male heroes of his fiction, seemed endlessly conflicted about his desire to assert a "masculine" autonomy against the regressive pull of comforting maternal dependency: alternately to cling to and distance himself from the "good"/"bad," rescuing and smothering, mother. His best stories are products of the inner psychic tension between the urge to succumb to the grief of disappointment and loss, and the impulse to inure, or inoculate, himself against the conscious recognition of emotional pain.

Appropriately, then, given the maternal and infantile origins of these authors' fixation at the stage of radical ambivalence, the solution some psychoanalysts have proposed to loosen the psyche from the grip of arrested development is to recognize that the mother (like the self and the world) possesses both positive and negative qualities. As James Masterson maintains, the healthy child must build up the

confidence that the world is neither a totally threatening nor a totally pleasurable place, but an arena of opposites: safety and danger, success and failure, comfort and pain, power and helplessness, companionship and loneliness. There will be moments of happiness and elation as well as times of frustration and sorrow. Most of all the child learns that his mother also embodies good and bad qualities. At times she rewards and comforts; at other times, she is distant, aloof, punishing. But the child discovers that his mother loves him with his emerging and separating self no matter what and that she sincerely wants him to explore the world and develop and grow in his own unique way. And as he does so, the real self emerges and develops its capacities to cope successfully with life. (Masterson, *Search for the Real Self,* 35)

Thus, the key to resolving this rapprochement-phase ambivalence, as became apparent early on in this book with the discussion of Melville's *Moby-Dick*, is not the kind of either/or thinking Ishmael, Ahab, Bulkington, and Pierre fell back upon, but an attitude and outlook of complementarity, simultaneity, and both-ness. This goal, as psychoanalysis might phrase it, is *object constancy*, through which people, and the world at large, are viewed not as parts that are either positive *or* negative, but as composite wholes.[13]

When the fantasy of the omnipotent mother is given up, so too, theoretically, is the belief in the possibility of total self-reliance and perfectibility. The primal separation from the gratifying, fantasy symbiotic mother must be mourned in order for notions of the inevitability of loss and transience finally to be accepted. When this illusion is deflated, so is the equally pernicious fantasy-illusion of an all-powerful, destructive, and threatening mother. Similarly, the abstract fantasy of the exalted, heroic paternal figure must be relinquished and mourned for. When the false expectations for the fulfillment of a paternal ideal are realized and grieved, that is when the paternal masculine self-object can be replaced by an attainable, though still primarily admirable, fallible father.

Through these psychological gestures of compromise and acceptance, gender difference, in effect, is also blurred in a healthy way. The purpose toward which I have applied feminism in this study, then, has been, in part, to unite individuals, both male and female, in the quest to enlarge the scope of human potential—not to reduce it by seeking to rigidly define, and thereby to further divide and restrict, the categories of gender identification and behavior. Certainly, the inability, prompted by an inflexible American idealism, to accept a blurring and blending of the boundaries between independence and dependence, good and evil, freedom and belonging, success and failure, and masculine and feminine, characterizes the literature of the traditional American male author, from the Puritans and the New Republic, through the Transcendentalists, Hawthorne, and Poe, to Hemingway in the twentieth century. The lesson to be learned by the individual, and collective, American male from an undoing of repressed grief and feminine identification, is that, just as all of one's life may be viewed as an ongoing process of separation from the mother, so, too, is there no point at which a man might say "now I am a 'man,' " or a woman might say "now I am a 'woman.' "[14]

Such a change in attitude should ultimately lead to the deflation of mother-loss and father-hunger as driving forces behind the repressed grief and unsatisfied desires of the American male. The result might also include a diminished emphasis on ego power, and a greater emphasis on finding more direct and overt outlets for one's feelings. Additionally, one can expect an exchange of symbolic displacements of repressed feelings for literal transcriptions of the author's inner and outer experiences (in which case, for example, the unconscious fantasy image of the woman/mother will no longer function as a scapegoat for male fears and desires). It might be of interest in the course of tracking the evolution of the American creative writer, to establish some correlation between the wave of expanded consciousness and self-awareness that swept through America in the latter half of the twentieth century, and the movement of its best and most representative literature from symbolic (or displaced) configurations of American life and ideology, toward a literature of socio-psychological realism and mimesis.

Given these prospective changes in attitude and perspective, future definitions of the American Dream may not be as heroic and grandiose as they have been in the past, but they possibly might encourage an American personality type that is more emotionally responsive and empathetic to the reality and energy of others. If self-esteem, as psychoanalysts have proposed, is indeed measured by the discrepancy between who one wishes to be and who one really is, then at stake here is the heightening of our individual and collective cultural confidence and self-esteem.[15] A recognition of one's weaknesses and limitations, while it may lower one's aspirations, ultimately serves to close that grievous and anxiety-provoking gap between the longed-for, and the attainable, self. To be sure, however, this kind of genuine self-love is not the same as the self-glorification of our culture's more pervasive inclination toward unhealthy narcissism.

Low self-esteem, at best, breeds loneliness, despondency, and a gnawing sense of self-loss; at worst, it breeds selfishness, anger, malicious competitiveness, and despair. An increased sense of self-esteem, however, fosters honesty, magnanimity, and above all, an ability to love that transcends neediness and compulsive desire. Despite the grandiosity and self-enshrinement of the American adolescent male (or, perhaps, as a consequence of these), as we have seen in the case of Melville, Twain, and Hemingway, he must periodically fight off a distressing sense of worthlessness and low self-esteem. Undoubtedly, as is also true for the adolescent American orphan-hero, the clearly manifested loneliness, despondency, fear of emotional vulnerability, and inability to give or receive love without fear and inhibitions, exhibited by these American writers, and by their fictional heroes, stemmed in part from their persisting and irksome sense of self-doubt: from their inability to bridge the gap between who they were, and the heroic, grandiose ego ideal toward which they aspired.

Overall, I have attempted to incorporate an elegiac consciousness into the traditional American myth of heroic aspirations, emotional inviolability, total self-reliance, and attainable utopias. In doing so, I hoped inadvertently to exhume the longed-for and yet repudiated corpse (or corpus) of the mother's body from the grave of regressive infantile fantasies in which it is buried within American literature. Psychotherapy, as Greg Mogenson suggests, "can be a grisly business,"[16] and the archetypal character of the American orphan-hero, with his perpetual family-romance yearning to wander, to grieve nostalgically for the lost good mother, and to seek out ceaselessly the foundling's heroic father, is itself the graveyard of his own unworked-through adolescent and infantile psychic conflicts. His "[a]nacronistic behavior," as Mogenson says of the patient in therapy who is essentially struggling "with a mourning process which has been indefinitely post-poned," is "merely a consequence of the failure of the patient to mourn losses" (264).

In summary, this study has been dedicated to discovering why and how three male American creative writers successfully sublimated their grief from early and subsequent experiences of loss into their art. For each, the writing of fiction served a cathartic, or one might say, therapeutic, function in that the final work of art produced became for them, in effect, a memorial to the losses which they could neither acknowledge consciously nor grieve openly. Their artistic products were elegiac monuments that provided an aesthetic outlet for a more direct cathartic experience of mourning and emotional expression. Through a reciprocal gesture of displaced mourning, the male reader of these typically American works of fiction participated vicariously in the psychological and emotional struggles of the perpetual adolescent orphan-hero as dramatized by these authors; and, as Freud, Norman Holland, and others have suggested, the aesthetic satisfaction, or pleasure, of immersing oneself in these fictionalized conflicts allowed the male reader to re-repress the griefs artfully displaced by Melville, Twain, and Hemingway into their art. Psychoanalytic theory, particularly object relations, preoedipal psychology, and feminist psychoanalytic theory, facilitated the timely undoing of a chronic (and a peculiarly American), form of repressed grief, denied emotional vulnerability, and repudiated feminine identification.

In embarking upon this work of psychoanalytic literary criticism, I was motivated by the desire to make these authors' predominantly "masculine" works of fiction accessible in a new way to "feminine" readers. Additionally, I was inspired by the related impulse to make the long-held American myths of optimism, tabooed grief, and willfully enforced perpetual regeneration understandable to a contemporary, feminist sensibility. In the course of this analytical investigation, I attempted to break down, or undo, an expanding matrix of indigenous American myths and cultural assumptions. I might list among these the following: the myth of the maternal figure as either a rescuer or a destroyer; the myth of an American notion of "masculinity" as independent of primitive emotional needs and ties, and as exclusive, or transcendent, of feminine, maternal, and infantile components; the myth that the attainment of "individualism" in America spontaneously eliminates relational and dependency needs; and the myth that the son may sever himself from the father without adverse consequences, in other words, without acknowledging radical familial and generational separations as significant and traumatic experiences of loss with which the young male can only come to terms through open grieving and mourning. Furthermore, I hoped to question the American suppositions that feelings can successfully and immutably be subordinated to will and self-rule, and that masculine self-esteem may indeed be based upon the fantasy of heroism and attainable perfection, rather than upon the mature acceptance of one's own, and the world's, shortcomings and limitations. In more general terms, I inadvertently sought to undo those repressions that for generations in America have sustained the belief that gain may be had without loss, that loss may stoically be endured without grief and mourning, and finally, as evidenced by the abiding literary renown of Melville, Twain, and Hemingway, that although literary greatness in America may indeed be won through the disavowal, or repression, of loss and grief, we should at the very least recognize the emotional sacrifices that were made, and the developmental problems that arose, in these authors' pursuit of a fundamentally tragic and personally self-destructive American notion of greatness.

Despite the differences elaborated upon at length in chapter 4 between the mythical figure of Sophocles' Oedipus and the American orphan-hero (primarily those having to do with the American author's reluctance to follow through with the boy's oedipal drives and impulses, which might enable him to initiate himself into the traditional, patriarchal, Western nuclear family), they have in common their orphanhood, their rebellious, stubborn independence, their pride and inability to depend on others, and their "monomaniacal thirst for knowledge": their "rationalistic and haughty perfectionism whereby comprehension is believed to conquer all."[17] D. H. Lawrence repeatedly recognized and pointed out to us these qualities in our best and most cherished male authors. Benjamin Franklin's "Each man his own master," Lawrence claims, "is but a puffing up of masterlessness."[18] Like Oedipus, J. Hector St. John de Crèvecoeur, Lawrence asserts, wanted only "to 'know'. To KNOW. Oh, insatiable American curiosity!" (37). Cooper's Deerslayer, similarly, was an "isolate, almost selfless, stoic, enduring man, who lives by death, by killing, but who is pure white" (69), and like these others, Deerslayer was himself an "*intellectual* savage" (38). What Poe wanted from the world, particularly from the beautiful women of his imagination such as Berenice and Ligeia, "is to analyze her, till he knows all her component parts, till he has got her all in his consciousness" (75).

To drive the mind incessantly to *know*, Lawrence implies, is not only "to suck the life out of" (76) the other, but also to suck the life and soul out of the loving and authentic self. In America, above all other nations, Lawrence declares, one finds "the pride of human conceit in KNOWLEDGE" (81). Hawthorne, too, "wanted to KNOW," and out of this perverse desire came "the birth of sin. Not *doing* it, but KNOWING about it" (91). Finally, both Ishmael and Ahab were "doomed . . . idealists"; they were pure-blooded American "monomaniacs of the idea," hunting down the great, unknowable, white whale: the symbol of "our white mental consciousness" (169). Like Oedipus, the heroism of the American orphan-hero resides in his emotional insularity and isolation, and in his masochistic thirst for knowledge at whatever cost to himself. One of the prevailing intentions throughout *The Grief Taboo in American Literature* has been not to deny this heroism, but to re-define this distinctly American notion of greatness as a menacing, emotionally paralyzing, and tragic heroism.

Though not conceived by a native American imagination, the adolescent figure of Peter Pan has come to stand for the narcissistic modern American male, who, as Dan Kiley writes in the subtitle to his book, *The Peter Pan Syndrome*, has "Never Grown Up."[19] Like Oedipus and the American orphan-hero, Peter was abandoned by his parents, and was shipped off to Never Never Land, where he became the leader of innumerable other "lost boys" like himself. As did Emerson and Thoreau, the Pan repressed his grief, channeled his sorrow into a valorization of loneliness and abandonment depression, and displaced these onto rebellious independence, emotional untouchability, and arrogant pride. Because he was only a boy, however, Peter's narcissism, grandiosity, and selfishness presented no real threat to society. Like Huckleberry Finn, as Kiley maintains about Barrie's story, "Peter and his legion of lost boys were plagued by loneliness. To cope with it, they had to find ways to turn the nightmare into sport. Since children are the consummate game players, it's no surprise that they camouflaged their loneliness with gaiety and trickery" (93). But, as Kiley perceptively points out, Peter's selfishness, insularity, rebelliousness, and arrogance mark him, and all of his similarly "lost" orphan companions, as potentially piratical: as budding, young, evil Captain Hooks-in-the-making.

Like Melville's Ishmael and Ahab, Peter Pan repressed his anger toward the parents who deserted him, and displaced his deep feelings of abandonment depression onto rebelliousness, angry protest, and suicidal longings; like Twain's Huckleberry Finn, he escaped the horrors of the world's, and of his own, repressed inner hostility by whitewashing them with a veneer of seemingly harmless, playful innocence; and finally, like Hemingway's male code heroes, and like Hemingway himself, Peter denied his own dependency needs, and the longing for love that accompanied them, by anesthetizing himself against emotional vulnerability and closing off the heart to the realities of grief and loss.

At the end of Act V, Scene I, Peter and his legion of boys defeat the cruel and heartless Captain Hook, who commits suicide by throwing himself overboard into the waiting jaws of a crocodile. At this point in his 1904 play, J. M. Barrie writes: *"The curtain rises to show* Peter *a very Napoleon on his ship. It must not rise again lest we see him on the poop in* Hook's *hat and cigars, and with a small iron claw."* [20] Was Peter the base and wicked Hook all along, rendered harmless and endearing merely by virtue of his jolly, carefree youthfulness? Was Mark Twain driven to confine Huckleberry Finn securely within the innocuous periphery of "innocent" boyhood, compelled to force him to wander endlessly always a step "ahead of" the adult, civilized world because he knew (perhaps unconsciously) what potential cruelty and heartlessness the perpetual male adolescent harbors within his mythical frame? How far from the haughty, demonical Ahab was the philosophy-crazed and emotionally repressed young Ishmael? And finally, how close to becoming the callous narrators of "After the Storm" and "A Natural History of the Dead" was Hemingway's young Nick Adams, with his obsessive taboo against grief and his defiant defenses against feminine identification and emotional vulnerability? The parodic nature of Hemingway's two stories, and the tragic, piteous fate of his later adult male heroes, Robert Jordan, Colonel Richard Cantwell, and Thomas Hudson, seem unmistakably to imply that Hemingway was keenly aware of the consequences of repressed grief and adolescent idealism carried to their extremes.

In real life the emotionally crippled American male—though harmless, endearing, and entertaining when young—does grow up, and, when he does, he carries with him the potential to infect his society and culture with his selfishness, emotional indifference, homophobia, and disdain, resentment, and envy toward women. Hence, what may be identified as heroism, even as tragic heroism, in the fiction of the American male author, does, perhaps, have the capacity to wield a menacing and dire influence in American society and culture. The taboo against grief, then, may well have pervasive repercussions that extend well beyond the covers of our most valued classic works of literature, in which merely the personal happiness of our mythical heroes is at stake. In American culture, we have yet to discover the extent of the injury and sadness precipitated by the innumerable losses for which, from our earliest Puritan beginnings to the present time, we have been reluctant to mourn.

Notes

Notes to Introduction

1. Perry Miller, *The New England Mind: From Colony to Province*, 9. Miller's views foreshadow innumerable studies which characterize Americans as lonely, alienated, and isolated from each other.
2. See in particular R. W. B. Lewis, *The American Adam: Innocence, Tragedy, and Tradition in the Nineteenth Century*, 5.
3. Helene Deutsch, "Absence of Grief," 13; and, Alexander Lowen, *Narcissism: Denial of the True Self*, 208.
4. Kaja Silverman, *Male Subjectivity at the Margins*, 2–3.
5. This study, in spirit, participates in a current trend in American literary criticism to expose the ways in which the American myth of optimism and rebirth has clouded a recognition of the underlying tragic, pernicious, and subversive elements in the American Dream and American democratic idealism. Sam B. Girgus, for example, in his recent book *Desire and the Political Unconscious: Eros and Ideology*, proposes that American ideology, as conveyed through the literature of America, undermines wholeness, permanence, and stability in a way that subverts the myth of the American Adam and America itself as a New World Garden. Peter Freese endeavors to correct faulty European notions about America as a melting pot, a mythical embodiment of assured success, and a limitless open frontier, in *'America': Dream or Nightmare? Reflections on a Composite Image*.

    Sacvan Bercovitch, Henry Nash Smith, and Quentin Anderson are three American literary critics who played a significant role in defining and upholding the myth of American idealism and optimism, but who courageously came to overturn a number of their own initial convictions about the positive repercussions of the American experiment. Quentin Anderson, who was one of the first cultural critics to point out the loneliness and alienation of the individual American "imperial self," in *The Imperial Self; An Essay in American Literature and Cultural History*, expands his initial premise to show in his more recent work, *Making Americans: An Essay on Individualism and Money*, how money in America enforces our isolation from each other and from our selves. In the essay, "Symbol and Ideal in *Virgin Land*," which is included in Sacvan Bercovitch and Myra Jehlen, eds., *Ideology and Classic American Literature* (Cambridge: Cambridge University Press, 1987), Smith speaks of "the guilt intrinsic to the national errand into the wilderness. Like my teachers and academic colleagues, I had in this fashion lost the capacity for facing up to the tragic dimensions of the Westward Movement."

    Whereas Bercovitch and Jehlen focus on the revisionary potential in an expanded political and social discourse of American ideology, the present study employs psychoanalytic discourse and the dynamics of the American male's developmental process to uncover and reach a personal and cultural understanding of the repressed grief and underlying detrimental consequences of American idealism that in the past have been covered-up, omitted, and defended against in American critical discourse, as in American fiction itself. However, unlike Cushing Strout in *Making American Tradition: Visions and Revisions from Ben Franklin to Alice Walker*, I do not attempt to refute or re-write the traditional American myth, but to acknowledge the tremendous impact—both positive and unfavorable—of the American democratic spirit on the personal lives and creative imaginations of American fiction writers. Specifically, Strout discusses what he calls the "Tocquevillian vision" of the traditional American canon, which, as he quite correctly notes, omits the authorial voices of Southern, black, and female writers, most of whom focus primarily on American social, rather than ideological, issues.

6. This accusation was leveled at Hemingway in a benign way by his life-long friend General Charles (Buck) Lanham, who related the exchange in a written correspondence to Irvin and Marilyn Yalom, dated August 22, 1967. Reprinted in the Yaloms's essay, "Ernest Hemingway—A Psychiatric View," 487. According to D. W. Winnicott, in *Deprivation and Delinquency*, adolescents, who generally avoid "compromise, especially the use of identifications and vicarious experience, must start from scratch, ignoring all that has been worked out in the past history of our culture. Adolescents can be seen struggling to start again as if they had nothing they could take over from anyone" (152). Furthermore, in "Adolescent Immaturity" (in *Home Is Where We Start From*), Winnicott suggests that: "One of the exciting things about adolescent boys and girls can be said to be their idealism. They have not yet settled down into disillusionment, and the corollary of this is that they are free to formulate ideal plans" (165).

7. This position is held by many developmental theorists, some of the first and most influential of whom include Robert J. Stoller in *Presentations of Gender*, Talcott Parsons in *Social Structure and Personality*, Nancy Chodorow in *The Reproduction of Mothering*, Jessica Benjamin in *Bonds of Love*, and Beatrice B. Whiting and John W. M. Whiting in *Children of Six Cultures*.

8. This is an historical evaluation of masculine identity development and does not necessarily represent a contemporary norm. Nor does it take into consideration alternative, progressive, and in some ways, preferable, gender identity structures. This study, in fact, is dedicated, in part, to confounding historical psychoanalytic and sociological notions of a "feminine"-exclusive masculinity.

9. While this study acknowledges the enormous impact that separation theories have had on the historical and psychological development of American culture, and recognizes as well the consequential tendency in psychoanalytic thinking alternatively to blame and idealize the mother—both forms of matriphobia in which all of one's problems are believed to stem from the mother's actions, attitudes, and behavior toward the child—my ultimate intention in working within these historically supportable, though undesirable, assumptions, is to de-mystify them by tracing them to a previously sanctioned, yet emotionally stifling and self-destructive, masculine idealization of heroic autonomy and emotionally repressive utopian thinking.

10. In pursuing this line of critical thought, I am following a precedent set by such literary critics as Kenneth Lynn, who advanced the idea that the "childish qualities of nineteenth-century American literature had their origins in the historical circumstances that fostered childishness in an entire civilization." See Lynn's "Adulthood in American Literature," 290.

11. According to Harvey A. Kaplan, in "The Psychopathology of Nostalgia": "The ego ideal is an extension of this thought in that it serves as a substitute for the original narcissistic perfection. Later, Freud wrote 'what man projects before him as his ideal is the substitute for the lost narcissism of his childhood in which he was his own ideal.'

The function of the ego ideal is to restore the lost narcissism of childhood. The ego ideal is comprised of identifications with parental figures seen in glorified perspective, and it expresses what one desires to be.

The ego ideal in its fulfillment of lost narcissism creates images and moves the individual to search the environment for objects which resemble these idealized images. If the individual lacks the capacity to surmount the frustrations of his environment— either due to personal conflicts or to emptiness of his environment—he will be driven to erect pathological ego ideal formations characterized by grandiose narcissistic fantasies that are directed toward his self esteem" (470–71).

12. As Kenneth Lynn points out, "most of the front-rank writers of nineteenth-century America grew up in families in which the father was either dead, missing, physically crippled, or financially inept," which, he continues, "suggests the possibility that fears about growing up affected their literary imaginations." See Lynn's, "Adulthood in American Literature," 290.

13. In *Absent Fathers, Lost Sons*, Guy Corneau remarks that: "Since the beginning of the industrial era, there has been less and less prolonged contact between fathers and sons," and that as of 1988 in the United States one in five children lives in a fatherless home (11). Based primarily on the work of Talcott Parsons, Nancy Chodorow contends, in *The Reproduction of Mothering: Psychoanalysis and the Sociology of Gender*, that in America a boy "must attempt to develop a masculine gender identification and learn the masculine role in the absence of a continuous and ongoing personal relationship to his father (and in the absence of a continuously available masculine role model). . . . Sociologically, boys in father-absent and normally father-remote families develop a sense of what it is to be masculine through identification with cultural images of masculinity and men chosen as masculine models" (176). For a discussion of the boy's dependency on the mother and distance from the father see also Talcott Parsons's *Essays in Sociological Theory*.

14. J. Laplanche and J.-B. Pontalis define the "oedipus complex" as an "[o]rganized body of loving and hostile wishes which the child experiences toward its parents. In its so-called *positive* form, the complex appears as in the story of *Oedipus Rex:* a desire for the death of the rival—the parent of the same sex—and a sexual desire for the parent of the opposite sex. In its *negative* form, we find the reverse picture: love for the parent of the same sex, and jealous hatred for the parent of the opposite sex." *The Language of Psycho-Analysis*, 282–83. The ego ideal, or the idealized image or object with which the individual wishes to identify, is believed by Peter Blos to be "the heir to the negative oedipus complex," that is to say, the wishful conception of what one would like to be, emerges from the same psychic impulse that strives to be like (and be in love with) the idealized figure of the (usually the same-sex) parent. See Blos's "The Function of the Ego Ideal in Adolescence," 94–95. Also see Blos's "The Genealogy of the Ego Ideal," in which he points out that the development of an "age-adequate, workable" (realistic or attainable) ego ideal requires a working-through of the negative oedipus complex. Thus, the negative oedipus complex is associated with the reality-testing phase of psychic growth, in which the individual comes to accept the compromises and limitations of reality, and in which he or she begins to formulate the "structuralization of the mature ego ideal" which "reduces excessive self and object idealizations to the level of more realistic self and object appraisals" (47, 57). Not only is some degree of "mourning" required in the positive oedipus complex (when the incestuous object of desire is given up), but it is also a part of healthy psychic growth when the individual suffers the grief and pain of "giving up infantile ideal states of the self." See Hans W. Loewald, "The Waning of the Oedipus Complex," 751–75; and

W. G. Joffe and Joseph Sandler, "Notes on Pain, Depression, and Individuation," 394–424.

15. As Ihab Hassan suggests, the "neurosis of innocence" that defines the ruling dialectic of American culture "is a regressive force" that interrupts the American hero's initiation process into maturity, and "prevents the self from participating fully in the world." See Ihab Hassan, *Radical Innocence: Studies in the American Novel,* 40.

16. Andrew Delbanco, *The Puritan Ordeal,* 97.

17. Thomas Paine, "Common Sense," in *The Essential Writings of Thomas Paine,* 23–72.

18. Benjamin Franklin, *Benjamin Franklin's Autobiography,* 66.

19. Andrew Delbanco points out that in Franklin's celebration of the rigid and immaculate process of self-creation, "every reader also feels a terrible vacuity in Franklin's scheme . . . a literally unutterable sense of isolation in Franklin's universe of individual calculation—a sense of loss for which he barely has a language." See Andrew Delbanco's *The Puritan Ordeal,* 246.

20. Alexis de Tocqueville, *Democracy in America,* 33.

21. Sampson Reed, "Observations on the Growth of the Mind," in *The Transcendentalists: An Anthology,* 56.

22. William Henry Furness, "Remarks on the Four Gospels," in *The Transcendentalists: An Anthology,* 126.

23. Ralph Waldo Emerson, *The Journals and Miscellaneous Notebooks,* 7: 202. Joyce W. Warren in *The American Narcissus: Individualism and Women in Nineteenth-Century American Fiction,* perceptively remarks that Emerson's uncompromising defiance is more appropriate in a "rebellious adolescent" than in a grown man, whose lingering adherence to such self-absorption can only result in a narrow outlook on life and an alienation from friends and relatives alike (27). Nevertheless, as Emerson states in the essay "Self-Reliance," he willingly subjugated any and all human ties to his insular search for self-fulfillment: "I shun father and mother and wife and brother when my genius calls me." See Ralph Waldo Emerson, "Self-Reliance," in *Essays and Lectures,* 262.

24. Gay Wilson Allen, *Waldo Emerson,* 226–27.

25. Ralph L. Rusk, ed., *The Letters of Ralph Waldo Emerson,* 3: 9.

26. Leon Edel points out that, as early as 1838, James Russell Lowell noted how "exquisitely amusing" it was to see "how [Thoreau] imitated Emerson's tone and manner. With my eyes shut I shouldn't know them apart"; and seventeen years later, according to another observer, Thoreau was "still tying to imitate his idol." "The Mystery of Walden Pond," in *Stuff of Sleep and Dreams,* 55.

27. Henry David Thoreau, *Walden and Civil Disobedience,* 5 and 7.

28. Leon Edel in "The Mystery of Walden Pond," believes that Thoreau's intense attachment to Walden Pond resulted from the fact that his mother had first introduced him to the place when he was a young boy, implying by this that Thoreau's love affair with Nature allowed him to relive throughout his life his satisfying—and never severed—emotional attachment to his mother. Landscapes such as Walden, Edel maintains, "revisit the dreams of our lives, and when they have been associated with some all-enveloping figure, the landscape itself can become a mother; and nature, as we know, is Mother Nature for us all" (53). But as Edel further points out, since "no man wants to think of himself as helpless," or as dependent on his mother, Thoreau rebelliously asserted a "longing to be free," and finally, in a full-blown defense against maternal dependency, he "made a myth of self-reliance" (62).

29. Henry David Thoreau, *The Journals of Henry David Thoreau,* vols. 7–20 of *The Writings of Henry David Thoreau,* 5: 199.

30. Henry David Thoreau, *Familiar Letters & Index*, in *The Writings of Henry David Thoreau*, 6: 42.

31. Walt Whitman, *Leaves of Grass*, 261. D. H. Lawrence was quick to recognize the regressive urge in Whitman's democratic equation: "Democracy. En Masse. One Identity" equals "delicious . . . death, death, death, death" and the immortal oneness of childhood and infancy. See D. H. Lawrence, *Studies in Classical American Literature*, 175.

32. As a number of biographers and critics have pointed out, however, in later life Whitman traded in his abstract idealism for a more personal and intimate emotional commitment to a few select companions and friends. According to Quentin Anderson in *Making Americans: An Essay on Individualism and Money*, the later Whitman "surrendered an imperium of selfhood for the sake of love and acknowledgment of his place in the history of his time" (199).

33. In illustrating how the underlying narrative of repressed grief can co-exist within a heterogeneous interpretive field, one might note, for example, that with a slight change in psychological emphasis, "Roger Malvin's Burial" may be read, as in the past it has been by critics such as Frederick Crews in *The Sins of the Father: Hawthorne's Psychological Themes*, and Simon O. Lesser in *Fiction and the Unconscious*, as a story of oedipal parricide in which the son murders the father for the prize of the daughter/wife. Similarly, Frederick Crews, and Peter Shaw ("Fathers, Sons, and the Ambiguities of Revolution in 'My Kinsman, Major Molineux,' " 559–76), have viewed "My Kinsman, Major Molineux" as the son's oedipal fantasy of competition and conquest in relation to the powerful father. Alternatively, the story may be linked with other works by Hawthorne, such as "The Hollow of Three Hills," and *Fanshawe*, as an example of Hawthorne's post-Gothic literary concerns, or of the strain of perversity in his creative imagination which inclined him toward an exploration of the issues of guilt, criminology, and universal depravity in his fiction. The tale may also be paired with "Young Goodman Brown," because of its depiction of a young man's initiation into evil, and its historical specificity as a portrayal of New England's popular insurrections against corrupt and despotic colonial statesmen and governors. More generally, the story has been seen as an allegory of the American Revolution, and as the mythical deposing of a king. For additional psychological readings of Hawthorne's works see Mark Van Doren, *Nathaniel Hawthorne;* Louis B. Salomon, "Hawthorne and His Father: A Conjecture"; and Hyatt H. Waggoner, *Hawthorne: A Critical Study*.

34. Lewis, *American Adam*, 6.

35. Stuart P. Sherman, *The Genius of America*, 35.

36. See Richard Poirier, *A World Elsewhere: The Place of Style in American Literature;* Charles Feidelson, Jr., *Symbolism and American Literature;* and, F. O. Matthiessen, *American Renaissance: Art and Expression in the Age of Emerson and Whitman*.

37. True liberty, Lawrence writes in *Studies in Classic American Literature*, "will only begin when Americans discover . . . the deepest *whole* self of man, the self in its wholeness, not idealistic halfness" (13). "American Democracy," he says, is "a form of self-murder, always" (59). In Hawthorne, Lawrence observes the "two halves of manhood"—the good-conscious half and the demon-repressed half—"mutually destroying one another" (106). Finally, about Melville's *Moby-Dick*, Lawrence asserts that "Melville knew. He knew his race was doomed. . . . The idealist, doomed. The spirit, doomed" (169).

38. Leslie A. Fiedler, *Love and Death in the American Novel*, 338.

39. Richard Chase, *The American Novel and Its Tradition*, 13.

40. Yvor Winters, *Maule's Curse: Seven Studies in the History of American Obscurantism*, 22.
41. Lewis, *American Adam*, 10.
42. See Murray Parkes, " 'Seeking' and 'Finding' a Lost Object: Evidence from Recent Studies of the Reaction to Bereavement"; and Erwin Stengel, "Studies on the Psychopathology of Compulsive Wandering."
43. See Martha Wolfenstein, "How Is Mourning Possible?" 113–14.
44. John Bowlby, "Pathological Mourning and Childhood Mourning," 535.
45. John Munder Ross, "Oedipus Revisited: Laius and the 'Laius Complex,' " 187.
46. *Mark Twain's Letters*, 49.
47. Herman Melville, "The Paradise of Bachelors and the Tartarus of Maids," in *The Piazza Tales and Other Prose Pieces*, vol. 9 of *The Writings of Herman Melville*, 322.
48. Ernest Hemingway, "Cross-Country Snow," in *In Our Time*, 110.
49. Mark Twain, "The $30,000 Bequest," in *Mark Twain's Short Stories*, 606.
50. In framing the moral of "The $30,000 Bequest," Twain may also have had a private bone to pick with his father who died when Twain was twelve years old, but not without leaving his family all but penniless, except for seventy-five acres of Tennessee Land that he swore on his death-bed would reap unimaginable financial profit in the years to come. As Twain writes in *The Autobiography of Mark Twain:* "it would soon make us all rich and happy." And so, he explains: "We straightway turned our waiting eyes upon Tennessee. . . . It kept us hoping and hoping during forty years and forsook us at last. It put our energies to sleep and made visionaries of us—dreamers and indolent" (24).
51. One should not circumvent too hastily the recognition of homoerotic elements or, as Leslie Fiedler phrases it in *Love and Death in the American Novel*, the "sacred marriage of males," as a psycho-social dynamic common to the three stories under consideration here. On the one hand, it might be argued, as Freud does in *Three Essays on the Theory of Sexuality* (1905), that the regressive inclination of the male characters in these tales leads to a reawakening of an original, or pregenital, "psychical hermaphrodism," or bisexual disposition (144). According to Freud, regression to the primitive stages of development can activate a person's unconscious homosexual potential. In a psychoanalytically related way, the regressive fantasies of Mr. and Mrs. Foster in Twain's story, in which they indulge in idealistic dreams of omnipotence and total hedonistic pleasure, additionally invite the implication that fantasies of preoedipal, or oral-anal, regression perhaps led Twain to conclude intuitively that gender difference between the Foster couple may be preempted, or at the very least viewed as irrelevant to their psychological drama. On the other hand, one might argue, as current studies of gender development have revealed, that there is an absence of "evidence to suggest that all males negotiate a homosexual phase of development," and therefore that "males should not be conceptualized as universally capable of homosexual 'regression' since there is no universally experienced homosexual phase of early childhood" (Friedman, *Male Homosexuality*, 233).

    This dispute with regard to American literature written by male authors—between the assertion of an adult male homoeroticism versus a regressive, pregenital psychological tendency—remains, however, in the realm of clinical research and theoretical speculation, and while I would acknowledge that a serious consideration of homoerotic issues in the fiction of Melville, Twain, and Hemingway is warranted, both from a literary and psychoanalytic perspective (particularly in view of the seemingly "homoerotic" relationships between Ishmael and Queequeg, Huckleberry Finn and Jim, and the male-male bonding in so much of Hemingway's fiction), I have deliberately chosen in this study to explore and pursue the interpretive possibilities that I believe may be gained by focusing on the latter, insufficiently explored, regressive pregenital approach.

52. Hemingway, *In Our Time*, 129.

53. Herman Melville, *Pierre; or, the Ambiguities*, vol. 7 of *The Writings of Herman Melville*, 87 and 167.

54. The term *code hero* originally was coined *not* by Hemingway himself but by his critics. Initially it was employed by such New Critics as Cleanth Brooks and Robert Penn Warren to describe the quality of a person's (particularly a sportsman's) ability to display "grace under pressure." It has been described both as a set of "game rules," and as a moral code that includes courage, dignity, and honor when faced with athletic, military, and philosophical challenges requiring mental and physical fortitude. Hemingway's cultural critics have used the term *code hero* to describe a person who, through ritualistic behavior and self-discipline, imposes meaning and order onto what the existentialist philosopher (and perhaps the emotionally depressed person as well) might view as a fundamentally aimless, destitute, and meaningless reality.

55. A. E. Hotchner, *Papa Hemingway: A Personal Memoir*, 293–94.

56. Mark Twain, "The Czar's Soliloquy," in Charles Neider, ed., *Mark Twain: Life As I Find It*, 272.

57. *Mark Twain—Howells Letters*, 248.

58. Mark Twain's letters, filed on microfilm in the Mark Twain Archives of the library at Elmira College in Elmira, New York.

59. The guilt Twain felt at not having been able to be at his daughter's bedside during her illness (he was touring Europe, and, in fact, had not seen Susy for over a year), undoubtedly rendered problematic his ability to work through and overcome his grief for this tragic personal loss.

60. Henry A. Murray, "Dead to the World: The Passions of Herman Melville," in *Essays in Self-Destruction*, 27–28. Rpt. in Edwin S. Shneidman, "The Deaths of Herman Melville," in *Melville and Hawthorne in the Berkshires*, 142–43. Murray's fascination with Melville culminated in a full-length work on him which remained incomplete at Murray's death; but if you stand outside the home in which Murray's widow still resides, you can see the sculpted figure of a whale perched on the eaves of the house.

Notes to Chapter 1

1. Herman Melville, *Pierre; or, the Ambiguities*, vol. 7 of *The Writings of Herman Melville*, 33.

2. For a summary discussion of the "rapprochement phase" of development see John B. McDevitt, "The Role of Internalization in the Development of Object Relations During the Separation-Individuation Phase"; and, M. S. Mahler, "Rapprochement Subphase of the Separation-Individuation Process," 487–506. During the rapprochement phase, according to McDevitt, on the one hand, the child "wants to fully exercise his new-found autonomy and independence; on the other hand, he painfully feels the loss of his former sense of omnipotence and is distressed by his relative helplessness" (332).

3. Daniel N. Stern, *Diary of a Baby*, 98.

4. Herman Melville, *Moby-Dick; or, The Whale*, vol. 6 of *The Writings of Herman Melville*, 414. All subsequent citations from *Moby-Dick; or, The Whale* will be to this edition and will be noted parenthetically.

5. Speaking of the sperm whale, Ishmael concludes that: "The whale, therefore, must see one distinct picture on this side, and another distinct picture on that side; while all between must be profound darkness and nothingness to him" (330). Later, Ishmael

adds that although man, unlike the whale, "can take in an undiscriminating sweep of things at one glance, it is quite impossible for him, attentively, and completely, to examine any two things—however large or however small—at one and the same instant of time . . ." (330).

6. Herman Melville, "Hawthorne and His Mosses," *The Writings of Herman Melville: The Piazza Tales & Other Prose Pieces: 1839–1860*, vol. 9, 239.

7. In this same spirit in which Melville valorized perpetual change and growth, and condemned stagnation and the comfort of complacency, he wrote to Nathaniel Hawthorne on November 17, 1851: "Lord, when shall we be done growing? As long as we have anything more to do, we have done nothing. . . . Lord, when shall we be done changing? Ah! it's a long stage, and no inn in sight, and night coming, and the body cold." Letter reprinted in *Moby-Dick* (Norton Critical Edition), 567. In an earlier letter to Hawthorne, Melville wrote of his own personal past: "Until I was twenty-five, I had no development at all. From my twenty-fifth year I date my life." Letter dated June 1(?), 1851. Reprinted in *Moby-Dick* (Norton Critical Edition), 559–60.

8. In Melville's *Pierre; or, the Ambiguities* (New York: Signet, 1979), as in *Moby-Dick*, the pivotal moment of crisis in the hero's life occurs when he is coldly rejected by the once omnipotent and all-fulfilling mother—the "pure and unimpairable" (16) Mary Glendinning—which gives to Pierre, as it gives to Pip and Ishmael, a "feeling entirely lonesome, and orphan-like," and he suddenly sees himself as "driven out an Ishmael into the desert, with no maternal Hagar to accompany and comfort him" (89). With Pierre's disillusionment in the abstract heroic father, its archaic prototype, the all-providing, utopian Paradise of the mother, symbolized not only by Mrs. Glendinning in the novel but by all of Saddle Meadows, is brought down as well, and Pierre experiences a long-postponed loss and grief in relation to them both. Yet, true to Melville's philosophy in *Moby-Dick*, the disappointments and grief that Pierre suffers are narcissistically embraced by him; he has "ringed himself in with the grief of Eternity" (304), and he comes to believe, as Ahab does, that his "topmost greatness lies" in his "topmost grief." Given this new outlook on things, Pierre's only recourse, as he sees it, is to become a writer.

9. Leo Bersani, "Incomparable America," in *Major Literary Characters: Ahab*, 221.

10. Through the "double-doom of his parents" (287), the "twice-disinherited" (199) Pierre also cuts himself off from all means of external parental support. He has become a "little toddler," who is for the first time "learning to stand by itself!" (296). Like Ishmael, Pierre enters what Melville describes with remarkable accuracy as the child's rapprochement phase of development, with its devastating grief from separation, lack of connectedness, and terrifying isolation. At first, Melville explains, the child: "shrieks and implores, and will not try to stand at all, unless both father and mother uphold it; then a little more bold, it must, as least, feel one parental hand, else again the cry and the tremble; long time is it ere by degrees this child comes to stand without any support" (296). But like the child who cannot yet tolerate such independence, who—like both Ishmael and Ahab—was traumatically and too soon forced away from the mother and out into the world, Pierre still "clings" and "clamors for the support of its mother the world, and its father the Deity" (296). At the close of the novel, however, Pierre is unable to reconcile "all the ambiguities which hemmed him in"—Isabel and Lucy, grief and joy, isolation and dependency, the city and the country—and he, like Ishmael, is trapped in the intense anxiety of a seemingly unresolvable rapprochement crisis. Bemoaning his fate of ambivalence, Pierre laments: "Oh, seems to me, there should be two ceaseless steeds for a bold man to ride,—the Land and the Sea; and like circus-men we should never dismount, but only be steadied

and rested by leaping from one to the other, while still, side by side, they both race round the sun" (348–49).

For Pierre it is "merely hell in both worlds" (360), but he rises to his fate, perceiving that true greatness lies in bearing the burden of his grief and ambivalence, and he resolves to "mold a trumpet of the flames, and, with my breath of flame, breathe back my defiance!" (360). Pierre is unable to receive catharsis through his grief and self-pity, however, because he has displaced his personal grief and gloom onto "all-stretchable philosophy" (339), and has narcissistically embraced that philosophy of nihilism in an attempt to achieve greatness as a martyr who, in the lonely isolation of an indefinite universe, grapples with the fire-spewing dragon of darkness and evil.

11. See John Bowlby's *Attachment,* and *Separation,* vols. 1 and 2 of his series *Attachment and Loss;* and D. W. Winnicott's discussion of "good enough" mothering in *Playing and Reality.* The "good-enough" mother, Winnicott explains, "is one who makes active adaptation to the infant's needs, an active adaptation that gradually lessens, according to the infant's growing ability to account for failure of adaptation and to tolerate the results of frustration" (10). According to Bowlby, mourning is essentially an act of self-preservation through which the individual hopes to come to terms with a disappointing reality and the injury that life has inflicted upon him or her through the loss of a loved one. This process demands a withdrawal of psychic attention away from reality onto the self. Such emotional withdrawal in a mother would have an adverse effect on her ability to empathize with her child to the degree that is necessary to function as what Winnicott describes as a "good-enough" mother. The effects of the mother's failure to respond and adapt adequately to the infant's needs might predictably result in "anxious and insecure attachment" behavior "or else a vehement assertion of self-sufficiency" in which the child grows up "to be tough and hard." In either case, a "prolonged absence of conscious grieving" is the likely consequence of such maternal deprivation (214–30).

12. Edmund Bergler identifies Melville's white whale as the "white-breast" of the dangerous, devouring "bad" pregenital mother against whom Ahab launches his enraged attacks. Bergler also points out that Melville's "*white whale* is reminiscent of the *white* skin of the mother," and hypothesizes: "Moby Dick equals monster or preoedipal mother." See "A Note on Herman Melville," 385–97. Melville's imaginative movement from adulthood back toward comforting preoedipal experience is described by Leslie Fiedler in *Love and Death in the American Novel,* as the removal of his subject "from the landbound world of history back toward the oceanic, which is to say, an archaic, or 'antemosaic' world of portents and monsters, unchanged since the days of creation" (382). Henry A. Murray contends "that the *imago* of the mother as well as the *imago* of the father is contained in the Whale" (414). See Murray, "In Nomine Diaboli," in *Critical Essays on Herman Melville's "Moby-Dick",* 408–20.

13. In the novel *Pierre; or, the Ambiguities,* that Melville began writing within a few weeks of completing *Moby-Dick,* one does not need the assistance of psychoanalysis to identify the central role played by the ambivalently loved mother, whom the son both desires to cling to and to identify with, and at the same time wishes to distance himself from, in an effort to establish his autonomy and separateness of self. Henry A. Murray, in his introduction to *Pierre,* maintains that the "entire novel, indeed, could be apperceived on one level as a young man's desperate attempt to break away from his matriarchal house of bondage." See Henry A. Murray's "Introduction," to *Pierre, or the Ambiguities* (Hendricks House), lv.

14. See McDevitt's "The Role of Internalization in the Development of Object Relations,"

in which he calls this a "negative outcome of the rapprochement-crisis"; and, he explains, if this "crisis leads to intense ambivalence and splitting of the object world into 'good' and 'bad,' the maternal representation may be internalized as an unassimilated, dissociated foreign body, as a hostile, 'bad' introject. The relationship with the actual mother is preserved, that is, protected from the child's hostility, by introjection of the representation of the 'bad' mother" (334).

15. That Moby Dick's aggression is a projection of Ahab's own hatred and anger toward the whale is a long-held notion in Melville criticism, just as the reciprocal quality of persecutory aggression is a standard tenet in psychoanalysis and object-relations theory, originating perhaps in Freud's discussion of aggression, guilt, and sado-masochism in *New Introductory Lectures on Psycho-Analysis* (1933[1932]), 22: 3–158.

16. The oedipal and preoedipal views are not contradictory here in that both primary (preoedipal) and secondary (oedipal) castration symbolize a gesture of the loss of, or forced separation from, the mother. Perhaps this explains why Melville's critics fall on both sides of this issue, often embracing a theoretical explanation that describes Moby Dick as both a maternal and a paternal agent. Robert K. Martin views Ahab as an aggressive, phallic, and logocentric symbolic construct in *Hero, Captain, and Stranger: Male Friendship, Social Critique, and Literary Form in the Sea Novels of Herman Melville*. David Leverenz sees the novel as a whole as a "projection of male penis envy," but also maintains that "Ahab rages to be beaten by an enormous symbol of both the father's and the mother's power, a sperm whale and milk-white breast, at once mutilating and abandoning." *Manhood and the American Renaissance*, 290–94. Similarly, Newton Arvin claims that Moby Dick "embodies neither the father merely nor the mother but, by a process of condensation, the *parental* principle inclusively." "The Whale," in *Herman Melville*, 151–93; rpt. in Hershel Parker and Harrison Hayford, eds., *"Moby-Dick" as Doubloon: Essays and Extracts (1851–1970)*, 211. However, since Ahab's traumatic experience of maternal deprivation is clearly stated by Melville, and since the absence of a real father figure in Ahab's young life suggests that oedipal competition with the father was not a substantial threat to his psychosexual development, it seems more likely that the agent of the symbolic castration Ahab suffers is not the father but the mother.

17. This phrase was coined by Helene Deutsch in her essay "Absence of Grief," 12–22. Deutsch concludes her study with the statement: "I suspect that many life stories which seem to be due to a masochistic attitude are simply the result of such strivings for the realization of unresolved affects" (21).

18. Janine Chasseguet-Smirgel, *Sexuality and Mind: The Role of the Father and the Mother in the Psyche*, 127.

19. Edward Stone, for example, in *A Certain Morbidness*, argues that "Ahab is not merely a creation apart from Ishmael but an extension of him" (32).

20. See Viggo W. Jensen and Thomas A. Petty, "The Fantasy of Being Rescued in Suicide." Jensen and Petty describe the "prototype for the relationship the suicidal person seeks with the rescuer" as a state that "probably existed originally between the infant and mother at a time when they shared a common ego, chiefly the mother's, and each responded directly to the unconscious of the other as though it were his own; this state is temporarily reinstated by regression in the patient contemplating suicide" (334). Whether or not this state ever actually existed in the life of the infant, even during its life in the womb, is questionable, as is the real existence of an "omnipotent" mother. I tend to concur with Daniel Stern, in *The Interpersonal World of the Infant*, who states that the omnipotent mother—either benevolent or hostile—is an imaginary figure belonging to a regressive fantasy. The dangers of viewing the mother as an

omnipotent figure, and the state of infancy as an experience of mother-child symbiosis devoid of agency on the part of the infant, is discussed by Nancy Chodorow in *Feminism and Psychoanalytic Theory*. Sydney Smith, in "The Golden Fantasy: A Regressive Reaction to Separation Anxiety," describes the regressive fantasy of omnipotence, and the fantasy omnipotent mother herself, as embodying the *wish* "to have all of one's needs met in a relationship hallowed by perfection . . . to be cared for so completely that no demand will be made on the patient except his capacity for passively taking in." Smith adds: "Implicit in the fantasy is the *notion* [my italics] that such a blissful state was at one time actual but now has been lost" (311). Specifically with regard to the rescue fantasy in suicide, Jensen and Petty maintain that the imagined omnipotent mother's "[f]ailure to come to his rescue probably would have been understood . . . as proof of [the mother's] abandonment" (331).

21. See James Masterson, *The Search for the Real Self.*
22. C. Murray Parkes, " 'Seeking' and 'Finding' a Lost Object: Evidence from Recent Studies of the Reaction to Bereavement," 188.
23. Erwin Stengel, "Studies on the Psychopathology of Compulsive Wandering," 254.
24. See McDevitt's "The Role of Internalization in the Development of Object Relations."
25. The womb imagery in Melville's early novels has been recognized by many of his critics. Charles J. Haberstroh, for example, points out how Tommo, in *Typee*, "can comfortably convert tomb to womb, and prison to 'Happy Valley' of tranquil security." *Melville and Male Identity*, 34. In *Mardi, Omoo*, and *Redburn* as well, Haberstroh writes, Melville succumbs to "the temptation to allow his narrator to fall into the role of dependent child in hopes of gaining support for him from individuals who would serve Melville's need to fictionally restore some of the security of his own childhood" (33). Helen Petrullo sees Tommo's entrance by sea into Nakuheva bay in *Typee* as a voyage into the amniotic universe of the mother's womb. See Petrullo's "The Neurotic Hero of *Typee*." Neal Tolchin, in *Mourning, Gender, and Creativity in the Art of Herman Melville,* builds on Petrullo's interpretation by viewing the entire island landscape as a "womb-like scene of a 'narrow valley, with its steep and close adjoining sides' " (57). In his essay, "*Moby-Dick:* The American National Epic," Richard Slotkin discusses Melville's "island" fantasies, which evoke "the dream-remembered, womblike haven of an innocent childhood, ruled and ordered by a maternal figure." In *Twentieth-Century Interpretations of "Moby-Dick"*, 15. Melville's "flight from home" in his novels, Frederick Rosenheim affirms, represents his birth fantasies and suggests his desire to go "back to mother, to the first voyage from her womb to her arms and breasts." See Rosenheim's "Flight from Home: Some Episodes in the Life of Herman Melville, 10.
26. Like "the universal cannibalism of the sea" (274) in *Moby-Dick*, the cannibalism of the natives in Melville's *Typee* and *Mardi* is explained by Rosenheim and Murray as Melville's image of the devouring oral-aggressive mother.
27. Henry A. Murray, "Introduction" to Melville's *Pierre; or, the Ambiguities*, xxvi.
28. Madelon Sprengnether recognizes in Freud's and Jung's conception of the mother imago "the simultaneously terrifying and renewing powers of the unconscious." *The Spectral Mother*, 98.
29. For one of the more comprehensive discussions of Melville's sources for *Moby-Dick*, see *Moby-Dick: or, The Whale* (Northwestern University Press/Newberry Edition).
30. As D. H. Lawrence remarked in *Studies in Classic American Literature*, Ahab's obsession is "the Gethsemane of the human soul seeking the last self-conquest, the last attainment of extended consciousness—infinite consciousness" (167).
31. Because of Melville's use of archaic pronouns in this paragraph, and his reference to

Ahab's reveries in the preceding paragraph, there is some confusion as to whether these are Ahab's or Ishmael's thoughts. Whether consciously or not, Melville seems to imply that Ahab and Ishmael share this utopian immortality fantasy.

32. The father, Chasseguet-Smirgel explains, "is absent from utopias, and the holding of children in common and the absence of inheritance which is also often mentioned lead to an effacing of the paternal image" (96).

33. Haberstroh, *Melville and Male Identity*, 17; Leon Howard, *Herman Melville: A Biography*, 16–17.

34. Frederick Rosenheim, in "Flight from Home," speaks of the "host of father figures" Melville "conjures up" in his fiction, all of whom "are idealized, powerful and protecting," as if to say that "father is not the weak, ineffectual bankrupt, incapable of protecting anybody, but is strong and powerful. He is also not the father who was unexcited about Herman's birth and thought him backward and slow but one who worships Herman and is ready to devote himself to Herman" (6–7).

35. If, in his novel, *Pierre*, as Henry Murray believes, "many years before Freud, Melville . . . discovered the Oedipus Complex" ("Introduction" to *Pierre*, xxxvii), Melville also demonstrated, through Pierre's tribulations, that an adolescent boy's ego-ideal identification with an abstract, heroic father image represents a continuation of his primitive infantile omnipotence and narcissism in relation to the archaic mother, and that when the moment of disillusionment with the heroic father arrives, it brings with it the grief of mother-loss in addition to the grief of father-hunger. Together these losses amount to a devastating narcissistic injury for Pierre, and awaken him not only to the threat of oedipal castration and the incest taboo, but also to his regressive desire to reunite with the mother.

36. Sigmund Freud, "A Disturbance of Memory on the Acropolis," in *Standard Edition* 22: 239–48. For Freud, to see the Parthenon temple was to feel the "guilt" or "filial piety" of the oedipal son's feeling toward the father of "undervaluation which took the place of the overvaluation of earlier childhood" (247–48).

37. Irving B. Harrison, "On the Maternal Origins of Awe." Also see Harrison's "On Freud's View of the Infant-Mother Relationship and of the Oceanic Feeling—Some Subjective Influences."

38. To the newborn infant, death, suffocation, and drowning are believed to be linked fears originating from the birth experience, which resurface again during weaning or removal from the breast. See Frank S. Caprio, "A Study of Some Psychological Reactions During Pre-Pubescence to the Idea of Death."

39. John Bowlby, in "Pathological Mourning and Childhood Mourning," speaks of protest as a distorted variation of expressed mourning. Searching and angry protesting directed at the lost object are, according to C. Murray Parkes, two common displaced grief responses. " 'Seeking' and 'Finding' a Lost Object: Evidence from Recent Studies of the Reaction to Bereavement," 187–201.

40. Haberstroh discusses Herman's losses in relation to his idealized father and older brother in *Melville and Male Identity*. Philip Young writes that Melville "had as a boy idolized his pious father," and analyzes Melville's "destruction of belief" in both his father and God. *The Private Melville*, 4. Leon Howard writes of Melville's ultimate disappointment with "a brilliant older brother and an idealized father" (*Herman Melville: A Biography*, 22). Newton Arvin attributes Melville's "emotional crisis" as a boy, characterized by "abandonment" and "desertion," to the fact that he was "[d]eprived of an idolized father on the very verge of adolescence" (*Herman Melville*, 23). The underlying premise of Neal Tolchin's analysis of grief in Melville's works is that

Herman's ambivalence toward his father before he died resulted in a "lifelong inability to finish mourning for his father" and a "deep need to work through conflicted grief" (*Mourning, Gender, and Creativity in the Art of Herman Melville*, xii, xvi). To attribute Melville's repression of grief to his identification with the repressed Victorian social codes of behavior endorsed by Melville's mother is, however, a reduction of a more profound psychological trauma to what more realistically may be identified as a supporting, yet less psychologically important, explanation for Melville's repressed grief. Henry A. Murray and Philip Young endorse the hypothesis that Herman's disillusionment in his idealized father was exacerbated when he discovered, in his late teens, that Allen Melville, like Pierre's father in Melville's *Pierre*, fathered an illegitimate daughter. See Young's discussion of this controversy in *The Private Melville*.

41. As John Bowlby writes: "Evidence at present available strongly suggests that adults whose mourning takes a pathological course are likely before their bereavement to have been prone to make affectional relationships . . . marked by a high degree of anxious attachment, suffused with overt or covert ambivalence." *Loss: Sadness and Depression*, vol. 3 of *Attachment and Loss*, 202. According to Helene Deutsch: "Psychoanalytic findings indicate that guilt feelings toward the lost object, as well as ambivalence, may disturb the normal course of mourning." ("Absence of Grief," 12–13).

42. John Bowlby, *Separation: Anxiety and Anger*, vol. 2 of *Attachment and Loss*, 213.

43. See Arvin's *Herman Melville*; Lewis Mumford's *Herman Melville*; Ludwig Lewishon's *The Story of American Literature*; Martin Leonard Pops's "In the Splendid Labyrinth: *Moby-Dick*," in *The Melville Archetype*; Edmund Bergler's essay, "A Note on Herman Melville," 385–97; Henry A. Murray's "Dead to the World: The Passions of Herman Melville," in *Essays in Self-Destruction*, 7–29; and, Frederick Rosenheim's "Flight from Home: Some Episodes in the Life of Herman Melville, 1–30.

44. One might add in support of this theory Henry A. Murray's observation that Herman's unusually early appearance of teeth at the age of three months infused his satisfying breastfeeding experience with an element of oral-aggressive trauma, and intensified Maria's desire to wean her infant early. Murray describes this event as Herman's "virtual expulsion from the paradise of his mother's embracing arms," and believes it accounts for his lifelong association of "deprivation and grief" with outward aggression toward the world and an inner aggression in the form of depression, guilt, a need for punishment, suicide, and emotional numbness ("Dead to the World," 17). In his short essay, "A Note on Herman Melville," Edmund Bergler perceives at the heart of *Moby-Dick* a drama characteristic of a child's masochistic attachment to the preoedipal mother, in which one can observe the "infant's fantasy of cruel, pre-Oedipal mother of earliest infancy" (387).

45. See Arvin's *Herman Melville*, 30.

46. Letter from Melville to Nathaniel Hawthorne, Nov. 17, 1851. Reprinted in *Moby-Dick* (Norton Critical Edition), 566.

Edmund Bergler believes that, in *Moby-Dick*, "Melville rescued himself from masochistic submission [to the devouring 'pre-Oedipal mother'] by denying it via identification with the fanatic and openly aggressive captain."

The oedipal theme of maternal incest in *Pierre*, Bergler maintains, is used merely as a defensive "countermeasure instituted" to protect Melville from "more deeply repressed oral-masochistic dangers" in relation to the persecuting "bad" mother ("A Note on Herman Melville," 388–91).

According to James F. Masterson, in *The Search for the Real Self*, Thomas Wolfe, in order to "deal with his feelings of disillusionment, betrayal, and loss," originating in a disturbed mother-infant relationship, "submerged himself in self-dramatization, fantasy, and a lifelong search for an omnipotent mother figure who would acknowledge his emerging self" (218). Wolfe, as I suggest about Melville, never matured emotionally past the stage of adolescence, and like Melville, Wolfe's infantile desire and aggression toward the disappointing and longed-for mother emerges in his creative writing process. Remarkably suggestive of Melville's feelings upon completing *Moby-Dick*, Wolfe once wrote after he had finished one of his own novels: "I have written it almost with a child's heart, it has come from me with a child's wonder and my pages are engraved not only with what is simple and plain but with monstrous evil as if the Devil were speaking with a child's tongue." Elizabeth Nowell, *Thomas Wolfe, A Biography*, 105–6.

47. Edwin S. Shneidman, "The Deaths of Herman Melville," in *Melville and Hawthorne in the Berkshires*, 118–43.

48. In a letter to Hawthorne, dated June 1?, 1851, Melville wrote that the literary reputation of his friend "is in the ascendant. My dear Sir, they begin to patronize. All Fame is patronage." As for himself, he proclaims, "Let me be infamous: there is no patronage in *that*. What 'reputation' H.M. has is horrible. Think of it! To go down to posterity is bad enough, any way; but to go down as a 'man who lived among the cannibals'!" Letter reprinted in *Moby-Dick* (Norton Critical Edition), 559. If, for Melville, greatness is directly a consequence of grief, then "Fame" can only be won by repudiating goodness and embracing evil. Perhaps, then, Melville counted upon the fact that he had written a "wicked book" as an assurance that he would earn for himself a place in posterity, even if the prize that was coming to him was not fame, but infamy; and it was this assurance that allowed him to feel, upon completing *Moby-Dick*, that he was "spotless as the lamb." Letter to Hawthorne, dated November 17, 1851. Reprinted in *Moby-Dick* (Norton Critical Edition), 566.

As Shneidman concludes his thoughts on Melville's relationship to death and fame:

Out of Melville's combination of his great sense of inner pride, his bravura inner life style, his imperious reaction to hostility and to criticism, his conscious and unconscious attrition of the social side of his literary life—out of all of these diverse elements grew his concern with death and annihilation and his enormous investment in his post-self. In this sense, Melville wrote not so much for his own time as he did for any appropriate (that is, any appreciating) time to follow—for what Leyda has called a "posthumous celestial glory." Melville was partially dead during much of his own life, but he more than compensated for that lugubrious limitation by writing in such a way that he could realistically plan to live mostly after he had died. 'On life and death this old man walked.' " ("The Deaths of Herman Melville," 143)

Notes to Chapter 2

1. Margaret Sanborn, *Mark Twain: The Bachelor Years*, 33.
2. Also see Albert Bigelow Paine, *Mark Twain: A Biography*, 1: 36.
3. Printed in the New York *American* (May 26, 1907); reprinted in *Mark Twain: Life As I Find It*, 388.
4. Mark Twain, in *Mark Twain's Notebook*, 240.
5. See Bernard De Voto's chapter, "Symbols of Despair," in *Mark Twain's America and Mark Twain at Work*.

6. See Twain's *New York Herald* interview (Oct. 16, 1900); reprinted in *Life As I Find It*, 334.
7. According to D. W. Winnicott, a transitional object becomes operable when one realizes that one's destructive impulse—which for Twain was his humor—does not in fact result in destruction, indicating that it is not outside the area of objects under the subject's mental control. *Playing and Reality*, 94.
8. Twain demonstrates this point in Chapter 7 of *Life on the Mississippi*, 47–49.
9. Van Wyck Brooks, *The Ordeal of Mark Twain*, 38.
10. Susan Gillman, *Dark Twins: Imposture and Identity in Mark Twain's America*, 6 and 93.
11. See reprinted *New York Herald* (Oct. 16, 1900) interview with Twain in *Life As I Find It*, 334; and Mark Twain, *The Autobiography of Mark Twain*, 157.
12. Rachel H. Varble, *Jane Clemens: The Story of Mark Twain's Mother*, 269.
13. See *The Autobiography of Mark Twain*, 248–49.
14. Erik Erikson, *Identity and the Life Cycle*, 142.
15. Mark Twain, "The Mysterious Stranger" (1899), in *The Mysterious Stranger*, 214.
16. Letter dated Nov. 12, 1870; reprinted in *Mark Twain's Letters*, 177–78.
17. Samuel and Doris Webster, "Whitewashing Jane Clemens," 531.
18. A. B. Paine describes Twain's childhood as "curious," and "full of weird, fantastic impressions and contradictory influences" (*Mark Twain: A Biography*, 1: 14). Rachel Varble characterizes the infant Sam as "a fury of a baby," adding: "Nothing agreed with him, nothing pleased him" (*Jane Clemens*, 122).
19. Mark Twain, "My First Lie, And How I Got Out Of It," in *The Man That Corrupted Hadleyburg and Other Essays and Stories*, Stormfield Edition of the *Writings of Mark Twain*, 159.
20. Although Guy Cardwell, in his biography of Twain, sensed that Mark Twain "sought to master the world in order to protect himself from it," and that he "felt himself to be emotionally alone, longed for affection and approval . . ." Cardwell never attempted to explore the psychological implication of these insights. *The Man Who Was Mark Twain*, 159.
21. In *The Autobiography of Mark Twain*, Twain is vague about identifying exactly what age he was when the stories he relates from his childhood occurred.
22. Forrest G. Robinson, *In Bad Faith: The Dynamics of Deception in Mark Twain's America*, 32.
23. Mark Twain, *The Adventures of Tom Sawyer*, vol. 4 of *The Works of Mark Twain*, 41.
24. Mark Twain, "Hunting the Deceitful Turkey," *Mark Twain's Short Stories*, 626.
25. It is interesting to note here that the astonishment which the boy in the story feels when he discovers that a "lame" creature was able to outwit him, mirrors Twain's amazement, expressed in *The Autobiography of Mark Twain*, over the fact that his mother, "who at forty was so delicate of body as to be accounted a confirmed invalid and destined to pass away soon," lived to the "mighty age" of eighty-eight (25).
26. D. W. Winnicott, "Stealing and Telling Lies," *The Child, the Family, and the Outside World*, 162–63.
27. Entry from Dec. 1897, in *Notebook*, 346.
28. Forrest Robinson recognizes the ancillary status of the game's content relative to its dynamic function—which is to discipline the child—when he concludes about the relationship between Tom and Aunt Polly:

The old woman's expectation that her nephew will break her rules is the indirect manifestation of the fact that she places great value on Tom's rebelliousness. To be sure, she is totally unaware of this contradictory wrinkle in her makeup. It is equally evident, however, that the rules are relatively unimportant except as occasions for the game, and that the game cannot begin until a rule has been broken. Paradoxically, then, Tom serves his aunt best when he seeks to escape detection in the violation of her orders. (*In Bad Faith*, 32)

29. Edith Jacobson, *The Self and the Object World*, 102.
30. In *The Autobiography of Mark Twain*, Twain also wrote: "I never knew Henry to do a vicious thing toward me or toward anyone else—but he frequently did righteous ones that cost me as heavily" (33).
31. In *Identity and the Life Cycle*, Erikson describes a "negative identity" as "an identity perversely based on all those identifications and roles which, at critical stages of development, had been presented to the individual as most undesirable or dangerous, and yet also as most real" (141).
32. Erikson writes that "self-esteem" is dependent on the "confidence that one's ability to maintain inner sameness and continuity . . . is matched by sameness and continuity of one's meaning for others" (*Identity*, 94).
33. Mark Twain, "On Training Children," in *Life As I Find It*, 210.
34. Mark Twain, "Which Was the Dream?" in *Mark Twain's Which Was the Dream? and Other Symbolic Writings of the Later Years*.
35. Although Twain described his father as "very grave" and "rather austere," which is far from "namby-pamby," he left the task of punishing his children to his wife; and as Twain remembers, his father only "laid his hand" on him twice, once for telling a lie, which astonished Twain. In retrospect, this, he says, "showed me how unsuspicious he was, for I knew I had told him a million before that" (*Notebook*, 271).
36. Charles W. Wahl, "Suicide as a Magical Act," in *Clues to Suicide*, 23.
37. The fragment, which appears in De Voto's *Mark Twain at Work*, was assigned the name, "Boy's Manuscript," by A. B. Paine, when he filed it among the Mark Twain Papers.
38. Coleman O. Parsons, "The Devil and Samuel Clemens," in *A Casebook on Mark Twain's Wound*, 187.
39. Although Twain says, in *The Autobiography of Mark Twain*, that the year was 1850, which would make him fifteen years old, he admits that he is not sure of the exact date (50).
40. Phyllis Greenacre, "The Family Romance of the Artist," 35.
41. A. B. Paine briefly relates this episode in Twain's life in *Mark Twain: A Biography* (1: 78–80).
42. Mark Twain, *The Prince and the Pauper*, eds., Victor Fischer et al., vol. 6 of *The Works of Mark Twain*, 54.
43. Judith Fetterley writes in her essay, "Mark Twain and the Anxiety of Entertainment," about the relationship of Mark Twain's "entertainers" with their audience. Fetterley suggests, about *Adventures of Huckleberry Finn*, that "Entertainment is salvation in St. Petersburg because it handles boredom, but it can't handle the loneliness and fear which are Huck's conditions" (219).
44. Mark Twain, *Mark Twain's Speeches*, vol 28 of the *Writings of Mark Twain*, 191–92.
45. Mark Twain, *Letters from the Earth*, 25.
46. There is a striking similarity here between the nature and motive of Twain's transference of his mother's qualities onto God and those of Martin Luther, whose projection of his father's behavior onto the Father in heaven signaled the moment of his transition from adolescence to maturity. In Erikson's psycho-historical study of Luther, he

speaks of young Martin's "doubt that the father, when he punishes you, is really guided by love and justice rather than by arbitrariness and malice." "This early doubt," Erikson explains, "was projected on the Father in heaven . . ." *Young Man Luther,* 58.

47. D. W. Winnicott, *Deprivation and Delinquency,* 84–144.

48. Twain does not mention the exact year, but the episode can be placed within his time frame in *The Autobiography* between 1864 and 1868 (.20).

49. Winnicott calls this part of adolescence "struggling through the doldrums" in "Struggling through the doldrums" (1963), *Deprivation,* 155.

50. From a letter to the Rev. Twichell, dated March 14, 1905 (*Mark Twain's Letters,* 2: 768).

51. See Freud's discussion of "tendentious jokes" in *Jokes and Their Relation to the Unconscious.* (*Standard Edition,* 8: 3–236.) Freud discusses what he calls Mark Twain's "economy of pity," in the section, "Jokes and the Species of the Comic," in this volume.

52. Spoken by the young narrator in Twain's *The Personal Recollections of Joan of Arc, by the Sieur de Conte,* Book I, 63.

53. *Mark Twain—Howells Letters,* 1: 248–49.

54. Letters of Mark Twain, filed on microfilm in the Mark Twain Archives at Elmira College in Elmira, New York. A. B. Paine, who traveled with Twain during the last years of the humorist's life, made note of his frequent outbursts of "profanity." One morning, for example, when they were in Washington, Paine overheard Twain in the bathroom wildly shouting: "God-damn the God-damned son-of-a-bitch that invented that faucet! I hope he'll roast in hell for a million years!" (*Notebook,* 396).

55. Letter to Twain's mother, dated Aug. 1886 (*Letters,* 2: 471).

56. In her essay "Mark Twain and the Anxiety of Entertainment," Judith Fetterley observes that the portrait of the entertainer in Twain's fiction is a solitary figure who is "flooded with anxiety, rage, contempt, and disavowal" (216), and whose jests, pranks, and performances reveal a thinly disguised hostility for his audience and a wish to annihilate them. Among those characters included in her study are Hank Morgan, Tom Sawyer, Pudd'nhead Wilson, and Huck Finn. The entertainer, she argues, fears being exposed as an "impostor" (222) by his audience whom he anticipates will discover this and turn on him at any moment.

57. See Appendix C, in Mark Twain, *Life on the Mississippi,* 369. Captain Basil Hall's book, *Travels in North America,* was first published in 1829.

58. From an interview with the New York *World,* October 1900. Reprinted in *Life As I Find It,* 342.

59. Letter to W. D. Howells, August 1898, *Letters,* 665.

60. Justin Kaplan, *Mr. Clemens and Mark Twain: A Biography,* 344.

61. "The Czar's Soliloquy" first appeared in the *North American Review* (March 1905), and was reprinted in *Life As I Find It,* 267–72.

62. Malcolm Bradbury's "Introduction" to *Pudd'nhead Wilson,* 24.

63. Twain notes that Stevenson's story of Dr. Jekyll and Mr. Hyde is "nearer" what he was aiming at, since each of Stevenson's doubles possessed "a conscience of its own" (*Notebook,* 348).

64. John Bowlby, *Loss: Sadness and Depression,* vol. 3 of *Attachment and Loss,* 226–28.

65. Mark Twain, "What Is Man?" in *What Is Man? and Other Essays,* 98.

66. In 1896, Twain wrote in his notebook: "My own luck has been curious all my literary life; I never could tell a lie anybody would doubt, or a truth anyone would believe" (283).

67. From a letter Twain wrote to the *Sacramento Union* in July of 1866. Reprinted in *On*

the Poetry of Mark Twain with Selections from His Verse, 56. In December 1907, Twain wrote the following about his good friend, and one of the men whom Twain most admired, Andrew Carnegie: "I like a man that does his own thinking and speaks out what he thinks, whether the world approve or not . . ." Bernard De Voto, ed., *Mark Twain in Eruption: Hitherto Unpublished Pages about Men and Events*, 45.

68. This is the general premise of Bowlby's work, *Loss: Sadness and Depression*. Among the childhood experiences of persons prone to chronic mourning is the "unsympathetic and critical attitude that a parent may take towards her child's natural desires for love, attention and support" (224).

Notes to Chapter 3

1. Mark Twain, *Mark Twain's Letters*, 665.
2. Mark Twain, "My Platonic Sweetheart" (1912), in *The Mysterious Stranger Manuscripts*, vol. 27 of *The Writings of Mark Twain*, 287–304. The story first appeared in *The Mysterious Stranger and Other Stories* (New York and London: Harper & Bros., 1922).
3. Letter to Father Fitz-Simon, June 5, 1908. *Mark Twain's Letters*, 2: 812.
4. See John Bowlby's *Loss;* and his essays "Pathological Mourning and Childhood Mourning"; and "Processes of Mourning."
5. See Helene Deutsch, "Absence of Grief"; and Edith Jacobson, *The Self and the Object World*.
6. See H. Donald Dunton, "The Child's Concept of Grief," in *Loss and Grief*, 358; Deutsch, "Absence of Grief," 12–4; and Bowlby, *Loss*. According to David Aberbach, the "attempt on the part of the unconscious to master the trauma in all its horror and to overcome it" may be made many years later, "[l]ong after the trauma" occurred. *Surviving Trauma: Loss, Literature, and Psychoanalysis*, 13. "The struggle for mastery over grief-ridden trauma" that is sometimes carried on throughout an entire lifetime, Aberbach adds, "is particularly evident among survivors who use creativity to confront and bear witness to the past and to find meaning in continued life" (2).
7. It should be mentioned at this point that symptoms of pathological mourning such as nostalgia, the belief in ghosts, an obsession with corpses and funerals, and so on, are distorted ways of experiencing grief. As Aberbach explains, "the denial of loss is a part of grief" (*Surviving Trauma*, 9). Thus, the inability to grieve, the denial of grief and loss, and the exhibition of pathological mourning symptoms, are, in effect, interchangeable.
8. Rachel Varble describes Henry in her biography of Jane Clemens as "reasonable, healthy, reliable, intelligent, obedient; a thorn in the flesh of his brother Sam." *Jane Clemens: The Story of Mark Twain's Mother*, 127. Henry's "reproachlessness," like that of the Model Boy of the village whom Twain speaks about in *Life on the Mississippi*, "was a standing reproach to every lad in the village. He was the admiration of all the mothers, and the detestation of all their sons" (319).
9. See Albert C. Cain et al., "Children's Disturbed Reactions to the Death of a Sibling"; and, Stephen P. Bank and Michael D. Kahn, *The Sibling Bond*, 281.
10. Mark Twain, "The Facts Concerning the Recent Carnival of Crime in Connecticut," in *Mark Twain's Short Stories*, 144–45.
11. Dunton, "The Child's Concept of Grief," *Loss and Grief*, 356.
12. Mark Twain, "A Dog's Tale," in *Mark Twain's Short Stories*, 554.
13. Twain as qtd. by Margaret Sanborn in *Mark Twain: The Bachelor Years*, 61. Sanborn also notes that Twain made the following record in his journal fifty years after Ben's death: "Dead brother Ben. My treachery to him" (61).

14. Martha Wolfenstein, "How Is Mourning Possible?" 121.
15. Mark Twain, *The Autobiography of Mark Twain*, 42. The relentless guilt which, much of the time, must have occupied the mind of Sam Clemens is perhaps most openly expressed in the description of his feelings after the accidental death by fire of the calaboose tramp when Sam was at the vulnerable, anniversary-reaction age of ten years old. As he relates the story, in *Life on the Mississippi*, Sam had given the man some matches one afternoon, and that evening the drunken man was arrested and jailed. That night the man's straw bed caught on fire, and he died clutching the bars of his cell and screaming for help in front of Sam's eyes. Apparently the Marshall, who was the only person who had the keys to release the victim, could not be located in time. Remembering this incident, Twain states that he believed himself "as guilty of the man's death as if I had given him the matches purposely that he might burn himself up with them" (326).
16. Twain as qtd. in Sanborn, *Mark Twain*, 49. This statement, made by Twain's mother, was also confirmed by A. B. Paine in *Mark Twain: A Biography*, 1: 35.
17. In "The Turning-Point of My Life" (in *What Is Man? and Other Essays*), Twain again tells the story of voluntarily contracting the measles that summer during which "a child died almost every day" (131). Living every day not knowing whether he would catch the disease or not, Twain writes that: "Life on these miserable terms was not worth living, and at last I made up my mind to get the disease and have it over, one way or another" (131). After he had accomplished this, he says: "Everybody believed I would die; but on the fourteenth day a change came for the worse and they were disappointed." Surviving this death-defying illness was what Twain came to refer to as "the turning-point of my life" (131).
18. Mark Twain, *Mark Twain's Notebook*, 363.
19. Twain writes of Henry's doctor's "mistake" in *The Autobiography of Mark Twain*, 101. A. B. Paine, in *Mark Twain: A Biography*, relates that Henry's physician, Dr. Peyton, had ordered Twain to remind the young night doctor to administer an eighth of a gram of morphine to Henry, which he did; and it was at that moment that Henry began his final decline. Paine concludes that Henry's "chance of life had been infinitesimal, and his death was not necessarily due to [an overdose of] the drug, but Samuel Clemens, unsparing in his self-blame, all his days carried the burden of it" (1: 143).
20. Mark Twain, "A Cat-Tale," in *Letters from the Earth*, 108.
21. The critical role which kinship between brothers can have on a writer's creativity was fully explored in a series of essays edited by Norman Kiell, entitled *Blood Brothers: Siblings as Writers*. In this study we see the effect of Evelyn Waugh's rivalrous hostility toward his younger brother, Alec, which can be seen in the comic cruelty exhibited in his work. The rivalry between Oscar and Willie Wilde closely resembles that between Sam and Henry Clemens, in that it takes the form, in Wilde's drama, *The Importance of Being Ernest*, of two brothers of divergent characters who are pitted against one another: the concerned, protective guardian, Jack, and the idle, irresponsible spendthrift, Algy. Jack Kerouac attributed his success as a writer to the spiritual influence of his deceased brother, Gerard, whose "spirit," he believed, actually wrote many of his books.
22. Bank and Kahn, *The Sibling Bond*, 283.
23. Mark Twain, "The Mysterious Stranger," in *The Mysterious Stranger & Other Stories*, 220.
24. Daniel G. Hoffman observes in his essay, "Black Magic—and White—in *Huckleberry Finn*," in *A Casebook on Mark Twain's Wound*, that, in Twain's mind and fiction,

death is never far from his superstitious imagination (311–34). Leslie Fiedler comments, in the essay "Faust in the Eden of Childhood" *(A Casebook on Mark Twain's Wound)*, on Twain's persistent belief that he carried the curse of death with him (277–300). Justin Kaplan raises the question of Twain's lifelong sense of guilt in *Mr. Clemens and Mark Twain* (337). And Bernard De Voto discusses, in *Mark Twain at Work*, his impression of Twain's works as a fiction of "dread" that is filled with body-snatching, revenge, death, and murder. He attempts to account for these issues in Twain's fiction by attributing them to the superstitious and death-related folklore of the slave population in the South to which Twain was exposed when he was a boy (See De Voto's chapter, "Noon and the Dark: *Huckleberry Finn*," 45).

25. Rachel Varble, *Jane Clemens: The Story of Mark Twain's Mother*, 17. It has been reported by one of Twain's biographers, A. B. Paine, in his 1912 biography of Twain, and by Twain himself in *The Autobiography of Mark Twain*, that Peggy's daughter, Jane, was also obsessive in her habit of accumulating and caring for crippled and ailing cats. Also see Varble, 45.

26. Varble relates that once the young Jane exclaimed about a forsaken house plant: "Poor darling, don't die! Drink this!" And once when she observed a dying mulberry tree being chopped down she demanded of its executioner: "Let it alone! It *wants* to live, can't you see?" (45). When Jane moved into a boarding house after her marriage to John Marshall Clemens, in 1823, she brought with her, much to his annoyance, three cats, one partially blind. Apparently she hoped, as Varble reported, "to save the kittens from the customary end" (96).

27. It has been said that Mark Twain's "Angel Fish," the bevy of pubescent girls whom he "collected" during the last decade of his life, and who he demanded wear white dresses and arrange their hair in pig-tails, were to him "reincarnations" of his dead daughter, Susy. As young Edith had for Jane Clemens, the Angel Fish allowed Twain to "keep his dead alive" and thereby indefinitely hold the experience of grief at a distance.

28. Varble explains that, after Ben's death, Jane became "painfully more solicitous" of her children's health, "giving rein to a bent already noticeable," and she would not even permit them to step on ant hills for fear of destroying the poor innocent creatures (145).

29. This episode in Sam's life was verified by several of Twain's biographers, including Paine and Sanborn, and by Twain himself, in "The Turning-Point of My Life" (in *Mark Twain in Eruption: Hitherto Unpublished Pages about Men and Events*, and in *The Autobiography of Mark Twain*).

30. Mark Twain, *The Autobiography of Mark Twain*, 77.

31. We hear the tale of the "drowned boy" in *Life on the Mississippi* (1883), and again in *Old Times on the Mississippi* (1875), and "The Mysterious Stranger" (1922), as well as in several of Twain's short stories.

32. Mark Twain, *Life on the Mississippi*, 313.

33. *Mark Twain's Letters*, 1: 40.

34. When Twain was a child he was strongly impressed by the Shoemaker's devilish claim that he had had a vision of the boy's sister Margaret's funeral procession before her death. In *The Autobiography of Mark Twain*, he tells of the dream that he had before Henry's death, in which the details surrounding the funeral preparations depicted in the dream conformed exactly to the details of the actual event. Although he claims that he omitted telling the story of the dream in *Life on the Mississippi*, because "I never wanted my mother to know about that dream" (*The Autobiography*, 101), according to Varble, who based her claim on eye-witness accounts, Sam not only told his mother

of the dream at the time, but reminded her of it when it so strangely appeared to have come true (Varble, 240).

35. Samuel and Doris Webster, "Whitewashing Jane Clemens."

36. No uncle of Twain's died that year, but his father did. On October 10, 1903, Twain made the note about witnessing the postmortem of his "uncle" ("Mark Twain Papers"). This observation has led A. B. Paine and Margaret Sanborn to conclude that Twain had merely repressed the true force of the traumatic episode, and that this notation was a screen memory of his father's postmortem which he had witnessed (Sanborn, 63). Twain also mentions the autopsy in "Villagers of 1840–3," written in 1897, and included in *Mark Twain's Hannibal, Huck and Tom: (Previously Unpublished Writings)*. Here Twain tells of the death of "Judge C." who "caught his death" and died of pneumonia, after which he states: *"The Autopsy,"* (40).

37. The manuscript of Orion's autobiography was believed to have been lost or stolen in Grand Central Station.

38. Mark Twain, *The Gilded Age: A Tale of Today*, 82.

39. *The Autobiography of Mark Twain*, 24.

40. Mark Twain, "The $30,000 Bequest," in *Mark Twain's Short Stories*, 606.

41. See also Twain's "Remarks on Copyright" delivered at the Hearing for the Congressional Committee on Patents, on December 7, 1906, in Washington, D.C. Reprinted in *Mark Twain Speaking*, 533–37. Here, Twain complains that the present "limited" copyright laws "merely take the author's property, merely takes from his children the bread and profit of that book." To support his argument, Twain compares an author of a book in which new ideas are discovered, to twelve Englishmen who go to South Africa. Eleven see nothing; only one sees a railroad running through the land that some day will lead to the building of a new, great city (536–37). This discovery, like any other inventive "idea," such as the washtub and the telephone, is one of many "symbols which represent ideas," just as books do. And he concludes: "A book *does* consist solely of ideas, from the base to the summit, *like any other property* of the author and his heirs forever and ever." (537). In another speech delivered to the House of Lords, on April 3, 1900, Twain similarly proposes:

> The limited copyright makes a distinction between an author's property and real estate, pretending that both are not created, produced and acquired in the same way. The man who purchases a landed estate has to earn the money by the superiority of his intellect; a book is the result of an author's own brain in the same manner—a combination and exploitation of his ideas (335).

42. Mark Twain, "Theodore Roosevelt," in *Mark Twain in Eruption*, 1.

43. A. B. Paine, *Mark Twain: A Biography*, 1: 75. Paine adds that Twain made this promise to his mother with gravity and sincerity.

44. David Kreuger, "Money, Meanings and Madness: A Psychoanalytic Perspective," 210.

45. The son's guilt at surpassing the father in some way (essentially tied in with the son's unresolved oedipal guilt and aggression in relation to the father), is the subject of Freud's essay, "A Disturbance of Memory on the Acropolis" (1936), in *Standard Edition*, 22: 239–48. Freud writes first of those people who "fall ill, or even go entirely to pieces, because an overwhelmingly powerful wish of theirs has been fulfilled" (243). Speaking personally, Freud surmises that the guilt and anxiety that he experienced during his visit to Athens was the result of his having traveled to a place that his father was himself never able to visit: "It seems as though the essence of success was to have got further than one's father, and as though to excel one's father was still something forbidden" (247).

46. In this respect Twain's contradictory family-romance fantasy resembled that of Rilke, who rebelled against all aspects of bourgeois life, while at the same time maintaining that he was of noble descent. See Phyllis Greenacre's "The Family Romance of the Artist," 26–29.

47. Mark Twain, *The American Claimant*, vol. 15 of *The Writings of Mark Twain*, 4.

48. In Twain's fiction one can see the adolescent's conflict of ambivalence acted out again and again through his fictional mastery of a game often played by boys during their key oedipal years, a game which D. W. Winnicott calls "I'm the King of the Castle," in which "the dirty rascal knocks the king over and in turn becomes the king" ("Adolescent Immaturity," in *Home is Where We Start From*, 150–66). Inevitably, another dirty rascal will overturn the king, so that eventually the dirty rascal and the king are symbolically interchangeable. For the boy who does and does not want to grow up, the triumph of becoming "king" invariably carries disappointment since it means that the rebellion is over and one has *become* the establishment that one had only a few moments earlier so vehemently detested. In Winnicott's words, once victory is attained, "Lost is all the imaginative activity and striving of immaturity. Rebellion no longer makes sense, and the adolescent who wins too early is caught in his own trap, must turn dictator, and must stand up waiting to be killed . . ." (160).

49. *Mark Twain's Notebook*, 217.

50. Jack Kleiner, "On Nostalgia," 473.

51. See Leslie Fiedler, *Love and Death in the American Novel;* Kenneth S. Lynn, *Mark Twain's Escape from Time;* and Coleman O. Parsons, "The Devil and Samuel Clemens," in *A Casebook on Mark Twain's Wound.*

52. Sigmund Freud, "The 'Uncanny,' " in *Standard Edition*, 17: 245.

53. Madelon Sprengnether, *The Spectral Mother: Freud, Feminism, and Psychoanalysis*, 231.

54. Fenichel and Fodor as discussed in Robert J. Lifton, "The Sense of Immortality: On Death and the Continuity of Life," 480.

55. Susan K. Harris, *Mark Twain's Escape from Time: A Study of Patterns and Images.*

56. Mark Twain, "Which Was the Dream?" in *Mark Twain's Which Was the Dream? & Other Symbolic Writings of Later Years.*

57. Bernard De Voto, "Symbols of Despair," in *Mark Twain at Work*, in *Mark Twain's America and Mark Twain at Work*, 109.

58. D. W. Winnicott, *Playing and Reality*, 20.

59. Wright Morris, "The Available Past," in *A Casebook on Mark Twain's Wound*, 275.

60. Stephen Cooper, " 'Good Rotten Material for Burial': The Overdetermined Death of Romance in *Life on the Mississippi.*"

61. Freud, "On Transience" (1916[1915]), *Standard Edition*, 14: 307.

Notes to Chapter 4

1. T. S. Eliot, "An Introduction to *Huckleberry Finn*," in *Adventures of Huckleberry Finn* (Norton Critical Edition), 329.

2. Frank W. Young, "The Function of Male Initiation Ceremonies," 391.

3. Bruno Bettelheim, *Symbolic Wounds: Puberty Rites and the Envious Male*, 224–25.

4. Mark Twain, *Adventures of Huckleberry Finn* (University of California Press/Bancroft Library), 274. All subsequent citations from *Adventures of Huckleberry Finn* refer to this edition, and will be noted parenthetically.

5. J. Laplanche & J.-B. Pontalis, *The Language of Psycho-Analysis*, 387.

6. Mark Twain, "The Raftsmen's Passage," in *Adventures of Huckleberry Finn* (Norton Critical Edition), 233.

7. In describing the childhood ambivalence toward the parents experienced by the creative artist who then goes on to engage in family-romance fantasies, Phyllis Greenacre refers to the "period in which good and bad . . . appear like black and white twins in so many relationships." The ambivalence toward the parents, Greenacre explains, is due to "grossly unresolved oedipal problems." "The Family Romance of the Artist," 9–11.

8. Twain appears to have had a similar personal myth of his own based on what psychoanalysis calls an "extensive life-pattern mirroring" of the father. He tended to view his successes with suspicion and passively accept his failures, which undoubtedly reminded him of the many failures of his own father. Twain always believed in his heart that, like his father, he "was born to indolence, idleness, procrastination, indifference—the qualities that constitute a shirk" (*The Autobiography of Mark Twain*, 40). George Pollock utilizes the term "nemesis" to describe those who believe they are destined to repeat the life pattern of a person who has died and for whose death they feel in some way responsible ("Anniversary Reactions, Trauma, and Mourning").

9. It is possible that Huck's emotional response to his father's disappearance originated in Twain's own sense of desertion, experienced when he discovered one day, at the age of four, that he had been left behind by his father when his family moved from Florida to Hannibal, Missouri. Describing this incident years later, Twain spoke of "the grisly deep silence" that overtook the empty house, and of the spooky black shadows that made him think that he was surrounded by ghosts and witches. See Margaret Sanborn's biography, *Mark Twain: The Bachelor Years*, 25. These manifestations of Twain's own projected aggressive thoughts toward his disappointing father are identical to Huck's own experience when he is alone in his room in the Widow's house late at night.

10. Edith Jacobson, *The Self and the Object World*, 204–16. Hans W. Loewald discusses the theme of guilt in a son's oedipal fantasy of parricide, specifically as it relates to outdistancing the father. "The Waning of the Oedipus Complex."

11. Otto Rank, "Feminine Psychology and Masculine Ideology," in *Beyond Psychology*, 240.

12. See Daniel Hoffman, "Black Magic—and White—in *Huckleberry Finn*," (1961) in *A Casebook on Mark Twain's Wound*, 104; Kenneth S. Lynn, *Mark Twain and Southwestern Humor*, 211; Peter G. Beidler, "The Raft Episode in *Huckleberry Finn*," in *Adventures of Huckleberry Finn* (Norton Critical Edition), 248; and, Harold Beaver, *Huckleberry Finn*, 84.

13. The single unswerving characteristic exhibited by Huck that sets him apart from those who move along the "current" of life, T. S. Eliot observes, is his insistence on being "true to himself" ("An Introduction to *Huckleberry Finn*," 331). This, according to Huck, is sanity, and as Twain himself once wrote: "The suicide seems to me the only sane person" (*Mark Twain's Notebook*, 368). Lionel Trilling, in his essay "The Greatness of *Huckleberry Finn*," in *Adventures of Huckleberry Finn* (Norton Critical Edition), 318–28, maintains that the "greatness" of the novel lies primarily "in its power of telling the truth." Trilling also perceives the psychological characteristic that, as D. W. Winnicott believes, separates adolescents from adults, when he writes that "adolescent children . . . are more concerned with not betraying themselves than with whether they smoke or not, or whether they do or do not sleep around. It can be seen that for them (as with small children, though it is more obscure here) the false solution is OUT." *Deprivation and Delinquency*, 112.

14. Greenacre, "The Family Romance of the Artist," 10.

15. Viggo W. Jensen and Thomas A. Petty, "The Fantasy of Being Rescued in Suicide."

16. Daniel Hoffman, for example, in "Black Magic—and White—in *Huckleberry Finn*,"

writes that Jim "is now free to take the place that Pap was never worthy to hold as Huck's spiritual father" (104). Also see Leslie Fiedler, "Come Back to the Raft Again, Huck Honey!" in *Adventures of Huckleberry Finn* (Norton Critical Edition), 418. See also Lionel Trilling, "The Greatness of *Huckleberry Finn*," 321; and Kenneth Lynn, *Mark Twain and Southwestern Humor*, 211.

17. Wilma Garcia suggests, in her study of mythology and American literature, that Jim plays the role of Huck's "male mother." Huck, she claims, is a "social outcast" who "needs a loving parent, but once he is separated from the repressive protection of the widow and her sister, he must look for nurturing outside the bounds of society." *Mothers and Others: Myths of the Female in the Works of Melville, Twain, and Hemingway*, 118–19.

18. See Harold Beaver, *Huckleberry Finn*, 73; Lionel Trilling, "The Greatness of *Huckleberry Finn*," 320; Wright Morris, "The Available Past," in *A Casebook on Mark Twain's Wound*, 275–76; and Kenneth Lynn, *Mark Twain and Southwestern Humor*, 187–89.

19. Susan K. Harris, *Mark Twain's Escape from Time: A Study of Patterns and Images*, 8.

20. Mark Twain, *A Tramp Abroad*, vol. 9 of *The Writings of Mark Twain*, 107.

21. Mark Twain, "Is Shakespeare Dead?" in *What Is Man? and Other Essays*, 330.

22. Sydney Smith, "The Golden Fantasy: A Regressive Reaction to Separation Anxiety," 311; and, Lloyd H. Silverman et al., *The Search for Oneness*, 1–6.

23. Roderick Peters, "Reflections on the Origin and Aim of Nostalgia." Nostalgia, Peters maintains, is:

> reminiscent of the "lost paradise" of mythology. In the paradise myths the "other" is there as creator, provider, container. There is perfect harmony, no discrepancy between need, or expectation, and provision or response. I believe that at a deep level in nostalgia the yearning is for the "other" to be there in that perfect way. The mother/infant dyadic experience is, or usually is, the first expression of the archetypal potentiality for creator/created, container/contained, provider/provided for to be experienced. Of course, the infant's experience with mother, whether *pre-partum* or *post-partum*, is not of a blissful, harmonious, clashless state, nor of its equally archetypally-based opposite, a chaotic hell. However, moments probably do approximate more or less closely to this archetypal constellation in both positive and negative poles. (137)

24. In Jack Kleiner, "On Nostalgia," 480. Also see N. Fodor, "Varieties of Nostalgia."

25. Roderick Peters, "Reflections on the Origin and Aim of Nostalgia," 147.

26. Bernard De Voto, *Mark Twain at Work*, 53.

27. Mark Twain, *The Adventures of Tom Sawyer*, vol. 4 of *The Works of Mark Twain*, 237.

28. Richard Poirier, *A World Elsewhere: The Place of Style in American Literature*, 177.

29. *Mark Twain's Letters*, 434.

30. See Talcott Parsons, "Family Structure and the Socialization of the Child," in Parsons and Bales, *Family Socialization and Interaction Process*, 35–131; and chapters 6 and 7 of Juliet Mitchell's, *Psychoanalysis and Feminism*, for a summary explanation of the "Oedipus complex" as it is understood by Freudian revisionists.

31. Julia Kristeva, *Powers of Horror*, 127–28.

32. Harold Beaver explores the novel as "a parody of Christian death and resurrection" and discusses Huck's nine different "impostures." *Huckleberry Finn*, 85.

33. As I discussed at length in the previous chapter, Mark Twain inherited his mother's inability to grieve over the deaths of his siblings and his father, and this incapacity to

grieve was exacerbated by the intense sibling rivalry that Twain felt toward his brothers and sister who died when he was a boy. Twain openly (although without real justification) blamed himself for both Ben's and Henry's death, as he blamed himself for the death from exposure of his own first child, Benjamin Lampton Clemens, many years later. Based on Twain's numerous autobiographical and fictional accounts of the deaths he experienced in childhood, guilt and death appeared to be synonymous in his imagination, which interfered with his ability to grieve and resulted in a lifetime of unresolved grief and pathological mourning.

34. Mark Twain, "The Damned Human Race," in *The Mysterious Stranger & Other Stories*, 174.

35. *Mark Twain's Notebook*, 301.

36. See James M. Cox, "The Uncomfortable Ending of *Huckleberry Finn*," in *Huckleberry Finn* (Norton Critical Edition), for a discussion of Huck's exchange of social for personal morality at the end of the novel, in which Huck "had not reached childhood's end, but had disclosed the lie of the adult world" 358.

37. As Harold Beaver writes, "Huck's voice, left to itself, was incapable of concluding anything," *Huckleberry Finn*, 55; also see Richard Poirier, *A World Elsewhere*, 191.

38. See Freud's discussion of his grandchild's *"fort-da"* game in which he describes the child's "instinctual renunciation (that is, the renunciation of instinctual satisfaction) which he had made in allowing his mother to go away without protesting," and the boy's use of the abstractions of symbolization and language as a replacement or "compensation" for her loss. *Beyond the Pleasure Principle* (1920), in *Standard Edition*, 18: 15.

39. Ernest Hemingway, *Green Hills of Africa*, 22. D. W. Winnicott also uses the word "cheating" in "The Absence of a Sense of Guilt" *(Deprivation and Delinquency)* to describe the adolescent's, baby's, and schizoid patient's attitude toward conforming to a self-betraying social—rather than personal and subjective—morality, when he writes that these individuals:

> are in some ways more moral than we are, but they are of course terribly uncomfortable. They perhaps prefer to remain uncomfortable and not to be "cured." Sanity spells compromise. That is what they feel to be wicked. Extra-marital intercourse is of no consequence to them as compared with betrayal of the self. And it is true (I think I could show you) that sane people relate to the world by what I call *cheating*. Or rather, if there is a sanity that is ethically respectable it arrived very early in the infancy of the individual when *cheating* was of no consequence. (111)

40. Norman Holland proposes, in *The Dynamics of Literary Response*: "We have seen how the 'willing suspension of disbelief,' that partial, encapsulated regression, creates a richer, longer kind of self than our ordinary one. We become a 'rind' of higher ego functions around a 'core' regressed to the very deep, primary at-oneness with the nurturing other—the text" (337).

41. James Masterson, *The Search for the Real Self*, 214–30.

42. Guy Cardwell, *The Man Who Was Mark Twain*, 159.

43. Van Wyck Brooks, *The Ordeal of Mark Twain*, 24.

44. Both Twain and his boy heroes appear to lack the kind of object constancy that is described in John Bowlby's definition of "immaturity," in volume 3 of his study on loss and mourning, *Separation: Anxiety and Anger*: "A person who approaches the world with confidence yet who, when in difficulty, is disposed to turn to trusted figures for support is often said to be mature. In contrast, both someone who is

326 Notes to Chapter 4

chronically anxious and permanently in need of support and someone who never trusts anyone are said to be immature" (209).

45. Mark Twain, "The Babies," in *Mark Twain's Speeches*, 2: 58.

46. Lee Clark Mitchell also senses in Twain's narrative that "the authority of words dictates far more than the shape of particular events" (" 'Nobody but Our Gang Warn't Around': The Authority of Language in *Huckleberry Finn*," in *New Essays on "Adventures of Huckleberry Finn"*), 83.

47. James Masterson, in his study of the lives of Jean-Paul Sartre, Edvard Munch, and Thomas Wolfe, explains how the artists' creativity "allows them to find and establish a segment of their real self that allows them to adapt to life" and to deal effectively with "feelings of abandonment and engulfment." As he says about Wolfe: "Writing became his escape from the abandonment feelings, and his daily life revolved around his need to write; but he could not write continuously," *The Search for the Real Self*, 226. It is safe to assume that this same dynamic was active in Twain's psychic life when, as he sometimes confessed, "I sit here—writing, busying myself, to keep my heart from breaking" *(The Autobiography of Mark Twain*, 48).

48. Roy Harvey Pearce, " 'The End. Yours Truly, Huck Finn': Postscript," in *Huckleberry Finn* (Norton Critical Edition), 361.

49. Karen Horney, *Neurosis and Human Growth*. Horney adds that "this dependency as a rule prevents suicide. If it were not for this dependency, suicide would be the logical outcome of self-hate" (114).

50. Mark Twain, "Talk about Twins" (1895), in *Life As I Find It*, 233.

51. Mark Twain, *The Tragedy of Pudd'nhead Wilson*, 303.

52. *Mark Twain's Notebook*, 212.

53. See section III, "The Purpose of Jokes," of Freud's *Jokes and Their Relation to the Unconscious* (1905), in *Standard Edition*, 8: 90–116.

Notes to Chapter 5

1. Quoted in Donald Jones, "Newspaper job in Toronto launched writer's career," *Toronto Star*, June 18, 1977.

2. Manic-depression is also referred to as "bi-polar depressive disorder." The main proponents of this psychiatric interpretation of Hemingway's personality are psychiatrists Philip Scharfer and Ronald Fieve, both of whom are interviewed by Denis Brian in *The True Gen*, 308–15. Fieve's interpretation of manic-depressive, or bi-polar, disorder is outlined in his book *Moodswing*.

3. Brian, *The True Gen*, 316–21.

4. Rovit, as quoted from an interview with Brian in *The True Gen*, 300.

5. Tom Dardis, *The Thirsty Muse: Alcohol and the American Writer*, 177. Dardis begins his discussion of Hemingway with the statement that alcohol indeed played a part in Hemingway's decline as a writer and in his personal life, but primarily because he could never admit he was a "rummy." Dardis explains that Hemingway believed "he'd mastered the art of drinking in his mid-teens" and falsely, and futilely, believed that alcohol "could dispel pain with no ill effects on the drinker" (159). Though alcohol gave Hemingway moments of relief, like throwing "gasoline on fire" it made his depression worse (166–67). By fueling his grandiosity alcohol served to "escalate his all-out machismo, which would grow to become a monstrous parody of itself" (172).

6. Irvin and Marilyn Yalom, in "Ernest Hemingway—A Psychiatric View," touch upon this hypothesis, which will be explored in detail throughout this chapter as it applies to Hemingway's fiction, when they propose that: "All traces of traits not fitting

[Hemingway's] idealized image had to be eliminated or squelched. The softer feminine side, the fearful parts, the dependent cravings—all had to go" (492).

7. The fact that Hemingway went to the front, where there was a real likelihood of being shot, was not the experienced heroism of a later Hemingway facing the possibility of death bravely, but rather, was representative of the naivete of a lingering adolescent ego-inflation and feeling of invincibility. See chapter 7 for a more detailed discussion of Hemingway's war wound as a signifier of lost invulnerability and immortality—a connection overtly stated by Colonel Richard Cantwell in *Across the River and Into the Trees*, who admits that his "first big" wound resulted in "the loss of the immortality . . . in a way, that is quite a lot to lose" (33). In terms of Hemingway's elevated idealism, Irvin and Marilyn Yalom rework Philip Young's theory of the return of a repressed castration anxiety as the reason for Hemingway's fictional re-enactions of his wounding during the war. (See Young's *Ernest Hemingway: A Reconsideration*.) The Yaloms explain that by "flaunting the danger, by recklessly re-exposing oneself to a similar threat, one is, in effect, denying to oneself that danger exists. Inwardly the ego employs repression and denial, outwardly the individual seems compelled to face the very thing he fears the most" ("Ernest Hemingway—A Psychiatric View," 492).

8. And this coming from the parents whose love a child always, secretly or otherwise, hopes—and by hoping, on some level believes—is unconditional. Developmental psychologists commonly agree that self-esteem and a secure, positive self-image are primarily a consequence of the child's belief that it is unconditionally loved by the parents or primary caretaker(s).

9. Traumatic loss as a contributing factor to the development of a depressive disorder is discussed by John Bowlby in *Loss*, Chapter 14. Bowlby bases his claims on the conclusions reached by G. W. Brown and T. Harris in *The Social Origins of Depression: A Study of Psychiatric Disorder in Women*.

10. See Bowlby, *Loss*, 262.

11. In an opposite, but similar, way, the currently popular anti-depressant drug, Prozac, is believed to mimic the same chemical and neurophysiological changes that result from an experience of well-being obtained from therapeutic counseling, or merely from incidents that produce a feeling of happiness, meaningfulness, or good fortune. See P. Kramer, *Listening to Prozac*.

12. Supporting the possibility that, regardless of the sequence of cause and effect, depression and ego-ideal disorders, or low self-esteem, go hand in hand, are clinical studies which show that lower self-concepts are prevalent among those with depressive disorders. See M. Harrow and M. J. Amdur, "Guilt and Depressive Disorders."

13. Calling upon Karen Horney's theory of personality, Irvin and Marilyn Yalom propose that "publicly and privately Hemingway invested inordinate psychic energy into fulfilling his idealized image," and that because he ultimately fell short of his ideal, owing to dependency needs, physical injury, and immaturely formed love relationships, he was forced to recognize "the discrepancy between what he wants to be and what he is in actuality," which resulted in self-hatred, paranoia, and finally, annihilation of the self through suicide. The Yaloms also maintain that "Hemingway's anxiety and depression stemmed in large part from his failure to actualize his idealized self" ("Ernest Hemingway—A Psychiatric View," 491). I am more apt to leave open the question of how precisely characterological and neurological factors combined to solidify and augment Hemingway's depression and negative self-image. Aside from this one point, I am in complete accord with the Yaloms' "clinical" assessment of Hemingway's aggrandized self-image and the resultant problems it created for him. The present

investigation of Hemingway's fiction, in fact, attempts to explore the full thematic, stylistic, and biographical implications of Hemingway's anxious relationship with an elevated, ideal, and heroic self-image, and in a sense carries to culmination the hypothesis set forth in "Ernest Hemingway—A Psychiatric View"—the only study on Hemingway that directly foreshadows the issues in these chapters of the psychoanalytic and literary significance of Hemingway's heroic, or grandiose, idealism.

14. The concept of an ego-ideal crisis thus provides an alternative, through object-relations theory, to the oedipal conflict, or castration anxiety theory, that has been applied to Hemingway's life and fiction by critics over the past few decades, particularly by Philip Young in *Ernest Hemingway: A Reconsideration.*

15. The ego ideal as maternal and pregenital in origin, and as a wish-fulfilling agency that provides a basis for an individual's self-esteem derived from narcissistic gratifications and identifications, is remarked upon at length in Edith Weigert's "The Superego and the Ego-Ideal." Annie Reich discusses ego ideal disturbances in relation to self-esteem in "Pathologic Forms of Self-Esteem Regulation." Peter Blos discusses the development of the ego ideal as it relates to adolescent narcissism and the negative Oedipus complex, in "The Genealogy of the Ego Ideal." Joseph Sandler et al. offer a summary of the use of the term "ego ideal" from Freud through 1963, in "The Ego Ideal and the Ideal Self."

16. For a psychoanalytic discussion of nostalgia see David S. Werman, "Normal and Pathological Nostalgia"; Jack Kleiner, "On Nostalgia"; Harvey A. Kaplan, "The Psychopathology of Nostalgia"; and Roderick Peters, "Reflections on the Origin and Aim of Nostalgia."

17. As Irvin and Marilyn Yalom point out in relation to Hemingway's narcissistic vulnerability in his relationships with women: "To love another is to expose oneself to the risk of painful separation or loss" ("Ernest Hemingway—A Psychiatric View," 489).

18. Ernest Hemingway, *Men Without Women*, 37. All subsequent citations from *Men Without Women* refer to this edition.

19. The term "opium" as a psychological, as well as a physical, "pain-killer," is used by Hemingway in the story "The Gambler, the Nun, and the Radio," in *Winner Take Nothing.*

20. General Lanham, as quoted by Denis Brian in *The True Gen*, 296.

21. General Lanham, Hemingway's good friend who remained close to him throughout his life, once made the comment that Hemingway was "frozen in adolescence." When Hemingway's fourth wife, Mary, passed on this remark to her husband, Hemingway replied: "Perhaps adolescence isn't such a bad place to be frozen" (See partial reprint of C. T. Lanham's correspondence with Irvin and Marilyn Yalom, written August 22, 1967, in "Ernest Hemingway—A Psychiatric View," 487). Indeed, Hemingway's intimate and prolonged personal concern with the vicissitudes of adolescence enabled him through his fiction to become one of America's greatest literary spokesmen for the pains, joys, and anxieties of a young American male in the process of growing up.

22. Joseph Defalco, in his study of the hero in Hemingway's short stories, uses as a guiding psychoanalytic principle the developmental theory that "destruction of the infantile father-image" is necessary for a boy's individuation process into maturity. And while he correctly, I believe, points out in story after story the boy's "recognition of the failure of the father" which "promotes regression" to infantile dependency, he labels this disillusionment as the Hemingway protagonist's heroic rebellion in the face of disappointment. *The Hero in Hemingway's Short Stories*, 45, 107, 198. What Defalco calls a "victory over the forces of compromise," and the healthy and mature "adjustment to contingencies" in life, I call the defensive repression, or taboo, of grief

and painful emotions. A real acceptance of life's contingencies and losses would probably have led Hemingway, and his protagonists, to accept loss and repudiate their self-deceptions. Instead, in both his later life and fiction, Hemingway becomes obsessed with loss, and with his attempts through nostalgic remembering and drinking to dispel the grief of loss and disillusionment. The later Hemingway, I believe, redoubled his defenses by increasing his drinking, his facade of machismo, and his emotional imperviousness.

23. See Lynn's *Hemingway*, 43, and Bernice Kert's *Hemingway Women*, 27.

24. In speaking about Grace's intense emotional suffocation and excessive mother-infant intimacy with her son, Kenneth Lynn suggests that at "some point" in Ernest's "edenic infancy he awakened to an understanding of the situation in which his mother had placed him." If Hemingway, later in life, displayed a serious lack of basic trust in relation to other people it was perhaps, Lynn proposes, "because he thought of himself as a victim of treachery long before he knew what to call it" (*Hemingway*, 43).

The essentially unsympathetic, if not outright critical, attitude that Hemingway's parents held toward all of their children's natural desires for love and support (particularly toward the precocious Ernest), may have, as John Bowlby suggests, inhibited their attachment behavior and encouraged them to bottle up their feelings. In such a situation, the child may then come, generally, "like his parents, to view his yearning for love as a weakness, his anger as a sin and his grief as childish" (Bowlby, *Loss*, 224–26). According to Bowlby, children who are exposed to this kind of deprivation in the parental relationship often "grow up to be tough and hard." Furthermore, Bowlby maintains, they "may become competent and to all appearances self-reliant, and they may go through life without overt sign of breakdown . . . whilst, especially in later years, they are at risk of depression, alcoholism and suicide" (225). Primarily, they will develop a pathological response to loss, in most cases manifested through a "prolonged absence of conscious grieving" (225).

25. Madelaine Hemingway Miller, *Ernie: Hemingway's "Sister 'Sunny' Remembers,"* 16.

26. See D. W. Winnicott, *Playing and Reality*.

27. Michael S. Reynolds, "Hemingway's Home: Depression and Suicide," 600.

28. Kenneth Johnston's *The Tip of the Iceberg: Hemingway and the Short Story*, 143. As Johnston writes, according to Carlos Baker, Hemingway also told Cowley "that his hatred of his mother was non-Freudian, that she was an all-time, All-American bitch" (143). Kenneth Lynn writes that by 1911 Ernest began to experience a "growing realization of his father's degrading subservience to Grace, for it resulted in a loss of respect, which was then intensified by Dr. Hemingway's abject departure from home in 1912 to take a 'rest cure' for his nerves" (*Hemingway*, 63).

29. Max Westbrook, "Grace under Pressure: Hemingway and the Summer of 1920," 93.

30. According to Harvey A. Kaplan in his essay "The Psychopathology of Nostalgia," the "function of the ego ideal is to restore the lost narcissism of childhood. The ego ideal is comprised of identifications with parental figures seen in glorified perspective . . . and it expresses what one desires to be." Quoting from S. Novey's "Some Philosophical Speculations about the Concept of the Genital Character," Kaplan explains that the "ego ideal is little more than the surface layer of an elaborate system of fantasies and beliefs. Related to this is a concept of a personal myth and extensive system of beliefs which are not what one would like to attain but what one feels one is" (91).

31. Leonard Kriegel, "Hemingway's Rites of Manhood," 416.

32. Wright Morris, *Earthly Delights, Unearthly Adornments*, 144.

33. Peter Blos, "The Function of the Ego Ideal in Adolescence," 96.

34. John Raeburn, *Fame Became of Him: Hemingway as Public Writer*, 166.

35. The Orpen fragment is an unpublished manuscript presently listed as #445 in the Hemingway archives at the John F. Kennedy Library in Boston. A short summary of the Orpen story is also given by Kenneth S. Lynn in *Hemingway,* 130–32, and by Peter Griffin in *Along with Youth,* 222–24.

36. The wish to deny one's insignificant origins and fabricate for oneself a more important background—or, in other words, to replace one's "little penis" with a "bigger phallus"—is also characteristic of Freud's "family-romance" fantasy. Like the erection of a grandiose ego ideal, the need for a family-romance fantasy, according to Freud, comes from the discrepancy between the idealized and real picture of the child's parents, who might otherwise serve as a successful ideal. (See Freud's essay, "Family Romances" (1909[1908]) in *Standard Edition,* 9: 237–41). Phyllis Greenacre discusses the theme of "family romance" in relation to the creative artist in her essay, "The Family Romance of the Artist."

37. According to Janine Chasseguet-Smirgel, when the little idealized penis is exposed as inferior, castration fears are newly confronted. The metaphors employed by Chasseguet-Smirgel to describe the vulnerable link between ego and ideal bear a significant relation to those imagined by Hemingway. As she explains, the "deeper the wound resulting from the lack of equation between narcissistic aspirations [ego ideal] and the real ego's situation, the more imperious will be the necessity to put into action efforts to bridge this fatal gap." *The Ego Ideal,* 97.

38. The connection between admitting emotions into the conscious psyche, which results from the breakdown of ritualized action, and the threat of chaos and death, has frequently been made by Hemingway's critics, including Peter Schwenger's observation that Nick "guards against his emotions as he would against death," ("The Masculine Mode," *Speaking of Gender,* 105); Frank McConnell's discussion of how Hemingway's and Nick's escape into style is a "last resort against chaos," ("Stalking Papa's Ghost: Hemingway's Presence in Contemporary American Writing," in *Ernest Hemingway: New Critical Essays,* 209); and John Griffith's determination that Hemingway's code heroes "use their rituals to avoid thinking about the terror that lurks just beyond their consciousness," "Rectitude in Hemingway's Fiction: How Rite Makes Right," in *In Our Time,* 168.

39. Leonard Kriegel alludes to this when he states with regard to Hemingway that "the need to prove his manhood was virtually conterminous with the craft he forged." "Hemingway's Rites of Manhood," 417.

40. Ernest Hemingway, *In Our Time,* 27. All subsequent citations from *In Our Time* refer to this edition.

41. Annie Reich, "Pathologic Forms of Self-Esteem Regulation," 220.

42. As the child becomes an adult, separation anxiety "may no longer be to the real mother, but to another person who represents security and approval." James Masterson, *The Search for the Real Self,* 69.

43. John Munder Ross uses the term "Laius Complex" to refer to the absent father's ambivalent impulse to both love and "put down" the son, which is mirrored by the son's ambivalence toward the father. See Ross, "Oedipus Revisited: Laius and the 'Laius Complex.' "

44. Edith Jacobson, *The Self and the Object World.* Jacobson defines self-esteem as the expression of the discrepancy or harmony between self-representation and the wishful concept of the self, or between the superego and the ego ideal (154–55).

45. Throughout Lynn's biography of Hemingway a special effort is made to expose the numerous lies Hemingway apparently told about his war experience (some of which, to Hemingway's credit, he admitted to later in life), thus dispelling the myth of

heroism Hemingway created around himself. Among other tales, Hemingway lied about having received bullet wounds, in addition to shell-fragment wounds, about carrying an Italian soldier on his back to a first-aid dugout, about joining the 65th Infantry as a first lieutenant after his tour of duty with the American Volunteer Ambulance Service ended, and about sleeping with the hostess of a hotel for a week during his vacation in Southern Italy. Lynn maintains that it was not only Hemingway who, like Krebs, felt compelled to lie in order to "feel justifiably proud of himself," but another set of "myth-lovers" (86)—Hemingway's later critics and American male readership—who seemed, equally, to need to believe in the grandiose masculine image that Hemingway fabricated. *Hemingway*, 82–92.

46. Peter Blos, "The Genealogy of the Ego Ideal." The first step in the development of the male ego ideal is the movement from primary narcissism to "delusional omnipotence shared with the mother." From the son's point of view, the mother of this second stage contains a phallic component. According to Blos, she embodies the "potency and power" of procreation, creativity, and omnipotent fantasy-making, or verbal imagination. For this reason she is an object of identification and envy to the male child, who wishes to possess her omnipotent, phallic powers (55).

47. Peter Griffin, *Less Than a Treason: Hemingway in Paris*, 73.

48. In the following statement made by Hemingway to W. G. Rogers, after reading Rogers's *When This You See, Remember Me: Gertrude Stein in Person* (1948), it is easy to detect a threatened masculinity in the defensive logic that Hemingway uses to describe his implied sexual attraction for Stein: "I liked her better before she cut her hair and that was sort of a turning point in all sorts of things. She used to talk to me about homosexuality and how it was fine in and for women and no good in men and I used to listen and learn and I always wanted to fuck her and she knew it and it was a good healthy feeling and made more sense than some of the talk." Quoted in Kenneth Lynn, *Hemingway*, 169.

49. "Mrs. Hemingstein" was one of many nick-names that Hemingway had for his mother's, and for his own, name.

50. See Peter Blos, "The Genealogy of the Ego Ideal," 56; and his full-length study, *On Adolescence*.

51. Mark Spilka, "Jake & Brett: Wounded Warriors," in *Brett Ashley*, 176–78, excerpted from Spilka's *Hemingway's Quarrel with Androgyny*.

52. See Robert Hopke, *Jung, Jungians & Homosexuality*, in which he maintains that "butch" women "serve to reinforce conformity to sex-role and gender categories" in society (110); and Marjorie Garber's discussion of Krafft-Ebing's "mannish" woman, *Vested Interests: Cross-Dressing and Cultural Anxiety*, 137–41.

53. Hemingway once claimed that the character of Brett was modeled on a man (Kenneth Lynn, *Hemingway*, 325). Tom Burnam in "Primitivism and Masculinity in the Work of Ernest Hemingway," makes the observation that "Hemingway's 'good' women seem really to be Hemingway men only slightly changed" (21). Robert Penn Warren concurs that Hemingway's "best women characters . . . are those who most nearly approximate the men; that is, they embody the masculine virtues and point of view characteristic of Hemingway's work." "Ernest Hemingway," in *Ernest Hemingway: Five Decades of Criticism*, 93.

54. Ernest Hemingway, *Men Without Women*, 119. All subsequent citations from *Men Without Women* refer to this edition.

55. Pamela Smiley identifies the problems in communication between Hemingway's men and women as one of "strong gender-linked language differences." "Gender-Linked Miscommunication in 'Hills Like White Elephants,' " 2.

56. Ernest Hemingway, *A Farewell to Arms*, 16–17. All subsequent citations from *A Farewell to Arms* refer to this edition.

57. Jean Markale also points out, in *Women of the Celts*, that in the mythical tales of Diarmaid and Grainne, and Tristan and Isolde, the male hero's act of falling in love is seen as a trap that permanently draws him away from the social and legal laws and institutions of patriarchal civilization, and labels him as a disloyal, treasonous criminal. The sexual union of Troilus and Cressida, and Othello and Desdemona, according to Janet Adelman in *Suffocating Mothers: Fantasies of Maternal Origin in Shakespeare's Plays, "Hamlet" to "The Tempest,"* signifies an engulfing and "dangerous return to the infant's first union with a nurturing maternal figure" (53) that destroys the hero's masculine identity, itself originally founded on the loss of the maternal figure.

58. About Catherine, Carlos Baker observes that for Frederic Henry: "Where she is, home is . . ." *(The Writer as Artist*, 112).

59. While Hemingway was writing the end of *A Farewell to Arms* his second wife, Pauline, gave birth to his son, Patrick, after a difficult labor and finally an emergency Cesarean section. See Meyers's *Hemingway: A Biography*, 208.

60. While it is impossible to say how many different versions of the ending to *A Farewell to Arms* Hemingway imagined, several alternative endings are preserved in the Hemingway archives at the John F. Kennedy Library in Boston.

61. Ernest Hemingway, *Winner Take Nothing*. All subsequent citations from *Winner Take Nothing* refer to this edition.

62. Gregory H. Hemingway, *Papa: A Personal Memoir*, 118.

63. Meyers, in *Hemingway: A Biography*, points out that Hemingway's son Leicester, like his son Gregory, "tried desperately and failed to please Hemingway" (482). Meyers cites Leicester's first wife who remarked that "Gregory is another one who wanted to emulate Ernest and fell short. He could never seem to get Ernest's approval and that's what he craved the most" (482).

Notes to Chapter 6

1. Tom Dardis, *The Thirsty Muse: Alcohol and the American Writer*, 171.

2. Ernest Hemingway, *Winner Take Nothing*, 6. All subsequent citations from *Winner Take Nothing* refer to this edition.

3. Ernest Hemingway, "The Snows of Kilimanjaro," in *The Snows of Kilimanjaro and Other Stories*, 3. All subsequent citations in the text refer to this edition.

4. Ernest Hemingway, "Fathers and Sons," in *Winner Take Nothing*, 152.

5. According to A. E. Hotchner, Hemingway confessed to him during a visit to Key West in 1955, that "The Snows of Kilimanjaro" was his most openly confessional work of fiction; that he "[n]ever wrote so directly about myself as in that story. The man is dying, and I got that pretty good, complete with handles, because I had been breathed upon by the Grim Reaper more than once and could write about that from the inside out." *Papa Hemingway: A Personal Memoir*, 158–59.

6. Ernest Hemingway, *Death in the Afternoon*, 122. All subsequent citations from *Death in the Afternoon* refer to this edition.

7. It may be remembered at this point that Hemingway had recently injured his arm in a car accident in 1930. He also, like Belmonte, had "feeble legs" from his wounding in the war, as he confessed an account of his skiing ability in *Green Hills of Africa*, "my legs were bad now and it was not worth the time you spent hunting good snow any more." *Green Hills of Africa*, 285. All subsequent citations from *Green Hills of Africa* refer to this edition.

8. Ernest Hemingway, *Across the River and Into the Trees*. All subsequent citations from *Across the River and Into the Trees* refer to this edition.
9. Peter Griffin, *Less Than a Treason*, 49, 100.
10. Ernest Hemingway, *Men Without Women*, 37.
11. The omitted passages from "A Natural History of the Dead" are on record in the Hemingway Archives of the John F. Kennedy Library in Boston.
12. As Grace later reported the story to her children, at the age of seven she went totally blind for several months as a result of a severe bout of scarlet fever. However, as Kenneth Lynn points out, "scarlet fever has seldom, if ever, been reported as a cause of blindness. What seems more likely is that she suffered a case of hysterical blindness as a result of the conflicted feelings stemming from the realization that she was expected to study music seriously." *Hemingway*, 31.
13. See, for one, Jeffrey Meyers's Appendix I in *Hemingway: A Biography*.
14. A. E. Hotchner, in *Papa Hemingway: A Personal Memoir*, reports that during Hemingway's last days in Havana he was informed by Cuban doctors that he was suffering from an uncommon disease, *keratitis sicca*, which, as he explains to his friend, resulted in the cornea of his eyes "drying up. Tear ducts dried up already" (234). A short time afterwards, however, when Hemingway visited a specialist in New York, he was told that he had no such disease, and that he merely needed a stronger pair of glasses. Hemingway's eyes, according to Hotchner, miraculously cleared up overnight, and he never bothered to fill his new prescription for glasses. Equally interesting is Hemingway's admission to Hotchner that while in Cuba, when he believed he was going blind, the "Only book in the joint with type big enough for me to read is *Tom Sawyer* . . . which is a great book but begins to pale on the ninth reading" (234). If it is remembered from chapter 3 of Twain's novel, Tom's inability to express his grief over his emotional deprivation and isolation resulted in the augmenting of that grief into a canker that infected his entire worldview. By repressing his grief, life itself became entirely devoid of meaning, and he wandered off to seek "desolate places that were in harmony with his spirit," fantasizing about suicide, and believing that by dying he would punish through guilt his offending Aunt Polly, who would see him as he really was: "a poor little sufferer, whose griefs were at an end" (Mark Twain, *The Adventures of Tom Sawyer*, vol. 4 of *The Works of Mark Twain*, 54).
15. Freud several times mentioned the use of "blindness" to represent castration, discussing the subject at greatest length in his analysis of E. T. A. Hoffmann's "The Sandman," in his essay "The 'Uncanny' " (1919) in *Standard Edition*, 17: 231–33.
16. Richard B. Hovey, "*Islands in the Stream*: Death and the Artist," 184.
17. Karl A. Menninger, *Man against Himself*, 23.
18. As Malcolm Cowley once said of Hemingway: "Ernesto never learned that you can't go back. He always tried to go back." (From a tape-recorded interview with Cowley included in a ninety-minute radio program on Hemingway produced by the Canadian Broadcasting Corporation. Available on LP recordings through CBC Publications, Toronto, Canada.)
19. Barbara Lounsberry, "*Green Hills of Africa*: Hemingway's Celebration of Memory," 26.
20. Jeffrey Meyers, for one, summarizes the reviews of the novel in *Hemingway: A Biography*, 339–42.
21. Earl Rovit, *Ernest Hemingway*, 141–42; Carole Moses, "Language as Theme in *For Whom the Bell Tolls*."
22. Ernest Hemingway, *For Whom the Bell Tolls*, 338–39. All subsequent citations from *For Whom the Bell Tolls* refer to this edition.

23. Michael S. Reynolds argues in "Hemingway's Home: Depression and Suicide," that: "Insomnia, erratic blood pressure, blinding headaches, and severe depression were the genetic heritage of Ernest Hemingway, his sisters and brothers. They carried it as a legacy from both sides of the family. . . . Marcelline had low blood pressure; Ernest, high blood pressure. Marcelline and Ernest both suffered from diabetes, and both went through periods of severe depression. Eventually three of the Hemingway children took their own lives: Ernest in 1961; Ursula in 1966; Leicester in 1982. Though Marcelline's death in 1963 was reported to be from natural causes, Leicester suspected suicide," 609.

24. Lawrence S. Kubie, "Multiple Determinants of Suicide," in *Essays in Self-Destruction,* 456.

25. Ernest Hemingway, *Islands in the Stream,* 237.

26. Roderick Peters, "Reflections on the Origin and Aim of Nostalgia," 136.

27. Ernst Kris (1956) "The Personal Myth: A Problem in Psychoanalytic Technique," in *The Selected Papers of Ernst Kris.*

28. Ernest Hemingway, *In Our Time,* 129.

29. While Freud might categorize Pablo within his psychoanalytic narrative as the reality-based superego, Lacan would perhaps describe Jordan's transformation as a subordination of a Desire for the Mother to the Law-of-the-Father. Although both psychoanalytic narratives would therefore judge Jordan's development as a movement toward "maturity," as it is defined by patriarchal psychoanalytic parameters, the far more important consequence of Jordan's development in terms of Hemingway's past fiction is that it paves the way for him toward his forgiveness of the ambivalently-loved father and hence toward an emotional reconciliation between the son and his image of the father.

Notes to Chapter 7

1. Jackson Benson, "Ernest Hemingway as Short Story Writer: Overview," in *The Short Stories of Ernest Hemingway: Critical Essays,* 290.

2. Carlos Baker, *The Writer as Artist,* 385.

3. Leo Schneiderman, "Hemingway: A Psychological Study," 36.

4. Joyce Carol Oates, "The Hemingway Mystique," in *(Women) Writer: Occasions and Opportunities,* 302.

5. Michael S. Reynolds, "Up Against the Crannied Wall: The Limits of Biography," *Hemingway: Essays of Reassessment,* 173.

6. Kenneth S. Lynn, *Hemingway,* 504.

7. John Barkham, "Trade Winds," *Saturday Review* 38 (Feb. 13, 1954): 6. Qtd. in John Raeburn, *Fame Became of Him: Hemingway as Public Writer,* 147.

8. John Raeburn, *Fame Became of Him: Hemingway as Public Writer,* 15.

9. Philip Young, "Hemingway: The Writer in Decline," in *Hemingway: A Revaluation,* 226.

10. See the chapter on Hemingway in Tom Dardis's *The Thirsty Muse: Alcohol and the American Writer,* 161.

11. Philip Scharfer and Ronald Fieve as quoted from an interview with Denis Brian in *The True Gen,* 310. Also see Ronald Fieve's book on manic-depression, *Moodswing.*

12. Otto Kernberg, *Borderline Conditions and Pathological Narcissism,* 227–30. These seemingly narcissistic traits might include the main problem of the disturbance of self-regard in connection with disturbed object relations, and the minor ones of "an unusual degree of self-reference in their interactions with other people, a great need to be loved and admired by others, and a curious apparent contradiction between a very

inflated concept of themselves and an inordinate need for tribute from others. Their emotional life is shallow. They experience little empathy for the feelings of others, they obtain very little enjoyment from life other than from the tributes they receive from others or from their own grandiose fantasies, and they feel restless and bored when external glitter wears off and no new sources feed their self-regard. They envy others, tend to idealize some people from whom they expect narcissistic supplies and to depreciate and treat with contempt those from whom they do not expect anything (often their former idols). In general, their relationships with other people are clearly exploitative and sometimes parasitic. It is as if they feel they have the right to control and possess others and to exploit them without guilt feelings—and, behind a surface which very often is charming and engaging, one senses coldness and ruthlessness. Very often such patients are considered to be dependent because they need so much tribute and adoration from others, but on a deeper level they are completely unable really to depend on anybody because of their deep distrust and depreciation of others" (227–28).

13. Bernice Kert, *Hemingway Women*, 375.

14. As Irvin and Marilyn Yalom maintain in "Ernest Hemingway—A Psychiatric View": "Of all the insults and injuries suffered by Hemingway, none was so grave, so irreparable to his psychic economy as the somatic decline of his advancing years. He had no easy way of befriending old age; no slot existed for the old man in the Hemingway code" (493).

15. Wright Morris, *Earthly Delights, Unearthly Adornments*, 146.

16. Gregory H. Hemingway, *Papa: A Personal Memoir*, 5.

17. See Lynn's *Hemingway*, 513; and, Jeffrey Meyers's Appendix I in *Hemingway: A Biography*.

18. David S. Werman defines "nostalgia" (as opposed to "homesickness") as "an experience with particular cognitive and affective components. The cognitive aspects consist of memories of a given place—rather than of objects—at a given time, and the affect associated with these memories is characteristically described as bittersweet." "Normal and Pathological Nostalgia," 388. This may suggest a reason why Hemingway envisioned Paris (a place), as his nostalgic "moveable feast," rather than his first wife, Hadley, the actual lost object itself. According to Harvey A. Kaplan, in "The Psychopathology of Nostalgia," nostalgia also mimics manic-depressive behavior in that, on the one hand, in a "psychoanalytic context, the meaning of nostalgia changes to become a variant of depression, an acute yearning for a union with the preoedipal mother, a saddening farewell to childhood, a defense against mourning, or a longing for a past forever lost. The mournful, grieving, despairing quality is stressed quite unlike the emotions that are portrayed in common usage." On the other hand, nostalgia may also be seen as "a universal affect that results in a heightened mental state, an enhancing, uplifting mood related to particular memories of the past. Nostalgia also entails the recognition and acceptance that this past can never return. There is an irrevocability, components of which can be characterized as sad or bittersweet. However, the mood is basically one of joyousness, producing an air of infatuation and a feeling of elation" (466, 465).

19. See Harvey A. Kaplan, "The Psychopathology of Nostalgia," 470; Sydney Smith, "The Golden Fantasy: A Regressive Reaction to Separation Anxiety"; Kernberg, *Borderline Conditions and Pathological Narcissism*, Chapters 8 & 9; and Jack Kleiner, "On Nostalgia."

20. Roderick Peters, "Reflections on the Origin and Aim of Nostalgia," 136.

21. Stanley W. Jackson, *Melancholia & Depression*, 373.

22. In Stanley W. Jackson, *Melancholia and Depression: From Hippocratic Times to Modern Times.* David S. Werman, "Normal and Pathological Nostalgia," 387–98. Kernberg adds, in *Borderline Conditions and Pathological Nostalgia*, that "the capacity for mourning over a lost good object or a lost ideal image of oneself, is an important prerequisite for emotional development and especially for the broadening and deepening of feelings" (237). See also Kaplan, "The Psychopathology of Nostalgia," 466.

23. In his study of Hemingway's developing career as a creative artist, Carlos Baker acutely identifies the critical psychological link between nostalgia and narcissism in Hemingway's later life. He writes:

    Nostalgia of various kinds and degrees shadowed and colored his perspectives on his past, romanticizing his fictional self-portraits and even giving prominent place to some of his own personal idiosyncrasies, as if he hoped to persuade readers to accept these, along with the rest, in lieu of the genuinely objective art he had once been able to achieve. Not only was he beginning to be impressed, like the legendary Narcissus, with the splendor of his reflected image, but he was also obliged to contend with the most dangerous problem of all—the same that he had clairvoyantly recognized in Joyce—the tendency to fall in love with the images he was making out of the materials that his life had foisted upon him. (*Writer as Artist*, 385)

24. See Werman, "Normal and Pathological Nostalgia," 395; and Kaplan, "The Psychopathology of Nostalgia," 473.

25. Jack Kleiner, "On Nostalgia," 494.

26. Robert E. Flemming, "The Endings of Hemingway's *Garden of Eden*," 201–2. Hemingway's complete hand-written manuscript of *The Garden of Eden* may be found at the John F. Kennedy Library in Boston.

27. Ernest Hemingway, letter to Col. Buck Lanham. June 12, 1948, quoted in Carlos Baker, *Ernest Hemingway: A Life Story*, 460.

28. Ernest Hemingway, *The Garden of Eden.* All subsequent citations from the published version of *The Garden of Eden* refer to this edition.

29. If it is remembered, as Harvey Kaplan writes in "The Psychopathology of Nostalgia," the ego ideal, like the family-romance fantasy of an idealized parent figure, is an "extension," or "substitute for the original," but lost, "narcissism of childhood" (470–71).

30. Among a long list of negative statements made against the novel is Richard B. Hovey's claim that it is Hemingway's "worst" book, and that much of the time it borders on "absurdity" ("*Islands in the Stream:* Death and the Artist," 189); and Philip Young's assertion that the Colonel's long conversations with Renata are "banal and downright embarrassing" ("Hemingway: The Writer in Decline," *Hemingway: A Revaluation*, 233).

31. Ernest Hemingway, *Across the River and Into the Trees*, 232. All subsequent citations in the text from *Across the River and Into the Trees* refer to this edition.

32. The unpublished Orpen manuscript is filed in the Hemingway Archives of the John F. Kennedy Library in Boston.

33. Ernest Hemingway, *A Moveable Feast.* All subsequent citations from *A Moveable Feast* refer to this edition.

34. As Hemingway wrote to a friend in 1950: "If you are lucky enough to have lived in Paris as a young man, then wherever you go for the rest of your life, it stays with you, for Paris is a moveable feast." See the epigram that opens the Scribner's editions of the novel.

35. John Bowlby, *Loss*, vol. 3 of his series *Attachment and Loss*, 239–40.

36. Ernest Hemingway, *Islands in the Stream,* 190. All subsequent citations from *Islands in the Stream* refer to this edition.
37. Richard Hovey diagnoses Hudson's problem as "melancholia" and "unbearable depression." *"Islands in the Stream:* Death and the Artist," 174.
38. Hovey recognizes, but does not satisfactorily attempt to explain, why Hemingway had to "finish off all three" of Hudson's sons in the novel. *"Islands in the Stream:* Death and the Artist," 179.
39. This is the focus of Gregory S. Sojka's "Art and Order in *Islands in the Stream,"* in *Hemingway: A Revaluation.*
40. Ibid., 264 and 266.
41. Richard B. Hovey, *"Islands in the Stream:* Death and the Artist," 182.
42. Tom Dardis, *The Thirsty Muse,* 10.
43. James A. Michener, *Literary Reflections: Michener on Michener, Hemingway, Capote and Others,* 120.
44. Ernest Hemingway, *The Old Man and the Sea,* 105. All subsequent citations from *The Old Man and the Sea* refer to this edition.
45. Hemingway, *Across the River and Into the Trees,* 55.
46. Ernest Hemingway, *The Snows of Kilimanjaro and Other Stories,* 3.
47. Sigmund Freud, (1942[1905 or 1906]) "Psychopathic Characters on the Stage," in *Standard Edition,* 7:305–10.
48. Jeffrey Meyers, *Hemingway: A Biography,* 461.

Notes to Conclusion

1. Joan Fleming and Sol Altschul, "Activation of Mourning and Growth by Psycho-Analysis," 429.
2. John Bowlby, *Loss: Sadness and Depression,* vol. 3 of *Attachment and Loss,* 137–38.
3. Verena Kast, *A Time to Mourn,* 73.
4. John Bowlby, in *Loss,* vol. 3 of his series *Attachment and Loss,* explains further about this aspect of distorted mourning that a "brief phase of numbing we now know to be very common following a bereavement; but we do not expect it to last more than a few days or perhaps a week. When it lasts for longer there is reason for unease; for example, we have seen how delay of a few weeks or months may presage chronic mourning. Abundant evidence now shows that delay, partial or complete, can last for longer than that, certainly for years or decades, and presumably in some cases for the rest of a person's life" (153).
5. Ralph Waldo Emerson, *The Journals and Miscellaneous Notebooks,* 4:67–68.
6. Joyce W. Warren, *The American Narcissus: Individualism and Women in Nineteenth-Century American Fiction,* 253–54.
7. Ernest Hemingway, "The Mother of a Queen," in *Winner Take Nothing,* 67.
8. Ralph Waldo Emerson, *The Early Lectures,* 2:279.
9. See Heinz Kohut's *The Restoration of the Self;* Christopher Lasch's *The Culture of Narcissism: American Life in an Age of Diminishing Expectations;* R. D. Laing's and A. Esterson's *Sanity, Madness and the Family;* James Masterson's *The Search for the Real Self: Unmasking the Personality Disorders of Our Age;* Erich Fromm's *Escape from Freedom,* and his later *The Sane Society;* and Robert Bly's *Iron John: A Book about Men.*
10. Nancy Chodorow, *The Reproduction of Mothering: Psychoanalysis and the Sociology of Gender,* 187.
11. Janine Chasseguet-Smirgel, *The Ego Ideal: A Psychoanalytic Essay on the Malady of the Ideal.* The consensus of psychoanalysts on the subject of the ego ideal (including

Ernest Jones, Edith Jacobson, Annie Reich, Jeanne Lampl de Groot, John M. Murray, and B. Grumberger) is that the ego ideal is the heir to primary narcissism, while the superego is heir to the Oedipus complex, and represents a person's set of internalized prohibitions. For those who project their ego ideal onto an abstract, grandiose, paternal substitute, and not onto the real, fallible (or castrating) father, the glorified, paternal, ideal self-object becomes an extension of the pregenital ideal object (the mother). In these cases of the perverse development of the ego ideal, illusions of narcissistic omnipotence and grandiloquence predominate, as the (paternal) ideal object has not been tempered by an acquired internal set of restrictive compromises and limitations (80, 104–5, 147–51).

12. Judith Viorst, *Necessary Losses: The Loves, Illusions, Dependencies and Impossible Expectations That All of Us Have to Give Up in Order to Grow*, 25.

13. Edith Jacobson, in *The Self and the Object World*, maintains: "Facilitating the gradual fusion of good and bad maternal images into a unified 'good' but also sometimes 'bad' mother, these shifts certainly assist the development of tension tolerance and of those feelings of pleasurable anticipation which introduce the category of time and secure the establishment of lasting emotional relations with the mother, i.e., of object constancy . . . the establishment of object and self constancy must be regarded as a very important prerequisite for both a healthy process of identification and normal superego formation. Conversely, the development of moral standards supports this merging of 'good' and 'bad' object and self images into concepts of total 'good and also bad' persons and a total 'good and also bad' self" (63, 66).

14. Bruno Bettelheim, in *Symbolic Wounds: Puberty Rites and the Envious Male*, used this phrasing in referring to the initiation of tribal boys into "manhood," which, unlike the girl's initiation into "womanhood," is not punctuated by overt biological signs such as menstruation and the development of breasts (242).

15. Chasseguet-Smirgel, *The Ego Ideal*, 147, 170–71.

16. Greg Mogenson, "The Psychotherapy of the Dead: Loss and Character Structure in Freud's Metapsychology," 262.

17. John Munder Ross, "Oedipus Revisited: Laius and the 'Laius Complex,' " 188.

18. D. H. Lawrence, *Studies in Classic American Literature*, 19.

19. Dan Kiley, *The Peter Pan Syndrome: Men Who Have Never Grown Up*.

20. J. M. Barrie's *Peter Pan*, as cited by Kiley, 33 (italics in original).

Bibliography

Primary Sources and Literary Criticism

Adelman, Janet. *Suffocating Mothers: Fantasies of Maternal Origin in Shakespeare's Plays, "Hamlet" to "The Tempest"*. New York: Routledge, 1992.

Allen, Gay Wilson. *Waldo Emerson*. New York: Viking Press, 1981.

Anderson, Quentin. *The Imperial Self: An Essay in American Literature and Cultural History*. New York: Knopf, 1971.

———. *Making Americans: An Essay on Individualism and Money*. New York: Harcourt Brace Jovanovich, 1992.

Arvin, Newton. "The Whale" in *Herman Melville*, 151–93. Edited by Newton Arvin. New York: W. Sloane Associates, 1950. Reprinted in Hershel Parker and Harrison Hayford, eds., *"Moby-Dick" as Doubloon: Essays and Extracts (1851–1970)*. New York: W. W. Norton, 1970.

Baker, Carlos. *Ernest Hemingway: A Life Story*. New York: Scribner's, 1969.

———. *The Writer as Artist*. Princeton: Princeton University Press, 1952.

Barkham, John. "Trade Winds." *Saturday Review* 38 (Feb. 13, 1954): 6–10.

Beaver, Harold. *Huckleberry Finn*. London: Unwin Hyman, 1987.

Beidler, Peter G. "The Raft Episode in *Huckleberry Finn*." In *Adventures of Huckleberry Finn*. Norton Critical Edition. New York: W. W. Norton, 1977.

Benson, Jackson. "Ernest Hemingway as Short Story Writer: Overview." In *The Short Stories of Ernest Hemingway: Critical Essays*. Edited by Jackson J. Benson. Durham, N.C.: Duke University Press, 1975.

Bergler, Edmund. "A Note on Herman Melville." *American Imago* 11 (Winter 1954): 385–97.

Bersani, Leo. "Incomparable America." In *Major Literary Characters: Ahab*, 210–28. Edited by Harold Bloom. New York: Chelsea House, 1991.

Bradbury, Malcolm. "Introduction." *Pudd'nhead Wilson*. New York: Penguin, 1986.

Brian, Denis. *The True Gen*. New York: Grove Press, 1988.

Brooks, Van Wyck. *The Ordeal of Mark Twain*. New York: Dutton, 1977.

Burnam, Tom. "Primitivism and Masculinity in the Work of Ernest Hemingway." *Modern Fiction Studies* 1 (Aug. 1955): 20–24.

Cardwell, Guy. *The Man Who Was Mark Twain*. New Haven: Yale University Press, 1991.

Chase, Richard. *The American Novel and Its Tradition*. Garden City: Doubleday, 1957.

Cooper, Stephen. " 'Good Rotten Material for Burial': The Overdetermined Death of Romance in *Life on the Mississippi*." *Literature and Medicine* 36: 78–89.

Cox, James M. "The Uncomfortable Ending of *Huckleberry Finn*." In *Adventures of Huckleberry Finn*. Norton Critical Edition. New York: W. W. Norton, 1977.

Crews, Frederick. *The Sins of the Father: Hawthorne's Psychological Themes*. Berkeley: University of California Press, 1966.

Dardis, Tom. *The Thirsty Muse: Alcohol and the American Writer*. New York: Ticknor & Fields, 1989.

de Tocqueville, Alexis. *Democracy in America*. Edited by Richard D. Heffner. New York: New American Library, 1956.

Defalco, Joseph. *The Hero in Hemingway's Short Stories*. Pittsburgh: University of Pittsburgh Press, 1963.

Delbanco, Andrew. *The Puritan Ordeal*. Cambridge, Mass.: Harvard University Press, 1989.

De Voto, Bernard. *Mark Twain at Work*. Boston: Houghton Mifflin, 1967.

————. *Mark Twain's America and Mark Twain at Work*. Boston: Houghton Mifflin, 1960.

————, ed. *Mark Twain in Eruption: Hitherto Unpublished Pages about Men and Events*. New York: Harper & Bros., 1940.

Edel, Leon. "The Mystery of Walden Pond." In *Stuff of Sleep and Dreams*. New York: Harper, 1982.

Eliot, T. S. "An Introduction to *Huckleberry Finn*." In *Adventures of Huckleberry Finn*. Edited by Sculley Bradley et al. Norton Critical Edition. New York: W. W. Norton, 1977.

Emerson, Ralph Waldo. *The Early Lectures*. Edited by Stephen E. Whicher et al. 3 vols. Cambridge, Mass: Harvard University Press, 1959–1972.

————. *Essays and Lectures*. Edited by Joel Porte. New York: Library of America, 1983.

————. *The Journals and Miscellaneous Notebooks*. Edited by William H. Gilman et al. 16 vols. Cambridge, Mass.: Harvard University Press, 1960–1982.

Feidelson, Charles, Jr. *Symbolism and American Literature*. Chicago: Chicago University Press, 1953.

Fetterley, Judith. "Mark Twain and the Anxiety of Entertainment." In *Critical Essays on Mark Twain: 1910–1980*. Edited by Louis J. Budd. Boston: G. K. Hall, 1983.

Fiedler, Leslie. "Faust in the Eden of Childhood." In *A Casebook on Mark Twain's Wound*. Edited by Lewis Leary. New York: Thomas Y. Crowell, 1962.

————. *Love and Death in the American Novel*. New York: Stein & Day, 1982.

Flemming, Robert E. "The Endings of Hemingway's *Garden of Eden*." *American Literature* 61 (May 1989): 261–70.

Franklin, Benjamin. *Benjamin Franklin's Autobiography*. Edited by J. A. Leo Lemay et al. Norton Critical Edition. New York: W. W. Norton, 1986.

Freese, Peter. *"America": Dream or Nightmare? Reflections on a Composite Image*. Essen: Verlag Die Blaue Eule, 1990.

Furness, William Henry. "Remarks on the Four Gospels." In *The Transcendentalists: An Anthology*, 124–28. Edited by Perry Miller. Cambridge, Mass.: Harvard University Press, 1950.

Garcia, Wilma. *Mothers and Others: Myths of the Female in the Works of Melville, Twain, and Hemingway*. New York: Peter Lang, 1984.

Gillman, Susan. *Dark Twins: Imposture and Identity in Mark Twain's America*. Chicago: Chicago University Press, 1989.

Girgus, Sam B. *Desire and the Political Unconscious: Eros and Ideology*. New York: St. Martin's Press, 1990.

Griffin, Peter. *Along with Youth*. New York: Oxford University Press, 1985.

————. *Less Than a Treason: Hemingway in Paris*. New York: Oxford University Press, 1990.

Griffith, John. "Rectitude in Hemingway's Fiction: How Rite Makes Right." In *In Our*

Time. Edited by Richard Astro and Jackson J. Benson. Corvallis: Oregon State University Press, 1974.

Haberstroh, Charles J. *Melville and Male Identity.* Rutherford, N.J.: Fairleigh Dickinson University Press, 1980.

Harris, Susan K. *Mark Twain's Escape from Time: A Study of Patterns and Images.* Columbia: University of Missouri Press, 1982.

Hassan, Ihab. *Radical Innocence: Studies in the American Novel.* Princeton: Princeton University Press, 1961.

Hayford, Harrison et al., eds. *Moby-Dick; or, The Whale.* Chicago and Evanston: Northwestern University Press, 1961.

Hemingway, Ernest. *Across the River and Into the Trees.* New York: Scribner's Sons, 1978.

———. *Death in the Afternoon.* New York: Scribner's Sons, 1960.

———. *A Farewell to Arms.* New York: Collier/Macmillan, 1986.

———. *For Whom the Bell Tolls.* New York: Scribner's Sons, 1968.

———. *The Garden of Eden,* MS. Hemingway Papers. John F. Kennedy Library. Boston, Mass.

———. *The Garden of Eden.* Edited by Tom Jenks. New York: Collier/Macmillan, 1986.

———. *Green Hills of Africa.* New York: Scribner's Sons, 1963.

———. *In Our Time.* Scribner Classic. New York: Collier/Macmillan, 1987.

———. Interview by Malcolm Cowley for the Canadian Broadcasting Corporation. Available on LP recordings through CBC Publications, Toronto, Canada.

———. *Islands in the Stream.* New York: Scribner's Sons, 1970.

———. *Men Without Women.* Scribner Classic. New York: Macmillan, 1986.

———. *A Moveable Feast.* New York: Macmillan, 1987.

———. *The Old Man and the Sea.* New York: Scribner's Sons, 1980.

———. "Orpen." MS. Hemingway Papers. John F. Kennedy Library. Boston, Mass.

———. *The Snows of Kilimanjaro and Other Stories.* New York: Collier/Macmillan, 1986.

———. *Winner Take Nothing.* Scribner Classic. New York: Macmillan, 1987.

Hemingway, Gregory H. *Papa: A Personal Memoir.* Boston: Houghton Mifflin, 1976.

Hoffman, Daniel G. "Black Magic—and White—in *Huckleberry Finn.*" In *A Casebook on Mark Twain's Wound.* Edited by Lewis Leary. New York: Thomas Y. Crowell, 1962.

Holland, Norman. *The Dynamics of Literary Response.* New York: Columbia University Press, 1989.

Hotchner, A. E. *Papa Hemingway: A Personal Memoir.* London: Weidenfeld and Nicolson, 1967.

Hovey, Richard B. "*Islands in the Stream:* Death and the Artist." *Hartford Studies in Literature* 12 (1980): 173–90.

Howard, Leon. *Herman Melville: A Biography.* Berkeley: University of California Press, 1951.

Johnston, Kenneth. *The Tip of the Iceberg: Hemingway and the Short Story.* Greenwood, Fla.: Penkevill Publishing, 1987.

Jones, Donald. "Newspaper Job in Toronto Launched Writer's Career." *Toronto Star,* June 18, 1977.

Kaplan, Justin. *Mr. Clemens and Mark Twain: A Biography.* New York: Simon & Schuster, 1966.

Kert, Bernice. *Hemingway Women.* New York: W. W. Norton, 1983.

Kiell, Norman. *Blood Brothers: Siblings as Writers.* New York: International Universities Press, 1983.

Kriegel, Leonard. "Hemingway's Rites of Manhood." *Partisan Review* 44 (1977): 416–30.

Lawrence, D. H. *Studies in Classic American Literature*. New York: Penguin, 1977.

Leverenz, David. *Manhood and the American Renaissance*. Ithaca: Cornell University Press, 1989.

Lewis, R. W. B. *The American Adam: Innocence, Tragedy, and Tradition in the Nineteenth Century*. Chicago: University of Chicago Press, 1955.

Lewishon, Ludwig. *The Story of American Literature*. New York: Modern Library, 1939.

Lounsberry, Barbara. "*Green Hills of Africa*: Hemingway's Celebration of Memory." *The Hemingway Review* 2 (Spring 1983): 23–31.

Lynn, Kenneth S. "Adulthood in American Literature." *Daedalus* (Fall 1976): 49–59.

———. *Hemingway*. New York: Simon & Schuster, 1987.

———. *Mark Twain and Southwestern Humor*. Boston: Little, Brown, 1959.

———. *Mark Twain's Escape From Time*. Columbia: University of Missouri Press, 1987.

Lyon, Isabel Van Kleck. *Diary*. In Papers. Filed on microfilm in the Mark Twain Archives, Elmira College Library. Elmira, New York.

Martin, Robert K. *Hero, Captain, and Stranger: Male Friendship, Social Critique, and Literary Form in the Sea Novels of Herman Melville*. Chapel Hill: University of North Carolina Press, 1986.

Matthiessen, F. O. *American Renaissance: Art and Expression in the Age of Emerson and Whitman*. New York: Oxford University Press, 1941.

McConnell, Frank. "Stalking Papa's Ghost: Hemingway's Presence in Contemporary American Writing." In *Ernest Hemingway: New Critical Essays*. Edited by A. Robert Lee. London: Vision, 1983.

Melville, Herman. "Hawthorne and His Mosses." In Vol. 9, *The Writings of Herman Melville: The Piazza Tales & Other Prose Pieces: 1839–1860*, 239–53. Evanston and Chicago: Northwestern University Press/The Newberry Library, 1987.

———. *Moby-Dick; Or, The Whale*. Edited by Harrison Hayford et al. Vol. 6 of *The Writings of Herman Melville*. Evanston and Chicago: Northwestern University Press/ The Newberry Library, 1988.

———. "The Paradise of Bachelors and the Tartarus of Maids." In *The Piazza Tales and Other Prose Pieces*. Vol. 9 of *The Writings of Herman Melville*. Evanston and Chicago: Northwestern University Press/The Newberry Library, 1987.

———. *Pierre; or, the Ambiguities*. Edited by Harrison Hayford et al. Vol. 7 of *The Writings of Herman Melville*. Evanston and Chicago: Northwestern University Press/ The Newberry Library, 1971.

Meyers, Jeffrey. *Hemingway: A Biography*. New York: Harper & Row, 1985.

Michener, James A. *Literary Reflections: Michener on Michener, Hemingway, Capote, and Others*. Austin: State House Press, 1993.

Miller, Madelaine Hemingway. *Ernie: Hemingway's "Sister 'Sunny' Remembers"*. New York: Crown, 1975.

Miller, Perry. *The New England Mind: From Colony to Province*. Cambridge, Mass.: Belknap Press of Harvard University Press, 1983.

Mitchell, Lee Clark. " 'Nobody but Our Gang Warn't Around': The Authority of Language in *Huckleberry Finn*." In *New Essays on "Adventures of Huckleberry Finn"*. Edited by Louis J. Budd. Cambridge: Cambridge University Press, 1987.

Morris, Wright. "The Available Past." In *A Casebook on Mark Twain's Wound*. Edited by Lewis Leary. New York: Thomas Y. Crowell, 1962.

———. *Earthly Delights, Unearthly Adornments*. New York: Harper & Row, 1978.

Moses, Carole. "Language as Theme in *For Whom the Bell Tolls*." *Fitzgerald/Hemingway Annual* (1978): 215–23.

Mumford, Lewis. *Herman Melville.* New York: Harcourt, Brace, 1929.

Murray, Henry A. "Dead to the World: The Passions of Herman Melville." In *Essays in Self- Destruction,* 7–29. Edited by Edwin S. Shneidman. New York: Science House, 1967.

———. "In Nomine Diaboli" In *Critical Essays on Herman Melville's "Moby-Dick",* 408–20. Edited by Brian Higgins and Hershel Parker. New York: G. K. Hall, 1992. Reprinted in *The New England Quarterly,* 24(Dec. 1951): 435–52.

———. "Introduction." *Pierre; or The Ambiguities.* Edited by H. A. Murray. New York: Hendricks House, 1949.

Nowell, Elizabeth. *Thomas Wolfe, A Biography.* New York: Doubleday, 1960.

Oates, Joyce Carol. "The Hemingway Mystique." In *(Women) Writer: Occasions and Opportunities.* New York: Dutton, 1988.

Paine, Albert Bigelow. *Mark Twain: A Biography.* 4 Vols. New York: Harper & Bros., 1912.

Paine, Thomas. "Common Sense." In *The Essential Writings of Thomas Paine,* 23–72. New York: Penguin/Meridian, 1984.

Parsons, Coleman O. "The Devil and Samuel Clemens." In *A Casebook on Mark Twain's Wound.* Edited by Lewis Leary. New York: Thomas Y. Crowell, 1962.

Pearce, Roy Harvey. " 'The End. Yours Truly, Huck Finn': Postscript." In *Adventures of Huckleberry Finn.* Norton Critical Edition. New York: W. W. Norton, 1977.

Petrullo, Helen. "The Neurotic Hero of *Typee.*" *American Imago* 12 (1955): 317–23.

Poirier, Richard. *A World Elsewhere: The Place of Style in American Literature.* New York: Oxford University Press, 1966.

Pops, Martin Leonard. "In the Splendid Labyrinth: *Moby-Dick.*" In *The Melville Archetype.* Kent, Ohio: Kent State University Press, 1970.

Raeburn, John. *Fame Became of Him: Hemingway as Public Writer.* Bloomington: Indiana University Press, 1984.

Reed, Sampson. "Observations on the Growth of the Mind." In *The Transcendentalists: An Anthology,* 53–58. Edited by Perry Miller. Cambridge, Mass.: Harvard University Press, 1950.

Reynolds, Michael S. "Hemingway's Home: Depression and Suicide." *American Literature* 57 (Dec. 1985): 600–610.

———. "Up Against the Crannied Wall: The Limits of Biography." In *Hemingway: Essays of Reassessment.* Edited by Frank Scafella. New York: Oxford University Press, 1991.

Robinson, Forrest G. *In Bad Faith: The Dynamics of Deception in Mark Twain's America.* Cambridge, Mass.: Harvard University Press, 1986.

Rosenheim, Frederick. "Flight from Home: Some Episodes in the Life of Herman Melville. *American Imago* 1 (Dec. 1940): 1–30.

Rovit, Earl. *Ernest Hemingway.* Boston: Twayne, 1963.

Rusk, Ralph L., ed. *The Letters of Ralph Waldo Emerson.* 6 vols. New York: Columbia University Press, 1939.

Salomon, Louis B. "Hawthorne and His Father: A Conjecture." *Literature and Psychology* 13 (Winter 1963): 12–16.

Sanborn, Margaret. *Mark Twain: The Bachelor Years.* New York: Doubleday, 1990.

Schneiderman, Leo. "Hemingway: A Psychological Study." *Connecticut Review* 6 (April 1973): 34-49.

Shaw, Peter. "Fathers, Sons, and the Ambiguities of Revolution in 'My Kinsman, Major Molineux.' " *New England Quarterly* 49 (Dec. 1976): 559–76.

Sherman, Stuart P. *The Genius of America.* New York: Scribner's, 1923.

Shneidman, Edwin S. "The Deaths of Herman Melville." In *Melville and Hawthorne in the Berkshires*, 118–43. Edited by Howard P. Vincent. Kent, Ohio: Kent State University Press, 1968.

Slotkin, Richard. "*Moby-Dick:* The American National Epic." In *Twentieth-Century Interpretations of "Moby-Dick"*. Edited by Michael T. Gilmore. Englewood Cliffs, N.J.: Prentice-Hall, 1977.

Smiley, Pamela. "Gender-Linked Miscommunication in 'Hills Like White Elephants.' " *The Hemingway Review* 2 (Fall 1988): 2–12.

Sojka, Gregory S. "Art and Order in *Islands in the Stream*." In *Hemingway: A Revaluation*. Edited by David R. Noble. Troy, N.Y.: Whitson Publishing, 1983.

Spilka, Mark. "Jake & Brett: Wounded Warriors." In *Brett Ashley*. Edited by Harold Bloom. New York: Chelsea House, 1991. Excerpted from Mark Spilka, *Hemingway's Quarrel with Androgyny*. Lincoln: University of Nebraska Press, 1990.

Sprengnether, Madelon. *The Spectral Mother: Freud, Feminism, and Psychoanalysis*. Ithaca: Cornell University Press, 1990.

Stone, Edward. *A Certain Morbidness*. Carbondale: Southern Illinois University Press, 1969.

Strout, Cushing. *Making American Tradition: Visions and Revisions from Ben Franklin to Alice Walker*. New Brunswick: Rutgers University Press, 1990.

Thoreau, Henry David. *Walden and Civil Disobedience*. Edited by Owen Thomas. Norton Critical Edition. New York: W. W. Norton, 1966.

———. *The Writings of Henry David Thoreau*. 1906. Walden Edition. 20 vols. Reprint. New York: AMS Press, 1968.

Tolchin, Neal. *Mourning, Gender, and Creativity in the Art of Herman Melville*. New Haven: Yale University Press, 1988.

Trilling, Lionel. "The Greatness of *Huckleberry Finn*." In *Adventures of Huckleberry Finn*. Norton Critical Edition. New York: W. W. Norton, 1977.

Twain, Mark. *Adventures of Huckleberry Finn*. Edited by Sculley Bradley et al. Norton Critical Edition. New York: W. W. Norton, 1977.

———. *Adventures of Huckleberry Finn*. Edited by Walter Blair and Victor Fischer. Berkeley: University of California Press/Bancroft Library, 1985.

———. *The Adventures of Tom Sawyer*. Vol. 4 of *The Works of Mark Twain*. Edited by John C. Gerber et al. Berkeley: University of California Press, 1980.

———. *The American Claimant*. Vol. 15 of *The Writings of Mark Twain*. Stormfield Edition. New York: Harper & Bros., 1924.

———. *The Autobiography of Mark Twain*. Edited by Charles Neider. New York: Harper Perennial, 1990.

———. *The Gilded Age: A Tale of Today*. Ontario: Penguin, 1985.

———. *Letters from the Earth*. Edited by Bernard De Voto. New York: Harper & Row, 1974.

———. *Life As I Find It*. Edited by Charles Neider. New York: Hanover House, 1961.

———. *Life on the Mississippi*. Edited by Willis Wager. Illustrated by Thomas Hart Benton, with an Introduction by Edward Wagenknecht. New York: The Limited Editions Club, 1944.

———. *The Man That Corrupted Hadleyburg and Other Essays and Stories*. New York: Harper & Bros., 1929.

———. *Mark Twain—William Dean Howells Letters*. Ed. Henry Nash Smith and William M. Gibson. 2 vols. Cambridge, Mass.: Belknap Press of Harvard University Press, 1960.

———. Mark Twain Papers. Bancroft Library, University of California, Berkeley.

————. *Mark Twain Speaking*. Edited by Paul Fatout. Iowa City: University of Iowa Press, 1976.

————. *Mark Twain's Hannibal, Huck and Tom: (Previously Unpublished Writings)*. Edited by Walter Blair. Berkeley: University of California Press, 1969.

————. *Mark Twain's Letters*. Arranged with comment by Albert Bigelow Paine. 2 vols. New York: Harper & Bros., 1917.

————. *Mark Twain's Notebook*. Edited by Albert Bigelow Paine. New York: Harpers & Bros., 1935.

————. *Mark Twain's Short Stories*. Edited with an Introduction by Justin Kaplan. New York: Signet Classic, 1985.

————. *Mark Twain's Speeches*. Vol. 28 of *The Writings of Mark Twain*. Stormfield Edition. New York: Harper & Row, 1929.

————. *Mark Twain's Which Was the Dream? & Other Symbolic Writings of Later Years*. Edited by John S. Tuckey. Berkeley & Los Angeles: University of California Press, 1967.

————. "My Platonic Sweetheart" (1912). In *The Mysterious Stranger Manuscripts*. The Definitive Edition of *The Writings of Mark Twain*, Edited by Albert Bigelow Paine. New York: Gabriel Wells, 1913. Vol. 27: 288–304. Originally printed in *The Mysterious Stranger and Other Stories*. New York and London: Harper & Bros., 1922.

————. *The Mysterious Stranger*. New York: Signet/New American Library, 1962.

————. *On the Poetry of Mark Twain with Selections from His Verse*. Edited by Arthur L. Scott. Urbana: University of Illinois Press, 1966.

————. *The Personal Recollections of Joan of Arc, by the Sieur de Conte*, Book I. New York: Harper & Row, 1924.

————. *The Prince and the Pauper*. Vol. 6 of *The Works of Mark Twain*. Edited by Victor Fischer et al. Berkeley: University of California Press, 1979.

————. *The Tragedy of Pudd'nhead Wilson*. New York: Penguin/New American Library, 1986.

————. *A Tramp Abroad*. Vol. 9 of *The Writings of Mark Twain*. Stormfield Edition. New York, London: Harper & Bros., 1929.

————. *What Is Man? and Other Essays*. New York and London: Harper & Bros., 1917.

Van Doren, Mark. *Nathaniel Hawthorne*. New York: W. Sloane, 1949.

Varble, Rachel H. *Jane Clemens: The Story of Mark Twain's Mother*. New York: Doubleday, 1964.

Waggoner, Hyatt H. *Hawthorne: A Critical Study*. Cambridge, Mass: Harvard University Press, 1955.

Warren, Joyce W. *The American Narcissus: Individualism and Women in Nineteenth-Century American Fiction*. New Brunswick: Rutgers University Press, 1989.

Warren, Robert Penn. "Ernest Hemingway." *Ernest Hemingway: Five Decades of Criticism*. Edited by Linda Welshimer Wagner. Ann Arbor: Michigan State University Press, 1974.

Webster, Samuel, and Doris Webster. "Whitewashing Jane Clemens." *The Bookman* 61 (July 1925): 531–35.

Westbrook, Max. "Grace under Pressure: Hemingway and the Summer of 1920." In *Ernest Hemingway: The Writer in Context*. Edited by James Nagel. Madison: University of Wisconsin Press, 1984.

Whitman, Walt. *Leaves of Grass*. Edited by Sculley Bradley et al. Norton Critical Edition. New York: W. W. Norton, 1973.

Winters, Yvor. *Maule's Curse: Seven Studies in the History of American Obscurantism*. New York: New Directions, 1938.

Yalom, Irvin, and Marilyn Yalom. "Ernest Hemingway—A Psychiatric View." *Archives of General Psychiatry* 24 (June 1971): 485–94.
Young, Philip. *Ernest Hemingway: A Reconsideration.* New York: Harcourt, Brace and World, 1966.
———. "Hemingway: The Writer in Decline." In *Hemingway: A Revaluation.* Edited by Donald R. Noble. Troy, N.Y.: Whitson Publishing, 1983.
———. *The Private Melville.* University Park: Penn State University Press, 1993.

Psychoanalytic Sources
Aberbach, David. *Surviving Trauma: Loss, Literature, and Psychoanalysis.* New Haven: Yale University Press, 1989.
Bank, Stephen P., and Kahn, Michael D. *The Sibling Bond.* New York: Basic Books, 1982.
Benjamin, Jessica. *Bonds of Love.* New York: Pantheon, 1988.
Bettelheim, Bruno. *Symbolic Wounds: Puberty Rites and the Envious Male.* Glencoe, Ill.: Free Press, 1954.
Blos, Peter. "The Function of the Ego Ideal in Adolescence." *The Psychoanalytic Study of the Child* 27 (1972): 93–97.
———. "The Genealogy of the Ego Ideal." *The Psychoanalytic Study of the Child* 29 (1974): 43-88.
———. *On Adolescence.* New York: Free Press of Glencoe, 1962.
Bly, Robert. *Iron John: A Book About Men.* New York: Vintage, 1992.
Bowlby, John. *Attachment and Loss.* 3 vols. New York: Basic Books, 1980.
———. "Pathological Mourning and Childhood Mourning." *Journal of the American PsychoanalyticAssociation* 11 (1963): 500–41.
———. "Processes of Mourning." *International Journal of Psycho-Analysis* 42 (1961): 317–40.
Brown, G. W., and Harris, T. *The Social Origins of Depression: A Study of Psychiatric Disorder in Women.* London: Tavistock Publishers, 1978.
Cain, Albert C. et al. "Children's Disturbed Reactions to the Death of a Sibling." *American Journal of Orthopsychiatry* 34 (1964): 741–52.
Caprio, Frank S. "A Study of Some Psychological Reactions During Pre-Pubescence to the Idea of Death." *Psychoanalytic Quarterly* 24 (1950): 495–505.
Chasseguet-Smirgel, Janine. *The Ego Ideal: A Psychoanalytic Essay on the Malady of the Ideal.* New York: W.W. Norton, 1985.
———. *Sexuality and Mind: The Role of the Father and the Mother in the Psyche.* New York: New York University Press, 1986.
Chodorow, Nancy. *The Reproduction of Mothering: Psychoanalysis and the Sociology of Gender.* Berkeley: University of California Press, 1979.
———. *Feminism and Psychoanalytic Theory.* New Haven: Yale University Press, 1989.
Corneau, Guy. *Absent Fathers, Lost Sons.* Boston: Shambhala, 1991.
Deutsch, Helene. "Absence of Grief." *Psychoanalytic Quarterly* 6 (1937): 12–22.
Dunton, H. Donald. "The Child's Concept of Grief." In *Loss and Grief,* 355–61. Edited by Bernard Schoenberg et al. New York: Columbia University Press, 1970.
Erikson, Erik. *Identity and the Life Cycle.* New York: W. W. Norton, 1980.
———. *Young Man Luther.* New York: W. W. Norton, 1962.
Fieve, Ronald. *Moodswing.* New York: Bantam, 1976.
Flemming, Joan, and Altschul, Sol. "Activation of Mourning and Growth by Psycho-Analysis." *International Journal of Psycho-Analysis* 44 (1963): 419–31.
Fodor, N. "Varieties of Nostalgia." *Psychoanalytic Review* 37 (1950): 25–38.

Freud, Sigmund. "A Disturbance of Memory on the Acropolis" (1936). *The Standard Edition of the Complete Psychological Works of Sigmund Freud.* 22: 239–48. Edited and Translated by James Strachey. London: Hogarth Press, 1986.

———. *Beyond the Pleasure Principle* (1920). *Standard Edition.* 18: 1–65. London: Hogarth Press, 1986.

———. "Family Romances" (1909[1908]). *Standard Edition.* 9: 237–41. London: Hogarth Press, 1986.

———. *Jokes and Their Relation to the Unconscious* (1905). *Standard Edition.* 8: 3–236. London: Hogarth Press, 1986.

———. "Mourning and Melancholia" (1917[1915]). *Standard Edition.* 14: 237–60. London: Hogarth Press, 1986.

———. *New Introductory Lectures on Psycho-Analysis* (1933[1932]). *Standard Edition.* 22: 3–158. London: Hogarth Press, 1986.

———. "On Transience" (1916[1915]). *Standard Edition.* 14: 303–8. London: Hogarth Press, 1986.

———. "Psychopathic Characters on the Stage" (1942[1905 or 1906]). *Standard Edition.* 7: 305–10. London: Hogarth Press, 1986.

———. *Three Essays on the Theory of Sexuality* (1905). *Standard Edition.* 7: 125–245. London: Hogarth Press, 1986.

———. "The 'Uncanny' " (1919). *Standard Edition.* 17: 217–52. London: Hogarth Press, 1986.

Friedman, Richard C. *Male Homosexuality: A Contemporary Psychoanalytic Perspective.* New Haven: Yale University Press, 1988.

Fromm, Erich. *Escape from Freedom.* New York: Avon, 1941.

———. *The Sane Society.* Greenwich, Conn.: Fawcett, 1955.

Garber, Marjorie. *Vested Interests: Cross-Dressing and Cultural Anxiety.* New York: Routledge, 1992.

Greenacre, Phyllis. "The Family Romance of the Artist." *The Psychoanalytic Study of the Child* 13 (1958): 9–36.

Harrison, Irving B. "On Freud's View of the Infant-Mother Relationship and of the Oceanic Feeling— Some Subjective Influences." *Journal of the American Psychoanalytic Association* 27 (1979): 399–421.

———. "On the Maternal Origins of Awe." *The Psychoanalytic Study of the Child* 30 (1975): 181–95.

Harrow, M., and Amdur, M. J. "Guilt and Depressive Disorders." *Archives of General Psychiatry* 25 (Sept. 1971): 240–46.

Hopke, Robert. *Jung, Jungians and Homosexuality.* Boston and London: Shambhala, 1991.

Horney, Karen. *Neurosis and Human Growth.* New York: W. W. Norton, 1950.

Jackson, Stanley W. *Melancholia and Depression: From Hippocratic Times to Modern Times.* New Haven: Yale University Press, 1986.

Jacobson, Edith. *The Self and the Object World.* Madison, Conn.: International Universities Press, 1986.

Jensen, Viggo W., and Petty, Thomas A. "The Fantasy of Being Rescued in Suicide." *Psychoanalytic Quarterly* 27 (1958): 327–39.

Joffe, W. G., and Sandler, Joseph. "Notes on Pain, Depression, and Individuation." *The Psychoanalytic Study of the Child* 20 (1965): 394–424.

Kaplan, Harvey A. "The Psychopathology of Nostalgia." *Psychoanalytic Review* 74 (Winter 1987): 465–86.

Kast, Verena. *A Time to Mourn.* New York: Atrium, 1988.

Kernberg, Otto. *Borderline Conditions and Pathological Narcissism.* Northvale, N.J.: Jason Aronson, 1985.

Kiley, Dan. *The Peter Pan Syndrome: Men Who Have Never Grown Up.* New York: Avon, 1983.

Kleiner, Jack. "On Nostalgia." *Bulletin of the Philadelphia Association of Psychoanalysts* 20 (1970): 11–30.

Kohut, Heinz. *The Restoration of the Self.* New York: International Universities Press, 1977.

Kramer, P. *Listening to Prozac.* New York: Penguin, 1993.

Kreuger, David. "Money, Meanings and Madness: A Psychoanalytic Perspective." *The Psychoanalytic Review* 78 (Summer 1991): 209–24.

Kris, Ernst. "The Personal Myth: A Problem in Psychoanalytic Technique" (1956). In *The Selected Papers of Ernst Kris,* 272–300. New Haven: Yale University Press, 1975.

Kristeva, Julia. "About Chinese Women." In *The Kristeva Reader,* 148–59. Edited by Toril Moi. New York: Columbia University Press, 1986.

———. *Powers of Horror: An Essay on Abjection.* New York: Columbia University Press, 1982.

Kubie, Lawrence S. "Multiple Determinants of Suicide." In *Essays in Self-Destruction,* 455–63. Edited by Edwin S. Shneidman et al. New York: Science House, 1967.

Laing, R. D., and Esterson, A. *Sanity, Madness and the Family.* London: Tavistock, 1964.

Laplanche, J., and Pontalis, J.-B. *The Language of Psycho-Analysis.* New York: W. W. Norton, 1973.

Lasch, Christopher. *The Culture of Narcissism: American Life in an Age of Diminishing Expectations.* New York: Warner, 1979.

Lesser, Simon O. *Fiction and the Unconscious.* Chicago: University of Chicago Press, 1957.

Lifton, Robert J. "The Sense of Immortality: On Death and the Continuity of Life." In *Death and Identity,* 171–99. Edited by Robert Fulton. Bowie, Md.: Charles Press, 1976.

Lowen, Alexander. *Narcissism: Denial of the True Self.* New York: Macmillan/Collier, 1985.

Lowewald, Hans W. "The Waning of the Oedipus Complex." *Journal of the American Psychoanalytic Association* 27 (1978): 751–75.

Mahler, M. S. "Rapprochement Subphase of the Separation-Individuation Process." *Psychoanalytic Quarterly* 41 (1972): 487–506.

Markale, Jean. *Women of the Celts.* Rochester, Vt.: Inner Traditions International, 1986.

Masterson, James. *The Search for the Real Self: Unmasking the Personality Disorders of Our Age.* New York: Macmillan, Free Press, 1988.

McDevitt, John B. "The Role of Internalization in the Development of Object Relations During the Separation-Individuation Phase." *Journal of the American Psychoanalytic Association* 27 (1979): 327–43.

Menninger, Karl A. *Man against Himself.* New York: Harcourt, Brace, 1938.

Mitchell, Juliet. *Psychoanalysis and Feminism.* New York: Vintage, 1974.

Mogenson, Greg. "The Psychotherapy of the Dead: Loss and Character Structure in Freud's Metapsychology." *American Imago* 45 (Fall 1988): 251–70.

Novey, S. "Some Philosophical Speculations about the Concept of the Genital Character." *International Journal of Psycho-Analysis* 36: 88–94.

Parkes, C. Murray. " 'Seeking' and 'Finding' a Lost Object: Evidence from Recent Studies of the Reaction to Bereavement." *Social Science and Medicine* 4 (1970): 187–201.

Parsons, Talcott. *Essays in Sociological Theory.* Glencoe, Ill.: Free Press, 1954.

———. "Family Structure and the Socialization of the Child." In *Family Socialization and Interaction Process*. Edited by Parsons and Bales. Glencoe, Ill.: Glencoe Free Press, 1955.

———. *Social Structure and Personality*. New York: Macmillan, Free Press, 1970.

Peters, Roderick. "Reflections on the Origin and Aim of Nostalgia." *Journal of Analytical Psychology* 30 (1985): 135–48.

Pollock, George. "Anniversary Reactions, Trauma, and Mourning." *The Psychoanalytic Quarterly* (July 1970): 347–69.

Rank, Otto. "Feminine Psychology and Masculine Ideology." In *Beyond Psychology*. New York: Dover, 1941.

Reich, Annie. "Pathologic Forms of Self-Esteem Regulation." *The Psychoanalytic Study of the Child* 15 (1960): 215–32.

Ross, John Munder. "Oedipus Revisited: Laius and the 'Laius Complex.' " *The Psychoanalytic Study of the Child* 37 (1982): 169–200.

Sandler, Joseph et al. "The Ego Ideal and the Ideal Self." *The Psychoanalytic Study of the Child* 18 (1963): 139–58.

Schwenger, Peter. "The Masculine Mode." *Speaking of Gender*. Edited by Elaine Showalter. New York: Routledge, 1989.

Silverman, Kaja. *Male Subjectivity at the Margins*. New York: Routledge Press, 1992.

Silverman, Lloyd H. et al. *The Search for Oneness*. New York: International Universities Press, 1982.

Smith, Sydney. "The Golden Fantasy: A Regressive Reaction to Separation Anxiety." *International Journal of Psycho-Analysis* 58 (1977): 311–24.

Stengel, Erwin. "Studies on the Psychopathology of Compulsive Wandering." *British Journal of Medical Psychiatry* 18 (1939): 250–54.

Stern, Daniel N. *Diary of a Baby*. New York: Basic Books, 1990.

———. *The Interpersonal World of the Infant*. New York: Basic Books, 1984.

Stoller, Robert J. *Presentations of Gender*. New Haven: Yale University Press, 1985.

Viorst, Judith. *Necessary Losses: The Loves, Illusions, Dependencies and Impossible Expectations That All of Us Have to Give Up in Order to Grow*. New York: Fawcett, 1986.

Wahl, Charles W. "Suicide as a Magical Act." In *Clues to Suicide*, 22–29. Edited by Edwin S. Shneidman and Norman L. Farberow. New York: McGraw-Hill, 1957.

Weigert, Edith. "The Superego and the Ego-Ideal." *International Journal of Psycho-Analysis* 43 (1962): 264–68.

Werman, David S. "Normal and Pathological Nostalgia." *Journal of the American Psychoanalytic Association* 25 (1977): 287–398.

Whiting, Beatrice B. and John W. M. *Children of Six Cultures*. Cambridge, Mass.: Harvard University Press, 1975.

Winnicott, D. W. *The Child, the Family, and the Outside World*. New York: Addison-Wesley, 1987.

———. *Deprivation and Delinquency*. London: Tavistock, 1984.

———. *Home Is Where We Start From*. New York: W. W. Norton, 1986.

———. *The Maturational Process and the Facilitating Environment*. Madison: International Universities Press, 1965.

———. *Playing and Reality*. New York: Tavistock, 1971.

Wolfenstein, Martha. "How Is Mourning Possible?" *The Psychoanalytic Study of the Child* 21 (1966): 93–123.

Young, Frank W. "The Function of Male Initiation Ceremonies." *American Journal of Sociology* 67 (Jan. 1962): 379–94.

Index